Talking Gender and Sexuality

Pragmatics & Beyond New Series

Volume 94

Talking Gender and Sexuality
Edited by Paul McIlvenny

Talking Gender and Sexuality

Edited by

Paul McIlvenny
Aalborg University

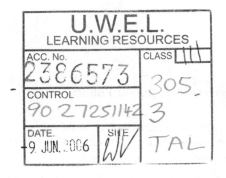
John Benjamins Publishing Company
Amsterdam/Philadelphia

™ The paper used in this publication meets the minimum requirements of American National Standard for Information Sciences – Permanence of Paper for Printed Library Materials, ANSI Z39.48-1984.

Library of Congress Cataloging-in-Publication Data

Talking gender and sexuality / edited by Paul McIlvenny.
     p. cm. (Pragmatics & Beyond, New Series, ISSN 0922-842X ; v. 94)
    Includes bibliographical references and index.
     1. Conversation analysis. 2. Language and sex. 3. Feminism. I. McIlvenny, Paul. II. Series.

P95.45.T356   2002
401.43--dc21   2002276251
ISBN 90 272 5114 2 (Eur.) / 1 58811 173 3 (US) (Hb; alk. paper)

John Benjamins Publishing Co. · P.O. Box 36224 · 1020 ME Amsterdam · The Netherlands
John Benjamins North America · P.O. Box 27519 · Philadelphia PA 19118-0519 · USA

Table of contents

Preface

In a convoluted fashion, this edited volume developed from a cosy international symposium on 'Talking Gender & Sexuality' that took place at Aalborg University, Denmark on November 5-6, 1999. In the end, all but one of the contributions to the book were selected from the many presentations given at (or submitted to) that symposium. The chapters are significantly revised versions of the original presentations, amended in the light of discussions at the symposium, the reviewers' and editor's comments, and the contributors' magnanimous reading of each other's drafts. Praise must be heaped on the contributors, who wrote such excellent articles, met my deadlines for submissions and revisions, and were thoroughly professional in their commitment to the project.

Thanks to the intrepid Johannes Wagner and the MOVIN (Micro-analysis Of Verbal/Visual INteraction) research organisation in Denmark for supporting, collegially and financially, the original symposium. I would also like to thank the symposium coordinator, Bente Vestergaard, and her assistant, Dorte Dewitz, as well as the Department of Languages and Intercultural Studies at Aalborg University for providing funds to support their part in the success of the symposium. My appreciation goes to the Pragmatics & Beyond New Series editor, Andreas Jucker, and the two anonymous readers of the manuscript, as well as Isja Conen, who capably fulfilled the role of publishing editor for John Benjamins. Recognition should also go to all the reviewers, including Alan Firth, Andrew Fish, Kirsten Gomard, Marjorie H. Goodwin, Elise Kärkkäinen, Arja Piirainen-Marsh and Pirkko Raudaskoski, for commenting at short notice and with alacrity on the first drafts. I express my gratitude to Sue Wilkinson for her generous advice in the early stages of the project and for providing exemplars of how to draft a prospectus for potential publishers.

Transcription conventions

The transcription conventions used in this book for rendering the nuances and details of spoken conversation reflect the standard that has emerged in conversation analysis. This evolving system has been developed chiefly by Gail Jefferson (1989: 193-196) and has undergone some modifications since the early studies, as can be seen from an inspection of the transcripts in Sacks, Schegloff and Jefferson (1974) and Sacks' (1995) *Lectures on Conversation*. See ten Have (1999: 75-98) and Hutchby and Wooffitt (1998: 73-92) for thorough discussions of the transcription practices in CA. A glossary is given below. For languages other than English (see chapters by Tainio and D'hondt in this volume) an interlinear gloss of the syntactic structure is provided, along with a free translation into English. Readers are referred to the individual chapters for the author's glossary of the additional notation conventions that they employ.

Symbol	Designation
A:	Current speaker (designated by a letter, a name or a category description).
CAPS	Capitalised letters indicate that a section of speech is louder than the surrounding speech.
<u>Under</u>scoring	Underlined fragments indicate stress or emphasis.
°soft°	Degree signs enclose speech that is quieter than the surrounding speech.
<fast>	Faster than surrounding speech.
>slow<	Slower than surrounding speech.
@voice@	The speech enclosed by the @s is said in an animated voice.
"voice"	Quotation voice.

erm::	A colon indicates a prolongation of the immediately prior sound. The number of colons tells the length of the prolongation.
.	A period indicates a falling intonation.
,	A comma indicates a continuing intonation.
?	A question mark indicates a rising intonation.
¿	An upside-down question mark indicates a rising intonation (more upwardly pronounced than a ',' but less so than a '?').
↑ *or* ↓	A marked shift into a higher or lower pitch in the utterance immediately following the arrow.
`no	A marked fall in pitch on a syllable.
Bu-	The dash marks a stop or cut-off in sound.
.hhh *or* hhh	An inbreath or outbreath. The length is indicated by the number of *h*s. A full stop prefixing a word indicates that it is pronounced with an inbreath (eg. *.joo* in Finnish).
hu, ha, he	Laugh particles. If enclosed in round brackets, eg. (h), then it occurs while talking.
(0.0)	Figures in rounded brackets represent absences of sound or activity, in steps of one tenth of a second.
(.)	A micropause (roughly 0.2 seconds or less).
oo[oooo] [oooo]oo	Overlap onset is marked with a single left square bracket and a single right square bracket marks where overlap terminates.
=	Latched utterances. There is no 'gap' between two utterances.
( ) *or* ( ):	An untranscribable passage or an unidentifiable speaker.
(guess) *or* (A):	A transcriber's guess of a dubious hearing or speaker identification.
((comment))	Comment by the transcriber.
→	An arrow in the margin draws the reader's attention to aspects of the analysis discussed in the text.

References

Have, Paul ten. 1999 *Doing Conversation Analysis: A Practical Guide*. London: Sage.

Hutchby, Ian and Wooffitt, Robin. 1998 *Conversation Analysis: Principles, Practices and Applications*. Cambridge: Polity.

Jefferson, Gail. 1989 "Preliminary notes on a possible metric which provides for a 'standard maximum' silence of approximately one second in conversation". In *Conversation: An Interdisciplinary Perspective*, D. Roger and P. Bull (eds), 166-196. Clevedon, Philadelphia: Multilingual Matters.

Sacks, Harvey. 1995 *Lectures on Conversation: Volumes I and II*. Oxford: Basil Blackwell.

Sacks, Harvey, Schegloff, Emanuel A. and Jefferson, Gail. 1974 "A simplest systematics for the organisation of turn-taking for conversation". *Language* 50: 696-735.

CHAPTER 1

Introduction

Researching talk, gender and sexuality*

Paul McIlvenny

1. Introduction

In the 1990s, a rich and enlightening debate took place concerning the best way to approach the study of language and gender. Scholars became increasingly critical of the essentialism of the predominant approaches to gender and spoken interaction, namely those often known as the *difference* and *dominance* paradigms. On the one hand, the difference model understands conversational interaction between 'the sexes' as comparable to that between two different (sub)cultures — for example, in the popularised dual-cultures model promoted by Tannen (1990) and others. On the other hand, the dominance model proposes that power relations and inequalities are reproduced in conversational interaction between men and women; see, for example, Fishman (1978) and Zimmerman and West (1975). The validity of, and the divisions between, the difference and dominance models have been keenly disputed and roundly criticised on many occasions (see, for example, Bing and Bergvall 1996, Cameron 1992a, 1992b, 1995, Crawford 1995, Eckert and McConnell-Ginet 1992, James and Clarke 1993, and Uchida 1992). Among other things, both were noted for their overbearing reductionism and naturalisation of 'two sexes', and their neglect of intra-gender differences. Cameron (1995: 39) surmises that "both dominance and difference represented particular moments in feminism: dominance was the moment of feminist outrage, of bearing witness to oppression in all aspects of women's lives, while difference was the moment of feminist celebration, reclaiming and revaluing women's distinctive cultural traditions."

If we survey the vast body of literature spread over several disciplines that constitutes language and gender studies over the last twenty five years (since

Lakoff 1975) and extract how gender (or sexuality) has been figured or modelled in relation to how people *talk*, we find that gender has tended to be seen as a variable attribute or essence of a speaker that is expressed in, or causes, certain linguistic behaviours, practices and/or actions in particular social contexts. Talk is simply a vehicle for the display of what are essentially independent, internal properties: one talks the way one does because one *is* a man or a woman, and talk is *reflective* of that essential difference. Thus, an asymmetrical relationship or distribution of work — for instance, in the use of a particular linguistic, pragmatic or discursive feature — indexes for the analyst that an inequality is operative and causal (see West 1996).

In opposition to this essentialist understanding of gender, feminist (socio)linguists began to develop new approaches that challenged the status quo in language and gender studies: see the contributions in, for example, Bergvall, Bing and Freed (1996), Bucholtz, Liang and Sutton (1999), Hall and Bucholtz (1995), Kotthoff and Wodak (1997a), Mills (1995) and Wodak (1997). Moreover, the promotion of a 'constructionist turn' in language and gender studies led to an increasing concern with gender as manifested in everyday activities and communication practices. Also, a new domain of inquiry emerged in the 1990s, namely the investigation of language use in relation to sexual orientation and the formation of sexual identities, with a predominantly linguistic focus on the marginalised speech of lesbian, gay, bisexual and transgendered (LGBT) interlocutors — see the work of Leap (1996) and the formative collections by Leap (1995) and Livia and Hall (1997a). This new domain has important repercussions both for how we study language and gender, and for the re-examination of the foundational premises of the field of sociolinguistics (Barrett 1997, though see Kulick 2000).

A consequence of the rethinking that has been generated by these developments is that *one of the profound theoretical challenges to how we understand and account for gender and sexuality — as a dynamic, performative engagement which is never complete — can be seen to match with the rich set of tools that have been developed for analysing the complexities of everyday practical language use, agency and identity in talk.* This book brings together a group of scholars from different disciplines (psychology, linguistics, sociology and communication science) who in their own way are drawing upon a bountiful methodological treasure chest developed over the last thirty years for analysing the richness and subtlety of talk and conversation — yet they are unhappy with how gender or sexuality has traditionally been ignored or misconceived in their respective fields, and so they have rummaged through a range of new theoretical resources for inspiration. The contributions to this book find their coherence in the confluence of four recent theoretical or methodological 'turns': first, the 'turn to interaction' in studies of social and cultural practice (the variants of conversation analysis); second, the 'turn to language' in social psychology (for example, in feminist discursive psychology); third, the 'turn to performativity' in gender and queer studies (the key proponents are Judith Butler and Eve Kosofsky Sedgwick); and lastly, the 'corporeal turn' across the humanities and social sciences to the analysis of situated (and virtual) embodiment. By weaving together these four turns, the book builds on the foundations of earlier research on language and gender, re-examines those very foundations in studies of spoken interaction and conversation, critically appraises this research to see if and how it 'translates' successfully into the study of sexuality in talk, and considers and promotes innovative alternatives that integrate the insights of recent feminist and queer theory with empirical studies of talk and conversation.

The chapters exemplify a collaborative engagement, from different theoretical and methodological positions, with foundational concepts such as performativity, agency, identity, difference, discourse, power, practice, desire and normativity. And these issues are addressed by focusing on the analysis of *talk* and *conversation* — the assumption being that talk is a fundamental set of practices in which normative and marginal genders and sexualities are worked into being, however contingently and temporarily. Indeed, their differentiation as well as their character as normative, marginal or transgressive are negotiated and accountable achievements. Nevertheless, the volume does not privilege so-called 'real' spoken talk materials, as opposed to more theatrical, textual or fictional examples. Thus, Sundén's chapter examines textually mediated talk, considering in a new light the performativity and embodiment of genders and sexualities in virtual conversational settings. The study of representations and mediations of talk is not only intrinsically interesting (see Kaplan 1996 and Volger 1998), it has also much to contribute, as Fish demonstrates in this volume, to our understanding of talk itself as a social and embodied practice imbued with ideologies, desires and fictional traces.

The first goal of the book is to introduce and discuss the principal theoretical and methodological questions concerning the role that different qualitative empirical analyses of talk can play for a feminist or queer-informed politics that is attentive to the everyday constitution of genders and sexualities. Chapters engage in debate over the commensurability or otherwise of conversation analytic, discursive and performative approaches to talking gender and sexuality. This involves a critical examination of the foundational tenets of the two primary approaches to conversation adopted by the authors, namely conversation analysis (CA) and discursive psychology (DP). Additionally, some authors provide incisive reviews of past and recent analyses of 'doing' gender and sexuality. Nevertheless, it is in the empirical studies of actual data fragments taken from recorded social interactions that we find the practical value of these methodological debates. Therefore, the second goal of the book is to use detailed empirical analyses of naturally occurring talk to uncover how gender and sexual identities, agencies and desires are contingently accomplished in conversational practices. A distinctive feature is that several of the chapters critically examine the operation of heterosexuality and heterosexism in talk (see Speer and Potter, Stokoe and Smithson, and Tainio), whilst another chapter specifically examines for the first time the interactional (in)visibility of lesbian interlocutors (Kitzinger). The book is also attentive to gender and sexuality in interaction with other crucial dimensions of social and cultural inequality, such as age (Tainio, Fish) and religion (D'hondt). Each empirical study highlights the power and relevance of a hands-on qualitative approach for critical studies of gender and sexuality in the social and human sciences.

The third goal is to pose the important question of what a critical theory of talk, gender and sexuality ought to look like that is sensitive to concerns with embodiment, agency, subjectivity and desire. Poststructuralist (and psychoanalytic) theories of discourse, desire and power can be used to complement and expand the analysis of talk in social interaction (Hepburn, McIlvenny). A renewed emphasis on desire and the 'unconscious' as appropriate (yet elusive) phenomena to study in social interaction leads one contributor (Fish) to probe the 'unsaid' and the 'dialogic unconscious' in conversation analysis itself. Such an emphasis has important methodological consequences when we wish to analyse the intertwined psychic and social lives of sexuality and gender in talk.

2.   Theories, terms and phenomena

Before we look more closely at the qualitative methods favoured in this book, and the crucial issues that pertain to those methods, we need to understand how feminism, queer theory and poststructuralism have radically altered how sex, gender and sexuality are to be understood, and thus what pertinent empirical research can and needs to be undertaken.

With the emergence in the 1980s of a robust critique of the biases of Enlightenment thought, some feminists began to engage with the predominantly male critics in order to bring *poststructuralist* and *postmodernist* thinking into dialogue with feminist principles (see Benhabib *et al.* 1995, Butler and Scott 1992 and Weedon 1987). Following hard on the heels of French poststructuralist feminism (Irigarary, Kristeva), and in tandem with the 'linguistic turn' in the social sciences and humanities, English-speaking postmodern feminist theorists have continued the inquiry into the category of 'woman', but with a healthier scepticism towards the 'totalising fictions' of feminism that necessarily exclude and marginalise 'different' women. For example, they argue that the search for an authentic women's speech overlooks the instability of gender divisions and the many differences between women. Instead, we need to emphasise the heterogeneity within given categories that are obscured by dualistic norms about social and cultural identity (see Elam 1994 for a discussion of feminism and deconstruction).

Michel Foucault's (1976) seminal work on discourse and sexuality has provided important tools for feminists to examine the political stakes in defining 'woman' as an originating identity. Following Foucault, Cameron (1995: 43) argues that feminist linguistics has produced a 'regime of truth', a normative discourse or dominant version of what it means to be a gendered speaker, that normalises women's exclusion from important communicative practices. From her perspective, the difference theorists in sociolinguistics, as well as the deficit and most dominance theorists, fail to address the question of where 'men' and 'women' come from. Gender is a problem to be explained, not a solution. She proposes, instead, that we focus on how subjects constantly negotiate the norms, behaviours and discourses that define masculinity and femininity for a particular community so as to produce themselves as gendered subjects. Hence, the essentialist notions of a 'men's style' or a 'women's language' need to be reformulated to allow for the possibility that men may use so-called women's language on particular occasions, and that some women and men do end up outside the gender norms identified by feminist linguistics.

Building on Foucault's genealogical approach, as well as a Derridean critique of speech act theory, Judith Butler (1990) introduced an influential 'performative turn' into feminist theorising so as to rethink gender *not* as what we are, *nor* a set of traits we have, but *an effect we produce by what we do*. Consequently, one becomes gendered by doing and talking gender. Gender has to be continually reaffirmed and displayed in spoken interaction, and through this contingently repeated citation, gender differentiation and gendered speech become naturalised, yet they are inherently unstable. Explicitly postmodern or poststructuralist approaches to gender *and* spoken interaction are not yet common nor clearly articulated, and in some cases scholars have been prematurely dissuasive (Kothoff and Wodak 1997b).[1] One reason for this may be that the critical attention to gender performativity and a politics of difference is often knotty and of a theoretical nature; it unsettles the traditional empirical studies, but leaves little from which to proceed. McElhinny (1993) presciently suggests that an ethnomethodologically-informed approach to conversation, similar to Goodwin's (1990), may enable us to show how the fluidity of gender identities and identifications in social interaction is managed. Indeed, such an approach is necessary in order to pose difficult questions to postmodern theories of language (see, for example, Salamensky 2001), which often gloss over or overlook the complexities and subtleties of social practice, the crucible in which structures of language *and* agency are interactively performed and forged.

Rethinking 'sex' and 'gender'

One result of the influx of poststructuralist thought into feminism is a rethinking of the modern distinction between 'sex' and 'gender' that is now entrenched in English-speaking industrialised nations, namely that sex is biological but gender is social and cultural (Ortner 1974, Stoller 1968). Although many feminists have found such a division to be productive for articulating a counter-sexist politics, the unfortunate consequence is that 'sex' has been naturalised and 'gender' has become socially essentialised.[2] In his provocative study of what he calls 'Gay Male English', Leap (1996) admits that he and many others have neglected gender in their research, such that we already 'know' in some sense what 'men' and 'women' are before we begin our research. Nevertheless, he sides with the dominant conception of gender as "socially constructed categories that give cultural representation to the biological differences between male and female" (xviii). Instead of considering gender as a category, as an identification or as expressive of sex in general, an alternative is to conceive of gender and sex as something we 'do', not 'are'. Recently, however, even approaches to 'doing' gender have tended to reify stereotypes of gender, for example, in accounts of how men 'do' masculinity by 'doing' masculine things (see Cameron 1998a and Stokoe and Smithson 2001 for criticisms of this trend).

With her hugely influential post-structuralist theory of gender performativity, Judith Butler (1990) challenges the usefulness of specifying and determining categories such as 'woman' because it is a provisional identity which inevitably excludes others. She does not take a stance in which gender is the expression of sex, nor one in which gender produces sex; instead, gender regulates sex as a natural condition of the body. Gender is "the discursive/cultural means by which 'sexed nature' or a 'natural sex' is produced and established as 'prediscursive', prior to culture, a politically neutral surface *on which* culture acts" (1990: 7, emphasis in the original). Moreover, not only does gender establish 'sex' in a pre-discursive domain, it establishes it as a duality, a binary norm. In her later book, *Bodies That Matter*, Butler (1993) revises her earlier emphasis which burdened gender, resulting in the absorption of a dematerialised 'sex'. Sex is now understood as a regulatory norm governing the materialisation of bodies over time. In this way, Butler's work more explicitly connects the reconfiguration of bodily gender with the possibility of discursive resignifications (Martin 1994).

In tandem with her notable critique of much of traditional language and gender scholarship, Deborah Cameron has cited and attempted to draw upon Butler's theory of gender performativity in several papers, one of which includes a loosely CA-informed, empirical analysis of sexist and homophobic talk among some male university students in the USA. Cameron (1997b: 48) argues that, in general, "the behaviour of men and women, whatever its substance may happen to be in any specific circumstance, is invariably read through a more general discourse on gender difference itself. That discourse is subsequently invoked to explain the pattern of gender differentiation in people's behaviour; whereas it might be more enlightening to say the discourse *constructs* the differentiation, makes it visible *as* differentiation." Thus, if people are who they are because of (among other things) the way they talk, an investigation of how people use linguistic resources to produce gender differentiation is needed. In reference to Butler's argument about performativity, Cameron (1997b: 49) concludes that "gender has constantly to be reaffirmed and publicly displayed by repeatedly performing particular acts in accordance with the cultural norms (themselves historically and socially constructed, and consequently variable) which define 'masculinity' and 'femininity'." Thus, in rendering action accountable to the normative discourse of gender difference, the differentiation between masculine and feminine is performatively constructed and made visible as differentiation. She argues that both analysts and conversationalists construct stories about themselves and others, with a view to performing certain kinds of gender identity. Other scholars who have attempted to bring the flavour of Butler's theorising to bear on language and gender studies include Rodino (1997) and Delph-Janiurek (1999).

Genders and queer sexualities

The most recent challenge to traditional conceptions of language and gender has been a queer one. At the same time as Judith Butler's *Gender Trouble* (1990) was serving as an important bridge for many scholars to a critique of the sex/gender system, a number of American scholars, for example Teresa de Lauretis (1991), were formulating a theoretical stance which has come to be known as *queer theory* or *queer studies*, an anti-essentialist, anti-assimilationist paradigm for the study of marginalised sexualities (see Jagose 1996, Bristow 1997 and Seidman 1996a for more details; see also de Lauretis 1999 for a review of its short and troubled history). De Lauretis articulated a queer theoretical perspective in which homo-sexualities are no longer seen as either merely transgressive or deviant vis-à-vis a proper, natural sexuality, or just another optional 'life-style'. Instead, they are social and cultural forms in their own right, whose "mode of functioning is both interactive and yet resistant, both participatory and yet distinct, claiming at once equality and difference, demanding political representation while insisting on its material and historical specificity" (1991: iii). Sedgwick (1993: xii) claims queer is "a continuing moment, movement, motive — recurrent, eddying, troublant.... across genders, across sexualities, across genres, across 'perversions.'" Queer can refer to "the open mesh of possibilities, gaps, overlaps, dissonances and resonances, lapses and excesses of meaning when the constituent elements of anyone's gender, of anyone's sexuality aren't made (or can't be made) to signify monolithically" (8-9). A recurrent theme is that queer is by definition, if not in practice, anti-essentialist, anti-separatist and anti-assimilationist. Also, it maintains a politics of practical action in which resistance and performance are key themes. Dramaturgical metaphors regularly appear in queer theory, but they accompany a shift to performance (over 'role' as reified noun) and a range of evocative imagery (Thorne 1995). Queer studies has been flourishing in certain locations since the early 1990s, yet sadly many academics have not read, nor have some even heard of this new radical social movement or the theoretical field of inquiry.

However, the relationship between feminism and queer theory is unsettled. Butler (1994) explicitly addresses the consequences of feminism *meeting* queer theory, particularly the charge that queer theory is requisitioning the study of sexuality for its own, and thus is cleaving a divide between itself and feminist analysis. Moreover, it has been pointed out by Epstein (1994) that much queer theory has unfortunately developed independently from social theory, and so is in danger of repeating its mistakes and findings. In the context of this volume, we need to ask if queer theory *meets* the study of spoken interaction.[3]

One of the disciplinary sites for the uptake of a queer theoretical perspective has been within the field of lavender linguistics (in the USA). In one of the first collections of lavender language scholarship, Leap (1995: vii) argues that the study of the construction of "lesbian and gay genders" in everyday language use in particular cultural and social domains is an important new linguistic enterprise. Issues of authenticity, passing and eroticised language play, as well as the salience of silence, non-verbal behaviour and gaze, are characteristic of a developing queer or lavender linguistics. A few collections have been published that engage predominantly with language and sexuality, including Harvey and Shalom (1997), Livia and Hall (1997a) and Leap (1995), as well as the special issue of *World Englishes* introduced by Leap (1998). Much as the sweep of feminist linguistics research can be traced back in dialectic relation to Lakoff's seminal work (1975) on language and woman's place, we currently see a broadening of the range of approaches applied in articles on queer language use, but so far the qualitative analysis of conversational materials has been overlooked or under-utilised.[4]

How to study the (conversational) performativity of gender and sexuality?

More often than not the work of Butler and other queer theorists has had only a superficial influence on language and gender studies — more a manifesto than a sustained theoretical reflection on 'performativity' and its ramifications. Rather than pursue Butler's project, some lavender language scholars have called for a return to Austin's conception of 'linguistic performativity' and the insights of speech act theory. We need to weigh up this call and to consider the issues involved for developing a perspective on 'doing' sexuality derived from empirical studies of talk as provided for by conversation analysis and discursive psychology.

The subtitle — "Bringing performativity back to linguistics" — of Livia and Hall's (1997b) catalytic introductory chapter to their collection *Queerly Phrased* unfortunately purports to claim a *proper* origin (a home) for theories of performativity. They take issue with the apparently exclusive focus on subjectivity in post-structuralist queer theory, and critique what they see as postmodernism's and Butler's "extreme cultural and linguistic relativity" and "linguistic determinism" (8). Unfortunately, their criticisms of Butler's purported radical relativism and determinism demonstrate their rather simplistic (mis)readings of Butler and Foucault on these issues (see McIlvenny in this volume).

It seems Livia and Hall wish to re-import the problematic notions of speaker intention and hearer uptake that can be found in some earlier versions of speech act theory (see Kulick 1999, 2000 for a trenchant critique). The difficulty with such a move is that linguists, in their 'bringing back', may discard important elements of queer performativity that may well challenge some of the core assumptions of sociolinguistics. There are also the attendant dangers of repeating the same 'mistakes' in a version of queer sociolinguistics as we now see were made (necessarily) over the last 30 years in feminist sociolinguistics. Moreover, a speech act theory approach is ill equipped to investigate performatives in interactional practices, as McIlvenny (this volume) and Speer and Potter (this volume) remind us.

For example, let us consider the almost mythical interpellation "It's a girl!", which is mentioned briefly in Judith Butler's writings, and which Livia and Hall (1997b) discuss in their introductory chapter to *Queerly Phrased*. With it we can locate a confluence of interests to do with sex, gender, normativity, interaction and talk that remain unaddressed from a (speech act) theoretical perspective. For queer theorists such as Butler (1993: 232), this apparently simple utterance is an initiatory transitive performative which not only names the 'girl', but invokes the normative process by which the 'girl' becomes a viable subject. Alternatively, using conversation analysis one could speculate that it could be understood as a news announcement — the medical determination and delivery of which sex category the infant is assigned — making conditionally relevant a news receipt token in second turn from the parent(s). Alternatively, it could be an assessment or evaluation of the 'normal sexedness' of the infant, which elicits a second assessment from the parent(s), such as "wonderful". It could also be thought of as a metaphorical summons, a calling into interactional being of the body of an infant, of how that body is to be addressed and to what it must answer. Of course, the baby does not answer the summons in next turn; instead, the answer to the summons is to be found in both the regulated expectability of many 'answers' and the full weight of social norms about gender and sex. Thus, gender and sex are intimately enmeshed and idealised in interaction from birth and, with ultrasound techniques, before. These suggestive analyses, of course, are only speculations or adumbrations, which remain hypothetical until further empirical and ethnographic study uncovers the interactional work that such singular performatives engage in actual situations. Even so, we can see the power of such an approach in contrast to a speech act model.

Recent studies that deploy a more sophisticated version of Butler for lavender linguistics include Bunzl's (2000) case study of 'inverted appellation' as linguistic drag in gay male conversation. Bunzl draws on Butler's early work that accounts for the cultural practice of drag as an instance of a paradigm for making gender trouble. His particular interest is in what he calls 'inverted appellation'; that is, cross-gender acts of naming in interpersonal communication (for example, third person pronouns, determiners and terms of address). He demonstrates how speakers can disalign interactional-grammatical resources from bodies/identities: how third person pronouns, for instance, can be dislocated from their supposed reference to always already gendered bodies. Bunzl's admixture of empirical analysis with performativity theory is bold and suggestive, but his analysis of actual inverted appellations in conversational interaction would be improved (or even transformed) by attending more closely to a conversation analytic emphasis on members' methods for adequately referring *in situ* to other members (following Sacks and Schegloff 1979 and Schegloff 1996b).

New topics: masculinity and heterosexuality

With the turn to the margins and alternative conceptions of gender and sexuality has come a fresh consideration of the corresponding norm or centre, namely masculinity and heterosexuality. The former has received the most attention in studies of language and gender, while the latter awaits a systematic treatment.

Feminist theories of language have most often maintained a critical stance on the language use of men, but few studies have explicitly problematised the normativity of deficit and difference models which imply that women, not men, should change their speech behaviour. In addition, studies of the diversity of men's conversational practices are few and far between, and those that exist tend to reify masculinity as conduct or presume it is an attribute wholly of men (see Halberstam 1998 for a critique). The focus on femininity and women's spoken interaction by feminist linguists is understandable, but with a relational approach to gender we need an understanding of 'hegemonic' masculinity that is more subtle than the abstract notion of a 'male oppressor' (or a male 'victim' in backlash men's studies). Some theorists (Connell 1995) argue that there has been a fragmentation of masculinity; indeed, there are complex power relations between men, in addition to those between men and women. A recent collection (Johnson and Meinhof 1997) explicitly addresses these issues. Papers by Cameron (1997b), Johnson and Finlay (1997) and Coates (1997) analyse informal men's talk and come to the conclusion that men and women do share linguistic and interactional resources — for example, turn organisation and gossip — but they draw upon them differentially; as a consequence, gossip as a speech genre is untied from its association with the 'feminine', while at the same time its specific use by men to construct hegemonic masculinity is documented. We need a richer understanding of how 'hegemonic' and other masculinities are performed in and through spoken interaction, often, but not necessarily, at the expense of others, including women and men (see Edley 2001, Speer 2001 and Wetherell and Edley 1999).

Feminism and women's studies have to a great extent challenged those masculine norms that marginalise and oppress women, but the literature on spoken interaction and gender has not really got to grips with the issue of *heterosexuality* in a sufficiently rigorous manner. Several contributions to this book focus their attention on heterosexuality as it is 'worked into being' in talk, a focus which is of very recent origin. One consequence of the contemporary wave of queer studies, notes Steven Seidman (1996b: 9), is a shift away from an exclusive preoccupation with homosexuality to a focus on "heterosexuality as a social and political organising principle." A flurry of activity in the 1990s (Wilkinson and Kitzinger 1993, Maynard and Purvis 1994, Richardson 1996, Steinberg, Epstein and Johnson 1997, Jackson 1999) has brought to our attention the unpoliticised nature and historicity of what is commonly accepted to be a timeless biological pre-disposition. Jonathan Katz's (1996) study of the invention of heterosexuality uncovers the hilariously ironic idea that in America the term 'heterosexuality' was first used in the 1890s to refer to a perversely excessive (male) 'sexual appetite' and a mental inclination to both sexes (a psychic hermaphrodism). According to Seidman (1991: 189), it was only in the early twentieth century that the concepts of heterosexuality and homosexuality emerged "as the master categories of a sexual regime that defined the individual's sexual and personal identity and normatively regulated intimate desire and behavior." Judith Butler, among others, has argued rather strongly that 'gender' only exists in the service of heterosexism (1993: 123). Terms such as 'compulsory heterosexuality' (Rich 1980) and the 'heterosexual social contract' (Wittig 1992) have emerged from the work of lesbian feminists. Nevertheless, Connell (1995: 394) points out that hegemonic heterosexuality is not a static system of sexual practice. Thus, as Katz (1996: 178-79) argues, if we challenge heterosexuality as the norm, we may discover that what society thinks of as the sex-normal, the sex-natural, the different-sex erotic and the specifically 'heterosexual', have a history of changing, often opposed, contradictory, and socially contested definitions. Katz (1996: 182) concludes that heterosexuality is invented *in* discourse as that which is *outside* discourse.

According to Seidman (1996: 12-13) queer theorists view heterosexuality and homosexuality "not simply as identities or social statuses but as categories of knowledge... a normative language" — which is why it is important for students of gender and sexuality in social interaction to critically examine heterosexuality, to study those conversational practices that contribute to ordering 'society' by sexualizing not only bodies, desires, acts, identities, social relations, but also knowledges, culture, and social institutions. Chrys Ingraham (1996: 168) makes the argument that even feminist sociological understandings of gender need to be re-examined for the ways in which they participate in the reproduction of what she calls "the heterosexual imaginary", which is "that way of thinking which conceals the operation of heterosexuality in structuring gender and closes off any critical analysis of heterosexuality as an organizing institution" (169). As these understandings are drafted, often wholesale, into research on language and gender, we urgently need to interrogate this straight imaginary.

Lesbian feminism since the 1970s has already mapped out some of the issues concerning heterosexuality. Rich (1980) points to the many structures in place to enforce heterosexuality and asserts that any resistance whatsoever to patriarchy places a woman somewhere in the lesbian continuum. The methodology Rich uses to expose her ideas, when applied to language, is useful in understanding the power of intimidation and coercion. A compulsory silence of women has been effected for centuries, and women's speech ridiculed (as lesbian women have been ridiculed) to the extent that both women and men believe that women have talked a lot (too much) when they manage to occupy no more than one third of the conversational space (Spender 1989). A true and good woman, under patriarchy, is supposed to be heterosexual and to embrace the public virtue of silence. To reject heterosexuality, or to break the taboo on public voice, is to invite scorn (see Kitzinger in this volume for an analysis of the subtleties of 'coming out' in public talk). More recently, Hollway (1984, 1995) and Gilfoyle, Wilson and Brown (1993) have focused on the oppressive discourses of heterosexuality that are manifested in men's verbal accounts of their sexual relations with women. Eckert (1996) has revealed the significance of the 'heterosexual marketplace' for the emergence of linguistic style in American elementary schools. And Cameron (1997b) has documented an especially homophobic version of male hetero-sexuality apparent in the 'gossip' of a group of American male students.[5]

3. Empirical approaches to researching talk, gender and sexuality

One important consequence of the rethinking that has been generated by the developments discussed in the previous section is that contemporary *performative* understandings of gender and sexuality may benefit from the application of those qualitative methods which have been refined in the analysis of agency, identity and *inter*-action in the practices of everyday talk. Two such empirical approaches to researching talk as social practice inform the contributions to this volume.[6] They are conversation analysis and discursive psychology, which are briefly introduced below.

Conversation analysis and gender

In the 1990s, a version of conversation analysis (CA) was finally established (and institutionalised) as a credible qualitative methodology through the publication of textbooks by Psathas (1995), Hutchby and Wooffitt (1998) and ten Have (1999), as well as through the increasing presence of conversation analytic research in any collection of articles or journal special issues on themes in interactional pragmatics, sociolinguistics, discourse as social interaction or qualitative research (see, for example, Silverman 1997, van Dijk 1997 and Tracy 1998). Conversation analysis has been inflected to varying degrees by the different fields and disciplines — for instance, linguistics, applied linguistics, anthropology, communication science and now feminism — which have taken it up as a useful methodology in various parts of the world. Consequently, the more 'sociological' concerns/antagonisms of ethnomethodology have often been laid aside and new issues have been raised. There are, nevertheless, increasingly sophisticated attempts to *translate* conversation analysis 'proper' — for example, with culturally-contexted conversation analysis (Moerman 1988, Sanders 1999) and discursive psychology (Potter and Wetherell 1987). Recently, there has been a broader return to membership categorisation analysis (MCA) as the lost sibling to sequential CA as it developed and became known after Sacks' death in 1975. Hester and Eglin (1997), Silverman (1998) and Lepper (2000) reconsider its worth and import for the analysis of methods of practical reasoning in conversational interaction. It is with this development, and the flurry of research on 'doing' social and cultural identity, that the relations between agency, membership, member, the subject, subjectivity and identity need to be thought through carefully.

Despite the plethora of studies that can be found under the rubric of conversation analysis, it is often pointed out that CA has not topicalised gender in talk. In fact, many practitioners have avoided the issue or castigated those who have entered into such a perilous endeavour. Nevertheless, a few notable scholars have broached the topic, starting with Harold Garfinkel, the founder of the field of ethnomethodology, a field to which CA has close affinities. In one of the first attempts to grapple with the naturalisation of 'sex status' as a practical matter, Garfinkel (1967) chose to study the progress of a pre-operative 'intersexed' patient in the 1950s. Although not expressly concerned with talk (though he did use interviews), Garfinkel used his marginal subject to breach the routine practical reasoning in language that solidifies the 'natural attitude' towards the 'sex status' — what we might nowadays call 'gender' — of members (see McIlvenny in this volume for further critical discussion).

With the emergence of a 'technology' for studying everyday conversation, we find that Harvey Sacks himself was not averse in his lectures to invoking the gender (or sexuality) of the participants in his analyses of a transcript. However, it was not until the mid 1970s that several studies brought a conversation analytic method to bear on the question of male dominance in cross-sex conversation (Fishman 1978, West and Zimmerman 1977, Zimmerman and West 1975). Although, strictly speaking, Fishman's work is limited in scope and is problematic as a contribution to conversation analysis (West 1996: fn7, 365), these studies put on the table in a dramatic way (with what appears to be clear statistical evidence that men specifically and categorically interrupt women) that the inspection of authentic conversational materials might reveal more about women's and men's speech than armchair speculation (cf. Lakoff 1975).

However, in one of the few explicit commentaries on an application of conversation analysis to the analysis of gender in talk, Schegloff (1987) finds cause to criticise the early approach to gender, dominance and interruption adopted by Zimmerman and West (1975), in which they reported an asymmetry of interruption between the sexes. Schegloff takes the study by Zimmerman and West as an exemplar of the foundational problem with conversational research that does *not* perform a comprehensive 'technical' analysis *before* importing 'macro-level' categories. Such research "aims to link an asymmetrical outcome in the talk to differential attributes of the participants of a macrorelevant type. What is commonly seen as differential between men and women in a finding such as this... is differential status or power, of which the interruptions are presumed to be a symbol and for which they are a vehicle" (214). From Schegloff's point of view, two methodological steps are required for an adequate analysis. The first step requires that one show that characterisations the investigator makes of the participants are grounded in the participants' own orientations in the interaction (215). The second step is to show that the differential attributes are conversation-specific, which in the early studies of gender in social interaction is not done in any straightforward way. Hence, he argues that Zimmerman and West must demonstrate that the interruption is adequately characterised as consequent on the macrolevel attributes, such as gender, in the data in question, otherwise there is no warrant for making such a claim, since the interruption could have easily have been simply an 'intra-interactional' issue for the participants themselves. On the basis of general studies of interruptions and overlaps in conversation, Schegloff demonstrates that in principle there are several possible accounts for competitive simultaneous talk that involve matters other than status or power tests altogether. Despite the legitimacy of his criticisms, Schegloff unfortunately invokes as his target a traditional approach to conceiving of gender in talk that has since been superseded. He assumes an approach that is only permitted to specify the conduct of fixed attribute roles — for instance, it is conversational activity that is to be "determined or effectuated by the attributes of the parties" (216) — and then he wisely dismisses it. West and Zimmerman's later work (1987) on 'doing' gender, examined by McIlvenny (this volume), does not fall into this category; instead, it is more concerned with how gender is accomplished in and through conversational work (see also West and Garcia 1988 and West and Fenstermaker 1993).

Other core CA scholars who have drawn upon Sacks' work or conversation analysis (as it developed after Sacks' death) in order to analyse gender or sexuality include Goodwin (1980, 1990, 1993, 1999), Watson and Weinberg (1982) and Jefferson (draft). Goodwin's (1990) exemplary work on talk as social activity among African-American children is well known and resists reduction to a simple dual-cultures socialisation model. In their membership categorisation analysis of the interactional construction of homosexual identity, Watson and Weinberg (1982) give one of the first analyses of the practical distinction between 'doing' and 'being' in accounts or disclosures of homosexuality in interview data. Jefferson (draft) is a genuine attempt to explore a tentative hypothesis that in 'male-female' interaction there is an asymmetry in one's response to the other's initiation of laughter. Well aware of the bias of using extrinsic categories such as 'male' and 'female' to characterise her participants, she concludes that there is little to support the generalisation in her limited corpus, and where an asymmetry exists in a piece of data it may easily be motivated by other interactional business. A number of studies have since been published that draw to some extent, with or without acknowledgement, on conversation analytic principles and/or findings to study talk, gender and sexuality.[7]

Feminist discursive psychology

The other anchor point for several chapters in this volume is the field of discursive psychology (DP: see Potter and Wetherell 1987, Edwards and Potter 1992), of which there are two main variants: the older poststructuralist-informed approach and the more recent CA-inspired approach. While both attend to the feminist project of intellectual, social and political change, the earlier feminist approach to social psychology draws heavily on a Foucauldian conception of discourse (see Wilkinson and Kitzinger 1995, Wetherell 1998 and Wetherell & Edley 1999). In common to both approaches, emotions, beliefs and opinions are *not* private things hiding inside the person: they are created by the language used to describe or account for them. For the earlier poststructuralist-informed approach, however, language is organised into discourses, and the discursive location of the individual frames one's 'personal' experience of self and subjectivity, yet language is an interactive activity which mediates sociocultural knowledge and is the medium in which identities and subjectivities are contested. From a feminist perspective, much of the social sense-making we are subjected to is the working through of ideological struggle between the discourses of legitimated, naturalised patriarchy and emergent, marginalised feminism. Hence, language is a key site for, and often the stake in, feminist resistance. The strength of this approach for studying gender and spoken interaction is that a diverse range of shifting and contentious discourses of masculinity and femininity can be demonstrated to be locally operative in situated performances of talk, with the result that particular ways of talking and being gendered are repressed or excluded (see Wilkinson and Kitzinger 1995). Empirical studies have concerned, for instance, adolescent talk about menstruation, the differences between male and female adult talk about sexual harassment (in Wilkinson and Kitzinger 1995), and the discourses of heterosexual desire manifested in women's talk (Hollway 1995). What these studies point to is the clash of discursive means and choices that women and men draw upon and make when engaging in the telling of opinions and experiences in spoken interaction. However, not all feminist social psychologists agree on the benefits to feminism of a poststructuralist discourse analytic approach; for example, some scholars argue that it is relativist and value-free, so it is not suited to a feminism that requires broad generalisations and political commitment (see Gill 1995, and Hepburn 2000 for discussion). Furthermore, as the chapter by Speer and Potter in this volume demonstrates, a divide has emerged between the poststructuralist inspired work of Wetherell, Edley and others, and the recent work of more CA-aligned discursive psychologists, such as Potter, Edwards, Hepburn and Speer (see Speer 2001 for further discussion of the relationship between CA and DP).

4.   Themes and issues

There are three key issues thematised by the studies presented in this book, each of which results from the central problematic of combining an empirical approach to understanding and describing talk (using conversation analysis or discursive psychology) with a post-structuralist or performative understanding of gender and sexuality. Many of the contributions use fine-grained, qualitative analyses of conversational materials, but not all agree on the appropriate phenomena to study or the methods to make claims about those phenomena. First, there is the question of the 'proper' object of analysis. What is it exactly that we should study? What does theory tell us? Second, there is the difficult problem of the limits of analysis. Should we remain open to 'unmotivated observation' in the first instance? Third, there is the urgent matter of the politics of qualitative methodologies such as CA. Is conversation itself inherently imbued with politics? And can CA, for example, be useful for other enterprises, such as feminism or queer studies?

The 'proper' object of analysis

Because of their common emphasis on constructionist versions of agency, contributors to this book reject a static model of gender or sexuality. Instead, attention is shifted to how gender and sexuality is 'done', 'figured' or 'framed' by co-conversationalists as an ongoing and contingent social practice. Several chapters investigate the best way to approach the study of gender and sexuality as identities or social categories (D'hondt, Fish, Stokoe and Smithson, and Tainio). Indeed, categorisation is a fundamental device by which all members of society constitute their social order. Widdicombe (1995: 112) argues that "category ascriptions, together with knowledge about the meaning of identities thereby made relevant, function as powerful mechanisms of social control, through the way they infuse individual's lives at the level of social interaction. They provide the means through which other people assume they already know something about members' selves and lives without speaking to them. And this is why resistance is a likely response." The emerging research on identity work and membership categorisation (for example, Antaki and Widdicombe 1998, Hester and Elgin 1997) prompts a much-needed review of local practices of subject-formation and subject-renewal in social life. An alternative interpretation of membership categorisation, in line with the feminist poststructuralist thought of Butler (1990), is that the 'I' and subjecthood is produced through performatively categorising others and being accountable to categorical distinctions that comprise a discourse. Thus, agency and subjection emerge through the contingency of the reiterative mutual constitution of membership categorisation and the sequential organisation of social/linguistic action. It is noteworthy that Butler (1997a: 27) contends that "a critical perspective on the kinds of language that govern the regulation and constitution of subjects becomes all the more imperative once we realize how inevitable is our dependency on the ways we are addressed in order to exercise any agency at all." Here we find a justification for focusing on the situated practices of categorisation and accountability in interaction.

However, Watson (1997) points out that work increasingly institutionalised under the name of 'conversation analysis' has become identified with sequential analysis, yet much of the latter does not topicalise what is implicit in its own analyses; that is, it draws upon members' notions of membership categories in its own methods, for example in the reification accompanying participant identification in transcripts (see Schegloff 1999a: 565-6 for a recent discussion of this "category shadow" problem). There is, nevertheless, also a danger that Sacks' notion of membership categorisation (and its structural binaries) can be used to reify categories and essentialize identities, thus eliding differences and covering over the continual recontextualisation of categories. The methodology of analysing the 'doing' of identity (and binaries) can render invisible the dynamic resistance to the epistemologies of identity (for instance, gender, gay or trans), and thus naturalise static 'everyday' conceptions. On the contrary, identity inconsistencies and lack of closure can be a resource for conversationalists (as Moerman 1993 and both D'hondt and Hepburn in this volume argue). Moreover, as Fish illustrates in this volume, accounts of talk practices can regulate identity much as talk practices do.

To what extent is 'identity' a normative ideal rather than a descriptive feature of experience? This is a difficult issue concerning the theoretical or ideological impact of humanism on the presentation and discussion of data and analysis in conversation analysis. In claiming to stick closely to the methods and practices of 'everyday life', there is a danger that a CA-type methodology can reproduce hegemonic power and beliefs as the 'natural attitude'. The accomplished integrity and coherence of identity and interaction in the analyst's carefully crafted fragments of 'everyday life' are taken as the practice of a community and the framework within which something can be said and made intelligible. So the rendering of a regulatory practice of what counts as 'doing' X becomes the normative definition of what X is because the practice's exclusions and omissions — people also deploy lay theories of the social — can easily become the analyst's too.

Another very important issue that all the contributors address is how gender and sexuality are made into 'natural objects'. That is, how they are naturalised as identities, attributes or relations, and insulated from inspection and contestation in everyday social interaction. To get a grip on how the hierarchies and alignments that compose commonsense notions of sex/gender and gender/sexuality are sustained, it is now becoming clear that what we need, along with the indispensable inquiry into marginal genders and sexualities, is a critical turn inwards to examine invisible norms and the most natural of categories: for example, the 'heterosexual'. Not simply to understand how the centre represents the margins (as 'Other') in and through language, but how the centre sees, hears and talks about itself as it constitutes itself as that very centre without a history, a name or a body. We need to shift the terminological emphasis so that we no longer think of deviation from the neutral (sociolinguistic) norm. Instead, we need to explicitly name the excessive and productive 'norm', and, finally, to rupture and decentre that norm which, in the words of Peggy McIntosh (1992), "confers dominance".

We can begin such an investigation by using the destabilising term 'homovestism' that has been coined to refer to the (perverse) masquerade of dressing as the same sex (the term 'homeovestism' was first used by Kaplan

1993). Katz (1996) argues that it can be extended productively to refer to the fallible yet insistent incitement to perform the same, the identity, that is transparent and naturalised. Katz calls for a novel in(tro)spection of "the feeling of being the same sex — the sex we think we are, the sex most of us desire to stay" (15). It is *conversational homovestism* — the feeling of speaking as the same sex — that we also need to examine and reflect on. Both the examination of the chronic constitution of the 'centre' or 'norm', and a parallel move to destabilise the binary hierarchies and enforced alignments of bodies, pleasures, desires, acts and language practices, are crucial steps towards developing a transformative, anti-essentialist study of talk, gender and sexuality.

Rather than restrict themselves to what actors explicitly 'orient' toward in their talk, Kitzinger (this volume) suggests that feminist conversation analysts should look specifically at what we could gloss as 'doing' naturalisation — the 'invisible' work done in talk — because it is "precisely the fact that sexist, heterosexist and racist assumptions are routinely incorporated into everyday conversations without anyone noticing or responding to them that way which is of interest."[8] The question then becomes: how does this failure to orient toward something actually constitute and reconstitute (hetero)sexism? In support of her point, Kitzinger cites Sacks' (1995, II: 185-6) analysis of everyday racism-in-action in a woman's account of her witnessing of an event. Garfinkel (1967) also gives some idea of the everyday routine operation of sexism-in-action. He points out that his study of Agnes reveals "the steps whereby society hides from its members its activities of organization and thus leads them to see its features as determinate and independent objects" (182). This theoretical position will be familiar to readers of Butler (1997b: 14), who argues for an understanding of citational performativity derived from Derrida in which "the term that claims to represent a prior reality reproduces retroactively that priority as an effect of its own operation." McHoul (1986: 69-70, my emphasis) reminds us, in agreement with Butler, that "Garfinkel uses the Agnes case to show that socio-sexual identity is, for 'normals' too, a continual problem of conduct to which countless unseen solutions are in operation everyday but to which neither *the member* nor *the investigator* has 'empirical' access except in special cases such as that of Agnes." The contentious issue of how can we make claims when we analyse how participants innocuously build in prejudiced assumptions and 'do' stereotypical categorisations in their talk in an unmarked and untopicalised fashion is taken up in the next section.

The limits of analysis

As we have seen above, one direction to follow would be to take a methodology such as conversation analysis or discursive psychology as given and then focus on 'discovering' those legitimate objects of study that might be said to be the substance or effect of 'doing' gender or sexuality (for example, Speer 1999 and Kitzinger this volume). A more critical approach would be to determine the limits of analysis in terms of what phenomena are outside its purview. For instance, Stokoe and Smithson (this volume) cautiously examine CA's claim that one must always anchor an adequate analysis in what the participants overtly display in their talk, and demonstrate that participants observably orient to gender or sexuality as a category. They ask if too much is lost by adhering to an examination of what the participants are doing in talk (see Weatherell 2000 for a similar argument). In her review of Ochs' (1992) work on indexicality and gender practices, McElhinny (1998b, 171, my emphasis) asks: "If part of the strategy for determining gender is assuming that gender is not always relevant, how do we determine and demonstrate *when* and *how* gender is relevant?" To provide an answer McElhinny cites Ortner (1989), who outlines how practice theories try to understand something a group of people did or believe, by attempting to locate the point of reference in a social practice from which the beliefs or actions emerge. Yet, for Ortner, this is not just a question of locating the actor's point of view. It is a question of seeking "the configuration of cultural forms, social relations, and historical processes that move people to act in the ways that produce the effects in question" (12). Schegloff, on the other hand, favours an approach that is grounded in what is demonstrably relevant to the participants. Any other approach, he claims, will inevitably import concerns that are relevant to the theorist or analyst, but not to the participants themselves. Thus, if a phenomenon is not relevant to the participants, or cannot be shown to be relevant, then it is not a valid object worthy of empirical study. For him it is only within the locus of situated accountability that a gendered analysis is warranted.[9]

Stokoe and Smithson (this volume) contend that this stance, when applied to the analysis of talk, implies that some explicit mention (or indexing) of a gender reference — for example, by using a pronoun, noun or name — is required. The issue is an ambivalent one since Schegloff (1997: 182) allows for the possibility of a non-explicit mention of a category term because an "orientation to gender can be manifested without being explicitly named or mentioned." Nevertheless, these alternative possibilities need to be enumerated and grounded in analyses of actual talk materials. There is also the question of whether the participants' overt reference is sufficient, since such a claim assumes a durable link between indexical grammatical resources and reference to irremediably 'sexed' bodies/persons (see Bunzl 2000 for a critique of this assumption). Moreover, relevancy can mean either situationally relevant for particular participants or an omni-relevant concern for participants on all occasions. If CA can arbitrate over the complete set of relevancies for participants on any given occasion, then this position implies that a large swath of 'phenomena' will be inappropriate objects of attention because they are beyond the limits of analysis. Indeed, with this methodological parsimony it appears that participants to a conversation are unnecessarily restricted both in their interests-at-hand and in their methods for performing social order.[10]

Is there a necessary limit to what can be said in analysis? And is all analysis haunted by its own 'unsaid'? Cameron (1998b: 452) claims that the task of the analyst, if she or he wishes to make claims that power is at work in an interaction, is "precisely to show what particular assumptions about gender and power relation *are likely to be at work* for the participants when they rule some interpretations in and others out." Following up on this point for both the participants and the analyst, Fish (this volume) demonstrates that even one of the founders of conversation analysis, Harvey Sacks, can unwittingly build in assumptions about gender and sexuality into his interpretation of a stretch of talk. Thus, the work of conversation analysis is not exempt from embodying taken-for-granted assumptions, which often include unexamined theoretical, empirical and ideological biases. One result is that if conversation analysis and ethnomethodology aims to topicalise and explicate members' practices, and if those practices themselves have a constitutive ideological dimension that is unintelligible in the practical discourse constituted by those practices, it may be that conversation analysis reproduces or replays that ideological dimension as a matter of course.

It would seem that CA can show *how* people 'do gender', and *how* conduct is normatively accountable, but it cannot explain *why* that conduct may be oppressive or say what other conduct is possible or desirable. However, as argued above, the 'natural' or 'ordinary' or 'everyday' are sites of contestation and struggle, and so we need to find ways to criticise apparently 'natural' or 'essential' categories. It should be possible to discover the gaps and contradictions in the regulatory practices of talk and make positive statements about repressions and exclusions. The question of whether CA can be supplemented by a more critical or interpretative perspective or whether CA's (largely implicit) social theory is incompatible with the aims of such a perspective is raised in the next section.

The politics of analysis

For many scholars it is disconcerting that in general the field of conversation analysis — an important and productive methodology for attending to the details of everyday life, the transparency of the natural, moral order and the shared practices by which that order is rendered accountable in talk — has had very little to say about gender, and next to nothing about sexuality, 'race', class, and the normalising of dominance and oppression. The result in many cases has been an overriding concern with 'doing' conformity to constitute 'the social order'. It is fruitful at this juncture to ask what ideological baggage conversation analysis brings with it, particularly with regard to power, agency, subjectivity and normativity. Moreover, it serves us well to go back and uncover just how much and in what ways scholars within the field have attempted to analyse gender and sexuality in talk (see both Kitzinger and McIlvenny in this volume).

Van Dijk (1990: 7) argues that many branches of discourse analysis, including CA, have paid more attention to the intricacies of the structures or strategies of text and talk itself than to "the conditioning or conditioned structures and processes of the social contexts of their actual use", which were often discussed merely in terms of conversational universals. For him, group and power differences, such as those of gender and sexuality, were often bracketed in the analysis of the minutiae of everyday talk. But the counter argument by Sharrock and Anderson (1986: 65) is that "sociologists of other persuasions have tried to find interest in such [conversational] materials by, for example, seeing conversational exchanges as (perhaps covert) struggles for power and control, thus linking ordinary talk to such recognised sociological themes as domination and control. Conversation analysts have resolutely resisted any attempt to endow the conversations they study with this kind of seeming importance.... The focal concern is with the analysis of the organisation of a commonplace activity." Compared to critical discourse analysis, for example, it seems that this is an ascetic approach indeed. However, although the resistance that Sharrock and Anderson speak of may be a worthy methodological principle, it does not mean that all theories of gender are antithetical to (a version of) CA, and vice versa. Indeed, McHoul (1986: 68) contends that "ethnomethodology's restraint in the domain of the political is not a necessary one — for if literal description is unavailable in any ideal sense, a purely descriptive sociology of everyday life is in equal jeopardy and the question of the political-moral grounds of analysis cannot but arise."

Another argument is that a politics might already be at work in the empiricist methodology of conversation analysis and that to obfuscate or deny such a politics in no way defuses the operation of power at work in the very practices of talk-in-interaction. Recently, one of the founders of CA, Schegloff (1997, 1999a, 1999b), has engaged on several occasions in an eye-opening debate with two discursive social psychologists, Margaret Wetherell (1998) and Michael Billig (1999a, 1999b). Billig argues that conversation analysis has a foundationalist and a participatory rhetoric behind its claims to be naively empiricist. However, one is led to believe from his criticisms of CA that there are no studies broadly conceived which have attempted to analyse or have discussed the problematics of power, gender and inequality in conversation. Even Schegloff seems to concur on this matter, though he is not against the possibility that such studies, properly carried out in a 'technical' fashion, could find pertinent structures or features of talk. Could it be then that conversation analysts have studiously avoided investigating such a possibility, or that it is very hard to investigate, or even that the phenomena in question happen so infrequently that it is not worth the effort? What is surprising is how little both discussants seem to know, or wish to bring to the attention of their readers, of not only contemporary issues and debates, but also prior work that has been undertaken already in which sex, gender or sexuality is a concern in the study of talk. For instance, neither of them refer in substance to the literature which has attempted to analyse gender and talk using conversation analytic principles and methods (for example, Watson and Weinberg 1982, Goodwin 1990, West and Fenstermaker 1995). Billig even ignores the work of feminists in his own department (see Kitzinger this volume), while Schegloff sticks close to his 'canon' of conversation analytic literature which has little if anything to say about gender. To be fair, in the first salvo of the debate Schegloff (1997) did refer favourably for the first time to the more recent work of West and Zimmerman (1987). This endorsement marks a shift from his previous (and justified) critique of Zimmerman and West's (1975) early studies of interruptions in cross-sex discourse.

Schegloff's (1997) paper which started the debate uses the analysis of gender in talk as an exemplar. His concern is with 'intrainteractional' phenomena (see Schegloff 1987), which are not necessarily tied to macro-level phenomena such as gender. He is at pains to point out that he does not want to preclude exploring for its own sake the technical richness of interaction — in fact, such a strategy may reap dividends for a critical discourse analysis. To further this goal he attempts to create a domain of interactional phenomena — the mundaneness of talk, its availability as a resource for all, its adequacy for all tasks — untied from politics. But we need to consider whose conversations are taken as the norm of power-free conversational labour beyond, or having priority over an analysis of gender and sexuality. According to Heritage (1984: 240), CA has "a central focus on casual conversation between peers, neighbours, etc. rather than, for example, looking directly at relationships involving dominance and subordination.... it is difficult, if not impossible, to explain specific features of such asymmetric interaction by reference to social attributes (eg. status, power, gender, ethnicity, etc.) without a clear knowledge of what is characteristic of ordinary talk between peers." But Heritage's phrasing and choice of examples is puzzling: is it so clear what is 'casual' and 'symmetric' about conversation between 'peers' and 'neighbours'? There is a real danger here that CA with its implicit emphasis on a model of conversation as primordially egalitarian inscribes liberal ideological notions of equality, opportunity and ability as norms of conduct (see McElhinny 1997).

A more pragmatic approach is to investigate in what ways a version of CA can be useful for other more politicised enterprises, such as feminism or queer studies. Kitzinger (this volume) argues that CA is not suitable for sex-differences research or an experimental or correlational paradigm, but it is well suited to social constructionist, postmodern, radical lesbian and queer approaches to sexuality and gender. Even Schegloff (1999a: 562) acknowledges that by paying attention to interaction in singular episodes produced within a matrix of turns organised into sequences — in which motives and intentions are inferred, identities made relevant, stances embodied and interpreted — then we can understand "what unwilling participants can do to manage that course to safer outcomes" and "how others might intervene to detoxify those settings."

5.   Overview of the chapters

The first contribution by **Celia Kitzinger** asks in bold terms if the apparently apolitical conversation analytic methodology has anything to say that could be of use for politicised (lesbian) feminists. Prompted and incited by the Billig/Schegloff debate on the relationship between critical discourse analysis and conversation analysis, Kitzinger finds Billig's "chivalrous defence" of his imperilled version of feminism against the naivety and 'ideology' of CA to be misplaced. She argues that his critique finds its target not just in CA but in many qualitative approaches in the social sciences, some of which have already been adopted by feminists. Rather than dismiss CA outright without a fair hearing, Kitzinger assesses its strengths in relation to the goals of particular feminisms, such as feminist social constructionism, for which it may be beneficial. She discusses the compatibility of its (largely implicit) social theory, the efficacy of its methodological principle to ground analysis in what participants themselves are doing, and the paucity of its analyses of so-called 'macro-' level phenomena. She concludes that a feminist conversation analysis is both feasible and desirable.

Kitzinger argues for a sincere consideration of what might also be dubbed a 'forensic' conversation analysis, one useful for certain feminist goals but where those goals are not wholly contained by CA. In other words, CA uncovers evidence of how and when the deed was done, revealing a parsimonious and unbiased 'truth', thus eliminating 'unscientific' speculation and hearsay. The evidence is then available for an assessment of what motivated such deeds. Therefore, for Kitzinger, conversation analysis has implications for feminist concerns and can illuminate how heterosexism, for example, operates as a situated practice, but *not why*. In her research, she has followed two possible strategies appropriate for a feminist conversation analysis. First, one can take the findings of CA's studies of everyday conversation and translate or extrapolate them to other settings that have not yet been studied or are difficult if not impossible to study because of ethical or privacy reasons (for instance, sexual refusals — see Kitzinger and Frith 1999). Such an approach can challenge the solidity of naturalised lay accounts of gendered verbal behaviour, and ground policy decisions in the 'actual facts' of conduct; otherwise, the well intentioned policy may unnecessarily exacerbate the situation it was designed to combat. Second, as she demonstrates in her chapter in this volume, one can investigate the sequential organisation of 'doing' sexuality in talk materials, such as practices in which sexual identity is made relevant (for example, in actual instances of 'coming out').

Kitzinger's 'wait and see' policy towards the status of CA as (an aid to) a critical methodology may go far — it is indeed an open question, since an empirical account of action cannot predict theoretically what actions and their associated conversational practices are relevant and consequential in mundane talk (Schegloff 1996a). Rather than decide beforehand, no matter how eager we may be to follow intuition and suspicion, she, like Speer and

Potter in this volume, prefers to 'discover' how such concepts as 'resistance', 'closeting', 'coming out', 'heterosexism' and so on, are manifested in talk itself.

Elizabeth Stokoe and **Janet Smithson** probe deeper into the limits of any analysis of (hetero)sexist talk that is based on the procedural and method-ological principles of particular versions of conversation analysis. Their moti-vation is grounded in the exasperation that many feminist scholars feel when CA fails to deliver an analysis that is congruent with what their intuitions tell them is going on in a particular stream of social interaction. They agree that CA is a useful methodology, but it has its limits, and these they wish to explore in relation to their data corpus. They pay particular attention to the quality of, and support for, the analyst's arguments based on data analysis, especially the grounding of the analysis in a demonstration of the participants' orientations. Their examples are drawn from focus group interviews conducted in Britain as part of an international study of young people's expectations about their future, and they include explicit references to the sexuality of others and reflexive orientations to homophobia or sexism. Stokoe and Smithson claim that there are also more implicit 'doings' that go unnoticed by the participants and are thus unavailable to a 'classic' (Schegloffian) CA analysis. They focus on the routine, mundane heterosexism — for instance, assuming a typical family to be heterosexual — that focus group participants (and even the inter-viewer) are complicit in 'passing by' without comment, repair work or reflex-ive attention.

While CA and ethnomethodology are founded on the project of uncover-ing how the 'natural attitude' is assembled in and through ordinary members' practices, there is a (less-often) repeated 'indifference' to the status of the practices, methods and procedures they study. Stokoe and Smithson challenge 'sequential' CA to provide a richly textured analysis of the sort of mundane heterosexism at work in their data, and they find it wanting in a number of respects. They suggest, instead, that the (feminist) analyst ought to draw upon membership categorisation analysis (MCA) — as first formulated by Sacks and elaborated recently as an alternative or supplement to sequential analysis in CA. They argue that the concerned analyst must inevitably draw upon her cultural knowledge and background to critique the inexplicit assumptions and inferences (what Fish in this volume would call the 'unsaid') of talk, which only the analyst has access to or an interest in. Although this stance is vulnerable to importing (and imposing) an analytic fiction (see Schegloff 1998, 1999a), their arguments are crucial for a general politics of conversa-tion. One could characterise their endeavour as desiring of a more critical edge so as to analyse the operation of naturalisation and hegemony in talk practices (what Butler 1997a has called the 'tacit performativity of power'), particularly those — such as heterosexism, whiteness and disability — that are fundamental to how we think of ourselves and others, but which for many people are still on the cusp of their everyday discursive consciousness.

Paul McIlvenny's chapter presents a thorough theoretical reflection on the similarities and differences between versions of conversation analysis and performative approaches to gender in feminism and queer studies. The 'performative turn' that has recently surfaced unevenly in studies of gender and sexuality in everyday language use is most often traceable to the work of the American feminist philosopher Judith Butler. In order to appreciate the need for comparison, McIlvenny introduces the relevance and complexity of Butler's poststructuralist understanding of 'performativity'. Butler borrows a Derridean twist to Austin's original notion of linguistic performativity and melds it with a Foucauldian conception of the discourses of sexuality in order to comprehend the ways in which gendered and sexed bodies are discursively constituted. Butler argues that gender performativity comprises not singular 'acts' but a stylised citational practice, a chronic reiteration without an original, by which discourse produces the phenomena that it regulates and concomitantly reproduces hegemonic heterosexist gender norms. Gender congeals through performative practices, though performativity is itself vulnerable to excitation, recitation or mis-citation, resulting in an 'undoing' or a displacement of gender.

McIlvenny argues that this turn to the performative in contemporary feminist and queer theory seems to have missed an opportunity to ground its theorising in an alternative 'empirical' account of conversational practice and action. A comparative theoretical approach is taken to resolve on what grounds conversation analysis might be an appropriate and helpful methodology for particularising the performative model of gender (and sexuality). He shows that the articulation of a perspective on performative gender can even be found in the writings of Harold Garfinkel, the founder of ethnomethodology, but the heteronormativity that underlies Garfinkel's study of the 'intersexed' Agnes is problematic. The sophisticated model of 'doing' gender proposed by West and Zimmerman (1987) is introduced and compared in a number of respects with Butler's version of gender performativity theory. He concludes that despite these few engaging attempts to document the practices of 'doing' sex and gender using ethnomethodological and conversation analytic methods, this work has its own problems regarding normativity, power, agency and subjectivity.

Moreover, there has been little attempt to consider whether or not it is an appropriate methodology for studying talk and *sexuality*.

Susan Speer and **Jonathan Potter** also engage substantively with some of the key ideas of Judith Butler, particularly those concerning the performative discourse of 'hate speech'. They argue that discursive psychology holds similar views to Butler regarding the theorisation of discourse, gender identity and prejudice, yet it differs on at least four crucial points. Ultimately, they advocate that discursive psychology can provide distinct advantages over Butler's abstract theorisation of the subject and agency as an effect of discourse or "decontextualised re-iterative acts" at the level of the utterance. Following a CA line, discursive psychology can examine in specific detail how heteronormative gender identities are locally occasioned and action oriented in segments of talk. Moreover, discursive psychology's anti-cognitivist stance provides a means to investigate hate speech and its resignification as interactional accomplishments by participants on particular occasions. Rather than regarding heterosexism, homophobia or other prejudices as psychic phenomena or features of the individual, they locate them as ongoing concerns of participants in conversational encounters. Importantly, they demonstrate their case with three examples, each drawn from a different interactional setting, that illustrate the local management of heterosexism in talk.

Liisa Tainio seeks to uncover some of the ways in which the sequential, grammatical and semantic aspects of talk and conversation can be taken into account in the study of gender, heterosexuality and sexual agency. She traces the complex weaving of sexual agency in and through the grammatical and semantic construction of agentivity in conversational interaction. By examining talk between speakers of the Finnish language, Tainio provides valuable comparative evidence of identity construction in a language quite different from English in many of its linguistic features (see also D'hondt's chapter). The speakers that interest her can be characterised along the dimensions of generation, gender and sexuality: they are aged heterosexual married couples, who are being interviewed by young students of both sexes. Talk in and about heterosexual relationships is an important but little studied domain that can supplement studies that focus on the ways in which many people routinely display their 'ordinariness' and achieve their status as 'normal' representatives of their gender in conversational interaction. Although there are very good grounds to challenge the implicit normative focus in traditional sociolinguistics on the language of heterosexuals or on language use in supposedly heterosexual settings (see Barrett 1997), work is still needed to uncover the operation of heterosexuality in talk. In contrast to Stokoe and Smithson, and Speer and Potter in this volume, Tainio brings a more propitious version of heterosexuality to the foreground in her analysis.

Tainio highlights how particular discourse identities, such as interviewee, are invoked and make visible other social identities, such as those organised around gender and generation. In an instance of sexual teasing, in which the participation framework is contingently realigned, she shows how sexual agency is renegotiated. She particularly examines the syntactic and semantic organisation of utterances to reveal in specific ways how semantic ambiguity is both a political and an interactional resource for negotiating sexual agency. Her findings go against the grain of what might, in more feminist enlightened times, be expected about how spouses from an older generation interact; for example, how patriarchal husbands dominate, and wives submit or acquiesce. With this subtle shift away from categorical statements of difference/dominance to the specific and contextual conversational work that participants engage in, we have more evidence with which to wear down the views of those who differentiate 'men' and 'women' or 'husband' and 'wife' in fixed and stereotypical ways. What we gain from such a feminist perspective is a more productive view of women's agency that is often elided by a focus on the patriarchal dividend.

Like Tainio, **Sigurd D'hondt** provides valuable comparative evidence of identity construction in talk in a non-English speaking culture. By examining a casual and seemingly fleeting conversation between speakers of Kiswahili in Dar es Salaam, Tanzania, D'hondt provides a snapshot of gender and desire in action. In the data extract, three male adolescents discuss a fourth adolescent, a female, who has just left the copresent gathering. One participant 'notices' a change in her appearance, which touches off speculation about her pregnant status and whether or not she has had an abortion or a miscarriage. Later her sexual status and availability are broached. D'hondt analyses in detail how particular discourses of religion and gender are juxtaposed and elaborated in the conversation of the three adolescents, and how the conflicting interpretative repertoires or modes of framing gender thereby invoke and 'talk into being' specific (religious, gendered and sexualised) identities with definite interactional consequences. Moreover, what might appear to be one coherent identity may appear in incommensurable versions in a single stretch of talk. By interpreting Goffman's notion of framing from a CA perspective, he provides a way to understand the gendering of talk as the articulation and framing of 'sex' (or "biological predispositions") that is accountably relevant to the interpretation of that talk.

Arguing against the institutional/mundane comparative procedure in CA that would narrowly construe gender identity as an institutional matter and reduce identity to an either/or issue, D'hondt takes gender to have an omni-relevant status in talk as a social activity. Following Wetherell (1998), he suggests that we open up the restricted notion of 'context' that is implied by the comparative procedure and consider also the "argumentative texture" of the data. In this vein, he uses membership categorisation analysis to make claims about the 'argumentative' forms of practical reasoning that inform the descriptions of others present or absent and their actions. By refashioning the relationship between talk and identity, he proposes that we examine moment-by-moment the way participants themselves accomplish the transformation of 'gender' into a feature that is accountably relevant to the production and interpretation of their talk.

Andrew Fish notes that CA has shied away from an analysis of the sort of unfathomable or non-empirical objects that psychology or psychoanalysis often entertains, such as the psyche, repression or the unconscious. As Schegloff (1999a: 567-8) acknowledges, conversation analysis as he understands it is not without *a priori* assumptions, nor is analysis the same as the thing analysed, but it is clear that its methodological principles trade in empirical accounts of social action; that is, it concerns what talk is doing for the participants themselves as they understand it, not in speculations about what they did not or could not say or do. Following other discursive psychologists (Edwards 1997) who are busy respecifying their phenomena of interest in interactional terms, Billig (1999c) has called for a reappraisal of the psyche and the unconscious in studies of dialogue and talk. Because language is inherently expressive and repressive, he prefers to see repression not as a mysterious mental or internal process but as practised in everyday conversation. Although Billig does not study authentic instances of everyday conversation, his analyses of dialogic repression at work in Freud's writings, case studies and reported conversations beg application to so-called 'real' data (if only to see if it works and brings analytical benefits). In his chapter, Fish makes the first step in this challenging task by asking us to look more closely at the assumptions and impositions — the 'unsaid' — that can accompany and haunt any analysis of sexual and gender identities in a stretch of talk. He focuses our attention on one famous example from the Harvey Sacks corpus, namely the telling of a dirty joke. Sacks used a transcript of an interaction between some adolescent boys to unravel the temporal and sequential organisation of a (re)telling of a 'dirty joke' by one of the boys to an uncompliant audience.

That the joke was told earlier to the boy by his younger sister is topicalised after the joke has been told on this occasion.

However, much like Garfinkel in his analysis of Agnes and her 'intersexed' status, Sacks was a prisoner of his cultural presumptions as well as his own analysis. Fish examines how Sacks' analysis — or academic fiction — unwittingly imposes unwarranted age and gender categorisations on the dirty joke that is retold by the adolescent boy. Sacks embeds superficial features of the boys' categorisational work in his own academic fiction, which he then translates into transcendental truths about little girls, their needs and their jokes, thus re-transmitting stereotyped categories and clichéd thinking. Fish traces this to the predilection for ignoring or distrusting members' own sophisticated and ambiguous use of the unsaid as a resource for 'doing' sex and gender in talk. He demonstrates that invoking sexuality and gender in talk routinely involves stereotyped categorisations of self and others that are available for imposition, manipulation, play and performance without ever being explicitly stated.

One of the key issues for an anti-assimilationist project is to determine how stereotypical notions of gender are routinely maintained, congealed and naturalised in social interaction, and, just as importantly, what they are doing in and through their deployment. Given that it is difficult for members of a culture to make explicit and describe the subtlety of what for them is already mundane and normal, this is not an easy task. **Alexa Hepburn** broaches the issue by examining interview materials in which notions of gender and sex difference are enrolled in teachers' variable accounts of bullying among pupils in mixed schools in Scotland. What is interesting in these materials is both the variability in the reports and descriptions produced by the teachers (see also D'hondt in this volume for a discussion of variability in identity categorisations), and the delicacy with which they attend and disattend the character of these gendered accounts as stereotypical or evaluative at the same time as they are incited as factually grounded or natural observations.

In a bold move, Hepburn draws upon Derrida's post-structuralist critique of language, logocentrism and epistemology to provide a richer understanding of the practical logic that informs a participant's enrolment of gender in the production of the discursive limits of conduct. This move provides further support for jettisoning a reductive psychological or cognitivist account that curtails further exploration (see also Speer and Potter in this volume); instead, she argues, one ought to focus on the richer and more proximate seam of interactional, figural and contextual features of talk. Discursive psychology — already with roots in poststructuralism — and conversation analysis supply important tools for revealing the different discursive strategies and conversational structures — for instance, extreme case formulations, three-part lists and active voicing — that participants use to enrol gender and constitute accounts as factual.

In the final chapter, **Jenny Sundén** examines the performativity of gender, sex and the body in what has been called, among other things, 'textual talk' or 'conversational writing', or more prosaically 'on-line typed-in interaction'. Her data is drawn from a long term ethnographic study of social interactions over the Internet in a particular social MUD, a text-based online virtual world in which users 'inhabit' characters and fictional spaces and engage in collaborative interactions and performances of identity. One of those identities that is both built into the software and discussed by the users is 'virtual' gender. To exchange messages, users are provided with a limited set of commands that automatically prefix an identification (and a verb) to any textual string typed by the user, and then the system sends it to the other users in the same 'conversational space'. But users can also name their characters, construct inspectable 'personal' descriptions and assign attributes to their characters, which other users can 'glance' at and which change the behaviour of the system. The attribute that interests Sundén is *@gender* that can take a range of forms — some quite utopian — which are adequate for characterising a member of the community (see Sacks 1972 for a discussion of membership categorisation devices). A particular choice (and that choice is not permanent) from one of these encoded membership categorisation sets has consequences both for how the software automatically uses pronouns to index a present user and how other users engage in pronominal reference to present and non-present users. What is important here is that the significance and import of gender and *@gender* in this virtual world is interactionally negotiable and performative.

Sundén considers how concepts like gender (and sexuality) apply to the conversational interactions in the MUD when it appears for all intents and purposes that those interactions are independent of the physical domain and the corporeal body. Indeed, it is common for both theorists and users to invoke a spiritual or transcendental discourse to account for their conduct online. She demonstrates that the familiar sex/gender dichotomy to be found in the so-called offline world (glossed in the riddle 'Is sex to gender as nature is to culture?'), migrates to straddle the permeable boundary between online and offline. Thus, gender is to be understood as the textual online incarnation of a sex which is grounded in the material body left behind in the physical world. Her data examples illustrate how users routinely deploy this perspective in accounting for their own conduct and that of other users. Sundén counters this discourse, however, by arguing that *both* sex and gender are discursive effects, which means that a more sophisticated understanding of (hetero)textuality, materiality and virtuality is needed in this context. Through careful readings of on-line conversations explicitly focusing on the writing (or typing) of sexed and gendered bodies, the author shows how immaterial bodies do matter, such that we cannot so easily separate textual and material realities.

6. Conclusion

The contributions in this volume contribute in significant ways to the mapping out of a fertile research landscape. Adventurous steps are made towards the productive alignment of the fine-grained empirical analysis of conversational materials with the contemporary aims of feminism and queer studies, as well as with the critical ambitions of discursive approaches to language, performativity, subjectivity, identity, desire and agency. Moreover, the contributions add to the impact of feminist theory, post-structuralist or otherwise, on the analysis of situated language use in conversational interaction, reflexively transforming how we think of and represent language and talk. Equally, the goals of feminism and queer studies are supplemented in novel ways by the volume's sophisticated interactional perspective on performativity and talk practices.

It is my hope that *Talking Gender and Sexuality* will enable readers to appreciate the theoretical and methodological complexities of researching talk, gender and sexuality using CA and DP — there are no easy solutions. Nevertheless, with the strong focus of the majority of the contributions on empirical materials and fine-grained analysis, readers can gain valuable insights in how to undertake the practical study of empirical materials themselves. The interdisciplinarity of the volume, particularly with the melding of performativity, discursive approaches and conversation analysis, provides us with new tools for describing and explaining an exciting domain of unforeseen and hitherto unexplored phenomena.

Notes

*   Thanks to Pirkko Raudaskoski, Susan Speer and Liisa Tainio for their suggestions to improve this introduction.

1.   Recently, some scholars have called for 'bridge building' between Foucauldian discourse theory and CA/ethnomethodology (Miller 1997). Although this is indeed a worthy enterprise, the focus so far has been on a certain structuralist period in Foucault's ideas — when he formulated his innovative perspective on disciplinary power, knowledge, subjection and discourse — that is particularly amenable to institutional analysis. John Heritage (1997: 179) suggests that "conversation analysis may end up with an affinity with a rather Foucauldian conception of power", yet nowhere is Foucault's (1976) later work on the history of sexuality and bio-power discussed.

2.   There has been plenty of critical discussion concerning how to conceive of 'sex' and 'gender' — for the debate in feminism, see Butler (1990), Delphy (1993), Epstein (1990), Matthieu (1996), Raynaud (1998) and Wittig (1992); in feminist sociolinguistics, see Cameron (1997a); in anthropology, see Nilsson (1996) and Stolcke (1993); and in sociology, see Hood-Williams (1996).

3.   This book suggests new directions to explore further the role that different qualitative empirical analyses of talk can play for a feminist or queer-informed politics that is attentive to the discursive construction of genders *and* sexualities. Although sexuality is not reducible to gender, there are good theoretical reasons to keep gender and sexuality in continuous dialogue, since the two concepts are in a mutually constitutive relationship of some complexity. For example, sexuality can be seen to articulate gender and the shaming of gender often reproduces a normative heterosexuality.

4.   Leap (1996) is ground-breaking and suggestive, but unfortunately it contains very few recorded examples of real conversations and lacks rigorous interactional analysis. This is true of much of the literature in lavender linguistics.

5.   These studies are important, but we should of course remain aware that there is the ever present danger of reinforcing a normative view of 'masculine' or 'heterosexual' conversational practices as superior or the norm (Barrett 1997), and of diverting funds from minority subjects and topics in feminist or queer linguistic research (Canaan and Griffin 1990).

6.   Although not used in this volume, it should be mentioned that recently a comprehensive approach to language and gender has emerged in the form of the communities of practice (CoP) model, first formulated with clarity by Eckert and McConnell-Ginet (1992). A thorough introduction to the notion of 'community of practice' can be found in Wenger (1998). When used to investigate language and gender as a social practice it offers the possibility to focus on the local construction of gender identity (see the special issue of *Language in Society* introduced by Holmes and Meyerhoff 1999). In a recent review of feminist contributions to linguistic anthropology and their relationship to practice theory, McElhinny (1998b) surveys the work of Sherry Ortner, who ties together the development of practice theory and feminist theory in anthropology. McElhinny claims that the two have been unified in linguistic anthropology to pioneer a feminist practice theory, but

without much visibility. Key figures in her canon are: Marjorie Goodwin (1990), Elinor Ochs (1992), and Eckert and McConnell-Ginet (1992).

A fourth approach, which does not feature in this collection except as provocateur, is critical discourse analysis (CDA) as promulgated by Fairclough (1995) among others. CDA draws on a rich conception of discourse as social practice following Pêcheux (1982) and Foucault (1972), but has had little engagement specifically with gender issues until recently (see Bergvall 1999 and Moonwomon-Baird 1996). One exemplary study can be found in Bergvall and Remlinger (1996), who direct attention to the reproduction of, and resistance to, traditional gendered social roles that men and women take on in the arena of university classroom interaction. They argue that CDA has a pivotal role as an educational tool to reveal how conversations evolve and how they might be improved by attending to the positive aspects of gendered behaviours in the classroom, without supposing a deficit or difference model. The CDA approach is also mentioned here since it has recently been the staging post for a debate over the politics of conversation analysis, a debate which has taken as its prime bone of contention the relevance of a descriptive analysis of talk and conversation to the critical analysis of gender (see Schegloff 1997, 1998 and Wetherell 1998).

7.   Besides those already mentioned, we should also include Ahrens (1997), Ainsworth-Vaughn (1992), Beach (2000), Bucholtz (1999), Cameron (1997b), Capps (1999), Conefrey (1997), Edwards (1998), Frith (1998), Frith and Kitzinger (1998), Garcia (1998), Gilfoyle, Wilson and Brown (1993), Gough (1998), Hall (1995), Hollander (1998), Hopper and LeBaron (1998), Kakava (1994), Kitzinger and Frith (1999), Kitzinger (2000a), Kitzinger (2000b), McElhinny (1998a), Mendoza-Denton (1999), Morgan and Wood (1999), Nilan (1994), Scott (2000), Stokoe (1998, 2000), Stokoe and Smithson (2001), Stringer and Hopper (1998), Widdicombe (1995), and Willott and Griffin (1997). Only a few as yet have topicalised sexuality (or desire) in talk, including Barrett (1999), Channell (1997), Cromwell (1995), Gaudio (1997), Gavey et al. (1999), Kitzinger (2000b), McIlvenny (2001), McPhillips and Braun (1999), and Speer and Potter (2000).

8.   Kitzinger's vernacular example of her experience while on holiday of the heterosexist practices of table seating illustrates not only that one must look carefully at how members accountably design their utterances, but that a 'feminist' (or 'queer') perspective might 'permit' or encourage analysts to ask better questions and articulate more richly the relations between entities — to find many ways to mix, confuse, and intermingle what 'members are doing out there' and 'what we say about them'. Her suggestive analysis shows that, in the case at hand, the 'invisibility' of participant orientations would simply be the result of a rigid, 'naïve' CA focus on the 'next-turn'. The more appropriate focus would be on the 'strategic' work practice of waiters in allocating appropriately sized tables, a practice which her improvised method ran into while she 'loitered' and 'learned' the (heterosexist) artfulness of waitering at the boundary between the mobile public and customers-to-be-seated. She then discovered an analytically noticeable 'non-occurrence' across a set of instances, which for the participants-as-customers would not have been 'accountably noticeable' in the design (or sequencing) of the turn.

9.   If we examine Schegloff's (1991) argument more closely and follow it to a logical conclusion, we find that there is in fact an array of possibilities for an analysis. If we use the letter (A) to refer to the availability of a category from a Pn adequate membership catego-

ry set, eg. [male, female] (see Sacks 1972), the letter (R) to refer to the situational relevance of a category description, as demonstrated in either (R1) speaker orientation, which means it is observable-reportable, or (R2) recipient orientation in a next turn. And let the letter (P) refer to the requirement of procedural consequentiality as defined by Schegloff. The theoretical combinations for a procedural analysis are as follows:

A and R1 and R2 and P are operable, which we can presume is Schegloff's ideal case for making a strong analytical claim.

A and R1 and R2 but *not* P, so that a category is noticed but is not consequential (except for the analyst).

A and R1 (but *not* R2) and P, which is potentially the case when a recipient misunderstands or mishears.

A and R1 (but *not* R2) and *not* P, which could arguably provide grounds for the analyst to still claim consequentiality for social ordering, eg. (hetero)sexism-in-action.

A but *not* R (neither R1 nor R2) and *not* P, which means there is no analytical warrant for using the descriptive category.

There are also some potential leaks and disturbances to this neat logic. For example, the assumed integrity of A could be compromised or subverted: [male, female] is hardly adequate in a social ordering which includes transgendered persons. Of course, these combinatorics are an abstract exercise in determining the logical limit of Schegloff's formulation of these concepts.

10.   Latour (1996) critiques ethnomethodology because by focusing on interaction per se ethnomethodologists fail to see the resources necessary for constructing "the social world". Contentiously, he also criticises the bounded notion of the 'everyday' that is foundational in ethnomethodology. Thus, because participants themselves are continually changing scale, displacing action and sharing agency, one cannot rely on the notion of a pure "participant orientation", uncontaminated by the 'social context' or the analyst. If one follows the participants, then one cannot stay within the local interaction.

References

Ahrens, Ulrike. 1997 "The interplay between interruptions and preference organization in conversation". In *Communicating Gender in Context*, H. Kotthoff and R. Wodak (eds), 79-106. Amsterdam: John Benjamins.

Ainsworth-Vaughn, Nancy. 1992 "Topic transitions in physician-patient interviews: Power, gender, and discourse". *Language in Society* 21(3): 409-426.

Antaki, Charles and Widdicombe, Sue (eds). 1998 *Identities in Talk*. London: Sage.

Barrett, Rusty. 1997 "The 'homo-genius' speech community". In *Queerly Phrased: Language, Gender and Sexuality*, A. Livia and K. Hall (eds), 181-201. New York: Oxford University Press.

Barrett, Rusty. 1999 "Indexing polymorphous identity in the speech of African American drag queens". In *Reinventing Identities: The Gendered Self in Discourse*, M. Bucholtz, A. Liang and L. Sutton (eds), 313-331. Oxford: Oxford University Press.

Beach, Wayne A. 2000 "Inviting collaborations in stories about a woman". *Language in Society* 29: 379-407.

Benhabib, Seyla, Butler, Judith, Cornell, Drucilla and Fraser, Nancy (eds). 1995 *Feminist Contentions: A Philosophical Exchange.* London: Routledge.

Bergvall, Victoria L. 1999 "Towards a comprehensive theory of language and gender". *Language in Society* 28: 273-293.

Bergvall, Victoria L., Bing, Janet M. and Freed, Alice F. (eds). 1996 *Rethinking Language and Gender Research: Theory and Method.* London: Longman.

Bergvall, Victoria L. and Remlinger, Kathryn A. 1996 "Reproduction, resistance and gender in educational discourse: The role of critical discourse analysis". *Discourse & Society* 7(4): 453-479.

Billig, Michael. 1999a "Whose terms? Whose ordinariness? Rhetoric and ideology in conversation analysis". *Discourse & Society* 10(4): 543—558.

Billig, Michael. 1999b "Conversation analysis and the claims of naivety". *Discourse & Society* 10(4): 572-576.

Billig, Michael. 1999c *Freudian Repression: Conversation Creating the Unconscious.* Cambridge: Cambridge University Press.

Bing, Janet M. and Bergvall, Victoria L. 1996 "The question of questions: Beyond binary thinking". In *Rethinking Language and Gender Research: Theory and Method*, V.L. Bergvall, J.M. Bing and A.F. Freed (eds), 1-30. London: Longman.

Bristow, Joseph. 1997 *Sexuality.* London: Routledge.

Bucholtz, Mary. 1995 "From mulatta to mestiza: Passing and the linguistic reshaping of ethnic identity". In *Gender Articulated: Language and the Socially Constructed Self*, K. Hall and M. Bucholtz (eds), 351-373. New York: Routledge.

Bucholtz, Mary. 1999 "'Why be normal?': Language and identity practices in a community of nerd girls". *Language in Society* 28: 203-223.

Bucholtz, Mary, Liang, Anita and Sutton, Laurel (eds). 1999 *Reinventing Identities: The Gendered Self in Discourse.* Oxford: Oxford University Press.

Bunzl, Matti. 2000 "Inverted appellation and discursive gender insubordination: An Austrian case study in gay male conversation". *Discourse & Society* 11(?): 207-236.

Butler, Judith. 1990 *Gender Trouble: Feminism and the Subversion of Identity.* London: Routledge.

Butler, Judith. 1993 *Bodies That Matter.* London: Routledge.

Butler, Judith. 1994 "Against proper objects". *Differences* 6(2-3): 1-26.

Butler, Judith. 1997a *Excitable Speech: A Politics of the Performative.* London: Routledge.

Butler, Judith. 1997b "Further reflections of conversations of our time". *Diacritics* 27(1): 13-15.

Butler, Judith and Scott, Joan (eds). 1992 *Feminists Theorise the Political.* London: Routledge.

Cameron, Deborah. 1992a "Review of Tannen's *You Just Don't Understand: Women and Men in Conversation*". *Feminism & Psychology* 2(3): 465-489.

Cameron, Deborah. 1992b "'Not gender difference but the difference gender makes' — Explanation in research on sex and language". *International Journal of Sociology of Language* 94: 13-26.

Cameron, Deborah. 1995 "Rethinking language and gender studies: Some issues for the 1990s". In *Language and Gender: Interdisciplinary Prespectives*, S. Mills (ed.), 31-44. London: Longman.

Cameron, Deborah. 1997a "Theoretical debates in feminist linguistics: Questions of sex and gender". In *Gender and Discourse*, R. Wodak (ed.), 21-36. London: Sage.

Cameron, Deborah. 1997b "Performing gender identity: Young men's talk and construction of heterosexual masculinity". In *Language and Masculinity*, S. Johnson and U. Meinhof (eds), 47-64. Oxford: Blackwell.

Cameron, Deborah. 1998a "Gender, language and discourse: A review essay". *Signs* 23(4): 945-973.

Cameron, Deborah. 1998b "'Is there any ketchup, Vera?': Gender, power and pragmatics". *Discourse & Society* 9(4): 437-455.

Canaan, Joyce E. and Griffin, Christine. 1990 "The new men's studies: Part of the problem or part of the solution?" In *Men, Masculinities and Social Theory*, J. Hearn and D. Morgan (eds), 206-214. London: Unwin Hyman.

Capps, Lisa. 1999 "Constructing the irrational woman: Narrative interaction and agoraphobic identity". In *Reinventing Identities: The Gendered Self in Discourse*, M. Bucholtz, A. Liang and L. Sutton (eds), 83-100. Oxford: Oxford University Press.

Channell, Joanna. 1997 "'I just called to say I love you': Love and desire on the telephone". In *Language and Desire: Encoding Sex, Romance and Intimacy*, K. Harvey and C. Shalom (eds), 143-169. London: Routledge.

Coates, Jennifer. 1997 "One-at-a-time: The organization of men's talk". In *Language and Masculinity*, S. Johnson and U. Meinhof (eds), 107-129. Oxford: Blackwell.

Conefrey, Theresa. 1997 "Gender, culture and authority in a university life sciences laboratory". *Discourse & Society* 8(3): 313-340.

Connell, R.W. 1995 *Masculinities*. Cambridge: Polity Press.

Crawford, Mary. 1995 *Talking Difference*. London: Sage.

Cromwell, Jason. 1995 "Talking about without talking about: The use of protective language among tranvestites and transsexuals". In *Beyond the Lavender Lexicon: Authenticity, Imagination, and Appropriation in Lesbian and Gay Languages*, W. Leap (ed.), 267-295. Amsterdam: Gordon & Breach.

Delph-Janiurek, Tom. 1999 "Sounding gender(ed): Vocal performances in English university teaching spaces". *Gender, Place & Culture* 6(2): 137-153.

Delphy, Christine. 1993 "Rethinking sex and gender". *Women's Studies International Forum* 16(11): 1-9.

Dijk, Teun A. van. 1990 "*Discourse & Society*: A new journal for a new research focus". *Discourse & Society* 1(1): 5-16.

Dijk, Teun A. van (ed.). 1997 *Discourse as Social Interaction*.[Discourse Studies: A Multidisciplinary Introduction Volume 2]. London: Sage.

Eckert, Penelope. 1996 "Vowels and nail polish: The emergence of linguistic style in the preadolescent heterosexual marketplace". In *Gender and Belief Systems: Proceedings of the Fourth Berkeley Women and Language Conference*, N. Warner, J. Ahlers, *et al.* (eds), 183-190. Berkeley, CA: Berkeley Women and Language Group.

Eckert, Penelope and McConnell-Ginet, Sally. 1992 "Think practically and look locally: Language and gender as community-based practice". *Annual Review of Anthropology* 21: 461-490.

Edley, Nigel. 2001 "Conversation analysis, discursive psychology and the study of ideology: A response to Susan Speer". *Feminism & Psychology* 11(1): 136-140.

Edwards, Derek. 1997 *Discourse and Cognition*. London: Sage.

Edwards, Derek. 1998 "The relevant thing about her: Social identity categories in use". In *Identities in Talk*, C. Antaki and S. Widdicombe (eds), 15-33. London: Sage.

Edwards, Derek and Potter, Jonathan. 1992 *Discursive Psychology*. London: Sage.

Elam, Diane. 1994 *Feminism and Deconstruction: Ms. en Abyme*. London: Routledge.

Epstein, Julia. 1990 "Either/or-neither/both: Sexual ambiguity and the ideology of gender". *Genders* 7: 99-142.

Epstein, Steven. 1994 "A queer encounter: Sociology and the study of sexuality". *Sociological Theory* 12(2): 188-202.

Fairclough, Norman. 1995 *Critical Discourse Analysis*. London: Longman.

Fishman, Pamela. 1978 "Interaction: The work women do". *Social Problems* 25: 397-406.

Foucault, Michel. 1972 *The Archaeology of Knowledge*. London: Tavistock.

Foucault, Michel. 1976 *The History of Sexuality, Volume One: An Introduction*. London: Penguin.

Frith, Hannah. 1998 "Constructing the 'other' through talk". *Feminism & Psychology* 8(4): 530-536.

Frith, Hannah and Kitzinger, Celia. 1998 "'Emotion work' as a participant resource: A feminist analysis of young women's talk-in-interaction". *Sociology* 32(2): 299-320.

Garcia, Angela. 1998 "The relevance of interactional and institutional contexts for the study of gender differences: A demonstrative case study". *Symbolic Interaction* 21(1): 35-58.

Garfinkel, Harold. 1967 *Studies in Ethnomethodology*. Cambridge: Polity Press.

Gaudio, Rudolf P. 1997 "Not talking straight in Hausa". In *Queerly Phrased: Language, Gender and Sexuality*, A. Livia and K. Hall (eds), 416-429. New York: Oxford University Press.

Gavey, Nicola, McPhillips, Kathryn and Braun, Virginia. 1999 "*Interruptus coitus*: Heterosexuals accounting for intercourse". *Sexualities* 2(1): 35-68.

Gilfoyle, Jackie, Wilson, Jonathan and Brown. 1993 "Sex, organs and audiotape: A discourse analytic approach to talking about heterosexual sex and relationships". In *Heterosexuality*, S. Wilkinson and C. Kitzinger (eds), 181-202. London: Sage.

Gill, Rosalind. 1995 "Relativism, reflexivity and politics: Interrogating discourse analysis from a feminst perspective". In *Feminism and Discourse: Psychological Perspectives*, S. Wilkinson and C. Kitzinger (eds), 165-186. London: Sage.

Goodwin, Marjorie Harness. 1980 "Directive/response speech sequences in girls' and boys' task activities". In *Woman and Language in Literature and Society*, S. McConnell-Ginet, R. Borker and N. Furman (eds), 157-173. New York: Praeger.

Goodwin, Marjorie Harness. 1990 *He-Said-She-Said: Talk as Social Organisation Among Black Children*. Bloomington, IN.: Indiana University Press.

Goodwin, Marjorie Harness. 1993 "Tactical uses of stories: Participation frameworks within girls' and boys' disputes". In *Gender and Conversational Interaction*, D. Tannen (ed.), 110-143. Oxford: Oxford University Press.

Goodwin, Marjorie Harness. 1999 "Constructing opposition within girls' games". In *Reinventing Identities: The Gendered Self in Discourse*, M. Bucholtz, A. Liang and L. Sutton (eds), 388-409. Oxford: Oxford University Press.

Gough, Brendan and Edwards, Gareth. 1998 "The beer talking: Four lads, a carry out and the reproduction of masculinities". *The Sociological Review* 46(3): 409-435.

Halberstam, Judith. 1998 *Female Masculinity*. Durham, NC: Duke University Press.

Hall, Kira. 1995 "Lip service on the fantasy lines". In *Gender Articulated: Language and the Socially Constructed Self*, K. Hall and M. Bucholtz (eds), 183-216. New York: Routledge.

Hall, Kira and Bucholtz, Mary (eds). 1995 *Gender Articulated: Language and the Socially Constructed Self*. New York: Routledge.

Harvey, Keith and Shalom, Celia (eds). 1997 *Language and Desire: Encoding Sex, Romance and Intimacy*. London: Routledge.

Have, Paul ten. 1999 *Doing Conversation Analysis: A Practical Guide*. London: Sage.

Hepburn, Alexa. 2000 "On the alleged incompatibility between feminism and relativism". *Feminism and Psychology* 10(1): 91-106.

Heritage, John. 1984 *Garfinkel and Ethnomethodology*. Cambridge: Polity Press.

Hester, Stephen and Eglin, Peter (eds). 1997 *Culture in Action: Studies in Membership Categorisation Analysis*. Washington, DC: University of America Press.

Hollander, Jocelyn. 1998 "Doing *Studs*: The performance of gender and sexuality on late-night television". In *Everyday Inequalities: Critical Inquiries*, J. O'Brien and J.A. Howard (eds), 43-71. Oxford: Blackwell.

Hollway, Wendy. 1984 "Women's power in heterosexual sex". *Women's Studies International Forum* 7(1): 63-68.

Hollway, Wendy. 1995 "Feminist discourses and women's heterosexual desire". In *Feminism and Discourse: Psychological Perspectives*, S. Wilkinson and C. Kitzinger (eds), 86-105. London: Sage.

Holmes, Janet and Meyerhoff, Miriam. 1999 "The community of practice: Theories and methodologies in language and gender research". *Language in Society* 28: 173-183.

Hood-Williams, John. 1996 "Goodbye to sex and gender". *The Sociological Review* 44(1): 1-16.

Hopper, Robert and LeBaron, Curtis. 1998 "How gender creeps into talk". *Research on Language and Social Interaction* 31(1): 59-74.

Hutchby, Ian and Wooffitt, Robin. 1998 *Conversation Analysis: Principles, Practices and Applications*. Cambridge: Polity.

Ingraham, Chrys. 1996 "The heterosexual imaginary: Feminist sociology and theories of gender". In *Queer Theory/Sociology*, S. Seidman (ed.), 168-193. Oxford: Basil Blackwell.

Jackson, Stevi. 1999 *Heterosexuality in Question*. London: Sage.

Jagose, Annamarie. 1996 *Queer Theory: An Introduction*. New York: New York University Press.

James, Deborah and Clarke, Sandra. 1993 "Women, men, and interruptions: A critical review". In *Gender and Conversational Interaction*, D. Tannen (ed.), 231-280. Oxford: Oxford University Press.

Jefferson, Gail. 1989 "Preliminary notes on a possible metric which provides for a 'standard maximum' silence of approximately one second in conversation". In *Conversation: An Interdisciplinary Perspective*, D. Roger and P. Bull (eds), 166-196. Clevedon, Philadelphia: Multilingual Matters.

Jefferson, Gail. draft "A note on laughter in 'male-female' interaction". Unpublished. Dated: April 5, 1997.

Johnson, Sally and Finlay, Frank. 1997 "Do men gossip? An analysis of football talk on television". In *Language and Masculinity*, S. Johnson and U. Meinhof (eds), 130-143. Oxford: Blackwell.

Johnson, Sally and Meinhof, Ulrike (eds). 1997 *Language and Masculinity*. Oxford: Blackwell.

Kakava, Christina. 1994 "'Do you want to get engage, baby?': The cultural construction of gender in Greek conversation". In *Cultural Performances: Proceedings of the Third Berkeley Women and Language Conference*, M. Bucholtz, A. Liang, L. Sutton and C. Hines (eds), 691-711. Berkeley, CA: Berkeley Women and Language Group.

Kaplan, Carla. 1996 *The Erotics of Talk: Women's Writing and Feminist Paradigms*. Oxford: Oxford University Press.

Kaplan, Louise. 1993 *Female Perversions: The Temptations of Madame Bovary*. New York: Doubleday.

Katz, Jonathan Ned. 1996 *The Invention of Heterosexuality*. New York: Plume.

Kitzinger, Celia. 2000a "How to resist an idiom". *Research on Language and Social Interaction* 33(2): 121-154.

Kitzinger, Celia. 2000b "Doing feminist conversation analysis". *Feminism & Psychology* 10(2): 163-194.

Kitzinger, Celia and Frith, Hannah. 1999 "Just say no? The use of conversation analysis in developing a feminist perspective on sexual refusal". *Discourse & Society* 10(3): 293-316.

Kotthoff, Helga and Wodak, Ruth (eds). 1997a *Communicating Gender in Context*. Amsterdam: John Benjamins.

Kotthoff, Helga and Wodak, Ruth. 1997b "Preface". In *Communicating Gender in Context*, H. Kotthoff and R. Wodak (eds), vii-xxv. Amsterdam: John Benjamins.

Kulick, Don. 1999 "Language & gender/sexuality". From the Language & Culture mailing list: Online Symposium. <http://www.language-culture.org/archives/subs/kulick-don/index.html>. [Nov 17, 1999].

Kulick, Don. 2000 "Gay and lesbian language". *Annual Review of Anthropology* 29: 243-285.

Lakoff, Robin. 1975 *Language and Woman's Place*. New York: Harper Row.

Latour, Bruno. 1996 "On interobjectivity". *Mind, Culture & Activity* 3(4): 228-245.

Lauretis, Teresa de. 1991 "Queer theory: Lesbian and gay sexualities — An introduction". *Differences* 4(2): iii-xviii.

Lauretis, Teresa de. 1999 "Gender symptoms, or, peeing like a man". *Social Semiotics* 9(2): 257-270.

Leap, William (ed.). 1995 *Beyond the Lavender Lexicon: Authenticity, Imagination, and Appropriation in Lesbian and Gay Languages*. Amsterdam: Gordon & Breach.

Leap, William. 1996 *Word's Out: Gay Men's English*. Minneapolis: University of Minnesota Press.

Leap, William. 1998 "Rethinking language and gender: Recent steps towards a lesbian, gay, bisexual and transgendered linguistics". *World Englishes* 17(2): 191-192.

Lepper, Georgia. 2000 *Categories in Text and Talk: A Practical Introduction to Categorization Analysis*. London: Sage.

Livia, Anna and Hall, Kira (eds). 1997a *Queerly Phrased: Language, Gender and Sexuality*. New York: Oxford University Press.

Livia, Anna and Hall, Kira. 1997b "'It's a girl': Bringing performativity back to linguistics". In *Queerly Phrased: Language, Gender and Sexuality*, A. Livia and K. Hall (eds), 3-18. New York: Oxford University Press.

Martin, Biddy. 1994 "Sexualities without genders and other queer utopias". *Diacritics* 24(2-3): 104-121.

Matthieu, Nicole-Claude. 1996 "Sexual, sexed and sex-class identities: Three ways of conceptualising the relationship between sex and gender". In *Sex in Question: French Material Feminism*, D. Leonard and L. Atkins (eds), 42-71. London: Taylor & Francis.

Maynard, Mary and Purvis, June (eds). 1995 *(Hetero)sexual Politics*. London: Taylor & Francis.

McElhinny, Bonnie. 1993 *We All Wear the Blue! Language, Gender and Police Work*. Unpublished PhD Dissertation. Stanford University.

McElhinny, Bonnie. 1997 "Ideologies of public and private language in sociolinguistics". In *Gender and Discourse*, R. Wodak (ed.), 106-139. London: Sage.

McElhinny, Bonnie. 1998a "Cooperative culture: Reconciling equality and difference in a multicultural women's co-operative". *Ethnos: Journal of Anthropology* 63(3): 164-189.

McElhinny, Bonnie. 1998b "Genealogies of gender theory: Practice theory and feminism in sociocultural and linguistic anthropology". *Social Analysis* 42(3): 164-189.

McHoul, Alec. 1986 "The getting of sexuality: Foucault, Garfinkel and the analysis of sexual discourse". *Theory, Culture & Society* 3(2): 65-79.

McIlvenny, Paul. 2001 "Do 'Opposites always attract'?: Doing gender/sexuality in intercultural encounters". In *Communicating Culture: Proceedings of the 3rd Nordic Symposium on Intercultural Communication, Oct 1996* [Language & Cultural Contact 28], K.G. Andersen (ed.), 81-99. Aalborg: Centre for Languages and Intercultural Studies, Aalborg University.

McIntosh, Peggy. 1992 "White privilege and male privilege: A personal account of coming to see correspondence through work in women's studies". In *Race, Class, and Gender: An Anthology*, M. Anderson and P.H. Collins (eds), 70-81. Belmont, CA: Wadsworth.

Mendoza-Denton, Norma. 1999 "Turn-initial *No*: Collaborative opposition among Latina adolescents". In *Reinventing Identities: The Gendered Self in Discourse*, M. Bucholtz, A. Liang and L. Sutton (eds), 273-292. Oxford: Oxford University Press.

Miller, Gale. 1997 "Building bridges: The possibility of analytic dialogue between ethnography, conversation analysis and Foucault". In *Qualitative Research: Theory, Method and Practice*, D. Silverman (ed.), 24-44. London: Sage.

Mills, Sara (ed.). 1995 *Language and Gender: Interdisciplinary Prespectives*. London: Longman.

Moerman, Michael. 1988 *Talking Culture*. Philadelphia: University of Pennsylvania Press.

Moerman, Michael. 1993 "Ariadne's thread and Indra's net: Reflections on ethnography, ethnicity, identity, culture, and interaction". *Research on Language and Social Interaction* 26(1): 85-98.

Moonwomon-Baird, Birch. 1996 "Lesbian conversation a site for ideological identity construction". In *Gender and Belief Systems: Proceedings of the Fourth Berkeley Women and Language Conference*, N. Warner, J. Ahlers, *et al.* (eds), 563-574. Berkeley, CA: Berkeley Women and Language Group.

Morgan, Ruth and Wood, Kathleen. 1995 "Lesbians in the living room: collusion, co-construction and co-narration in conversation". In *Beyond the Lavender Lexicon: Authenticity, Imagination, and Appropriation in Lesbian and Gay Languages*, W. Leap (ed.), 235-248. Amsterdam: Gordon & Breach.

Nilan, Pam. 1994 "Gender as positioned identity maintenance in everyday discourse". *Social Semiotics* 4(1-2): 139-162.

Nilsson, Frida. 1996 "The breakdown of the sex/gender distinction in anthropological discourse". *NORA: Nordic Journal of Women's Studies*(2): 114-127.

Ochs, Elinor. 1992 "Indexing gender". In *Rethinking Context: Language as an Interactive Phenomenon*, A. Duranti and C. Goodwin (eds), 335-358. Cambridge: Cambridge University Press.

Ortner, Sherry. 1974 "Is female to male as nature is to culture?" In *Woman, Culture, and Society*, M.Z. Rosaldo and L. Lamphere (eds), 67-87. Stanford, CA: Stanford University Press.

Ortner, Sherry. 1989 *High Religion: A Cultural and Political History of Sherpa Buddhism*. Princeton, NJ: Princeton University Press.

Pêcheux, Michel. 1982 *Language, Semantics and Ideology: Stating the Obvious*. London: Macmillan.

Potter, Jonathan and Wetherell, Margaret. 1987 *Discourse and Social Psychology: Beyond Attitudes and Behaviour*. London: Sage.

Psathas, George. 1995 *Conversation Analysis: The Study of Talk-in-interaction*. London: Sage.

Raynaud, Claudine. 1998 "Sex or gender? Double-crosses, double-binds". *European Journal of English Studies* 2(3): 267-284.

Rich, Adrienne. 1980 "Compulsory heterosexuality and lesbian existence". *Signs* 5(4): 631-660.

Richardson, Diane (ed.). 1996 *Theorising Heterosexuality: Telling It Straight*. Buckingham: Open University Press.

Rodino, Michelle. 1997 "Breaking the binaries: Reconceptualising gender and Its relationship to language in computer-mediated communication". *Journal of Computer-Mediated Communication* 3(3). [Online]. Available: <http://jcmc.huji.ac.il/vol3/issue3/rodino.html>. [Apr 24, 1998].

Sacks, Harvey. 1972 "An initial investigation of the usability of conversational data for doing sociology". In *Studies in Social Interaction*, D. Sudnow (ed.), 31-74. New York: Free Press.

Sacks, Harvey. 1978 "Some technical considerations of a dirty joke". In *Studies in the Organisation of Conversational Interaction*, J. Schenkein (ed.), 249-269. London: Academic Press.

Sacks, Harvey. 1995 *Lectures on Conversation: Volumes I and II*. Oxford: Basil Blackwell.

Sacks, Harvey and Schegloff, Emanuel A. 1979 "Two preferences in the organisation of reference to persons in conversation and their interaction". In *Everyday Language*, G. Psathas (ed.), 15-21. Boston: Irvington.

Salamensky, S.I. (ed.). 2001 *Talk Talk Talk: The Cultural Life of Everyday Conversation*. New York: Routledge.

Sanders, Robert E. 1999 "The impossibility of a culturally contexted conversation analysis: On simultaneous, distinct types of pragmatic meaning". *Research on Language and Social Interaction* 32(1-2): 129-140.

Schegloff, Emanuel A. 1987 "Between micro and macro: Contexts and other connections". In *The Micro-Macro Link*, J. Alexander, B. Giesen, R. Munch and N. Smelser (eds), 207-234. Berkeley, CA: University of California Press.

Schegloff, Emanuel A. 1991 "Reflections on talk and social structure". In *Talk and Social Structure*, D. Boden and D. Zimmerman (eds), 44-70. Cambridge: Polity Press.

Schegloff, Emanuel A. 1996a "Confirming allusions: An empirical account of action". *American Journal of Sociology* 102(1): 161-216.

Schegloff, Emanuel A. 1996b "Some practices for referring to persons in talk-in-interaction: A partial sketch of a systematics". In *Studies in Anaphora*, B. Fox (ed.), 437-485. Amsterdam: John Benjamins.

Schegloff, Emanuel A. 1997 "Whose text? Whose context?" *Discourse & Society* 8(2): 165-187.

Schegloff, Emanuel A. 1998 "Reply to Wetherell". *Discourse & Society* 9(3): 413-416.

Schegloff, Emanuel A. 1999a "'Schegloff's texts' as 'Billig's data': A critical reply". *Discourse & Society* 10(4): 558-572.

Schegloff, Emanuel A. 1999b "Naivety vs. sophistication or discipline vs. self-indulgence: A rejoinder to Billig". *Discourse & Society* 10(4): 577-582.

Scott, Karla D. 2000 "Crossing cultural borders: 'Girl' and 'look' as markers of identity in black women's language use". *Discourse & Society* 11(2): 237-248.

Sedgwick, Eve Kosofsky. 1993 "Queer performativity". *GLQ: A Journal of Lesbian and Gay Studies* 1: 1-16.

Seidman, Steven. 1991 *Romantic Longings: Love in America, 1830-1980*. New York: Routledge.

Seidman, Steven (ed.). 1996a *Queer Theory/Sociology*. Oxford: Basil Blackwell.

Seidman, Steven. 1996b "Introduction". In *Queer Theory/Sociology*, S. Seidman (ed.), 1-29. Oxford: Basil Blackwell.

Sharrock, Wes and Anderson, Bob. 1986 *The Ethnomethodologists*. London: Tavistock.

Silverman, David (ed.). 1997 *Qualitative Research: Theory, Method and Practice*. London: Sage.

Silverman, David. 1998 *Harvey Sacks: Social Science and Conversation Analysis*. Cambridge: Polity Press.

Speer, Susan A. 1999 "Feminism and conversation analysis: An oxymoron?" *Feminism & Psychology* 9(4): 471-478.

Speer, Susan A. 2001 "Reconsidering the concept of hegemonic masculinity: Discursive psychology, conversation analysis and participants' orientations". *Feminism & Psychology* 11(1): 107-135.

Speer, Susan A. and Potter, Jonathan. 2000 "The management of 'heterosexist' talk: Conversational resources and prejudiced claims". *Discourse & Society* 11(4): 543-572.

Spender, Dale. 1989 *The Writing or the Sex?* New York: Pergamon Press.

Steinberg, Deborah Lynn, Epstein, Debbie and Johnson, Richard (eds). 1997 *Border Patrols: Policing the Boundaries of Heterosexuality.* London: Cassell.

Stokoe, Elizabeth H. 1998 "Talking about gender: The conversational construction of gender categories in academic discourse". *Discourse & Society* 9(2): 217-240.

Stokoe, Elizabeth H. 2000 "Towards a conversation analytic approach to gender and discourse". *Feminism & Psychology* 12(4): 552-563.

Stokoe, Elizabeth H. and Smithson, Janet. 2001 "Making gender relevant: Conversation analysis and gender categories in interaction". *Discourse & Society* 12(2): 243-269.

Stolcke, Verena. 1993 "Is sex to gender as race is to ethnicity?" In *Gendered Anthropology*, T.d. Valle (ed.), 17-37. London: Routledge.

Stoller, Robert. 1968 *Sex and Gender, Vol I: Splitting: A Case of Female Masculinity.* London: The Hogarth Press.

Stringer, Jeffrey L. and Hopper, Robert. 1998 "Generic *he* in conversation?" *Quarterly Journal of Speech* 84: 209-221.

Tannen, Deborah. 1990 *You Just Don't Understand: Women and Men in Conversation.* New York: Ballantine Books.

Thorne, Barrie. 1995 "On West & Fenstermaker's 'Doing difference'". *Gender & Society* 9(4): 497-499.

Tracy, Karen. 1998 "Analyzing context: Framing the discussion". *Research on Language and Social Interaction* 31(1): 1-28.

Uchida, Aki. 1992 "When 'difference' is 'dominance': A critique of the 'anti-power-based' cultural approach to sex differences". *Language in Society* 21: 547-568.

Volger, Candace. 1998 "Sex and talk". *Critical Inquiry* 24: 328-365.

Watson, D.R. and Weinberg, T.S. 1982 "Interviews and the interactional construction of accounts of homosexual identity". *Social Analysis* 11: 56-78.

Watson, Rod. 1997 "Some general reflections on 'categorization' and 'sequence' in the analysis of conversation". In *Culture in Action: Studies in Membership Categorisation Analysis*, S. Hester and P. Eglin (eds), 49-75. Washington, DC: University of America Press.

Weatherell, Ann. 2000 "Gender relevance in talk-in-interaction and discourse". *Discourse & Society* 11(2): 286-288.

Weedon, Chris. 1987 *Feminist Practice and Poststructuralist Theory.* Oxford: Blackwell.

Wenger, Etienne. 1998 *Communities of Practice.* Cambridge: Cambridge University Press.

West, Candace. 1996 "Goffman in feminist perspective". *Sociological Persepctives* 39(3): 353-369.

West, Candace and Fenstermaker, Sarah. 1993 "Power, inequality, and the accomplishment of gender: An ethnomethodological view". In *Theory on Gender/Feminism on Theory*, P. England (ed.), 151-173. New York: Aldine de Gruyter.

West, Candace and Fenstermaker, Sarah. 1995 "Doing difference". *Gender & Society* 9(1): 8-37.

West, Candace and Garcia, Angela. 1988 "Conversational shift work: A study of topical transition between men and women". *Social Problems* 35: 551-575.

West, Candace and Zimmerman, Don. 1977 "Women's place in everyday talk: Reflections on parent-child interaction". *Social Problems* 24: 521-529.

West, Candace and Zimmerman, Don. 1987 "Doing gender". *Gender & Society* 1: 125-151.

Wetherell, Margaret. 1998 "Positioning and interpretative repertoires: Conversation analysis and post-structuralism in dialogue". *Discourse & Society* 9(3): 387-412.

Wetherell, Margaret and Edley, Nigel. 1999 "Negotiating hegemonic masculinity: Imaginary positions and psycho-discursive practices". *Feminism & Psychology* 9(3): 335-356.

Widdicombe, Sue. 1995 "Identity, politics and talk: A case for the mundane and the everyday". In *Feminism and Discourse: Psychological Perspectives*, S. Wilkinson and C. Kitzinger (eds), 106-127. London: Sage.

Wilkinson, Sue and Kitzinger, Celia (eds). 1993 *Heterosexuality*. London: Sage.

Wilkinson, Sue and Kitzinger, Celia (eds). 1995 *Feminism and Discourse: Psychological Perspectives*. London: Sage.

Willott, Sara and Griffin, Christine. 1997 "'Wham bam, am I a man?': Unemployed men talk about masculinities". *Feminism & Psychology* 7(1): 107-128.

Wittig, Monique. 1992 *The Straight Mind and Other Essays*. London: Harvester Wheatsheaf.

Wodak, Ruth (ed.). 1997 *Gender and Discourse*. London: Sage.

Zimmerman, Don and West, Candace. 1975 "Sex roles, interruptions and silences in conversations". In *Language and Sex: Difference and Dominance*, B. Thorne and N. Henley (eds), 105-129. Rowley, M.A.: Newbury House.

CHAPTER 2

Doing feminist conversation analysis[*]

Celia Kitzinger

Feminism is a politics predicated upon the belief that women are oppressed; it is a social movement dedicated to political change. Issues that have preoccupied feminists include: violence against women, childhood sexual abuse and recovered memories, acquaintance rape, sexual harassment, the beauty myth, compulsory heterosexuality, women's health and reproductive rights, equal opportunities for women in the workplace, and the end of heteropatriarchal domination.

Conversation analysis (CA) is the academic study of talk-in-interaction, as identified, in particular, with the works of its founder, Harvey Sacks, in conjunction with Emanuel Schegloff and Gail Jefferson. Issues that have preoccupied conversation analysts include: the projectability of turn constructional units, the onset of overlap in turn-taking organisation, turn allocation techniques, the syntax of sentences in progress, sequence organisation, preference structures, and the organisation of repair in conversation.

It is, then, not immediately apparent, on the basis of the foregoing descriptions of 'feminism' and 'conversation analysis', just what would be involved in 'doing feminist conversation analysis', and it is perhaps no surprise that some feminist and critical researchers (for example, Billig 1999, Wetherell 1998) have expressed considerable reservations about the value of CA for feminist work — even suggesting that feminism and CA are 'oxymorons' (Speer 1999). Of course, it is true that CA has not hitherto been notable for its contributions to feminist or lesbian perspectives, but CA hardly stands out in this regard. The core texts on a whole range of other analytic approaches across the social sciences (including, for example, experimental design, psychoanalysis, survey technique, oral history, content analysis, ethnography, grounded theory, psychometric testing, repertory grids and Q methodology) remain largely silent about feminist issues — and yet feminists have found ways of adapting these powerful methods and using them for our own purposes. In the long history of debate about what constitute appropriate feminist methodologies, there is (so far) not one single methodology which feminists have agreed has to be discarded as fundamentally incompatible with feminism (see Reinharz 1992). The pattern has rather been that particular approaches (for example, experimental, psychoanalytic or postmodern work) have become established without feminist involvement and consequently have been roundly criticised as sexist by feminists who initially dismiss the entire approach ("the master's tools will never demolish the master's house"). Subsequently, other feminists working *within* those approaches have found imaginative and creative ways to address those feminist criticisms, to make gender and sexuality visible, and to use the master's tools for feminist purposes — and the approach then becomes firmly established as a recognised and accepted way of 'doing feminism' in the academy. To those feminists who would discard CA as anti-feminist, then, I would urge caution, if for no other reason simply on the basis of our prior experience of rashly dismissing other approaches as fundamentally anti-feminist, and having later to 'reclaim' them for feminism.

Moreover, from the earliest development of CA in the 1970s, there has always been some feminist interest in CA, and this interest has grown enormously in recent years since the publication of Sacks' (1995) *Lectures on Conversation* and the wider availability of resources on doing CA (Hutchby and Wooffitt 1998, ten Have 1999, Psathas 1995). It is unfortunate that Billig's recent critique of CA, which is framed up in part as a chivalrous defence of feminism against the demonised figure of Schegloff, nowhere cites feminist involvement in CA or engages with feminist claims that CA is of use to us. He overlooks classic feminist work drawing on CA, such as West and Zimmerman's exploration of interruptions in cross-sex conversations, (West 1979, West and Zimmerman 1977, Zimmerman and West 1975) and Goodwin's (1990) analyses of girls' talk, as well as more recent feminist uses of CA carried out by feminists based in his own Department, and by others who have presented their work at Loughborough's Discourse and Rhetoric Group, of which Billig is a founding member (for example, Frith 1998, Frith and Kitzinger 1998, Kitzinger and Frith 1999, Speer 1999, 2001, Stokoe 1998). Moreover, in arguing that CA incorporates into its basic premises ideas that are fundamentally antithetical to feminist (and other critical) values, Billig's article assumes a narrow and restrictive model of feminism which is seriously at variance with (and renders invisible) the full range and variety of feminisms across the social sciences. In responding to Billig's critique of CA,

Schegloff (1999: 559) has taken him to task for various "misunderstandings or misreadings" of CA: to that charge I would add a failure to appreciate the range of contemporary feminist theory around gender and sexuality.

This article is not, however, intended as a direct response to Billig's claims, but rather aims to address those of his concerns which strike me as being more generally shared, and which are often been raised (in conversation rather than in print) in critical and feminist academic contexts. These key criticisms are: (1) the extent to which CA's underlying and often unarticulated social theory is compatible with feminism (or other critical perspectives); (2) the difficulty of reconciling CA's emphasis on 'participants' orientations' with the analyst's own preoccupations with gender, class, sexuality, and power when these are not apparently attended to by participants themselves; and (3) CA's apparent obsession with the minute details of mundane everyday talk, to the exclusion of broader social and political realities. I will first present a theoretical discussion of these three (overlapping) 'troubles with CA', and then offer a concrete illustration drawn from an ongoing conversation analytic study of talk in which people 'come out' as lesbian, gay, bisexual or as having (had) same sex sexual experiences. My theoretical argument and my practical example converge in the claim that it is, ironically, *precisely those three features of CA which are critiqued as anti-feminist which in fact offer the most exciting potential for feminist-informed conversation analytic work.*

1. The trouble with conversation analysis is...

Conversation analysis is a relatively well-defined field, with a clearly visible set of core contributors (Sacks, Schegloff and Jefferson key amongst them) whose work defines the centre of the field. By contrast, feminist and critical approaches are much more diffuse and heterogeneous, and there is no single agreed upon feminist (or critical) theory, methodology, epistemology or ontology: feminist work embraces the experimental and the experiential, the positivist and the postmodern. This heterogeneity of feminist and critical perspectives means that CA is open to attack on a bewildering array of contradictory points from critics of different persuasions. It is clearly not the case that CA is (or can readily be made) compatible with all variants of feminist research. As I will suggest below, it is not generally well suited to sex-differences research, to experimental or correlational paradigms, to work seeking to uncover individual affects or cognitions, nor to use within structural-functionalist or essentialist feminisms.

All these approaches flourish under the rich variety of feminist research today — and they are unlikely to find CA suited to their purposes. But feminist research *also* includes social constructionist, ethnomethodological, postmodern, radical lesbian and queer approaches to sexuality and gender — and for these feminists, as I will show, CA has much more to offer.

The critics of CA (cited above) sometimes appear to imagine that they can locate it in opposition to some imagined monolithic 'feminism', which has one single politically correct line. In fact, it is striking that criticisms of CA are also very often equally applicable as criticisms of particular kinds of feminisms. For example, both CA and ethnomethodological feminisms are accused of lacking a proper appreciation of social-structural forces that constrain and shape behaviour, and of focusing excessively on the mundane and relatively 'trivial' aspects of our lives at the expense of larger systems of institutionalised power and control; and both CA and post-modern feminism are accused of being dense and impenetrable, and of mystifying ordinary people's everyday experience with jargon-ridden prose. My aim here is not to defend the 'trivial' or the 'jargon-ridden', but rather to contextualise these criticisms of CA within the ongoing feminist debates. We need to replace a simplistic CA/feminism dichotomy with a more sophisticated engagement with *feminist* discussions about the appropriate conceptualisations of social structure and individual agency, the relationship of power to subjective understandings, and the role of the mundane 'micro' events of everyday life in relation to oppression. In what follows, I have tried to lay out some of the groundwork for those discussions to take place.

(1) CA's social theory

CA emerged in the context of, and embodies, many of the ideas of ethnomethodology — the sociological theory developed by Garfinkel and his collaborators in the 1960s (from which terms like 'member' and 'participant' derive). Garfinkel (1967) rejected the dominant sociological paradigm of his day, as articulated in the work of Talcott Parsons, which explained human action as the result of institutionalised systems of norms, rules and values which are internalised by individuals. For Garfinkel, this approach portrays social actors merely as victims at the mercy of external social forces. For ethnomethodologists, social facts like power and oppression are *accomplishments* (Garfinkel 1967); instead of being already existing 'things', they are processes continually created and sustained (and resisted) through the practices of members in interaction. Ethnomethodology offered a model of people as agents, and of a social order grounded in contingent, embodied, ongoing interpretative work — an interest in how people *do* social order, rather in how they are animated by it, in how everyday reality is produced by those engaging in it. It is, as Heritage (1984: 2) points out, "an important prophylactic against the mystifying consequences of 'grand theorizing' and 'abstracted empiricism'". (For more information about the relationship between ethnomethodology and CA, see Turner's 1974 *Ethnomethodology*, which includes chapters by both Sacks and Schegloff, and Psathas 1979 for a collection of work inspired both by Garfinkel and by Sacks.) For Harvey Sacks, the founder of CA, talk-in-interaction was simply one commonplace site of human interaction which could be studied for what it revealed about the production of social order. Talk as such is not given any *principled* primacy in CA: the key interest of CA is not in talk as *language*, but in talk as *action* — that is, in what people *do* with talk. CA "describes methods persons use in doing social life" (Sacks, quoted in Psathas 1995: 53).

It is this underlying ethnomethodological theory which is singled out by Billig (1999: 543) as conveying "a participatory view of the world", with which he finds himself (and thinks feminists should find ourselves) in profound disagreement. CA's focus on the ordinary world of everyday conversation, and its use of terms like 'co-conversationalist', 'participant' and 'member' convey, says Billig (1999: 552), "an essentially non-critical view of the social world", and support an "assumption that the conversational situation can be considered as a sociologically neutral place" (554), "in which equal rights of speakership are often assumed" (550). According to Billig, this ethnomethodological stance makes CA incompatible with feminism at the most basic level, in what he calls its "foundational rhetoric".

Billig's critique is not, of course, uniquely a critique of CA, but rather of the full range of sociological approaches (including ethnomethodology, symbolic interactionism, labelling theory, interpretivist approaches and social constructionism) which theorise people (including women) as active participants in the construction of the social world, and which set themselves in opposition to structural functionalist models of the social order. In other words, it is equally a critique of a great deal of specifically *feminist* work. Feminist ethnomethodology is cited in most feminist methods texts (see Gould 1980: 465, Reinharz 1992) and the approach has been used to study (for example) the construction of gender (Kessler and McKenna 1978; see also Crawford 2000), mental illness (Smith 1987), sexual harassment (Wise and Stanley 1987) and prostitution (Davidson 1996). Like ethnomethodological work more generally, this feminist research uses terms like 'member' and 'participant', and focuses on women as active co-constructors of meaning, rather than simply positing us as the pre-defined victims of a heteropatriarchal social system.

In conclusion, then, CA does not commit us to an 'uncritical' view of the social world, but it does commit us to a broadly ethnomethodological one in which people are understood not simply as victims of an all-powerful social order but also as agents actively engaged in methodical and sanctioned procedures for producing or resisting, colluding with or transgressing, the taken-for-granted social world. Some feminists have certainly criticised ethnomethodology for having too loose and flexible a version of power, for attributing more agency to women than can be reconciled with the operations of heteropatriarchal power, and for offering excessively 'individualistic' solutions to social problems (see Wise and Stanley 1987: 202-208 for discussion of these criticisms). CA is potentially open to the same criticisms, but it should be noted that they are criticisms not of CA per se, but rather criticisms of particular kinds approaches to research, including specifically *feminist* approaches. Rather than counterposing some imaginary unified 'feminism' on one side and CA/ethnomethodology on the other, we need to relate CA's social theory to, and engage with, wider feminist and critical discussions about social structure and human agency.

(2) Participant vs. analyst orientations

Feminism has always been deeply concerned with recovering women's own meanings and understandings about the world. The goal of feminist social science has been envisioned as "to address women's lives and experiences *in their own terms*, to create theory grounded in the actual experience and language of women" (Du Bois 1983: 108, emphasis in original). In much feminist research, the author states explicitly that she is trying to avoid the imposition of her own meanings or interpretations — that it is her participants' voices we hear in her work, not her own analytic preoccupations. CA makes remarkably similar claims: it "seeks to remain faithful to members' perspectives" (Psathas 1995: 49) and to privilege in its analysis "the orientations, meanings, interpretations, understandings etc. of the *participants*" (Schegloff 1997: 166). Here, then, we might expect a happy fit between feminism and CA. And indeed, CA's concern with "participants' own orientations to the meaning making practices of everyday life" has been described as a 'main reason' for adopting it within critical psychology (Forrester 1999: 34).

There are, however, two problems for (some) feminists with the conversation analytic version of 'participants' orientations': first, it is incompatible with the traditional treatment of gender as a sociological variable, and second, it raises difficulties for the analyst who 'hears' in the data oppressions and power abuses not 'oriented' to by the participants. I will deal with these two issues separately.

First, in contradistinction to the feminist version of 'participant orientation', the CA version means that neither gender nor any other sociological variable can be considered in relation to the talk unless the participants themselves can be shown to orient to it. Unless participants themselves make gender relevant then, from a CA perspective, for the analyst to do so is to engage in what Schegloff (1997: 167) has called an act of "theoretical imperialism", which imposes the analyst's preoccupation on to the participants' talk. Simply the fact that the speaker *is* a woman is not sufficient to justify analysing her talk *as* a woman, "because she is, by the same token, a Californian, Jewish, a mediator, a former weaver, my wife, and many others" (Schegloff 1997: 165). Many CA studies do not even report the gender of speakers: talk issues from the mouths of disembodied subjects called A, B and C.

There a huge academic (and popular) industry — including work by many feminists — exploring whether and how talk is constructed differently by people of different genders and sexualities and claiming that women speak "in a different voice" (Gilligan 1982); that men "just don't understand" (Tannen 1990); that we are more 'co-operative speakers' than are men (Maltz and Borker 1983, Tannen 1990); that we use tag questions (Lakoff 1975) and minimal responses (Fellegy 1995) differently; that talk between lesbian couples is more symmetrical than that between heterosexual couples (Day and Morse 1981) or that lesbians talk differently from heterosexual women, and gay men from straight men, in relation to pitch, grammatical variation and lexical items (Jacobs 1996). All of it is "illicit" (Billig 1999: 545) from a CA perspective because it imposes the analysts' categories ('male', 'female', 'heterosexual', 'lesbian' and so on) on the data, without troubling to show that the participants themselves are oriented to doing gender or sexuality in the talk.

Many feminists have been critical of sex differences research as a feminist approach (Kitzinger 1994), and have increasingly emphasised the need to get "beyond binary thinking" (Bing and Bergvall 1996) and to understand how genders (and sexualities) are socially constructed rather than being pre-existing natural facts. Sex differences research presumes the already-existing a-priori categories of 'men' and 'women' or 'heterosexuals' and 'homosexuals', but if we are to take seriously the idea that gender and sexuality are socially constructed and continually produced and reproduced in social interaction (including, although not limited to, talk) then, instead of claiming that women talk 'like this' and men 'like that' as markers of their pre-existing identities, we need to explore how ways of talking actively *produce* speakers as males or females. Rather than seeing language use as marking a gender or sexual identity which exists prior to the act of speaking, we can understand language use as one way of producing this identity. Instead of how you talk depends on who you already are, who you are and who you are taken to be, depends on your repeated performance over time of the talk that constitutes that identity (Butler 1990, 1997). Instead of 'how do women and men talk differently?', we can ask how particular forms of talk contribute to the production of people as 'women' and as 'men' (Cameron 1996). There is remarkably little conversation analytic work analysing naturalistic data in which gender and sexuality just 'happen' to be present, not as pre-existing properties of people, nor as responses to formal questions about 'masculinity' and 'femininity', but realised, made relevant, in interaction through what Elinor Ochs (1992) has referred to as "indexing gender" (though see Hopper and LeBaron 1998). This would be a useful approach for feminists to take. The idea that genders and sexualities are constructed through interaction has a long intellectual history within feminism, and finds contemporary resonance in what postmodern and queer theory have referred to as 'performativity' (Sedgwick 1990, Butler 1993). From this perspective, then, CA (while not compatible with essentialist feminism) is entirely compatible with (indeed, offers a method for) social constructionist, postmodern and queer theories which treat gender and sexuality as accomplishments rather than as pre-given categories.

Second, as Billig points out, one implication of CA's stricture to focus on 'participant orientations' is the prohibition of particular analytic moves predicated upon the analyst's prior categorisation of speakers as 'men' and 'women'.

> Feminist analysts might be predisposed to 'hear' the operation of unequal gender power in interchanges between men and women. Unless the participants themselves can be heard to 'orientate' to gender issues, then this hearing of gender will be illicit (or unmandated). ... [A]nalysts must not introduce these concerns if the participants have not done so (Billig 1999: 545).

Suppose, we, as analysts, *do* hear the "operation of unequal gender power" in a particular conversation, and suppose further that we have no evidence that either conversationalist hears it that way. It could perhaps be an instance of what we would want to label 'sexual harassment' but for both harasser and victim it is treated as 'just life' and not oriented to as anything out of the ordinary (see Kitzinger and Thomas 1995 and Mott and Condor 1997 for examples). Or it could perhaps be an instance of what we might want to label 'heterosexism', but for the heterosexuals involved, it is just business as usual — they fail to notice their heterosexual privilege in any way (see Kitzinger 1990). So these are not instances in which a victim protests, or a speaker notices and makes moves to redress or to bolster an act of oppression. Instead, the surface calm of the conversation is entirely untroubled by any apparent awareness that unequal power has been exercised. In this situation, what can we say — either as feminists, or as conversation analysts? What warrant (if any) do we have for our claim that an act of oppression has taken place, if the participants do not orient to it as such?

Conversation analysts by and large have not been particularly interested in pursuing this question: CA usually ends with the analysis of the partici pants' orientations, and as most conversation analysts do not bring their politics into their research, that is all that is seen to be required. Feminists, by contrast, have been quite concerned about the relationship between their (feminist) analysis of their participants' actions and the (generally non-feminist) way in which participants themselves interpret the same behaviours. As I have discussed elsewhere (Kitzinger and Wilkinson 1997), the desire to present politicised analyses of non-politicised participants, while still somehow 'validating their realities' has led to unresolved dilemmas in feminist work. Far from involving the imposition of a new and fundamentally anti-feminist requirement, then, the emphasis on participant orientations in CA simply presents feminists with an old problem in a new guise.

From my own perspective, it would be unbearably limiting to use CA if it meant that I could only describe as 'sexist' or 'heterosexist' or 'racist' those forms of talk to which actors orient as such. Indeed, it is *precisely the fact that sexist, heterosexist and racist assumptions are routinely incorporated into everyday conversations* without anyone noticing or responding to them that way which is of interest to me. How is it, for example, that an unquestioned set of mundane heterosexual assumptions regularly surfaces in talk in which participants do not notice (or orient to) their own heterosexual privilege, and how does precisely this failure to orient constitute and reconstitute heterosexist reality? These questions can be addressed without violating the precepts of CA — as evidenced by Sack's analysis of a telephone conversation between two white women, Estelle and Jeanelle, neither of whom orient in any way to the white privilege and class privilege, *yet Sacks draws our attention to precisely these features.* In the data he presents, Estelle recounts to Jeanelle a story about driving past a shop, and seeing two police cars there, which she interprets as doing their legitimate business of trying to prevent a "colored lady" from going "in the main entrance where the silver is". Here is what Sacks, the founder of CA, has to say about it:

> In her report there's, eg., no hint of any interest in stopping and helping out, or getting worried about what's going to happen. More importantly, there's no hint that she had any fear that somehow, eg., that policemen was about to turn to her and ask her what she was doing there. The massive comfort in her innocence, and in that legitimate audience status that she has, is something that we should give real attention to, in at least this way. It's the kind of thing that we know can be readily shaken. There are times and places where some Estelle would not feel at all that comfortable, but, passing such a scene — and you can readily imagine it — she would figure "oh my God here I am, the first thing that happens is they're going to figure I'm involved". And that never dawns on our Estelle. And until it dawns on her she can have no sense of an empathy with, eg., a kid in the ghetto. Her sense of innocence affects the whole way she sees the scene. ... What are the conditions that would lead somebody like Estelle here to at least have it cross her mind that somebody else might see her and wonder what in the world is Estelle doing there, or that when the cop turns around with his gun he's going to shoot her or tell her to halt. ... This lady is not designing a right-wing report. All she's doing is reporting what she saw (Sacks 1995, II: 185-186).

Precisely by giving careful attention to Estelle's own orientation to the events she is recounting, Sacks is able to analyse her account as an instance of mundane, ordinary, everyday racism-in-action.

It is also worth considering what we take to be instances of 'orientation to gender' — what 'count' as such, from a conversation analytic perspective. In Sacks' example of orientation to 'race', as in Schegloff's (1997) example of orientation to 'gender' ("Ladies last!"), terms like 'colored' or 'ladies' clearly index and can be used to sustain the analyst's claim that race/gender are being invoked. It is, however, far from obvious that it is *only* when participants make use of such explicit terms ('colored', 'lady', 'man', 'he/she' and so on) that we as analysts can make the claim that race/gender and so on are relevant to the interaction. While not offering the kind of rigorous counter-evidence I would prefer, a personal anecdote (based on field notes taken at the time, rather than tape-recordings of the interactions) offers some indication of how politically-conscious conversation analysts might develop explorations of the relevance of gender/sexuality/ethnicity when these are *not* indexed with the specific terminology which makes their relevance apparent. My (female) partner and I, at our holiday hotel, were greeted at the restaurant entrance every morning for ten days by a different person, and asked two questions: the first question addressed the issue of the number of people for whom a table was required, and the second addressed the issue of whether this table should be in the smoking or the non-smoking section of the restaurant. After a few mornings it struck me that, while the second question seemed sensible enough (they could not tell just by looking at us whether we were smokers or non-smokers), it did seem odd that, confronted with two people standing in front of them at the entrance to the dining room, they nonetheless always asked how many people we were. The form of this question varied ("is it two people?", "just two people?", "for two people?", "only two people?", "*how* many people?"), but most forms incorporated some awareness on the part of the person asking the question that there were in fact two people standing in front of them, and in several forms, the question incorporated an implication that two was an insufficient number ("just", "only"), and that more might have been expected — although, as it happens, about half of the tables on any given morning were occupied by two, and only two, persons. Curious as to whether this question was routine, I loitered at the entrance one morning and observed the entrance and pre-seating exchanges of 20 parties, of whom 18 (10 of them male/female couples, none of them same-sex couples) were asked *only* whether they would prefer smoking or non-smoking tables. The numbers question was raised with a man on his own ("just one?") and with a family with a large number of children ("how many?"). So my partner and I were the only party amongst those I observed consisting of two people who were asked to specify or confirm how many we were — and only we, and a solo breakfaster, were asked a question which implied that our number was insufficient. We were also the only party composed of two persons of the same sex. My analysis of the question about how many people we were is, then, that it derived from the questioner's observation that we were two people, but two people of the same sex, and that we therefore did not constitute a normatively complete 'couple' and that perhaps our numerical insufficiency might be accounted for by tardy husbands whose imminent arrival would complete our party. This (admittedly anecdotal) example is offered as an instance of the way in which an orientation to gender — here, specifically to the fact that two people are of the same sex — can be present in an interaction which does not use terms like 'lady', 'girl', 'man' and so on (on the contrary, the gender-neutral term 'people' was *always* used). It illustrates, too, the everyday mundane heterosexism of which many more overt instances had arisen over the course of the same holiday — the customer relations person who asked if we liked our hotel rooms and when we said yes, replied "next time bring your boyfriends"; or the salespeople in a silk shop who encouraged us to send our husbands in for tailor-made suits. These are the overt and explicit examples of the expectation that we two were representative of more than two, that each of us is half of some other couple, that we stood for four people in total.

The CA injunction to take participants' orientations seriously, then, offers some important challenges for developing a more politically sensitive approach to gender/sexuality/ethnicity and so on in talk, and raises for feminists a familiar set of dilemmas about how both to be responsive to our participants' concerns, and at the same time to develop a feminist analysis with which they may well be in disagreement. Different feminists have resolved these dilemmas in different ways, and some of these ways are less compatible with CA than are others. Here, as elsewhere, the underlying principles of CA intersect in crosscutting ways with the various different strands of feminist research, and need to be discussed in that context.

(3) The 'micro-macro' distinction

Feminist and critical psychologists often view conversation analysts as narrowly focused on 'just talk' and as ignoring the world of social institutions and brute force. This is also, of course, an accusation which has been levelled against discourse analysts — but CA, even more than DA, is seen as suffering from "seduction with the 'data'" (Forrester 1999: 34) and represented as nitpicking, obsessively concerned with the minute details of in-breaths and hesitations, and as unable to see beyond the 'micro-' level of the 0.2 second pause, to the 'macro-' level of oppression. According to feminist psychologist Margaret Wetherell (1998: 402), "the problem with conversational analysts is that they rarely raise their eyes from the next turn in the conversation." For feminists, 'context' means the social, cultural, and historical setting within which talk takes place, the institutional or hierarchical relationship of the people talking, and their location in the social order. For conversation analysts, 'context' is often reducible to the immediately preceding and subsequent turns in the conversation, from which, indeed, they may rarely raise their eyes.

But then, most conversation analysts are not feminists or critical theorists (neither, of course, are most experimentalists, or content analysts or grounded theorists), and we cannot look to current practices and expect to see feminism already in place. Rather, knowing that, of course, as feminists, we will inevitably want to focus on issues of power and oppression, the appropriate question is what, if anything, CA's 'micro' perspective has to offer us in that regard.

There is nothing intrinsic to feminist or critical approaches which mandates a cavalier attitude to the data. Feminism and careful attention to the details of talk are not incompatible — and CA's focus on talk finds resonance in a great deal of feminist interest in talk and its role in the construction of genders and sexualities. Certainly, genders and sexualities are accomplished in many ways other than through talk: through the surgeon's knife, the queer basher's fist, the sexual harasser's leer, the 'glass ceiling' in the workplace, and the images on the banners and buttons at the gay pride march — but they are also produced through talk. A feminist conversation analysis would use this focus on talk to uncover the practical reasoning through which the taken-for-granted world is accomplished (and resisted) — the resources members have for sustaining a social world in which there are 'women' and 'men', 'heterosexuals' and 'homosexuals', 'normal people' and the rest of us.

The small details of talk are important because CA has established beyond reasonable doubt that people use the tiny details of talk (micro-pauses, mm hms, restarts, in-breaths and the rest) to conduct and understand the course of their interactions.

> A main thrust of the research here is the finding that far from its being the case that 'social experience [comes] at us too fast' for adequate treatment, speakers and hearers, with respect to the most mundane features of talk and interaction, orient to delicate and rather complex features of the unfolding activity in what Sacks has referred to as 'utterance time' (ie. the standard pacing of talk) (Turner 1974: 11).

It is not that conversation analysts suddenly decided they had an absorbing interest in micro-analysing talk and wanted to spend their lives measuring pauses in tenths of a second, or analysing the sequential implicativeness of false starts and hesitations, or the difference between 'uh huh' and 'yes' in backchannel communication. It is that these apparently tiny and insignificant details *are relevant to the participants* in the conversation, and systematically effect what they do next, and how they do it. If we want to understand what people are saying to each other, and how they come to say it, and what it means to them, then we, as analysts, have to attend to their talk *at the same level of detail that they do.* Unless we do so, we run a serious risk of doing violence to the meaning of the data we are analysing. We can harness CA's careful and sophisticated description of the methods people use to do things in talk, and use them as resources in developing our own feminist analyses.

In conclusion, then, I have argued that CA is clearly compatible with, and usable for, certain kinds of feminist research. It does not fit well with sex differences research or with essentialist feminisms in which, for example, the assumption is made that women's talk is always produced by them *as women* and is always structured by and bears the marks of their oppression. It is, however, compatible with ethnomethodology, and with the later developments of social constructionism, post-modernism and queer theory, which see genders and sexualities as produced and reproduced through ordinary every day interactions — including conversation. This makes CA a useful technique for understanding how, in our ordinary, mundane interactions, we produce the social order we inhabit — in other words, how we 'do' power and powerlessness, oppression and resistance. Billig (1999: 550) is simply wrong in his claim that CA "assumes equal rights of speakership". As Schegloff points out, it "does not *presume* an equalitarian society, but merely *allows* one" — and it also allows for *in*equalities, such that ordinary conversation:

> can thereby become a canvas on which the practices end up having painted a picture of inequality, or exclusion, or oppression, or asymmetry without a sense of oppression... Those who take conversation or other talk in interaction to be basically an arena of oppression should undertake to *show* that; the available tools of analysis do not preclude that showing (Schegloff 1999: 564).

Finally, a conversation analytic approach permits, as a social structural one does not, a proper appreciation of resistance and subversion. As feminists and queer theorists have repeatedly emphasised of late, women, lesbians, gay men, bisexual and transgendered folk are not simply victims of an overarching heteropatriarchal world order. We also resist and subvert it — and, of course, we are also sometimes complicit with the very processes by which we are oppressed (see Kitzinger and Frith 1999 on young women's resistance to the advice to 'just say no' to sexual encounters, and Kitzinger 2000 for a conversation analysis of resistance to 'thinking positive' in the talk of breast cancer patients). CA offers the opportunity to render concepts like 'oppression', 'resistance' and 'complicity' less opaque than they sometimes appear in some postmodern theorizing, and instead to reveal them as concrete practices visible in talk.

2. Conversation analysis and coming out: or How to come out without anyone noticing[1]

There is an enormous literature on 'coming out' to others as lesbian, gay, bisexual or as having (had) same-sex sexual experiences. There is substantial *quantitative* research in which coming out to others (or, more accurately, self-report of having come out to others on some kind of questionnaire measures or "disclosure scales") is correlated with self-esteem, mental health or levels of social support (for example, Franke and Leary 1991, Schachar and Gilbert 1983), generating findings such as "the more widely a woman disclosed her sexual orientation the less anxiety, more positive affectivity, and greater self-esteem she reported" (Jordan and Deluty 1998: 41-2). In quantitative research like this, the actual experience of 'coming out' is subordinated to an investigation of its psychological and social sequelae. *Qualitative* work on coming out relies overwhelmingly on retrospective self-report: lesbians and gay men are asked, in interviews, to describe how they came out, and this is usually taken as a (more or less) adequate reflection of how their coming out was actually done (for example, Edgar 1994, Cain 1996). This naturalistic approach to 'coming out' stories treats interviewees as informants transparently revealing truths about themselves and their world — 'telling it how it really was' (for example, Gagné, Tweksbury and McGaughey 1997, Shakespeare 1999). Other work treats retrospective self-report as a form of sexual story telling (for example, Plummer 1995) and investigates them for their 'narrative iconicity' (Wood 1997) or 'creation of coherence' (Liang 1997). What does not exist in the literature is any study in which 'coming out' — the act of disclosure itself — is the primary data source, that is in which 'coming out' is actually captured as a live event.

By accident, I happen to have (so far) twelve instances of 'coming out' on audiotape. They come from a variety of sources including focus groups and training sessions, but most (including the two presented here) are taken from small group seminar sessions with undergraduate students, run as part of a "Human Sexualities" course at a British university, recorded, with students' signed permission and informed consent, for ongoing research by several members of the department on how sexuality is produced through talk.[2] My interest, as a feminist, in these coming out data was initially prompted by what seemed a bewildering absence of response to the 'comings out' on the part of the audience (including, in four cases, me). In what I have come to think of as the mundane form of everyday coming out for people in relatively safe environments, nobody expresses disgust, talks about hell fire and damnation, or accuses anyone of being a disgusting pervert — but equally, nobody says "congratulations!" or "that's wonderful" (as I would have liked to have done) or gives any indication that they have even registered the information. The absence of response is striking — to the extent that a reviewer of an earlier draft of this chapter commented, "in these interactions, the homosexuality aspects are not treated — by speakers or hearers — as 'coming out' — so how does the author justify her hearing?'

I 'hear' these as 'comings out' on the basis of my own, and others' reported experiences of everyday life for lesbians and gay men in a heterosexist world (see, for example, Coyle and Kitzinger 2002, Kitzinger 1987, Kitzinger and Wilkinson 1995, Peel 2001). Coming out is not a 'one off' event but something about which decisions have to be made repeatedly, over and over, sometimes several times a day, to different audiences in different contexts, in the face of the repeated assumption of heterosexuality. Although the one-off announcements to parents or 'confessions' to spouses are the popularly represented and 'dramatic' forms of 'coming out', the mundane, everyday 'comings out' (to the locksmith who suggests I ask my husband to rehang a door, to the leisure centre receptionist questioning my 'couples discount' form completed with two women's names, to the friendly taxi driver who asks if my partner and I are sisters) are numerically by far the most common. The reviewer asks, "Isn't 'coming out' all about newsworthiness and announcing something new?", against which I counterpose my own experience of trying, repeatedly, to manage and challenge these everyday assumptions of my heterosexuality while precisely *not* treating — nor forcing the other to treat — my thereby revealed lesbianism as a 'newsworthy' issue. But this discussion is to pre-empt the findings I want to report: my claim at this stage is only that they are 'comings out' in the sense that a speaker revealed (however they revealed it) their sexuality to someone who had not previously known it. How that revelation was managed, and how others responded, is what I set out to discover — an undertaking which could not have been embarked upon if I had insisted upon a prior operational definition of 'coming out' as an activity necessarily (by definitional fiat) carried out, or responded to, in a particular predetermined manner.

In addition to my own 'member's knowledge', I brought to my data analysis other (untaped) discussions with the students who were coming out in these settings, or who had been the audiences for the comings out of others, about their experiences. I knew from the very people who provided the data that these taped moments of 'coming out' were intensely important experiences. Coming out was extensively discussed beforehand, experienced as important and significant at the time, and considered newsworthy enough to report to other people afterwards — and yet, at the time the coming out was being done, nobody (me included) reacted to it in this way. There is virtually nothing in the lesbian and gay research literature which addresses the issue of lack of response, nor is there any consideration of the political implications of these 'non-responses' to comings out. These, then, are the data extracts to which I am currently applying conversation analytic techniques in an attempt to gain a better understanding of how comings out (in these cases, mundane, everyday comings out) are achieved and reacted to.

In this first example, I am leading a seminar discussion on intersexuality and the students are discussing how they would feel if they learned that someone they were attracted to was intersex, and the implications of that for their sexual identities. In this context, an undergraduate ('Linda') comes out as having found herself attracted to a woman a few years before. Other than a few 'mm's in response to this information, neither I nor any other students in the group give any reaction at all. I have cropped the transcript at the point where I launch into an account of sexual script theory.

Linda comes out

```
01  Kate:   I think it would change y- your concept of (0.2)
02          of (.) w- what it is that attracts you to somebody
03          (0.2) and i- their sex would n-not not be that feature,
04          perhaps¿
05          (1.0)
06  Kate:   Have I explained what I mean? I'm not sure whether I've
07          said what I me(hh)an
08  CK:     So y- (0.4) inst- (.) I mean, >I think a lot of lesbians
09          and gay people use that argument anyway which is that
10          it's not< (.)
11  Kate:   [mmm]
12  CK:     [the    ] sex, it's the person [I  think]
13  Kate:                                  [Yeah, I ]
14          think my brain w'ld, it'd do it that way.=
15  Linda:  =It does, it does have an effect on you because (0.2)
16          if you've thought of yourself as heterosexual (1.0)
17          and you (.) >suddenly find yourself attracted to a woman
18          °it happened to me,< (0.2) a few years ago°
```

19		it's <u>very</u> (0.8) dis<u>turb</u>ing, [in a] way it's=
20	CK:	[mm]
21	Linda:	=it's (0.2) makes you very anxious (.)
22		because you then don't know how you're supposed to respond=
23	CK:	=mm[mm=
24	Linda:	=[and (.) if you e- found out that your partner was an
25		intersex you would wonder (.) >how do I respond to this
26		person sexually< I don't <u>know</u> (.) how to approach, how
27		to be romantic how to (.) wh<u>at</u> this person expects
28		from <u>me</u>, whereas if you (.) think of- you know of
29		yourself as <u>heterosexual</u>, then you <u>know</u> (0.2) the
30		responses you <u>know</u> how to interact.
31		[So it's those kind of]
32	CK:	[There's a sort of set of] <u>guidelines</u>, aren't there,
33	(?):	mmm
34	CK:	for how to (.) how to <u>do</u> sexual interaction

In this extract, then, Linda tells us that she was sexually attracted to a woman a few years ago, and it creates barely a ripple on the surface of the conversation about intersex.

In the second example, it is the teaching assistant running the seminar discussion ('Pat') who comes out as having been heterosexual and now being lesbian. The extract is taken from about half an hour into the seminar, and students are supposed to be evaluating different theories of sexuality: as the extract opens, Pat is discussing the criteria upon which they might base this evaluation. Again, there is apparently no response at all. I have cropped the extract at the point at which the students move off into a discussion about conversion therapies for homosexuality.

Pat comes out

01	Pat:	So: (0.4) um, (0.4) th- that's another thing to kind of
02		think about t- and to be aware of when you're kind of
03		ev<u>alu</u>ating different theories of (.) of of sexuality
04		is y'know (.) is it explaining simply who
05		people chose to (.) or who people have <u>sex</u> with (.)
06		or is it explaining (.) .hh you know I mean what people
07		often refer as a kind of a lifestyle, y'know,
08		how they live their lives, who they live with and so on.
09		.hhh um (2.0) I mean living (0.4) living with a woman is
10		quite different from living with a ma:n I think.

```
11          (0.2)
12          I mean, I've been heterosexual and I'm now lesbian
13          and I certainly experience being in a relationship with
14          a woman as very different from being in a relationship
15          with a man .hhh and (.) it's not just kind of hinged around
16          (0.4) kind of the sex and who you're sleeping with
17          <there's a whole kind of (.) there's a whole big aspect of
18          sexuality and sexual identity that I think theories often
19          (.) miss out on and they reduce it to questions of who
20          you're sleeping with and not >you know< more broadly who you
21          are um (.) oka:y, w- what evidence is there that sexuality
22          can change?
23          (0.2)
24   Dave:  There was that Exodus thing
25   Pat:   uh huh
26   Dave:  um (0.2) it's like a christian organisation I think that
27          focuses on the fact that um homosexuality is a sin (.)
28   Pat:   uh huh
```

Many of Harvey Sacks' *Lectures on Conversation* are devoted to explorations of how people methodically achieve recognizable conversational actions without paying some negative price associated with them: how to avoid giving your name without refusing to give it; how to avoid giving help without refusing it; how to get help without requesting it; how to talk in a therapy session without revealing yourself. Part of what my analysis suggests is that many of us have developed a technique which could be called 'How to come out without anybody noticing'.

CA asks that we understand these 'coming out' utterances not only as a matter of information transfer from the person coming out to their co-conversationalists, but also as actions in interactional sequence. Conveying new information is not the same thing as announcing news: not all new information conveyed is set up by speakers to be treated as news by the person to whom it is told. There is, for example, a substantial CA literature on breaking 'bad news' (for example, of serious diagnoses and deaths) which shows a range of devices used to avoid one person being heard to tell another bad news, while also ensuring that the information is imparted. In ordinary conversation, news telling can be organised so that the recipient, rather than the bearer of the news, ends up pronouncing it (Schegloff 1988), and clinicians presenting parents with a diagnosis of mental retardation in their child use particular strategies to present the diagnosis as a simple 'confirmation' of something the parent already knows (Maynard 1992). So, although the comings out I have collected do, as it happens (as I know from subsequent discussions with the people involved), convey new information to the listeners about the speakers' sexuality, the first thing to observe, from a CA perspective, is that speakers are not doing 'news-announcement'. Undoubtedly, there are some comings out which do news-announcement, and which we can recognise as such: they begin with classic phrases (pre-announcements) like "Mum, I've got something to tell you," or "Guess what? I'm gay". News announcement normatively makes relevant from the recipient an acknowledgement of news receipt and assessment of the information so conveyed. When 'comings out' are done as news announcement, then, they would make relevant assessments which can be anything from "Oh no! it'll kill your father" to "Oh, that's wonderful, I'm so pleased for you". But neither Linda, Pat, nor any of the other ten comings out I am analysing, do news announcements. Instead, information about the speaker's sexuality is conveyed as an aside, as a list item, or as passing instance or illustration of some other point altogether. *Not* presenting information about one's sexuality as news has decisive consequences for shaping the course of the talk's development. If it is not announced as news, recipients have to work hard to receive it as such.

There's something else, though, about the construction of this coming out talk which makes audience response unlikely, and that is the location of the information in the turn-taking organisation. Turn-taking organisation is one of those classic areas of CA with which feminists and other radicals are often most impatient — but it offers a powerful tool for understanding why it is that these recipients of comings out do not react. Information about the speaker's sexuality is often deeply embedded within turn constructional units in ways that would render as interruptive, any acknowledgement or assessment of this information from a co-conversationalist.

In Sacks, Schegloff and Jefferson's (1974) classic paper on turn-taking, they propose a model for conversation which seeks to explain the practices people use for ensuring — with systematic and orderly exceptions explainable by the theory itself — how it is that people in conversation overwhelmingly speak one at a time. The model proposes the existence of turn constructional units (TCUs) which can be whole sentences, phrases, sometimes just words, but which are recognizable (in context) as potentially constituting a complete turn. Each speaker is initially entitled to just *one* of these: after that, another speaker has the right (sometimes the obligation) to speak next. The model is complex and sophisticated, and I have oversimplified it radically, but the key point of relevance here is that the turn-taking organisation is not organised to be indifferent to the size of the turns parties take: rather, its "underlying (though supercessable) organisation is designed to minimize turn size" (Schegloff 1982: 73) and consequently we need to understand long turns, with lengthy and/or multiple TCUs, as "achievements and accomplishments" (73) which have overcome the inherent bias of the system.

In the coming out episodes, the speaker, the one who is coming out, uses *long* TCUs, and *many* TCUs — and as CA shows us, that is something which has to be worked at: it does not just happen. Conversation analysts have documented some of the techniques people use when they want to keep speaking for a long time. Long TCUs can be accomplished by using particular sentence structures (such as 'if/then' constructions) which are hearably not complete until a second part of the sentence (such as the 'then' part) has been produced. People can project a long TCU simply by taking a big in-breath: studies show that in-breaths put hearers on the alert for a long (possibly multi-unit) turn. Multi-unit turns can be secured at the beginning of a speaker's turn by making a bid to tell a story ('Did you hear about the time when...'); by using a list launcher ('four things...'); and by using 'markedly first verbs' (like 'I thought...' or 'I tried...') which are regularly used to mark things incorrectly thought, or unsuccessfully tried, and therefore project accounts of what is now known, or an account of failure). Speakers may also employ methodical devices for achieving multi-unit turns during the course of their talk. They may 'rush through' a possible transition point — talking right through the intersection between one TCU and the next, not pausing to take a breath until a point of maximum grammatical control (that is, where it is obvious that the speaker is not complete). Even more radically, speakers sometimes prevent the end of a TCU (and hence possible speaker transition) from occurring simply by not uttering the last word or syllable of the TCU. (For all this, and more, see Schegloff 1982.) While critics have poured scorn on the turn-taking organisation research as a tedious political irrelevance which could only obscure the operation of power (see, for example, Billig's 1999 deeply flawed claims in relation to turn-taking and rape), Schegloff (1999: 563) has said that:

> those committed to analyzing forms of inequality and oppression in interaction might do better to harness this account of turn-taking organisation as a *resource* for their undertaking than to complain of it as an ideological distraction.

And that is exactly what we can do here.

If we look back at Linda's coming out, we see that she embeds her coming out in the middle of an 'if/then' structure (though the 'then' is not actually spoken) which projects the first possible transition place to well *after* her coming out. In addition, at line 19, at exactly the point where the TCU is reaching possible completion, and speaker transition becomes relevant, she augments it with another unit which acts as a 'pivot' to get her across the transition place from the end of one TUC into the beginning of the next. The pivot ("in a way", line 19) is both the last part of one TCU and the beginning of the next TCU: "it's very disturbing in a way"/ "In a way it's it's makes you very anxious". By using the pivot to get her across the possible transition space, Linda again postpones her co-conversationalists' opportunity to offer any acknowledgement or appraisal of the information she has imparted. After using an "and" (line 24) to indicate 'still not finished', she then launches another TCU which again uses an 'if/then' structure (and a listing device) to maximally extend the turn. By the time CK, who is leading the seminar group, comes in at the next possible transition place — and note that even here Linda keeps talking (lines 31 and 32 are in overlap) — it is way too late to respond to "it happened to me a few years ago" (line 18). In sum, Linda actively uses the turn-taking organisation of conversation to extend her turn beyond her coming out moment to decrease the likelihood of anyone offering an assessment of, or any other response to it. And in fact no one does.

We see a similar example of an extended turn construction in Pat's talk. She begins by making a general point about the difference between living with a woman and living with a man, and her 'coming out' is nicely embedded as a sort of 'take me, for instance', following which she continues her turn, filling the relevant slot in which the recipient would otherwise be expected to respond, with a clearly audible in-breath and an "and" (line 14), which indicates that she is not yet finished, so warding off challenge, questions, or assessment, and subsequently pausing only at places in her talk which are clearly grammatically incomplete (lines 15, 16 and 18). At line 20, she reaches the projectable end of her TCU "and not more broadly who you are" — and intonationally it is clear that some ending is required (such as 'spending your life with', for example). But Pat does not supply any ending: she simply fails to complete her TCU (thereby avoiding possible speaker transition relevance), signals topic change with an 'okay', and asks a question — which makes sequentially relevant an answer to the question so posed, and not any comments, questions or assessment related to her earlier statement that she's 'been heterosexual' and is 'now lesbian'. Like Linda, Pat uses the turn-taking system of conversation to make discussion of her coming out unlikely. And, indeed, nobody does discuss it. As with Linda's coming out, it is not treated as a noticeable, commentable-upon piece of information.

So, what political relevance can be derived from this conversation analysis of the turn-taking structure of coming out talk? Linda and Pat (and others in data not presented here) are coming out, but they are using the turn-taking organisation to avoid their sexuality becoming topicalised, and they are conveying information about their sexuality in a 'not-new' format (as an instance or example of something else). The design of these comings out is attentive to, and hence can be used to explore, the conditions of our oppression in (at least) two ways.

First, they are attentive to the accusation of 'flaunting it' — to the complaint 'I don't mind gays but why must they be so blatant?' Their construction as 'not-news', as conversational asides, and their embeddedness in long turns, is precisely designed *not* to flaunt, not to draw attention to, not to make an issue of it — to slip it into the conversation so as to make it public, but in a way that is demonstrably relevant to the conversation, displayed as being an instance or piece of evidence in support of some other point. Another reason why coming out might be done in this way is in order to mark some kind of resistance to the whole idea of coming out, to the notion that it should be necessary, that unless we announce as newsworthy our difference from a presumed heterosexual norm, then we can legitimately be assumed to be heterosexual. As recent theorists have suggested, there is a sense in which coming out colludes with the notion that before we came out, we were hiding, and that in letting other people know our sexuality, we are revealing the past deception of the closet. By making lesbianism an aside, an instance, a deliberately casual exemplar of something else, these young women may be invoking and constructing the notion that that is indeed all it is (or all it should be), that — in fact — there is nothing of note *to* 'flaunt'. Coming out in a way that clearly avoids 'flaunting' sexuality as a newsworthy, commentable-upon piece of information can be seen, then, both as collusion with the heterosexual imperative *not* to be public about our sexuality, but equally as a resistance to the whole notion that our sexuality can be assumed to be heterosexual unless we announce to the contrary.

Second, there is a protective element in these comings out: they are both protective of others and self-protective. By embedding information about the speaker's sexuality in the middle of turn construction units or in following them with multiple TCUs, speakers protect the recipients from having to produce a response. Both the location of the information, and its structure as 'not news' (as an aside, for instance) provides for recipients to hear it and yet not have to deal with it there and then. Hearers are insulated by subsequent talk against the potential shock value of the information they are receiving. It is a way in which speakers protect others from being potentially crass recipients of the delicate information conveyed — and, of course, protect themselves from having to deal with such potentially crass responses. In continuing to analyse these data, I hope to develop a better understanding of the politics of coming out in everyday situations.

3.   Doing feminist conversation analysis

Feminist (and LGBT) scholars have used a variety of different approaches for developing theory and practice in relation to coming out. The social science literature on this topic includes a great deal of qualitative work (analysed using thematic analysis, discourse analysis, grounded theory, narrative approaches and so on) as well as quantitative work (for instance, surveys, questionnaires, tests and experiments). What unites these disparate studies as 'feminist' — across a range of different epistemological, methodological and ontological assumptions — is their commitment to creating social and political change. In this paper, I have demonstrated that CA, too, can be used for feminist purposes.

As we have seen, 'the trouble with CA...', according to feminist and radical critics, is three-fold: its (ethnomethodological) social theory; its emphasis on participant rather than analyst orientations; and its attention on the micro-details of interaction. In applying CA to coming out, I have illustrated how these alleged 'troubles' are in fact strengths which enable the development of a clearly feminist analysis.

First, the social theory of CA means that my analyses were based on an ethnomethodological concern with member's methods for doing 'coming out', as that knowledge is displayed *in action*, that is through what they actually say and do. When 'doing coming out', people are conceptualised as active agents and participants in the world, rather than simply as victims of heteropatriarchal society.

Second, in line with the CA focus on 'participant orientations', analysis is not framed up as a sex (or sexualities) differences study. Instead of subordinating the data analysis to already existing *a priori* categories of gender, sexuality or other dimensions of social power, the aim was to explore how genders, sexualities and power are accomplished in interaction. The studies show how actions (such as comings out) are actively designed in relation to the actions of others — and in the design of those actions, and in others' responses to them, we as analysts can see the everyday (sexist and heterosexist) world under construction. In feminist conversation analysis, oppression and resistance are not simply abstract theoretical concepts but become visible as concrete practices of social members in interaction. In the 'coming out' research, for example — as in Sacks' Estelle and Jeanelle example — nothing much happens, and it was precisely how it is that nothing much gets to happen, how the conversation is constructed as 'business as usual' which provided the analytic interest.

Finally, these analyses would simply not have been possible without a fine-grained analysis of the data at the level of which participants themselves produce and respond to the talk. The conversation analytic work on sequence organisation, and turn-taking, requires analysts to be sensitive to micro-pauses, in-breaths, intonational changes and other small details of talk, because these are relevant to the participants and are part of the mundane way in which the social order is routinely produced and reproduced.

In conclusion, I hope I have made a case for including CA amongst our array of analytic approaches. As feminists we need to understand and to counter overt violence, legal discrimination, and institutionalised oppression — but the politics of the personal means understanding too the routine everyday talk through which we collude with (or resist) the social order.

Notes

* This chapter is a revised and condensed version of an article previously published under the same title in *Feminism & Psychology* (2000) 10: 163-193.

1. I am enormously grateful to Professor Emmanuel Schegloff, from whose inspired and enthusiastic teaching I have learnt everything I know about CA, and on the basis of which I embarked on the 'coming out' analysis presented here. He should in no way be held responsible, of course, for the use I have made of his ideas, and all errors and inaccuracies are mine alone.

2. With thanks to Virginia Braun, Victoria Clarke, Elizabeth Peel and Sue Wilkinson for passing on to me the audiotapes of these coming out episodes, without which this research would not, of course, have been possible.

References

Billig, Michael. 1999 "Whose terms? Whose ordinariness? Rhetoric and ideology in conversation analysis". *Discourse & Society* 10(4): 543-558.

Bing, Janet M. and Bergvall, Victoria L. 1996 "The question of questions: Beyond binary thinking". In *Rethinking Language and Gender Research: Theory and Method*, V.L. Bergvall, J.M. Bing and A.F. Freed (eds), 1-30. London: Longman.

Butler, Judith. 1990 *Gender Trouble: Feminism and the Subversion of Identity*. London: Routledge.

Butler, Judith. 1993 *Bodies That Matter*. London: Routledge.

Butler, Judith. 1997 *Excitable Speech: A Politics of the Performative*. London: Routledge.

Cain, Roy. 1996 "Heterosexism and self-disclosure in the social work classroom". *Journal of Social Work Education* 32: 65-76.

Cameron, Deborah. 1996 "The Language-Gender Interface: Challenging Co-optation". In *Rethinking Language and Gender Research: Theory and Method*, V. Bergvall, J. Bing and A.F. Freed (eds), 31-53. London: Longman.

Coyle, Adrian and Kitzinger, Celia (eds). 2002 *Lesbian and Gay Psychology*. Oxford: Blackwell.

Crawford, Mary (ed.). 2000 "The social construction of gender: Reappraisal of Kessler and McKenna", *Feminism & Psychology*. 10(1): 7-10.

Davidson, Julie O'Connell. 1996 "Prostitution and the contours of control". In *Sexual Cultures*, J. Weeks and J. Holland (eds), 102-128. London: Macmillan.

Day, Connie L. and Morse, Ben W. 1981 "Communication patterns in established lesbian relationships". In *Gayspeak: Gay Male and Lesbian Communication*, J.W. Chesebro (ed.), 64-78. New York: Pilgrim.

Du Bois, Barbara. 1983 "Passionate scholarship: Notes on values, knowing and method in feminist social science". In *Theories of Women's Studies*, G. Bowles and R.D. Klein (eds), 27-43. London: Routledge & Kegan Paul.

Edgar, Timothy. 1994 "Self-disclosure strategies of the stigmatized: Strategies and outcomes for the revelation of sexual orientation". In *Queer Words, Queer Images: Communication and the Construction of Homosexuality*, R.J. Ringer (ed.), 221-237. New York: New York University Press.

Fellegy, Anna M. 1995 "Patterns and functions of minimal response". *American Speech* 70: 186-198.

Forrester, Michael A. 1999 "Conversation analysis: A reflexive methodology for critical psychology". *Annual Review of Critical Psychology* 1: 34-49.

Franke, Rachel and Leary, Mark R. 1991 "Disclosure of sexual orientation by lesbians and gay men". *Journal of Social and Clinical Psychology* 10: 262-269.

Frith, Hannah. 1998 "Constructing the 'other' through talk". *Feminism & Psychology* 8(4): 530-536.

Frith, Hannah and Kitzinger, Celia. 1998 "'Emotion work' as a participant resource: A feminist analysis of young women's talk-in-interaction". *Sociology* 32(2): 299-320.

Gagne, Patricia, Tewksbury, Richard and McGaughey, Deanna. 1997 "Coming out and crossing over: Identity formation and proclamation in a transgender community". *Gender & Society* 11(4): 478-508.

Garfinkel, Harold. 1967 *Studies in Ethnomethodology*. Cambridge: Polity Press.

Gilligan, Carol. 1982 *In a Different Voice*. Cambridge, MA: Harvard University Press.

Goodwin, Marjorie Harness. 1990 *He-Said-She-Said: Talk as Social Organisation Among Black Children*. Bloomington, IN: Indiana University Press.

Gould, Meredith Gould. 1980 "The new sociology" *Signs* 5(3): 459-468.

Have, Paul ten. 1999 *Doing Conversation Analysis: A Practical Guide*. London: Sage.

Heritage, John. 1984 *Garfinkel and Ethnomethodology*. Cambridge: Polity Press.

Hopper, Robert and LeBaron, Curtis. 1998 "How gender creeps into talk". *Research on Language and Social Interaction* 31(1): 59-74.

Hutchby, Ian and Wooffitt, Robin. 1998 *Conversation Analysis: Principles, Practices and Applications*. Cambridge: Polity.

Jacobs, Greg. 1996 "Lesbian and gay male language use: A critical review of the literature". *American Speech* 71: 49-71.

Jordan, Karen M. and Deluty, Robert H. 1998 "Coming out for lesbian women: Its relation to anxiety, positive affectivity, self-esteem, and social support". *Journal of Homosexuality* 35: 41-63.

Kessler, Suzanne and McKenna, Wendy. 1978 *Gender: An Ethnomethodological Approach*. New York: John Wiley.

Kitzinger, Celia. 1987 *The Social Construction of Lesbianism*. London: Sage.

Kitzinger, Celia. 1990 "Heterosexism in psychology". *The Psychologist* 3(9): 391-392.

Kitzinger, Celia. 1994 "Sex differences research: Feminist perspectives". *Feminism & Psychology* 4(2): 330-336.

Kitzinger, Celia. 2000 "How to resist an idiom" *Research on Language and Social Interaction* 33: 121-154.

Kitzinger, Celia and Frith, Hannah. 1999 "Just say no? The use of conversation analysis in developing a feminist perspective on sexual refusal". *Discourse & Society* 10(3): 293-316.

Kitzinger, Celia and Thomas, Alison. 1995 "Sexual Harrassment: A Discursive Approach". In *Feminism and Discourse: Psychological Perspectives*, S. Wilkinson and C. Kitzinger (eds), 32-48. London: Sage.

Kitzinger, Celia and Wilkinson, Sue. 1995 "Transitions from heterosexuality to lesbianism: The discursive production of lesbian identities". *Developmental Psychology* 31(1): 95-104.

Kitzinger, Celia and Wilkinson, Sue. 1997 "Validating women's experience? Dilemmas in feminist research". *Feminism & Psychology* 7(4): 566-574.

Lakoff, Robin. 1975 *Language and Woman's Place*. New York: Harper and Row.

Liang, A.C. 1997 "The creation of coherence in coming-out stories". In *Queerly Phrased: Language, Gender and Sexuality*, A. Livia and K. Hall (eds), 287-309. Oxford: Oxford University Press.

Maltz, Daniel N. and Borker, Ruth A. 1982 "A cultural approach to male-female miscommunication". In *Language and Social Identity*, J.J. Gumperz and J. Cook-Gumperz (eds), 196-216. Cambridge: Cambridge University Press.

Maynard, Douglas W. 1992 "On clinicians co-implicating recipients' perspectives in the delivery of diagnostic news". In *Talk at Work: Interaction in Institutional Settings*, P. Drew and J. Heritage (eds), 331-358. Cambridge: Cambridge University Press.

Mott, Helen and Condor, Susan. 1997 "Sexual harassment and the working lives of secretaries". In *Sexual Harassment: Contemporary Feminist Perspectives*, A.M. Thomas and C. Kitzinger (eds), 49-90. Buckingham: Open University Press.

Ochs, Elinor. 1992 "Indexing gender". In *Rethinking Context: Language as an Interactive Phenomenon*, A. Duranti and C. Goodwin (eds), 335-358. Cambridge: Cambridge University Press.

Peel, Elizabeth. 2001 "Mundane heterosexism: Understanding incidents of the everyday", *Women's Studies International Forum* 24(5): 541-554.

Plummer, Ken. 1995 *Telling Sexual Stories: Power, Change and Social Worlds*. London: Routledge.

Psathas, George (ed.). 1979 *Everyday Language: Studies in Ethnomethodology*. New York: Irvington.

Psathas, George. 1995 *Conversation Analysis: The Study of Talk-in-Interaction*. London: Sage.

Reinhartz, Shulamit. 1992 *Feminist Methods in Social Research*. New York: Oxford University Press.

Sacks, Harvey. 1995 *Lectures on Conversation: Volumes I and II*. Oxford: Basil Blackwell.

Sacks, Harvey, Schegloff, Emanuel A. and Jefferson, Gail. 1974 "A simplest systematics for the organisation of turn-taking for conversation". *Language* 50: 696-735.

Schachar, Sandra A. and Gilbert, Lucia A. 1983 "Working lesbians: Role conflicts and coping strategies". *Psychology of Women Quarterly* 7: 244-256.

Schegloff, Emanuel A. 1982 "Discourse as an interactional achievement: Some uses of 'uh huh' and other things that come between sentences". In *Analyzing Discourse: Text and Talk* [Georgetown University Roundtable on Languages and Linguistics 1981], D. Tannen (ed.), 71-93. Washington, DC: Georgetown University Press.

Schegloff, Emanuel A. 1988 "On an actual virtual servo-mechanism for guessing bad news: A single case conjecture". *Social Problems* 35(4): 442-457.

Schegloff, Emanuel A. 1997 "Whose text? Whose context?" *Discourse & Society* 8(2): 165-187.

Schegloff, Emanuel A. 1999 "'Schegloff's texts' as 'Billig's data': A critical reply". *Discourse & Society* 10(4): 558-572.

Sedgwick, Eve Kosofsky. 1990 *The Epistemology of the Closet*. Berkeley, London: Harvester Wheatsheaf.

Shakespeare, Tom. 1999 "Coming out and coming home". *Journal of Gay, Lesbian and Bisexual Identity* 4(1): 39-51.

Smith, Dorothy. 1987 *The Everyday World as Problematic: A Feminist Sociology*. Boston MA: Northeastern University Press.

Speer, Susan A. 1999 "Feminism and conversation analysis: An oxymoron?" *Feminism & Psychology* 9(4): 471-478.

Speer, Susan A. 2001 "Reconsidering the concept of hegemonic masculinity: Discursive psychology, conversation analysis and participants' orientations". *Feminism & Psychology* 11(1): 107-135.

Stokoe, Elizabeth H. 1998 "Talking about gender: The conversational construction of gender categories in academic discourse". *Discourse & Society* 9(2): 217-240.

Tannen, Deborah. 1990 *You Just Don't Understand: Women and Men in Conversation.* New York: Ballantine Books.

Turner, Roy. 1974 "Introduction". In *Ethnomethodology: Selected Readings*, R. Turner (ed.), 7-12. London: Penguin.

West, Candace. 1979 "Against our will: Male interruptions of females in cross-sex conversations". In *Language, Sex and Gender: Does "La Différence" make a Difference?* [Annals of the New York Academy of Sciences, Vol 327], J. Orasanu, M.K. Slater and L.L. Adler (eds), 81-100. New York: New York Academy of Sciences.

West, Candace and Zimmerman, Don H. 1977 "Women's place in everyday talk: Reflections on parent-child interactions". *Social Problems* 521-529.

Wetherell, Margaret. 1998 "Positioning and interpretative repertoires: Conversation analysis and post-structuralism in dialogue". *Discourse & Society* 9(3): 387-412.

Wise, Sue and Stanley, Liz. 1987 *Georgie Porgie: Sexual Harassment in Everyday Life.* London: Pandora.

Wood, Kathleen M. 1997 "Narrative iconicity in electronic-mail lesbian coming out stories", *Queerly Phrased: Language, Gender and Sexuality*, A. Livia and K. Hall (eds), 257-273. Oxford: Oxford University Press.

Zimmerman, Don and West, Candace. 1975 "Sex roles, interruptions and silences in conversations". In *Language and Sex: Difference and Dominance*, B. Thorne and N. Henley (eds), 105-129. Rowley, M.A.: Newbury House.

CHAPTER 3

Gender and sexuality in talk-in-interaction

Considering conversation analytic perspectives

Elizabeth H. Stokoe and Janet Smithson

1. Introduction

In this chapter, we critically evaluate conversation analytic (CA) approaches to the study of the gender, sexuality and language from a feminist perspective. Rather than attempting to characterize interactional styles, we explore instead the ways that participants in interaction orient to gender and sexuality categories. In so doing, we explore the CA position that in order to warrant claims about the relevance of such sociological variables to interaction, they must be shown to be demonstrably relevant to the participants.

We drew on focus group interactions to explore these issues. The transcribed data was analysed using conversation and membership categorization analysis. We explored the complex ways that speakers assembled membership categories as well as their sequential organisation. We found that gender and sexuality was 'made relevant' to interaction in two related ways. First, we focused on instances in which gender and sexuality was procedurally relevant for speakers, as evidenced through discursive phenomenon such as repair, disclaimers and 'troubling' orientations to such categories. Second, we analysed instances in which the relevance of sexuality to interaction could be evidenced only by drawing upon the analyst's cultural knowledge. In these instances, issues of sexuality were pertinent to us as analysts but could not be evidenced as relevant to speakers. We explore the consequences of our analyses for feminist researchers using CA. We question whether CA, in its strictest implementation, is adequate to address feminist concerns, especially in the context of recent developments in feminist conversation analysis.

2.   Gender, sexuality and discourse

Identifying the relevance of gender and sexuality to social interaction continues to stimulate debate across the social sciences. When feminist language and gender research began in the 1970s, the emphasis was upon defining speech styles and attributing them to men or women. Three theoretical frameworks governed a field that emerged as a distinct body of inquiry: deficit (for example, Lakoff 1973), dominance (for example, Fishman 1978) and cultural difference (for example, Tannen 1990). Slower to emerge as a field, studies of language and sexuality opted for a similar approach, aiming to link sexual identities to language styles and identify, for example, 'gay men's English' (Leap 1996) or lesbian women's speech (Moonwomon-Baird 1997).

Criticisms of early language and gender research and the three frameworks are well documented (see Crawford 1995). A fundamental assumption of many studies is an essentialist treatment of gender. Gender is theorised as a property of individuals and, in studies of interaction, is treated as an unproblematic sociolinguistic variable that can be correlated with various language behaviours. Feminist commentators subsequently rejected this as an underpinning epistemology, instead locating gender in interactions (Bohan 1993). Recent studies that attempt to link sexual identity to language have fallen foul of similar censure. For example, linking sexual identity categories such as 'gay' to speech styles essentialises sexuality in the same way that gender was essentialised in speech style studies (Kulick 1999). Critical rethinking across both fields has led to a focus on the performative nature of gender and sexuality and their status as 'emergent properties' of social interaction (for example, Bucholtz, Liang and Sutton 1999, Butler 1990, West and Zimmerman 1987). These newer understandings of gender and sexuality have been developed via methods such as discursive and conversation analysis (for example, Edley and Wetherell 1999, Kitzinger 2000, Stokoe 1998).

Consequently, there has been a considerable shift in the gender, sexuality and discourse arena, away from a study of interactional differences between groups of men and women, to a focus on the discursive articulation of gendered and sexual identities. Although this new direction is welcome, the constructionist strand has prompted its own critical commentary. For example, Cameron (1998) argues that some of this newer work confounds a so-called 'critical' position with analytic explanation that perpetuates gender dualism. Similarly, Stokoe (2000) suggests that some writers blend a constructionist stance with cultural (essentialist) feminism.[1] For example, in her analyses of women's talk, Coates (1996) bases her descriptions of how the participants 'do femininity' by pointing to instances in which they talk about what could be glossed as 'female' things (their appearance, being at the mercy of their hormones). Conversely, men perform masculinity by adopting a particular conversational style and by talking about impersonal, factually based topics (Coates 1997, Tannen 1999). Both Coates and Tannen start their analysis by looking at the talk of one gender and assume, for example, that there is something about *women's* talk that performs femininity. Kulick (1999) makes a similar point about language and sexuality research in which analysts look only at the talk of a particular pre-categorised group of people. By examining the talk of gay men, "the only people whose language is analysed are people who explicitly self-identify as queer, so we start out 'knowing' the identities whose very constitution ought to be precisely the issue under investigation" (1999: 6). In Coates' and Tannen's articles, they also 'start out knowing the identities' of the women and men whose identities they claim are constituted in interaction, resulting in a tautological argument (Kulick 1999).

Gender, sexuality and conversation analysis

Finding the best way to approach the study of language, gender and sexuality is a complex problem. Particularly troublesome is how best to make claims about the relevance of such identities to social interaction without sliding into essentialist claims about particular groups of people. One solution is to interrogate gender and sexual identity categories *as they appear in people's talk*, using ethnomethodological principles and the related methodologies of membership categorisation analysis (MCA) and sequential conversation analysis (SCA).[2] These methodological traditions, although often discussed quite separately, may be used fruitfully together to investigate the procedural consequentiality of categories-in-interaction (see also D'hondt this volume, Housley 2000, Lepper 2000, Nilan 1994, 1995, Stokoe and Smithson 2001, Tainio this volume, Watson 1997).

Across both analytic traditions, the focus is upon what participants, or *members*, orient to in their discussions, rather than seeking to impose identity categories (such as 'woman', 'gay man') onto the analysis of patterns in discursive data. Summarising the fundamental assumption of this position, Schegloff (1992: 196, emphasis in original) writes:

> showing that some orientation to context is demonstrably relevant to the
> participants is important … in order to ensure that what informs the analy-

sis is what is relevant to *the participants in its target event*, and not what is relevant in the first instance to its academic analysts by virtue of the set of analytic and theoretical commitments which they bring to their work.

So in order to warrant a claim that any interactional identity or sociological variable is relevant in conversation, analysts must be able to demonstrate its *relevance for speakers*. With specific reference to gender categories, Schegloff (1998: 415) argues that "rather than beginning with gender ideologies ... the analysis might begin by addressing what the parties to the interaction understand themselves to be doing in it". This framework, as well as constituting a welcome directional shift for language and gender studies, provides a more politically effective position from which to make claims about the relevance of 'gender' and 'sexuality' to talk – a position that is not steeped in gender difference or underpinned by essentialism.

This 'analytic mentality' is echoed throughout in the CA literature and also in discursive psychology (for example, Antaki 1995, Antaki and Widdicombe 1998, Speer and Potter 2000, Speer and Potter this volume). It has also been applied in the small body of work that explores members' practices of gender categorisation (for example, Edwards 1998, Hopper and LeBaron 1998, Philipsen 1990/1991, Stringer and Hopper 1998, Stokoe 1998, 2000). In LeBaron's words,

> we should not ... say "oh, look, here's a man and a woman talking; let's look at how they talk; oh, we can make these conclusions about gendered communication". But rather we should say, "gender only becomes an issue when the participants themselves make it one and we can point to different things about that" (Le Baron, participating in transcribed discussion in Tracy 1998: 15).

We agree that CA is a useful tool for making claims about the relevance of social categories to talk-in-interaction because such claims are grounded in speakers' orientations.[3] This is in sharp contrast to other work in the gender and language field, in which analysts' assumptions and categories are imposed onto the analysis. However, the application of CA to the study of gender and other social categories has recently become the focus of heated discussion (Billig 1999, van Dijk 1999, Kitzinger 2000, Schegloff 1997, 1998, 1999a, 1999b, Speer 2001, Speer and Potter 2000, this volume, Stokoe 2000, Weatherall 2000, Wetherell 1998). The main thrust of the debate centres on the implied 'narrowness' of the CA stance on the role and meaning of 'context', 'relevance' and 'participants' orientations'. In this chapter, we set out and explore in detail some of these issues, grounding our arguments in the analysis of conversational data. We examine several fragments of focus group data in which speakers invoke gender and sexuality categories. In so doing, we address the following questions:

– Is it *fruitful* to rely on orientations to gender and sexuality solely in participants' terms?

– Related to this, we ask what, precisely, *counts* as an orientation to sexuality or gender? We suggest that the actual discursive practices of 'making relevant' or 'orienting to' conversational phenomenon need further definition.

– Does the conversation analyst *unavoidably* and thus properly draw upon broader contextual and cultural knowledge in the pursuit of talk's explication?

– How should (feminist) conversation analysts treat interactions in which gender and sexuality (and particularly sexist and heterosexist assumptions) are 'unnoticed' by participants but are relevant in the maintenance of heteronormativity?

Overall, we suggest that culture and common-sense knowledge, of both members and analysts, are unacknowledged resources in CA. We shall address these points in turn throughout the rest of the chapter.

Conversation analysis and the context debate

As described earlier, in order to make claims about the relevance of social categories to talk-in-interaction, conversation analysts must ground their claims entirely in participants' orientations to the phenomenon under study. This position is linked to CA's 'analytic mentality' that requires researchers to consider their data without pre-selecting concepts and theories to test or explore (Hester and Eglin 1997). If we extend this line of argument, it follows that the wider cultural context is irrelevant in analysis unless we can demonstrate its procedural relevance to speakers. This position is stated perhaps most strongly by Sanders (1999: 130), who claims that "in principle, necessarily, culture is an unapparent and functionally unimportant element of routine everyday interactions".

Although many conversation analysts adopt this approach, others are critical of such a stance for a variety of reasons. The locus of debate is set out by Watson (1992: xiv) in his question: "how far is extra-textual material necessary to the carrying on of analysis at the level of concreteness common to ethnomethodology [and] conversation analysis?" There are at least two conflicting perspectives on this issue. Whereas Schegloff, Sanders and others would argue a 'fundamentalist' stance against importing background knowledge, others argue in favour of analysts 'raising their eyes' from the text on the page to consider the broader argumentative texture that surrounds any fragment of discourse data (Wetherell 1998). As a result, CA is often described as having 'a restricted notion of context' (Tracy 1998). The upshot of this line of criticism is that a 'complete and scholarly' conversation analysis should draw upon other theoretical frameworks such as post-structuralism (for example, Wetherell 1998), social constructionism (Buttny 1993, Abell and Stokoe 2001), discursive psychology (Speer and Potter this volume) or ethnography (Bilmes 1993, Moerman 1988). In other words, analysts properly draw upon cultural, ethnographic and subjective background knowledge in the explication of members' interactional practices.

An alternative solution to the 'restricted notion of context' problem is to dismantle CA's claims to an unmotivated 'analytic mentality'. Instead, we argue that regardless of such claims researchers use their background knowledge, either acknowledged or unacknowledged, in the process of doing analysis (Stokoe and Smithson 2001). A similar position is suggested by Arminen (2000: 436), who argues that rather than seeking explicitly to link CA with, say, ethnography, researchers should "acknowledge the fact that CA studies use knowledge of the context anyway, either overtly or tacitly". Criticising a recent collection of CA studies of identity (Ankaki and Widdicombe 1998), Kiesling (2000: 506) also argues that although analysts claim to focus solely on the endogenous orientations of speakers, they "draw on all kinds of implicit cultural knowledge in their analyses. This means that 'making relevant' relies on the analysts' cultural knowledge, and thus external context."

A further way of solving this problem is to revisit CA's notion of 'member' and extend it explicitly to include the analyst. Whilst many conversation analysts explain how speakers-as-members display cultural knowledge and tacit sense-making procedures in their interactions, they have a restricted notion of who 'members' are. Typically, when writers talk about members, they refer only to participants in the fragments of transcript they analyse. They rarely include the analyst as a member. As Cicourel (1992: 294) writes: "the investigator's ability to comprehend [conversational] exchanges is assumed to be self-evident and is seldom if ever an aspect of the analysis". Like all debates, however, there are some commentators who take a different position, acknowledging that the import of analysts' common-sense knowledge into analysis is inevitable because they are members of the culture that produces the talk (Arminen 2000). Although CA aims to explicate what participants do in interaction, in so doing "we need to have some access to the *interpretative and inferential* resources which the participants are relying on" (Hutchby and Wooffitt 1998: 113, emphasis added). These resources include the analysts' contextual knowledge.

We argue that analysts are *also* members and display their own sense-making procedures in analysis. It therefore follows that analysts might bring to bear different versions of common-sense knowledge, and what feminists treat as common-sense is likely to differ from what non-feminist researchers do (Billig 1991, Smithson 1999). So if analysts draw upon their member's knowledge of interactions, then their own position and agenda is necessarily woven into analysis. As ten Have (1999: 35) concludes, "the researcher's own comprehension, 'as a member', so to speak, is also and inevitably involved".

Gender and participants' orientations

Related to the 'restricted notion of context' problem is the issue of 'partici-pants' orientations' itself. We have two related points to make about this: is such a position tenable, and what does it mean practically – what 'counts' as a participants' orientation? First, a criticism of the position itself. What hap-pens if speakers do not explicitly make relevant an aspect of context, yet the analyst wants to make a claim that the talk is gendered, sexist or heterosexist? What can be said about stretches of talk that are problematic for the analyst but not explicitly for the speaker? As Frith (1998: 535) points out, CA's reliance on individuals' explicit orientation to phenomena is troubled as it "raises the question of whether all the dimensions [of the phenomena] will be interactionally displayed". This issue is also discussed by Beach (2000), who analyses a conversation between two men about an absent woman. Towards the end of his paper, he asks if the analysis can support a claim that the talk is sexist, speculating that many readers will 'see' sexism in the data. However, there is no evidence that the issue of 'sexism' is demonstrably relevant for the speakers. Beach characterises the problem in terms of a "critical distinction between observer-imposed and evaluated social order (e.g., "This interaction is clearly sexist") versus the analytical demonstration that such order is demonstrably relevant (and thus procedurally consequential) for interaction-al participants" (401). We could treat the talk as 'sexism as a practical activi-ty', or 'doing sexism' but only "storified as inappropriate and 'sexist' by oth-ers" (402). As a result, CA is often accused of incorporating an 'unbearably limiting' and 'intolerably impoverished notion of participant orientations'

(Kitzinger 2000, D'hondt this volume; see also Billig 1999, Wetherell 1998), in which claims about racism, sexism or heterosexism can be made only if the speakers demonstrate the relevance of such social phenomenon.

But do conversation analysts restrict themselves to such a limited criteria for claiming relevance? Our second concern with 'participants orientations' centres around what the term means practically – what counts as a 'participants' orientation', 'making relevant', 'attending to' or 'noticing' gender and sexuality in interaction? Many commentators use these terms interchangeably but, as we have discussed elsewhere (Stokoe and Smithson 2001), the actual discursive practices involved remain unspecified. Conversation analysts describe both explicit and implicit ways that speakers might demonstrate their orientation to gender. But what mechanisms are involved in this process, for both speakers and analysts? Kiesling (2000: 506) also writes about this 'frustrating' problem noting that, in the Antaki and Widdicombe collection, "no author gives a systematic account of this relevance-making".

For some analysts, a definition of 'what counts' can be gleaned from analyses in which participants *use explicitly a gender reference* such as 'ladies' (Schegloff 1997: 182), 'woman' and 'girl' (Edwards 1998), 'she', 'Mrs' and 'a lady' (Philipsen 1990/1991) or a generic 'he' (Stringer and Hopper 1998). In most of these examples, procedural consequentiality for speakers can be demonstrated in the way that the references are 'noticed' through, for example, self-repairing one gender reference to another. Hopper and LeBaron (1998) note that such repairs are oriented to the need for gender-inclusive language, thus promoting the relevance of gender as part of the conversational context. When a speaker troubles such a reference, gender becomes the axis around which the conversation proceeds.

So 'what counts' as an orientation to gender can perhaps be defined as the explicit mention of a gender reference. However, as we noted above, this sort of definition is restrictive for, as Ochs (1992) points out, few words in the English language exclusively index gender. Schegloff acknowledges the potential limitations of such a narrow definition: "explicit mention of a category term … is by no means necessary to establish the relevant orientation by the participants … orientation to gender can be manifested without being explicitly named or mentioned" (1997: 182). Similarly, Hopper and LeBaron (1998: 171, emphasis added) suggest that "gender can be indexed as a relevant part of the context by *ambiguous* words with *possible* references to sexuality…" or by including references to gendered activities (they give the example of 'car mechanics'). But these sorts of indexes are problematic for if something is implicit or ambiguous in conversation it is up to the analyst to reveal something that, logically, is not evidenced directly. The analyst must therefore draw on some form of contextual knowledge to speculate on the meaning of such references. For example, Hopper and LeBaron (1998) argue that the activity 'car mechanic' indexes male gender. But there is nothing intrinsic in this term that indexes gender; this example can only be given (and any subsequent analysis performed on it) if the analyst imports something of their own background knowledge about gendered references and activities. But, as we have seen, there is little consensus about the status of background knowledge in CA.

A consensus seems even more remote when we split conversation analysis into sequential CA (SCA, represented by Schegloff and colleagues) and another strand of ethnomethodological inquiry called membership categorisation analysis (MCA). MCA is based on Sacks' earlier writings and has had a "slower and more restrained development" than SCA (Lepper 2000). Few general CA texts engage with MCA since the majority of research focuses on sequential and organisational issues in interaction (for example, preference structures and adjacency pairs).[4] In contrast, MCA focuses on the local management of speakers' categorizations of themselves and others, treating talk as culture-in-action.

MCA is organised around the notion of the Membership Categorisation Device (MCD). According to Sacks, the MCD explains how categories may be hearably linked together by native speakers of a culture. For example, he provides the now-classic example taken from data in which a child says: 'The baby cried. The mommy picked it up' (Sacks 1972). Sacks claimed that we hear links between mommy and baby, specifically that the mommy is in fact the mommy of the baby. He aimed to provide an explanatory apparatus — the MCD — that allows this 'fact' to occur. In this case, the MCD of 'family' allows the categories 'mommy' and 'baby' to be linked together. Categories (including 'members') are therefore linked to particular actions ('category-bound activities' or CBAs) such that there are 'common-sense' expectations about what constitutes a 'mommy's' or 'baby's' normative behaviour. Moreover, Sacks argued that categories are 'inference-rich', which means, for example, that from the category of 'wife' one can infer 'being heterosexual' and 'running a household' (Tainio this volume). A crucial feature of MCA is that "a strip of text may tell you which membership category is to be heard, or it may require you to make an *inference* about what membership category is relevant" (Lepper 2000: 15, emphasis in original). Similarly, when we consider Sacks' notion of the 'standardised relational pair' (for example, parent-child, man-women, mother-father) the rule of application is that mentioning one pair-part is sufficient basis for *inferring* the presence of the other. In sum, for MCA, the analyst will necessarily draw on extra-textual information – their own background knowledge – to explicate fully the sense-making orientations of the speakers.

As we can see from Lepper's description, users of MCA appear to adopt a less restricted notion of culture and background knowledge than SCA: "they are entirely happy to work within the margins of cultural familiarity that Sacks [then] allowed himself ... and ... to call upon what they know is conventionally associated with membership of various categories" (Antaki and Widdicombe 1998: 10). Schegloff, in his introduction to Sacks' (1992) lectures, criticises MCA for precisely these reasons, arguing that it risks 'promiscuity' in analysis by importing researchers' categories into the analysis. Sacks later dropped MCA because of this potential for 'wild' analysis, in which the interpretations of the analyst might prevail over the evidence in the talk (Lepper 2000). However, we argue that MCA provides a promising solution to the problem of contextual knowledge and the restricted notion of participants' categories. Given that a key feature is its more inclusive approach to the contextual and cultural location of interaction, it may be fruitful in exploring the relevance of gender and sexuality to interaction.

3. Method

Having set out the above theoretical arguments, we now move on to explore them in relation to conversational data. The fragments of data that we draw upon are based on video or audiotaped recordings of interactions in focus group discussions. The discussions came from a large-scale project on young adults' expectations of the future, including their employment and family orientations.[5] Part of this project involved running focus groups in five European States (Sweden, Norway, Ireland, Portugal and the U.K.). Each group involved 6-10 people between the ages of 18 and 30 from a variety of backgrounds. Twenty percent of the participants were from ethnic minority backgrounds. The focus groups, which lasted about one-and-a-half hours, followed a semi-structured guide, and they discussed current and future employment and 'career' paths, relationships and expectations of support for future work and family roles. Although it is unlikely that all the participants were heterosexual, none positioned themselves explicitly as lesbian, gay or bisexual in the discussions. The groups were mainly single-sex groups of people at similar 'life stages', that is, all were university students, in training or in professional jobs. This chapter draws on the British sub-section of the data. The recorded data were transcribed in detail according to the conventions developed in CA (see appendix at the front of the book). The transcripts were read repeatedly in conjunction with the recorded data. Turns-at-talk were considered for the sense-making orientations of the participants. We focused on instances of talk in which sexuality was made relevant to the discussion.

4. Analysis

In order to explore the issues set out in the first part of this chapter, we apply conversation analytic procedures to examine instances of talk in which issues of gender and sexuality are demonstrably relevant for speakers. For each data fragment, we explore the complex ways that speakers assemble membership categories, link members to actions and define the conditions for assigned membership as they establish themselves and others as members of particular categorisation devices. We also consider the sequential organisation of speakers' categorisations and their interactional function as they actively produce the conversational order. In so doing, we consider the sorts of commentary on discourse and sexuality that versions of conversation analysis can stimulate and investigate the ways that gender and sexuality are 'made relevant' to interaction. In the first section of the analysis (Extracts 1-4), we focus on instances in the data where gender and sexuality can be evidenced as procedurally relevant to speakers. Each extract is analysed in turn, followed by a general commentary on the first section of analysis. In the second section (Extracts 5-7), we analyse instances where, although gender's relevance can be evidenced from participants' orientations, the relevance of (hetero)sexuality can be inferred only by drawing upon the analyst's background knowledge to explicate the categorisations made. However, we argue that such a strategy is warranted in order to explicate fully the cultural relevance of speakers' implicit category knowledge.

Gender and sexuality as procedurally relevant to speakers

In Extract 1, we examine an extract from a discussion between a group of male university students about ideals of parenting.[6] The men have been talking about marriage, cohabiting parents and lone parents. We focus on the way that gender and sexuality are invoked as the participants formulate member-ship categorisation devices and the activities that are linked to the different collections. G, H and B are students; M is the focus group moderator.

Extract 1: Male university students

```
 1  G:       as lo:ng as they've got a suppo:rtive atmosphere (.) with good
 2    →      morals from both sexes=
 3  H:       =I think that's the most important thing (0.5) it doesn't
 4           really matter if they are living together >or anything like
 5           that< (.) but (.) just as long (.) I think if they have both
 6           parents (.) I mean I do find it difficult for single parents
 7           (.) and >I don't think there's anything wrong with it< (0.5)
 8           but I do reckon it's difficult for the child and they don't get
 9           the full support that they need
10  M:   →  so ↑how about if you have gay couples like (.) G just
11           mentioned that it's impo↑rtant for the child to have role
12    →      models of both sexes  (.) but (.) does anyone here have a
13    →      strong opinion on whether gay parents should be allowed to have
14           children?
15  H:   →  I hate myself for sa↑ying this (.) but I don't think that even
16    →      though it's far more open (.) I don't think that having gay
17           couples is right for bringing up the child (.) I don't think
18           it's normal in society it won't be accepted and it might be
19    →      different (.) I shouldn't really be saying that but I do still
20           believe that (.) I don't think it's right=
21  G:       =I just don't see it a problem at all=
22  B:       =I don't see a problem with it (.) I just (.) what again (.) I
23           see the problem would be when the child is at school
```

We start our analysis of this extract with the following question in mind: how best to make claims about the relevance of particular categories to interaction? A quite simple observation based on this data fragment is that gender and sex-uality may be analysed, in participants' terms, at the level of talk-in-interac-tion, rather than as a feature of the speaker's 'essentialised' identity. Throughout this extract, references to the "sexes" (lines 2 and 12) and "gay" (lines 10, 13 and 16), and their subsequent discussion, demonstrate the rele-vance of such categories to the interaction.

In particular, the participants' orientation to the need to account for their position in relation to "gay parents" (lines 3, 15, 21 and 22) promotes sexuality as the axis around which the conversation proceeds. A general finding of discourse analytic work is that speakers might preface or suffix talk which might be treated as 'risky' with disclaimers such as 'I'm not sexist, but ...' (for example, van Dijk *et al.* 1997, Potter and Wetherell 1987). Examining such disclaimers and their sequential location displays the speakers' awareness that the upcoming (or preceding) stretch of talk is somehow problematic, requiring some careful framing or accountability work. In Extract 1, the speakers position 'gay parents' as 'other' by discussing 'it' as an objective and external issue, separate from their everyday lives. They all treat the moderator's question (lines 10-14) as a request for an opinion and attend explicitly to their potential heterosexism, each in a different way. H surrounds his evaluations of gay parents with disclaimers: "I hate myself for saying this" and "I shouldn't really be saying that" (lines 15 and 19). G takes a different position, stating that he does not "see it [gay parenting] as a problem at all" (line 21). B ratifies G's evaluation but adds that problems might arise "when the child is at school" (line 23). This cautious management of giving opinions marks 'gay parents' as a potential trouble source and, as membership categorisation analysts tell us, common-sense knowledge or culture is displayed when speakers problematise some aspect of the interaction (Hester and Eglin 1997; see also Abell and Stokoe 2001).

There are several other features worth exploring in this extract. Focusing on the participants' articulation of categorical evaluations, we can see a 'partitioning' in the collectivity of 'parents' being constructed as the interaction proceeds and a moral hierarchy being developed. If we draw on Sack's rules of application for building MCDs, we can see that in lines 1-2, G assembles the 'family' MCD as comprising 'both sexes'. The pro-term "they've" (line 1) refers to 'children' and, from here, we can suggest that the relevant category environment (or 'context') includes family, parents, mother, father, and so on. However, in order to make this claim we need to draw on our knowledge of (hetero)normative family relations as these categorisations are not explicit in this stretch of talk. This may be problematic for sequential conversation analysts but not for MCA for, as we discussed earlier, analysts may be required to "make an *inference* about what membership category is relevant" (Lepper 2000).

H builds on G's turn arguing "that's the most important thing", where "that's" can be indexically linked to G's comment about "both sexes". H's turn is complicated by the shifting referents of the pro-term "they". At line 4 it refers to 'parents' whereas at lines 5, 8 and 9 it refers to 'the child/ren'. Across his turns (lines 3-9 and 15-20), H assembles a hierarchy of 'parents', from 'both' at the top, 'single parents' in the middle to 'gay parents' at the bottom. Categorisation is bound up with moral and hierarchical structures such that, in the ongoing construction of MCDs, there are 'morally flavoured' activities that both constitute and reflect social and cultural divisions (Jayyusi 1984, Lepper 2000, Nilan 1995). This requires unpacking in some detail.

First, when considering the sequential location of each categorisation, 'both parents' is followed by the categorical evaluation of 'single' and 'gay' parents, thus locating 'both' at the top of the hierarchy. H's turn is also linked indexically to G's in that 'children' need a 'supportive atmosphere' from 'both sexes'. 'Both parents' therefore implies 'both sexes', which is in turn linked to the category bound activity of 'full support'. In contrast, H weaves into his evaluation of 'single parents' the disclaimer "I don't think there's anything wrong with it (0.5) but…", again orienting to potential trouble with being negative about single parents. Similarly, disclaimers frame H's discussion of 'gay parents' as we discussed above. But although conversation analysis enables us to identify this 'trouble', it cannot explain *why* talking about gay parents might be controversial (see Wetherell 1998). Some background knowledge about the heteronormative assumptions around parenting in western culture must be imported.

Second, when exploring the categorisations made in assembling the hierarchy we can find instances of cross-membership and cross-category activities which problematise the normative order of social life (Nilan 1995). Here, the problem is that 'gay' people have engaged in a cross-category activity (parenting). The category 'gay' resists candidate membership of the category 'parent'. This is because the category bound activities (CBAs) of 'parent' that H and G have described ("supportive atmosphere", "full support") excludes 'gay parents'. The contrasting CBAs for 'gay parents' exclude being "normal in society" and being "accepted" (line 18). Overall, we can claim that this moral hierarchy is something that the speakers themselves are oriented to as they comment on categories of parents being "right" (lines 17, 20), "normal in society" and "accepted" (line 18), "allowed" (line 13) and "wrong" (line 7).

The second fragment comes from a discussion between men aged between 18 and 25 on a vocational training course. The group has been discussing training and job prospects, work and non-work priorities. In Extract 2, they are responding to the question "When it comes to being a man or a woman these days, do you think when it comes to getting jobs, do you think it is harder or easier if you're a man or a woman?" Glossing the preceding turns at talk, the men have been arguing that there is too much protection for sexual harassment against women, of which women take advantage. B is a trainee hairdresser.

Extract 2: Male vocational training course participants

```
 1  M:       Do yo:u agree with that as well (.) how about in your career (.)
 2     →     because >you could call it< a traditional one wo↑men to go in to
 3     →     (.) do you think it's ha:rder being a man in that one?
 4  B: →     Well I think >with the ladies< they tend to get pregnant so they
 5           leave the business for about 4 or 5 months (0.5) so the clients
 6           go elsewhere so it's harder for them to get back in but most of
 7     →     the girls who are determined (.) they'll end up running a salon
 8     →     (.) there are quite a lot of gays in hair-dressing as well so you
 9     →     find most of them don't have boyfriends (1.0) most of my friends
10     _     who are hairdressers are just taking drugs (.) raving till god
11           knows what hour (.) yeah (0.5) you do get quite a lot of
12           prejudice for being a hairdresser (.) my boss tends to employ
13     →     gorgeous looking girls
```

In the first turn, the moderator introduces gender, as a dichotomous social category, with the categories 'women' and 'man'. B takes this up at lines 4, 7 and 13, continuing to discuss 'ladies' and 'girls'. Gender is therefore procedurally relevant to the interaction. At lines 8-9, B makes sexuality 'the relevant thing' about the people he is discussing when he says: "there are quite a lot of gays in hair-dressing as well" (see Edwards 1998). B positions the 'gays' in hairdressing as 'other' at line 9 with his use of the pro-term 'them': "you find most of *them* don't have boyfriends". Sexuality is demonstrably relevant to conversational interaction, though, in Schegloff's (1992) terms, it is not necessarily *procedurally relevant* to the ensuing talk. In other words, although a sexuality reference term is used – 'gay' – the other participants in the focus group interaction do not pursue sexuality as a relevant concern in the following turns at talk.

Membership categorisation analysis of the extract reveals more about the relevance of gender and sexuality to the interaction. In his work on MCDs, Sacks (1992, I: 249) points out that "many activities are taken by Members to be done by some particular or several particular categories of Members where the categories are categories from membership categorisation devices." The activity being discussed in the above extract is 'hairdressing', about which the speaker constructs a series of complex categorical evaluations. He partitions firstly the collectivity of 'hairdressers' into the categories 'ladies' and 'girls' (lines 4 and 7), each of which are sequentially associated with different defining category-bound activities. So, there are 'ladies' who "get pregnant so they leave the business" and there are 'girls' who are "determined they'll end up running a salon". The categories 'girls' and 'ladies' are likely to have different 'category bound activities' associated with them. As Edwards (1998) notes, these might include normative assumptions about age or marital status, with the category of 'girl' arguably being different status than that of 'ladies'. Next, there are 'gays' who "don't have boyfriends". So far, B makes it clear that the criteria to be eligible in the category 'hairdresser' includes being "determined" or single-minded, which for a 'girl' excludes being a mother or, if you are a gay man, excludes being in a serious relationship. All of these categories can be contrasted in the next part of B's turn with "my friends" and "my boss" (lines 9-12), the category-bound activities being 'taking drugs', 'raving' and 'employing gorgeous looking girls', all of which could be glossed as activities inconsequential to hairdressing. In contrast, the 'ladies', 'girls' and 'gays' are discussed in terms of the practical considerations relevant to being a hairdresser.

The following extract is from a discussion between a group of women on a vocational training course. The group is responding to the moderator's question "Do you think there's any difference for men and women these days when it comes to getting a job, getting on in it?" They are arguing that there is still discrimination against women, which men do not realise. H, a woman and a trainee hairdresser, also indexes homosexuality.

Extract 3: Female vocational training course participants

```
1   M:    How about in your job (.) in hairdressing (.) are there many
2         men in that=
3   H:    =not a lot (.) there's a lot more wo↑men than men
4   M:    Do you think that makes it ha:rd for the men?
5   H:    Sometimes (.) cos people look at a man (.) and he's a
6    →    hairdresser (.) they'll take him as a poof and you do get that
7         a lot (.) but that's other men
```

In her first turn the moderator, by querying gender in a discussion about the activity of hairdressing, infers that being categorised both as 'men' and 'hairdressers' is an issue worthy of discussion. H takes this up, assembling the category 'hairdresser' as a largely feminised category. However, when asked if "this makes it hard for the men" (where 'this' refers indexically to "more women than men"), H orients to *sexuality* as the salient reason to explain why things might be hard for male hairdressers: "people look at a man (.) and he's a hairdresser (.) they'll take him as a poof" (lines 5-6). This series of categorisations – 'man', 'hairdresser', 'poof' – is interesting in the way that H makes such an evaluation of a person's sexual/gender identity based on their profession into something normative and routine.

First, the term 'poof' indexes sexuality, as it is a pejorative term for homosexual men. However, in order to explicate fully this categorisation, the cultural knowledge of the analyst is again necessary. A reviewer of this chapter pointed out that the term 'poof' would need to be explained for an American audience, thus supporting our point that 'what counts' as an orientation to sexuality (or gender) will often require going beyond the orientations of the speakers. Second, although H orients to sexuality, she does not attend to the possible heterosexism of her own use of the term 'poof'. Unlike in Extract 1, for example, she does not disclaim a potentially negative 'take' on what is said. This is particularly interesting because H *does* disclaim the categorisation she is building in the final line "but that's other men" – in other words, it is *other non-hairdressing men* who might assume that all male hairdressers are 'poofs'. As in Extract 1, where sexual identity was contrasted with parenting, H orients to her accountability in evaluating sexual identity alongside another activity: hairdressing. In so doing, H displays her cultural knowledge that the category of 'male hairdressers' is associated with being 'a poof'. Sacks' rules of application for MCDs includes the fact that something salient about one member of a collectivity can be taken as shared by all members. In other words, all male hairdressers are (or might be) gay. This is treated implicitly as problematic – that is, (heterosexual) male hairdressers do not want to be assumed to be gay. This can in turn be made sense of only by importing cultural knowledge about heterosexism in western society.

Finally in the first section of analysis, Extract 4 comes from the group of male university students who are discussing whether or not there is a stigma attached to being the child of a single parent. We focus on the turn of one participant, C.

Extract 4: Male university students

```
1    C:      I mean you are looking (.) 20 years ago and there was >the
2            single parent thing< where (.) a mother having a child would
3            give it up to ado:ption rather than face the stigma (.) and one
4    →       of the big questions now is (.) sort of gay parents (.) so I
5            think attitudes have changed so much over the past few decades
6            I don't think it's a big issue (.) I don't think kids think
7            about that to be honest (.) they are just too busy thinking
8            about toys and TV programmes and all the other things (.)
9            stimuli in their life (.) rather than social issues
```

An important feature of membership categorisation devices is their function as the building blocks of culture and society (Hester and Eglin 1997). The categorisation process constitutes and maintains social and cultural boundaries. Consequently they are sites of social change, as speakers assemble new MCDs and new versions of old MCDs (Nilan 1995). We can see this process at work in the above fragment. C explores a temporal shift in what constitutes 'social issues' through his categorisation of 'single parents' as associated with 'stigma' and, more specifically, in the combination of 'mother'-'child'-'adoption'. These categorisations are linked to the time periods "20 years ago" and "past few decades", in contrast to "now" when 'single parents' are no longer "a big issue". This is because "now" the "big question" is to do with gay parenting. At line 4, "gay parents" functions as a replacement category for 'single parents', which we can follow indexically as the stigmatised group that might 'now' be a 'social issue'.

We can make one or two other comments about this extract. C uses the term 'gay' as a generic term for gay men and lesbian parents, which is arguably problematic in the same way that the generic 'he' is used to refer to men and women. The term 'gay' excludes lesbians but is used without trouble in the above fragment of talk. However, we can only comment on the problematic use of generic 'gay' if we draw upon our knowledge of lesbian feminist politics – this might not be salient for other researchers. Also potentially problematic is C's gender index at line 2 when he discusses "the single parent thing where a mother ...". As we have noted elsewhere (Stokoe and Smithson 2001), speakers in this corpus regularly use generic gendered category terms: in this case, the generic female parent. In so doing, he infers that membership of the category 'single parent' is exclusively female. This is in contrast to other instances in our data in which speakers orient to a gender-neutral account of parenting through their repairs around categorisations such as 'mother, or father'.

Commentary on Extracts 1-4

In each of the Extracts 1-4, categories of gender and sexuality were demonstrably relevant at particular moments, to both the moderator and participants, and thus to conversational action. This claim is arguably grounded in the orientations of the speakers rather than in the analysts' *a priori* assumptions about the way gender and sexual identities might influence conversational behaviour or discourse patterns. Accordingly, 'what counts' as an index of or orientation to sexuality might be defined as the explicit mentioning of a gender or sexuality reference such as 'woman', 'man', 'sexes', 'gay' or 'poof'. From here, we can inspect the data to find out at what *sequential* point the references are occasioned. In some instances, although a gender or sexuality reference was mentioned, it did not become the axis around which the conversation proceeded (for example, 'gay' in Extract 2). In contrast, procedural consequentiality for speakers was evidenced through the 'troubling' of talk about sexuality (for example, use of disclaimers and accounting for opinions expressed in Extracts 1 and 3) and through the differential use of gender categories (for example, 'ladies' and 'girls' in Extract 2).

Sequential analysis therefore allows us to follow the course of talk to a repair, to shift between categories or a disclaimer, but does not allow us to account for such phenomena (Arminen 2000). In other words, although we can see speakers disclaiming their (heterosexist) opinions, or using different gender categories, we cannot say why this might happen without knowledge of the cultural context (see Wetherell 1998). For example, if we want to comment on the status of the gender categories 'girls' and ladies' (as in Extract 2), we need to draw upon our background and extra-textual knowledge about the category bound activities that are conventionally associated with them. SCA does not permit further analytic commentary or speculation as to the status of such categories. It cannot tell us *what* the status actually is. This can be done only by importing the background knowledge that culturally competent members, including the analyst, have available to them. Perhaps the use and status of terms like 'girls' and 'ladies' (which can be 'offensive' and 'politically incorrect' when describing adult women) is more salient for feminist than non-feminist researchers.

We suggest that MCA extends SCA in analytically useful ways. For example, evaluating the 'moral flavour' of an account, incorporating a 'relevant category environment' and so on, both require and allow the analyst's explicit cultural familiarity with the data. As we emphasised at various points in the analysis, our commentary required the import of extra-textual knowledge about sexuality reference terms. We, as feminists, suggest that analysis becomes more interesting and politically effective with this additional commentary and simply pointing out the relevance of sexuality to the speakers is not the most interesting aspect of the data. But to get to this more interesting commentary, one must go beyond describing data in participants' own terms. We continue to explore these issues in the second part of the analysis.

Gender and sexuality as procedurally relevant to speakers?

In the first analytic section, we focused on instances in which speakers invoked gender and sexuality references. Such explicit orientations were generally rare in our data, particularly to sexuality and sexual identity. The use of indexes such as 'gay' and 'poof' and the 'troubling' of talk around sexual identity were far outweighed by a more implicit sexuality, which we explore in this section. Across the data corpus, normative discourses of heterosexuality emerged (see Smithson 2000). This may have been partly due to the focus group context, which deals with public accounts (Kitzinger 1994) and partly due to the focus of this research project, which sought to explore 'orientations' and discourses rather than individuals' practices and experiences. While the moderator tried to avoid heterosexist language by, for example, using the word 'partner' instead of 'boy/girlfriend', it is possible that by making 'family' the whole focus of the research, the research team inadvertently adopted a heterosexist bias, which was shared by some of the groups. Similar heterosexist bias was exhibited in the focus groups and individual interviews in all five countries. The moderator both colluded with and challenged these assumptions. Extract 5 comes from a group of professional men in their late 20s, none of whom have children.

Extract 5: Male professional workers

```
 1  M:      so does everyone here actually want to stay at home (.) and look
 2           after children (.) and think that would be feasible?
 3  (?):     °yeah°
 4  M:      do you think that's easy for men to do (.) do you think they
 5           would get trouble from employers for that (.) or from other men?
 6  D:      it depends what area of work you do (.) I don't think within this
 7           area of work you would (.) maybe (.) but other areas are sort of
 8           um (.) stereotyped (0.5) maybe you would
 9  W:      I mean if my brother came home and said he wanted to do
             that he'd
10           just be laughed out of the office where he works (.) cos he works
11           in like the steel industry (.) I mean (.) in this type of
12           environment it's almost positively encouraged (0.5) it's like one
13           of your job descriptions
14  M:      How about in your job S (.) Is that acceptable?
15  S:      I mean if (.) it would be the same as (.) with most people (.) the
16           woman's staying at home with the kids (.) cos that's (.) to be
17           honest (.) that's the norm (.) and I'm not saying it doesn't work
```

18   the other way round (.) but say I took what (.) let's say (.) to
19   bring the kid up to the age when they're going to school (.) that's
20   4 years let's say taken out (.) that would set me back a hell of a
21   long way to get back into working

The procedural relevance of gender starts with the moderator's question at line 4: "do you think that's easy for men to do". From here, a series of complex categorisations are developed between the moderator and focus group participants as they nominate the activities that are bound to the categories of 'women' and 'men'. For example, S links 'woman' to "staying at home" and to "kids" and evaluates this in terms of a social "norm" (lines 15-17). This is contrasted with the problems for men who are associated with such activities. S links the pro-term 'I' (which, as with the moderator's pro-term "here" at line 1, refers to 'men') to being "set back a hell of a long way".

The group treat as shared knowledge the assumption that the normative family, as constructed by speaker S at line 17, equals a dyadic heterosexual parental unit. The categories belonging to the MCD 'family' rely on implied category knowledge on the part of the other participants, the moderator and, by extension, the analyst. Neither the participants nor the moderator challenge this by, say, pointing out that in a gay couple there is no woman to stay at home with the kids. Interestingly, S attends to and disclaims the potential *sexism* of his remarks (thus orienting to gender) at lines 17-18 – "I'm not saying it doesn't work the other way round" – but fails to orient to the potential heterosexism in his description of normative family relations. This seems to be relevant to the analyst alone; it is not demonstrable as procedurally relevant to the participants.

The talk in Extract 5 is an example of what Braun (2000: 134) calls "heterosexism by commission" – "the explicit articulation of heterosexist assumptions". In her female focus group data, she points to instances in which talk about women becomes talk about heterosexual women, thus excluding lesbian women. However, the extent to which these assumptions are explicit is problematic. Rather than being 'explicitly articulated', we suggest that it is in the implicit and unchallenged (by the analyst or other participants) discussion of parenting that the heterosexism occurs — something Braun calls "heterosexism by omission". In the above conversation about parenting, something hegemonic is implicitly passed by and thus goes unnoticed – necessarily unnoticed for it to succeed. This is something that analysts, however, can make available by drawing upon using their cultural knowledge (see also Fish this volume, Kitzinger 2000).

A further example of this sort of mundane heterosexism occurs in the following extract, taken from the same group of university student men as in Extract 4. This extract occurs a few turns after Extract 4. The men have just been discussing whether a child of gay or lesbian parents would be teased at school. The moderator moves the topic on.

Extract 6: Male university students

```
 1  M:    Right (.) OK moving on now imagine in the future you do have
 2         children (.) with or without a partner (.) do you have any
 3         opinion on how you would want them to be brought up (.)
 4         would you still imagine carrying on working (.) who do
 5         you think should be looking after the child when it's very
 6         small (.) does anyone (.) you presumably do have some opinions
 7         on this (.) but has anyone thought about these issues at all
 8         (.) can you imagine if you had children what would be best for
 9         them?
10  G:    you need the right atmosphere to be brought up in=
11  M:    =Mhmm
12  C:    it's quite difficult (.) I think one of the parents would have
13         to take a large percentage of the child on board (.) purely for
14         the fact that one's going to have to be the bread-winner if you
15         like (.) I think it would be very difficult for both parents to
16         get part time jobs that would fit in with each other and the
17         child (.) that's just an unfortunate thing (.) whether it be
18    →    the father or the mother (.) I don't think it even makes any
19         difference
21  B:    it would depend on who makes the most money probably
22  C:    yeah (.) probably would
```

In the moderator's long first question (lines 1-9), she uses the gender and sexuality-neutral reference 'partner' to introduce the issue of childcare and working parents. In line 18, C makes explicit an interpretation of what may have been a relevant category environment in the participants' prior turns. He provides a candidate understanding of what a family comprises – a 'mother' and 'father' – which is appropriate for the rhetorical point being made (he is not being sexist). By collecting together these categories, C assembles the MCD of 'family' in a very particular way that implicitly excludes other types of families. As Nilan (1995: 71) argues, "one function of categorisation work in ordinary conversation appears to be the maintenance of existing social/cultural categories, in part by constantly defining and affirming the conditions for assigned membership." Here, the nominated categories display an orientation to the potential sexism of the discussion, but, in so doing, they display heterofamilial assumptions. However, neither he nor the moderator make troublesome the potential heterosexist 'take' on what he says by, for example, saying "whether it be the father or mother or one partner in a homosexual relationship". Sexuality is relevant to this discussion but in an implicit and unnoticed way.

Finally, Extract 7 provides an example of heterosexism on the part of the researcher. It comes from a group of young university student women. They have been discussing whether they would like children, and if so what sort of childcare they would prefer.

Extract 7: Female university students

```
 1  M:       what sort of conditions would it take for most of you to have
 2            children (.) would you want to be married (.) some of you were
 3            saying earlier=
 4  (?):      =yes definitely=
 5  (?):      =yeah (.) I'd be married definitely=
 6  M:        =and how about financially (.) do you think it's important to
 7            be financially stable=
 8  (?):      =yes definitely stable
 9  M:        so would it be important to have a secure job or have a partner
10            in a secure job or something like that?
11  (?):      [yes (yeah)
12  (?):      [yes definitely
13  H:        no job is secure though (.) if you stopped working and you
14            wanted to return five years later it's not going to be there=
15  A:        =which is why you need to be married to someone who has got a
16            secure job=
17  H:        =or who is earning lots of money=
18  (?):      =yeah
19  M:   →    so you are all getting into rich husbands
20  L:        yes that's what we are getting at (laughter) the solution
```

Again, the moderator and participants collude in the construction of a shared context for their discussion. As the group comprises all females (including the moderator), the indexical and pro-terms 'you', 'I' and 'we' refer to the perceptually available category of 'women' (Jayyusi 1984). Additionally, the moderator's first question, "what sort of conditions would it take for most of you to have children (.) would you want to be married", implies that each of the present group could pursue such a category-bound performative act (Sedgwick

1993). In the U.K., marriage is still the (official and legal) preserve of hetero-sexuals. Here, then, 'marriage' is a category bound activity that is tied to 'you' (women) and 'children'. As the mention of one category from an MCD can imply the presence of another (for example, family, men), we can claim that these categories constitute the relevant category environment for the sur-rounding discussion.

This assertion does however rest on a particular set of analytic assump-tions. While marriage is only legal for heterosexual couples in the U.K., there are examples of gay and lesbian marriage, both in other countries, and infor-mally (without legal status) in the U.K., of which young people may be aware. The analyst does not have intimate access to the cultural knowledge the speak-ers rely on in their talk; however, their knowledge is perhaps displayed at line 19 in which the moderator makes explicit what may have been assumed in the preceding turns: "so you are all getting into rich husbands". This prompts laughter and ratifying comments from the participants. 'Husband' is part of the standardised relational pair 'husband-wife', although in order to bring 'wife' into the analysis requires contextual knowledge. Taken together, this sequential series of categorisations provides evidence that the group's taken-as-shared assumption is that the relationships and circumstances under dis-cussion are based around heterosexuality. Sexuality is therefore relevant to the discussion, but evidence for such a claim requires going beyond explicit men-tion of a sexuality reference term.

Commentary on Extracts 5-7

If we compare the three extracts in this part of the analysis, all are framed along heteronormative lines. This type of discussion has been termed 'closeting inter-action' (McIlvenny 2001), which describes how heteronormativity gets prac-tised in talk. In order for it to be possible for a speaker to 'come out' or be 'outed' as homo- or bisexual, 'closets' have to be formed and negotiated. In Extracts 5-7, we can see the collaborative construction of the 'closet' and presumed het-erosexuality of the speakers through discussions based on heteronormative assumptions about parenting, marriage and the family. Although explicit het-erosexism needs to be framed and negotiated carefully (Extract 1), as with explicitly sexist remarks (Extracts 5 and 6), the heterosexual norm needs no such management. Indeed, it goes unnoticed by both participants and the mod-erator, only to be revealed in this analysis. As Bohan (1996: 39) concludes, het-erosexism is "so pervasive, so taken for granted, as to escape notice".

How can we square this necessarily implicit notion with an analytic approach that requires evidence from the explicit orientation of the speakers? In formulations of CA such as Edwards (1998), Schegloff (1997) or Hopper and LeBaron (1998), gender relevance is evidenced through troubling, repairs and noticing sequences. To a certain extent, sexuality can be evidenced in the same ways. But to evidence the relevance of heterosexuality to conversation – problematic for us as feminist researchers, but 'business as usual' for the speakers involved – we have drawn upon our interpretative resources and cultural knowledge (Kitzinger 2000). Kitzinger argues that a return to Sacks' early work allows the researcher to analyse things that are 'unsaid and passed by' in interaction. This stance does, however, remain incongruent with other versions of CA in which explicit orientations are required to warrant claims of relevance.

5. Discussion: Gender, sexuality, participants' categories and analysts' cultural knowledge

In this chapter, we have explored different approaches to the study of language, gender and sexuality. Rather than attempting to characterise speaker's interactional styles, we have used conversation analysis to investigate how gender and sexuality are made relevant to interaction. In so doing, we asked four related questions that arise from our use of CA as feminists. We shall answer each in turn.

First, we asked whether it is fruitful to rely on orientations to gender and sexuality solely in participants' terms. Related to this, we asked what, precisely, *counts* as an orientation to sexuality or gender? We suggested that the discursive practices of 'making relevant' or 'orienting to' conversational phenomenon needed further definition. From our analysis, we found that gender and sexuality could be evidenced as relevant to conversational business if a gender or sexuality reference term was invoked and in some way 'oriented to' by speakers. So, for example, framing a discussion of 'gay parenting' with disclaimers along the lines of 'I hate myself for saying this, but …' displayed the speaker's orientation to the need to account for the ensuing opinion. But although CA can evidence the issue of 'gay parenting' as relevant to speakers, it cannot tell us why such an issue might need to be disclaimed in this way. To interpret such a move, the analyst must draw upon their cultural knowledge around issues of discussing sexuality in negative ways. Analysing conversational data without considering the wider social context leaves a gap between technical analysis and that which is relevant socially for speakers (Pomerantz 1989). As Arminen (2000: 436) points out, "in any context, CA may disclose the sequential course of talk, but parties' orientations to their talk might be enlightened by [contextual] details without access to which the analyst's explication of the practice may seem 'bloodless', impersonal and unimportant" (see also Wetherell 1998). Membership categorisation analysis can reveal the knowledge used when speakers assemble categories such as gender and sexuality. Nilan (1995) argues that the categorisation process is fundamental in maintaining wider social and cultural boundaries. Speakers' micro-level orientations therefore constitute ideologies that are in turn recycled in talk. To answer the first question, then, we argue that analysts should start with participants' orientations but also use their knowledge of the context to add texture and social relevance to the analysis.

Addressing the second related question of 'what counts' as an orientation to gender or sexuality, we found that although procedural relevance to speakers could be demonstrated (as described above), in other instances the relevance of (hetero)sexuality could be made explicit only by drawing on extratextual information. We suggested that by including the analyst in the category of 'member' allows her/him to display her/his own cultural knowledge in the analytic process. 'What counts', therefore, includes the speakers' *and analysts'* orientations to categories in the data. As Arminen (2000: 454) has noted, "CA practitioners ... might benefit from paying closer attention to background knowledge and sets of beliefs that may be the relevant sources informing the ways subjects apparently, but perhaps not obviously, design their actions". We argued that the heteronormative backdrop that informed participants' discussions in the focus group data could be revealed partly by using membership categorisation analysis because it allows the analyst to use her/his interpretative and inferential resources. Consequently, we argue that conversation analysts draw *properly* upon their broader contextual and cultural knowledge in the pursuit of talk's explication and so answer our third question.

We conclude that a strict sequential implementation of conversation analysis may be inadequate to address feminist concerns, especially when dealing with interactions in which gender and sexuality (and particularly sexist and heterosexist assumptions) are 'unnoticed' by participants. However, if we draw on other approaches such as membership categorisation analysis, an ethnomethodological framework can work well to inform us about the social and political relevance of micro-level interaction. An approach that incorporates the analysts' sense-making orientations as well as the participants' – one that aims to reveal the 'passed by' and implicit context of interaction – and acknowledges cultural and background knowledge as a resource provides the most fruitful framework for studying the links between gender, sexuality and discourse.

Notes

1. Stokoe (2000) has made a similar point about some gender and language theorists who write from an ethnomethodological perspective. These writers use sequential conversation analysis (SCA) to explore how patriarchy is realised at the micro-level of interaction. In other words, as men arguably dominate in society, they also dominate micro-level interaction. Men 'do masculinity' by interrupting women speakers and denying their rights to interaction. West and Garcia (1988, see also Ainsworth-Vaughn 1992) found that men make unwarranted or unilateral topic shifts whereas women produce collaborative shifts. Other gendered interactional patterns have been found including women's competence as active listeners (West 1995), men and women's different use of directives (Goodwin 1990, West 1998), women's increased conversational work and men's domination through silence (De Francisco 1991) and men's use of 'put-downs' and interruptions of women (Conefrey 1997). However, these studies link gender to, for example, interruption, talk time, topic initiation and topic maintenance. Conversation is analysed for particular interactional patterns that are then linked unproblematically to gender. This application of sequential conversation analysis to what ten Have (1999) calls 'non-CA purposes' is problematic because such studies correlate gender (as a 'fixed' property) with a pre-defined category (such as 'interruption'). Gender is therefore implicitly essentialised, which runs contrary to the ethnomethodological position that gender is something one 'does', not something one 'has'. These studies confound their underlying ethnomethodological stance, that gender is 'done', by linking gender to interaction practices. In this sense, gender remains a dichotomy in which contrasting things can be said about women and men.

2. For the purposes of this chapter, we will use the general term 'conversation analysis' unless referring specifically to sequential aspects of talk or membership categorisation analytic procedures.

3. Conversation analysts have until recently had little to say about the relevance of sexuality to interaction (but see Braun 2000, Kitzinger 2000, Speer and Potter 2000).

4. Although MCA and SCA comprise different research trajectories, some commentators argue that a comprehensive theory of interaction should use both approaches simultaneously (for example, D'hondt this volume, Watson 1997).

5. The research was carried out by the second author as part of a research project 'The Reconciliation of Future Work and Family Life. Understanding and Supporting the Family and Employment Orientations of Young People in Europe'. This project was co-funded by D.G.V. of the European Commission as part of the Fourth Medium Term Community Action Programme on Equal Opportunities for Women and Men. The research was designed and also carried out, in their respective countries, by Julia Brannen, (Thomas Coram Research Unit, University of London), Ann Nilsen (University of Bergen), Pat

O'Connor (University of Limerick), Maria das Dos Guerreiros (ISCTE, Portugal), Clarissa Kugelberg (University of Uppsala) and Suzan Lewis (Manchester Metropolitan University).

6. All names have been changed. The moderator (M) was also the main researcher on this project and one of the authors of this chapter.

References

Abell, Jackie and Stokoe, Elizabeth H. 2001 "Broadcasting the royal role: Constructing culturally situated identities in Princess Diana's 'Panorama' interview". *British Journal of Social Psychology* 40: 417-435.

Ainsworth-Vaughn, Nancy. 1992 "Topic transitions in physician-patient interviews: Power, gender, and discourse change". *Language in Society* 21: 409-426.

Antaki, Charles. 1995 "Conversation analysis and social psychology". *British Psychological Society Social Psychology Section Newsletter* Winter: 21-34.

Antaki, Charles and Widdicombe, Sue (eds). 1998 *Identities in Talk*. London: Sage.

Arminen, Ilkka. 2000 "On the context sensitivity of institutional interaction". *Discourse and Society* 11(4): 435-458.

Beach, Wayne A. 2000 "Inviting collaborations in stories about a woman". *Language in Society* 29: 379-407.

Billig, Michael. 1991 *Ideology and Opinions: Studies in Rhetorical Psychology*. London: Sage.

Billig, Michael. 1999 "Whose terms? Whose ordinariness? Rhetoric and ideology in conversation analysis". *Discourse and Society* 10: 543-558.

Bilmes, Jack. 1993 "Ethnomethodology, culture, and implicature: Toward an empirical pragmatics". *Pragmatics*, 3: 387-409.

Bohan, Janice S. 1993 "Regarding gender: Essentialism, constructionism and feminist psychology". *Psychology of Women Quarterly* 17: 5-21.

Bohan, Janice S. 1996 *Psychology and Sexual Orientation*. London: Routledge.

Braun, Virginia. 2000 "Heterosexism in Focus Group Research: Collusion and Challenge". *Feminism and Psychology* 10(1): 133-140.

Bucholtz, Mary, Liang, A.C. and Sutton, Laurel A. (eds). 1999 *Reinventing Identities: The Gendered Self in Discourse*. Oxford: Oxford University Press.

Butler, Judith. 1990 "Performative Acts and Gender Constitution: An Essay in Phenomenology and Feminist Theory". In *Performing Feminisms*, S. Case (ed.), 270-282. Baltimore: The Johns Hopkins University Press.

Buttny, Richard. 1993 *Social Accountability in Communication*. London: Sage.

Cameron, Deborah. 1998 "Gender, language and discourse: A review essay". *Signs* 23(4): 945-973.

Cicourel, Aaron. 1992 "The interpenetration of communicative contexts: Examples from medical encounters". In *Rethinking Context: Language as an Interactive Phenomenon*, A. Duranti and C. Goodwin (eds), 291-310. Cambridge: Cambridge University Press.

Coates, Jennifer. 1996 *Women Talk*. Oxford: Blackwell.

Coates, Jennifer. 1997 "Competing discourses of femininity". In *Communicating Gender in Context*, H. Kotthoff and R. Wodak (eds), 285-314. Amsterdam: John Benjamins.

Conefrey, Theresa. 1997 "Gender, Culture and Authority in a University Life Sciences Laboratory". *Discourse and Society* 8(3): 313-340.

Crawford, Mary. 1995 *Talking Difference: On Gender and Language*. London: Sage.

De Francisco, Victoria L. 1991 "The sounds of silence: How men silence women in marital relations". *Discourse and Society* 2(4): 413-423.

Dijk, Teun A. van. 1999 "Critical discourse analysis and conversation analysis". *Discourse & Society* 10(4): 459-60.

Dijk, Teun A. van, Ting-Toomey, Stella, Smithson, Geneva, and Troutman, Denise. 1997 "Discourse, ethnicity, culture and racism". In *Discourse as Social Interaction*, T.A. van Dijk (ed.), 144-180. London: Sage.

Edley, Nigel and Wetherell, Margaret. 1999 "Imagined futures: Young men's talk about fatherhood and domestic life". *British Journal of Social Psychology* 38: 181-194.

Edwards, Derek. 1998 "The relevant thing about her: Social identity categories in use". In *Identities in Talk*, C. Antaki and S. Widdicombe (eds), 15-33. London: Sage.

Fishman, Pamela. 1978 "Interaction: The work women do". *Social Problems* 25: 397-406.

Frith, Hannah. 1998 "Constructing the 'other' through talk". *Feminism and Psychology* 8(4): 530-536.

Goodwin, Marjorie H. 1990 *He-Said-She-Said: Talk as Social Organisation Among Black Children*. Bloomington: Indiana University Press.

Have, Paul ten. 1999 *Doing Conversation Analysis*. London: Sage.

Hester, Stephen and Eglin, Peter (eds). 1997 *Culture in Action: Membership Categorisation Analysis*. Boston: University Press of America.

Hopper, Robert and LeBaron, Curtis. 1998 "How gender creeps into talk". *Research on Language and Social Interaction* 31(3): 59-74.

Housley, William. 2000 "Category work and knowledgeability within multidisciplinary team meetings". *Text* 20(1): 83-107.

Hutchby, Ian and Wooffitt, Robin. 1998 *Conversation Analysis*. Cambridge: Polity.

Jayyusi, Lena. 1984 *Categorisation and the Moral Order*. London: Routledge.

Kiesling, Scott. 2000 "Review of Charles Antaki and Sue Widdicombe (eds) (1998). *Identities in Talk*". *Discourse Studies* 2(4): 506-508.

Kitzinger, Celia. 2000 "Doing feminist conversation analysis". *Feminism and Psychology* 10(2): 163-193.

Kitzinger, Jenny. 1994 "The methodology of focus groups: The importance of interaction between research participants". *Sociology of Health and Illness*, 16:103-121.

Kulick, Don. 1999 "Language & gender/sexuality". *Language & Culture mailing list: Online Symposium*. <http://www.language-culture.org/archives/subs/kulick-don/index.html>. [June 20, 2000].

Lakoff, Robin. 1973 "Language and woman's place". *Language in Society* 2: 45-79.

Leap, William. 1996 *Word's Out: Gay Men's English*. Minneapolis: University of Minnesota Press.

Lepper, Georgia. 2000 *Categories in Text and Talk*. London: Sage.

McIlvenny, Paul. 2001 "Do 'opposites always attract'?: Doing gender/sexuality in intercultural encounters". In *Communicating Culture: Proceedings of the 3rd Nordic Symposium on Intercultural Communication, Oct 1996* [Language & Cultural Contact 28], K.G. Andersen (ed.), 81-99. Aalborg: Centre for Languages and Intercultural Studies, Aalborg University.

Moerman, Michael. 1988 *Talking Culture.* Philadelphia: University of Pennsylvania Press

Moonwomon-Baird, Birch. 1997 "Toward the study of lesbian speech". In *Queerly Phrased: Language, Gender and Sexuality*, A. Livia and K. Hall (eds), 202-213. Oxford: Oxford University Press.

Nilan, Pam. 1994 "Gender as positioned identity maintenance in everyday discourse". *Social Semiotics* 4(1-2): 139-163.

Nilan, Pam. 1995 "Membership categorization devices under construction: Social identity boundary maintenance in everyday discourse". *Australian Review of Applied Linguistics.* 18(1): 69-94.

Ochs, Elinor. 1992 "Indexing gender". In *Rethinking Context*, A. Duranti and C. Goodwin (eds), 335-358. Cambridge: Cambridge University Press.

Philipsen, Gerry. 1990/1991 "Situated meaning, Ethnography and conversation analysis". *Research on Language and Social Interaction* 24: 225-238.

Pomerantz, Anita. 1989 "Epilogue". *Western Journal of Speech Communication* 53: 242-246.

Potter, Jonathan and Wetherell, Margaret. 1987 *Discourse and Social Psychology: Beyond Attitudes and Behaviour.* London: Sage.

Sacks, Harvey. 1992 *Lectures on Conversation* (Vols. I and II, edited by Gail Jefferson). Oxford: Blackwell.

Sanders, Robert E. 1999 "The impossibility of a culturally contexted conversation analysis: On simultaneous, distinct types of pragmatic meaning". *Research on Language and Social Interaction* 32(1&2): 129-140.

Schegloff, Emanuel A. 1992 "In Another Context". In *Rethinking Context: Language as an Interactive Phenomenon*, A. Duranti and C. Goodwin (eds), 191-227. Cambridge: Cambridge University Press.

Schegloff, Emanuel A. 1997 "Whose text? Whose context?" *Discourse & Society* 8(2): 165-187.

Schegloff, Emanuel A. 1998 "Reply to Wetherell". *Discourse & Society* 9(3): 413-6.

Schegloff, Emanuel A. 1999a "'Schegloff's Texts' as 'Billig's Data': A Critical Reply". *Discourse & Society* 10(4): 558-72.

Schegloff, Emanuel A. 1999b "Naivety vs. sophistication or discipline vs. self-indulgence: A rejoinder to Billig". *Discourse & Society* 10(4): 577-82.

Sedgwick, Eve Kosofsky. 1993 "Queer performativity". *GLQ: A Journal of Lesbian and Gay Studies* 1: 1-16.

Smithson, Janet. 1999 "Equal choices, different futures: Young adults talk about work and family expectations". *Psychology of Women Section Review* 1(2): 43-57.

Smithson, Janet. 2000 "Using and analysing focus groups: Limitations and possibilities". *International Journal of Social Science Methodology: Theory and Practice* 3(2): 103-119.

Speer, Susan A. 2001 "Reconsidering the concept of hegemonic masculinity: Discursive psychology, conversation analysis, and participants' orientations". *Feminism and Psychology* 11(1): 107-135.

Speer, Susan A. and Potter, Jonathan. 2000 "The management of heterosexist talk: Conversational resources and prejudiced claims". *Discourse and Society* 11(4): 543-572.

Stokoe, Elizabeth H. 1998 "Talking about gender: The conversational construction of gender categories in academic discourse". *Discourse and Society* 9(2): 217-240.

Stokoe, Elizabeth H. 2000 "Towards a conversation analytic approach to gender and discourse". *Feminism and Psychology* 10(4): 552-563.

Stokoe, Elizabeth H. and Smithson, Janet. 2001 "Making gender relevant: Conversation analysis and gender categories in interaction". *Discourse and Society* 12(2): 243-269.

Stringer, Jeffrey L. and Hopper, Robert. 1998 "Generic *he* in conversation?" *Quarterly Journal of Speech* 84: 209-221.

Tannen, Deborah. 1990 *You Just Don't Understand! Women and Men in Conversation.* London: Virago.

Tannen, Deborah. 1999 "The display of (gendered) identities in talk at work". In *Reinventing Identities: The Gendered Self in Discourse,* M. Bucholtz, A.C. Liang and L.A. Sutton (eds), 221-240. Oxford: Oxford University Press.

Tracy, Karen. 1998 "Analysing context: Framing the discussion". *Research in Language and Social Interaction* 31(1). 1-28.

Watson, Graham. 1992 "Introduction". In *Text in Context: Contributions to Ethnomethodology,* G. Watson and R.M. Seiler (eds), xiv-xxvi. London: Sage.

Watson, Rodney. 1997 "Some general reflections on 'categorization' and 'sequence' in the analysis of conversation". In *Culture in Action: Membership Categorisation Analysis,* S. Hester and P. Eglin (eds), 49-75. Boston: University Press of America.

Weatherall, Ann. 2000 "Gender relevance in talk-in-interaction and discourse". *Discourse and Society* 11(2): 286-288.

West, Candace. 1995 "Women's competence in conversation". *Discourse and Society* 6(1): 107-131.

West, Candace. 1998 "Not just doctor's orders: Directive-response sequences in patients' visits to women and men physicians". In *The Sociolinguistics Reader: Gender and Discourse,* J. Cheshire and P. Trudgill (eds), 99-126. London: Arnold.

West, Candace and Garcia, Angela. 1988 "Conversational shift work: A study of topical transitions between women and men". *Social Problems* 35: 551-575.

West, Candace and Zimmerman, Don H. 1987 "Doing gender". *Gender and Society* 1: 125-151.

Wetherell, Margaret. 1998 "Positioning and interpretative repertoires: Conversation analysis and post-structuralism in dialogue". *Discourse and Society* 9(3): 387-412.

CHAPTER 4

Critical reflections on performativity and the 'un/doing' of gender and sexuality in talk*

Paul McIlvenny

1. Introduction

Recently, scholars have tried to coax conversation analysis (CA) from being an empirical or descriptive discipline to becoming a critical one by reflecting on the ideological assumptions behind its 'objective' analyses of 'everyday' conduct (Billig 1999a, 1999b, Hutchby 1999 and Wetherell 1998). I have also been provoked by the unfortunate separation of politics and analysis that often appears to go with a 'naïve empiricism' in much of CA. But another motivation for revisiting and (re)theorising the analysis of talk, social interaction and discursive practice has come in the form of the productive challenge posed by feminist and queer theories that conceive of gender (and sexuality) as something we 'do', not 'are'. This view is representative of the 'performative turn' that can be traced in many fields and disciplines, with distinctive histories and trajectories. The source of this recent 'turn' is most often traceable in the first instance to the work of the feminist philosopher Judith Butler. Butler's (1990) troubling of how we think of gender and identity has worked through into many fields, including cultural studies (Bell 1999), literary studies (Sedgwick 1993c), performance theory (Parker and Sedgwick 1995a), philosophy (Benhabib et al. 1995), sociology (Esterberg 1996), as well as feminist socio-linguistics (Cameron 1997a, 1997b) and the relatively new field of queer or 'lavender' linguistics (Leap 1996: 159-163, Livia and Hall 1997; see also Kulick 1999, 2000 for a critique). Although the 'performative turn' has surfaced slowly and unevenly in studies of gender and sexuality in everyday language use, it is clear that the 'turn' is in part responsible for the reinvigoration of the analysis of agency and identity.

At first glance, however, it may seem that the recent developments in queer theory, especially the poststructuralist theorising of Judith Butler and Eve Kosofsky Sedgwick (1990, 1993b), are distant from the concerns of CA, yet a surprising number of crisscrossings emerge when we consider the complex questions of agency, subjectivity, identity, normativity and power. Even though it is not renowned for dealing with gender and sexuality, the field of CA is adept at fine-grained analysis of the complexities of practical action, agency and identity in talk. Because of this focus we need to consider carefully in what ways CA might be relevant and applicable to feminism and queer studies, especially with regard to developing an appropriate methodology for analysing the performativity of sexuality in talk (see also Speer and Potter in this volume). In this chapter I examine how notions of 'doing', particularly the 'doing' of gender and sexuality, in studies of talk-in-interaction are similar to and different from the notion of 'performativity' in the work of Judith Butler, particularly her argument that gender identity "is performatively constituted by the very 'expressions' that are said to be its results" (1990: 25). Some of the basic tenets of both are explicitly compared in the hope that we can find suggestive new directions by bringing CA and 'post-identity' gender theory into dialogue.

To do justice to the variety and contemporary relevance of past work, a critical review is undertaken of the early foundations of a perspective on conversational performativity or 'doing' gender in the writings of Garfinkel, Kessler and McKenna, Sacks, and Schegloff. The prime focus for comparison, however, is the model of 'doing' gender first proposed by West and Zimmerman (1987). Although there are a few early studies that use a (pseudo) conversation analytic framework to analyse gender in conversation (Zimmerman and West 1975, Fishman 1978), the lineage of serious work investigating the practices of 'doing' gender in talk is not as well known as it should be, and does not seem to have generated very many follow-up studies. West and Zimmerman's (1987) ground-breaking theoretical discussion of 'doing' gender is increasingly cited, and it has been critiqued in feminist academic journals, but its relationship to Butler's theory and its contribution to ethnomethodology or conversation analysis have not yet been fully appraised. Likewise, although Butler's work has had great impact on certain fields, there has been little sustained criticism of Butler from the perspective of empirical studies of conversation, discourse and language use.

2.   Do we need another 'performative turn'?

There is not the space in this chapter to even begin to appraise the broad sweep of notions of performance and performativity that can be found in the social and human sciences. Traditions that have examined the nature of 'performance' or 'performativity' include activity theory (Vygotsky), anthropology (Hall 1999), performance theory (Carlson 1996), philosophy (Austin 1962), practice theory (Bourdieu 1977) and sociology (Goffman 1959). They have all offered models and theories to explain how it is that one is 'doing' something by engaging in a particular action, behaviour or practice. Often these are premised on a distinction between 'being' (as well as 'meaning' or 'saying') and 'doing', which can be traced to a number of sources, including Nietzsche, Sartre, Wittgenstein, Ryle and Schutz. I propose that we can see in the 'turn' to performativity at least four distinct but related and increasingly radical senses. First, it has the sense of acting (or 'doing') as the result of particular behaviours, signs or uses of language (P1) — a sense which is common in accounts of linguistic performativity and anthropological performance. Second, it refers to norms, order or structure that are expressed, accomplished or constructed through certain rituals, practices and/or procedures (P2) — for example, in social constructionist theories. Third, it is a bringing into 'being' (and thus establishing as an origin) as a retrospective effect of particular behaviours, actions, practices and/or relations (P3) — what we may call an interpellation or discursive effect. Fourth, it can be understood in an extended sense as a way of inhabiting norms or relations that alters those norms or extends those relations to include other entities and thus transforms our sense of what is real, what is social and what is liveable (P4) — for example, in the domain of cosmopolitics. There is a further sense in which performativity is a concept with important theoretical repercussions. It can apply not just to the objects of study, but also to the research itself (see Ashmore 1989 and Lynch 2000 for extended discussions of reflexivity), with the result that research studies performatively constitute their objects of study (see also Foucault 1972).

With the spread of the 'performative turn' we see the emergence of a variety of approaches to accounting for how gender (and now sexuality) is produced and reproduced in everyday language practices. For many scholars, gender is no longer seen as a 'fixed' property or attribute of individuals that is manifested in asymmetrical linguistic or communicative behaviours by those individuals (Bing and Bergvall 1996). West and Zimmerman (1987), whose model is detailed later, ask that we try *not* to think how always already gendered subjects effect appropriate behaviours, but how persons have propensities and differential opportunities to perform certain practices and activities in order to be seen as gendered. Lorber (1987: 124) suggests that "*gender* is fundamental, institionalized, and enduring; yet, because members of social groups must constantly (whether they realise it or not) 'do' gender to maintain their proper status, the seeds of change are ever present." In reference to conversational styles, Cameron (1995: 43) recommends that "instead of saying simply that these styles are produced by women and men as markers of their gender affiliation, we could say that the styles themselves are produced as masculine and feminine, and that individuals make varying accommodations to those styles in the process of producing *themselves* as gendered subjects." These sources are indicative of an increasingly common, anti-essentialist emphasis on gender as a performance or set of practices by which one produces oneself and is constituted as a gendered subject.

The general shift among feminists to an understanding of gender as a performative effect gave a warrant for social constructionists to discover agency in gender as a social practice, where earlier it had been missed or precluded. And it also provided opportunities to think of *not* becoming, of *un*doing, of possibly contesting gender's reified status (Lorber 1991, 2000). Moreover, a renewed conception of gender and agency is conceivable that moves away from theories that postulate 'women as victims' (see Kitzinger 2000 and Gardiner 1995). However, there are inconsistencies and misunderstandings in the adoption of a notion of gender performativity; for instance, it can be easily reduced to a mode of socialisation that perpetuates gender dualism (see Cameron 1998 and Stokoe and Smithson 2000). It has, unfortunately, become too simple to say that someone or some group is 'doing' gender and to regard the activities or practices of speakers as implacably co-extensive with their gender effects.

3.   Butler's theory of gender performativity

Judith Butler's distinctively feminist post-structuralist challenge to normative gender and sexuality has inspired many, both academics and activists, since she first published *Gender Trouble* in 1990. Her writings have had a major influence on many fields and disciplines, but not as yet in ethnomethodology or conversation analysis (nor in discursive psychology; see Speer and Potter this volume). Nevertheless, many of the citations are rather superficial and tend to reproduce a restricted (even corrupted) set of readings. Exploring Butler's work in more detail is important for at least two reasons: first, her theoretical sophistication concerning conceptions of agency, subjection, power and performativity may serve us well in considerations of how we 'do' gender and sexuality in talk; second, her work does not stand isolated, so it is valuable to trace the parallels to her ideas in studies of talk, gender and sexuality over the last forty years.

Judith Butler's *Gender Trouble* was first published in 1990, and as a measure of its significance and popularity the volume has been reissued with a new preface in a special tenth anniversary edition (1999a). A primary goal of *Gender Trouble* was an immanent critique of the identity politics and essentialising practices of feminists over the category of 'woman'. In her new preface (1999a: xx) she describes her dogged attempts to 'denaturalise' gender and a presumptive heterosexuality. To found a notion of performativity with which to go beyond an expressive model of gender, Butler acknowledges her debt to Derrida's reading of Kafka in which the anticipation of the law produces the very phenomenon that it anticipates (xiv). If we look back to Butler's (1988) early work on performativity we find a syncretic mixture of other sources, including Nietzsche (to claim a doing behind which there is no being), Simone de Beauvoir, as well as anthropological and dramaturgical notions of performance (to bring an understanding of collective and ritual social drama), which lead her to a reconsideration of gender as a performance.

In this early work, Butler (1988: 519) also discusses the phenomenological tradition of constitutive 'acts' and considers the performance metaphors lurking behind a philosophy of action. Her radical claim that gender can be neither true nor false, even though it is rendered stable, polarised and discrete, hints at Austin's (1962) original formulation of the 'performative'/'constative' distinction. Despite the credit going to Butler for harnessing the notion of performativity, it appears that it was only after the publication of *Gender Trouble* that Sedgwick (1993a) expanded on the notion of queer performativity and deployed Austin's original notion of performative so as to clarify how to do things with words non-referentially.[1] Prompted by Sedgwick, Butler (1993a) pursued further the relation between queer and performativity, bringing in Derrida's critique of Austin's and Searle's understanding of performatives in order to elucidate the relations between intention, citation, iterability and authenticity.

Formulating a theory of linguistic action, Austin (1962) examined a particular class of utterances — first person, singular, present, indicative —

which do not describe a doing or state a doing, but *do it*. This set of utterances came to represent performativity (P1) for Austin. Another analytical philosopher, John Searle, took up the baton of what became known as speech act theory (Searle 1969), and developed it towards a broad theory of communicative language use as part of a theory of intentional action, whereupon an extended debate took place between Jacques Derrida (1977a, 1977b) and Searle (1977). In his philosophical discussion of performativity and metalanguage, Lee (1997: 13) notes that with a deconstructive turn Derrida sets Austin against himself: "he uses Austin's deconstruction of the centrality of the representational model of speech to deconstruct the very notions of intention and convention that Austin and Searle use to interpret how speech acts work." Derrida (1977a, 191) asks, "isn't it true that what Austin excludes as anomaly, exception, 'nonserious', *citation*..., [is] the determined modification of a general citationality — or rather, a general iterability — without which there would not even be a 'successful' performative?"

Following on from Derrida's subtle critique of Austin's 'violent' exclusion of 'parasitic' citations from the category of 'real' performatives, Butler (1993b) argues that gender performativity comprises not singular 'acts' but a stylised citational practice, a chronic reiteration without an original. Thus, the binding power of an act is not derived from the intention of the speaker, but from the (re)citation of a prior chain of acts which are implied in a present act. Whereas Austin tends to treat the speaker as if s/he were all but coextensive with the power by which the individual speech act is initiated and authorised, Butler argues that the subject is constituted through a regulated process of repetition, and thus agency is located within the possibility of variation on that repetition. However, because of the nature of performativity, there abides an inescapable weakness with the operation of the ideal norm: the inevitable failure to legislate or contain it. Gender congeals through performative practices, but performativity is itself vulnerable to excitation, recitation or mis-citation, resulting in an 'undoing' or a displacement of gender.

In order to challenge our conventional understandings of gender, Butler melds this revised notion of performativity with a Foucauldian conception of the discourses of sexuality (Foucault 1976), and thus she seeks to comprehend the ways in which gender identity is performative, and gendered and sexed bodies are discursively constituted. In his early work, Foucault (1972: 49) argues that discourses are "practices that systematically form the objects of which they speak." Subjects are performatively produced in discourse, as discursive effects of productive power relations. Discourses produce limits on what is 'knowable'. Mills (1997: 17) summarises this conception of discourse as "something which produces something else (an utterance, a concept, an effect), rather than something which exists in and of itself and can be analysed in isolation." Thus, Butler moves towards a discursive performativity (P3), following Foucault, rather than a specifically linguistic performativity (P1) in which language is understood as action that performatively "induces a set of effects through its implied relation to linguistic convention" (1999a: xxv).

I have hinted at Eve Kosfosky Sedgwick's role in the development of queer performativity. Let me say a little more because she explores specifically and positively how particular queer (or noncanonical) utterances are performative. Sedgwick (1993a) suggests, for instance, that a consideration of the stigmatising performative 'Shame on you' may better serve a theory of queer performativity. This performative is dissimilar in many ways to the defining core of Austin's theory: it has no explicit first person pronoun and is verbless, "which implies a first person whose singular/plural status, whose past/present/future status, and indeed whose agency/passivity can only be questioned rather than presumed" (4). Sedgwick's more detailed exploration of particular types of performatives as they relate to queer matters is suggestive, but it suffers from some of the same problems as does speech act theory. For instance, her reflections on the performative act of shaming may turn out to be inappropriate to actual practices of shaming in conversational interaction. Nevertheless, her insights suggest that conversation analysts may find something 'queer' going on when they look for phenomena in which participants are doing 'witnessing' or avoiding agency or transforming recipiency in the production of injurious talk.

4.   Eight comparative questions

What I wish to do now is to explain something of the force of Butler's conception of gender performativity, but in such a manner that we can then compare it with notions such as reflexivity, accountability and 'doing' gender in ethnomethodology and conversation analysis, which are explained later. Such an undertaking is not to be found explicitly in the ethnomethodological nor conversation analytic literature, nor in Butler's work itself. On the other hand, there are hints of possible connections between ethnomethodology and Butler. In one of her first papers on gender performativity, Butler (1988: 519) refers to the antecedent phenomenological theory of 'acts' (P2) — espoused

by Edmund Husserl, Maurice Merleau-Ponty and George Herbert Mead —
which "among others, seeks to explain the mundane way in which social
agents *constitute* social reality through language, gesture, and all manner of
symbolic social sign." Husserl and Merleau-Ponty are notable precursors to
some of the basic ideas to be found in Garfinkel and ethnomethodology
(Heritage 1984). In addition, both Butler and CA have a mutual interest in
problematising speech act theory. Another oblique connection can be found
when Butler (1988: 528) briefly criticises Goffman for positing a self that
assumes and exchanges various 'roles' within the complex social expectations
of the 'game' of modern life. Garfinkel (1967) also criticises Goffman's dramaturgical notion of strategic role: it is both too explicit and too special.
Goffman's notion of gender as strategic display may veer towards the performative, but it remains only a game, a ploy of essentialised actors.[2] Besides
these indirect connections, there is little in the way of explicit comparison
between Butler and ethnomethodology or conversation analysis, a situation
which I hope to rectify in this chapter.

I propose that points of contact between CA and gender performativity
theory as articulated by Butler (and Sedgwick) can be profitably traced through
a consideration of eight questions that address key issues centring on the
nature of the subject, agency, interaction, categorisation, context, social order,
constructionism and gender/sexuality. The questions discussed in the following sections are formulated in Butler's theoretical terminology; the questions
are returned to later from the perspective of ethnomethodology and CA.

(1) Who is the subject of a performative act?

When considering how one acts performatively or non-performatively, it is
important not to misread Butler and suppose that the force of a performative
(what it does) derives from the subject or the intention of the subject who
utters it, nor to reduce performativity to a theatrical performance behind
which lies a 'real' essence or self who chooses to act. Butler (1988) begins her
essay on performative acts and gender constitution by citing some of the different ways that philosophers have engaged with a discourse of 'acts'.
Unfortunately, the theatrical and phenomenological models "assume the existence of a choosing and constituting agent prior to language (who poses as the
sole source of its constituting acts)" (519), and thus they take the gendered self
to be prior to its acts, when in fact it is a "compelling illusion" (520). Indeed,
performativity is a name for something everyone does in order to be gendered,

and Butler intends this in the strong sense that one cannot be an intelligible subject (our humanity is at issue) without 'doing' gender.

In order to reconsider the individualist assumptions underlying the phenomenological view of constituting acts, Butler proposes that 'acts' cannot be reduced to the domain of a sovereign subject. It is true that there are "individual ways of *doing* one's gender, but *that* one does it, and that one does it *in accord with* certain sanctions and proscriptions, is clearly not a fully individual matter" (1988: 525). Butler (1997) develops a richer notion of *social interpellation* and the social (simultaneous with the discursive) iterability of the utterance. She argues that the performative is not a singular act used by an already established subject, but "one of the powerful and insidious ways in which subjects are called into social being from diffuse social quarters, inaugurated into sociality by a variety of diffuse and powerful interpellations" (160). In a recent interview, she describes her interest "in the Althusserian problem of how, one might say, a speech act brings a subject into being, and then how that very subject comes to speak, reiterating the discursive conditions of its own emergence" (Bell 1999b: 165). Althusser gives her interpellation, the prototypical discursive act by which subjects are constituted, while Austin provides a way of understanding the speech acts of that subject. She points out that a critical perspective on the kinds of language that govern the regulation and constitution of subjects is imperative because we are inevitably dependent on the ways we are addressed in order to exercise any agency at all.

(2) What type of work goes into a performative act? And what role has the audience for such an act?

We can legitimately ask not only who the 'subject' of a performative is, but also how a performative 'works', in the sense of how the relevance of a performative citation and its trajectory is displayed, recognised or negotiated *in situ*. Butler (1995: 205) points out that "it is not simply that the speech act takes place *within* a practice, but that the act is itself a ritualized practice. What this means, then, is that a performative 'works' to the extent that it *draws on and covers over* the constitutive conventions by which it is mobilized." Although Butler's emphasis has shifted to performativity as repetition and ritual, there is still a tendency for her to focus on the provisional success of an individual performative act (seen also as an act of consciousness that founds both a gendered subject and an imaginary gender). More recently, Butler (1997) has dealt with the possibilities for agency when one is interpellated by a speaker;

however, despite Butler's (1993a) critical attention to the voluntaristic impulses of gender performativity, it is not clear how a range of different subjects (such as participant, audience or witness) rather than the singular 'acting' subject come into play, or are interpellated in a poststructuralist sense.

Parker and Sedgwick (1995b: 10, my emphasis) appreciate the problem and recommend that, "Austin-like, the obliquity of queer reception needs and struggles to explicate the relations on the *thither* side of 'I do'", which they see as necessary in order to explore the possible grounds and performative potential of refusing, fracturing and warping (see Foster 1998 for an alternative analysis of gender in terms of the figure of a choreography). Sedgwick (1993a: 3) opens up to the possibility of not only the interpellation of others present — witnesses, for instance — but also of the deconstruction of 'the performer', of refocusing on a "populous and contested scene in which we examine the quality and structuration of the bonds that unite auditors or link them to speakers and interrogate the space of reception" (7-9). As shown later, this is precisely what conversation analysts such as West and Zimmerman (1987) have already begun to explore from an interactional perspective.

(3) By what practices are others performatively constituted?

This question is important to ask because the relationship between everyday practices of categorising other persons and the procedural formation of (discourse, social and cultural) identity has come to prominence in recent debates in conversation analysis (see D'hondt, Fish and Tainio in this volume). With the theory of gender performativity we find that naming and interpellation are key performatives by which a subject comes into existence. Butler (1997) revamps Althusser to recast in linguistic terms the idea that one comes to 'be' through a dependency on the Other, "to the extent that the terms by which recognition is regulated, allocated, and refused are part of larger social rituals of interpellation" (26). She also considers the performative force of insulting, of injurious naming in relation to illocutionary force. Yet she is careful to point out how agency is possible in the field of the discursive constitution of the subject. One is not fixed when one is inaugurated as a subject of speech that insults. For Butler, categorisation is an inherently political act and has exclusionary effects. Because a performative calls a subject into being, makes a subject intelligible, then it follows that because one is called in one way and not another, those other forms of subjectivity are unavailable. And it is even possible not to be called, to be outside intelligibility, which for Butler is a constitutive condition of intelligibility itself. With poststructuralist conceptions of agency as discursive effect, we can understand better the complexity of the construction of collective and individual differences; how, that is, hierarchies and inequalities are produced.

(4) What status does context have in the theory of performativity?

In her writings, Butler is at pains to emphasise the contingent nature of action as a process of reiteration, such that action, subject, and context are refigured. She argues that "understanding performativity as a renewable action without clear origin or end suggests that speech is finally constrained neither by its specific speaker nor its *originating context*" (1997: 40, my emphasis). Performativity has its own social temporality by which, she argues following Derrida, agency remains enabled precisely by the contexts from which it inevitably breaks. She does not imply a contextual determinism here, since the citationality of discourse can work to enhance and intensify our sense of responsibility for it, not absolve us of responsibility. Thus, the performative subject who speaks is accountable to the manner in which such speech is repeated — for reinvigorating such speech, as well as re-establishing the contexts and negotiating the legacies of usage that constrain and enable the speakers' speech (27).

(5) How is the durability of the performative effect (of gender) achieved over singular occasions?

If gender or sexuality is an identity effect constituted by a non-referential performative, then how exactly is it created, made recognisable, attributed, maintained and made durable? In other words, how does the stylised repetition of acts institute a recognizable gender identity, one that is seen as natural and necessary? Butler (1995: 205, emphasis in original) contends that if a performative provisionally succeeds then "it is not because an intention successfully governs the action of speech, but only because that action echoes prior actions, and *accumulates the force of authority through the repetition or citation of a prior and authoritative set of practices.*" The power of the performative is indeed that it covers over the constitutive conventions by which it is mobilised, such that gender *feels* natural (a position we can compare with Garfinkel's 'discovery' of the 'natural attitude' of sex status). Recently, following Bourdieu (1991), Butler (1997: 143) argues that "ordinary language records and preserves social oppositions, and yet it does so in a way that is not readily transparent. Those oppositions are sedimented within ordinary language and a theoretical reconstruction of that very process of sedimentation is necessary in order to understand them at all." However, the specific practices by which a 'covering over' is accomplished and made unnoticeable are rarely delineated by Butler, except when exposed by a misperformance.

(6) If gender and agency are discursive effects, a sedimentation of acts of gendering, then how can this naturalisation be exposed and transformed?

Although one may resign oneself to the naturalising effects of gender, of crucial importance to Butler's theorising is a reconsideration of the politics of the performative, with the aim of resisting or subverting the operation of a coercive heteronormativity. Rather than see agency as confined or restricted by a sovereign subject or by an external force or structure, the possibility of agency is opened up in the very process of the contingent reiterability that is inherent in performativity. Thus, recitations can also be resignifications. Since the publication of *Gender Trouble* and her essay "Imitation and gender insubordination" (1991), drag has become the archetypal subversive act that is most associated with Butler, both positively and negatively. But drag is simply a useful example for Butler to challenge the distinction between 'gender reality' — what she refers to as the "naturalized knowledge of gender" — and the unreal, inauthentic or imaginary. Drag can and does, according to Butler, disrupt the categories through which we see gender in bodies, with the result that the reality of gender is put into crisis. In no way, however, is drag an exemplary trans-situational subversive act. And even if gender can be rendered ambiguous in drag, it may not disturb or reorient normative sexuality at all.

(7) Does the theory of performativity take a constructionist stance?

Vasterling (1999) argues that Butler has a sophisticated constructionist stance, which cannot be accused of linguistic monism or determinism (cf. Livia and Hall 1997, who tar Butler with the brush of linguistic determinism). It is clear from Butler's arguments that the claim that language 'constructs' the subject does not entail that language fully determines the subject, and the claim that agency is the effect of discursive conditions does not entail that these conditions control the use of agency. Butler (1993b) makes a careful statement of her position against both linguistic monism and a simple constructionism. She argues that constructionism can lead to linguistic idealism or discursive monism,

which are generative and deterministic. On the other hand, the view that discourse constructs the subject is too simply a reversal of terms. To counter the
idea that everything is discursively constructed, as if there is a deterministic relation between discourse and its effects that denies agency, she develops an
account of the relation between the discursive and the non-discursive which
complicates the construction of both 'subjects' and 'acts'. Construction is neither a single act nor a causal process initiated by a subject culminating in a set
of fixed effects (1993b: 10). Butler tentatively explores the limits of constructionism in terms of the violent divide between bodies that matter and other
abjected bodies that are less intelligible to the symbolic order of compulsory
normalisation because they are 'outside' discourse (and yet constitutive of it).

If, as Butler (1990: 276) suggests, acts are collective and not fully an individual matter, then what theories are available to give a better understanding
of just how agency is delegated and translated? In a recent interview, Butler
(1999b: 297) reflects upon her performative theory of gender as about "a certain way of inhabiting norms that alters the norms and alters our sense of
what is real and what is liveable." This formulation suggests a broader and
more 'worldly' performative conception of social ordering (P4) — see Law
(1999) and Latour (2000). For example, Bowers and Iwi (1993: 364) contend
that "we perform the social by defining it". A society comes into being in the
way that it does "*precisely through* the associations actors make as they recruit
others to their definition of it" (364, emphasis in the original). Society is not
to be described but achieved; thus, there are many competing versions of the
social. A performative version of society does not privilege one version over
another, nor does it have to commit to individualism or social constructionism. It is not idealist since it requires great effort to secure the endurance of a
version, and it is not substantively relativist because not all constructions are
equally possible.

(8) How are gender and sexuality figured in a theory of performativity?

In its sophisticated analysis of the relationship between and limits of sex, gender and sexuality, Butler's theory of gender performativity clearly shines. For
her there is no origin of gender and no original sex. The so-called prediscursive 'sex' is a result or effect of the apparatus of cultural construction designated by gender (1990: 7). Indeed, the implied correlation or distinction
between sex and gender, which has become a widely-held belief in feminism
since the 1970s, serves to enforce a compulsory heterosexuality. Gender dif-

ference is the product of a series of normative regulatory practices that work to secure a binary sexual model and to marginalise other forms of desire or object-choice. Butler (1990: fn16, 151) uses the term 'heterosexual matrix' to designate the "grid of cultural intelligibility through which bodies, genders and desires are naturalised... to characterize a hegemonic discursive/epistemic model of gender intelligibility that assumes that for bodies to cohere and make sense there must be a stable sex expressed through a stable gender (masculine expresses male, feminine expresses female) that is oppositionally and hierarchically defined through the compulsory practice of heterosexuality." In her later work (1993b), the more forgiving term 'heterosexual hegemony' is used to emphasise that it is malleable and open to rearticulation.

5. Tracing performativity and gender in ethnomethodology and conversation analysis

In this section, I consider whether or not an anti-essentialist and anti-foundationalist notion of performativity as elaborated by Butler is congruent with notions of practical action that have been proffered within ethnomethodology and conversation analysis. Attention is paid to those studies that engage with gender (and sexuality) as a relevant practice. It may seem anachronistic to return at this stage to the early studies by Garfinkel (and Kessler and McKenna), but given the recent attention to conversation analysis as a relevant methodology for new audiences — feminists or queer studies scholars, for example — I feel it is fruitful for three reasons to trace not only the work of one of the founders of conversation analysis, Harvey Sacks, but also the development of the companion field of ethnomethodology. First, among scholars turning to CA there is often an initial reductive tendency ushered in by a lack of broad knowledge of the subtleties and varieties of conversation analysis and their fraught relationship with versions of ethnomethodology. Second, one of Garfinkel's principal studies was of the management of 'sex-status' in interviews with an 'intersexed' person. Third, Garfinkel's studies, as well as Sacks', contain elements that have since been forgotten, glossed over or rejected, but which may have contemporary relevance for understanding the genealogy of 'doing' gender.

Reflexivity and accountability in Garfinkel's study of 'Agnes'

The early foundations of a perspective on 'doing' gender are seen in some of the writings of Harold Garfinkel.[3] In Garfinkel's (1967) widely cited study of an 'intersexed' person under the pseudonym 'Agnes', we find many interesting theoretical assumptions and presumptions. For the medical doctors and Garfinkel, Agnes was an 'inter-sexed' person who had requested sex-reassignment surgery. Using Agnes as his breaching subject, Garfinkel hoped to make observable *that* and *how* 'normal sexuality' is accomplished through witnessable displays of talk and conduct. He concludes that "from the standpoint of persons who regard themselves as normally sexed, their environment has a perceivedly normal sex composition. This composition is rigorously dichotomized into the 'natural', ie. *moral,* entities of male and female" (116, emphasis in original).[4] As a result of the many interviews and tests at the clinic, it was determined that Agnes was not a transsexual, she was 'intersexed', and so re-assignment surgery was permitted. However, after Agnes' post-operative revelations (reported in an appendix to Garfinkel's book) in which it becomes clear that she had in effect 'deceived' them, she came to be seen by the doctors as having always been 'transsexual'. The irony of the case is that Garfinkel fell for the 'member' who passed as 'naturally' of the female sex ('trapped in the wrong body') in order to have science efface all that visibly remained of a 'natural' masculine sex.

The Agnes study is often cited since it embodies in one of its earliest forms Garfinkel's position on the 'incarnate' or reflexive character of member's practices in ordinary settings. In his comprehensive treatment of the origins of ethnomethodology, Heritage (1984) has tracked the developments and innovations that Garfinkel introduced to a new theory of social action, one which views social action as fundamentally organised with respect to its *reflexivity* and *accountability.* Heritage demonstrates that although Garfinkel draws upon Schutz and the notion of phenomenological constitution (traditionally understood from an observer's point of view), what Garfinkel added was to see things in the light of actors engaged in practical action, such that their actions can be seen to contribute reflexively to the sense of the activity they are engaged in.[5] Lynch (1993: 1) describes ethnomethodology as "a way to investigate the genealogical relationship between social practices and accounts of those practices." To appreciate one such fundamental relationship we only need to consider the oft-quoted phrasing by Garfinkel (1967: 1) of a foundational principle of symmetry in which "the activities whereby members produce and manage settings of ordinary everyday affairs are identical with members' procedures for making those settings 'account-able'." It is the 'reflexive' or 'incarnate' character of accounting practices — the reflexive accountability of action for participants themselves — that allows social order to be built out of behaviour as part and parcel of the production of that behaviour.

With regard to the 'reproduction' of gender or what Garfinkel calls 'sex status', Heritage (1984: 181) claims that Garfinkel has given us "a profound analysis of gender [sex status] considered as a produced institutional fact"; that is, the reproduced differentiation of culturally specific 'males' and 'females'.[6] In Butler's terms, the reflexivity of accountability to gender installs (or naturalises, and thus conceals) for the members themselves a set of norms (or 'natural attitude') as an imaginary origin or stable background for conduct, despite the fallacy of that origin. With this formulation we can see a performative relation between conduct and social order (P3). Garfinkel, however, does not use the term 'performative' to characterise his theoretical project, though he does refer to a notion of "performative character" in a footnote in which he describes Agnes' descriptions of normal sexuality as turned into "exhibitions which, as much as anything, distinguished for us her talk about normal sexuality from the talk about normal sexuality by normals" (1967: fn9, 182). Here, Garfinkel is willing to maintain a distinction between 'passing' as impression management — a continual process of coming to terms with practical circumstances as a texture of relevances — and the conduct of those 'natural normals' who just are *bona fida* members. Garfinkel seems to be proposing that an intersubjective self is the 'interiority' which is the accomplishment of 'normals'; others are merely inauthentic performances (exhibits) of accountable selves. In other words, 'normals' circumscribe what is routine and they accomplish that routine coherently (see Garfinkel 1967: 173-75). He does not reach the more radical conclusion that everyone is passing (cf. Kessler and McKenna 1978: 18).

Doing 'male' and 'female' in Kessler and McKenna

Kessler and McKenna's (1978) groundbreaking, explicitly social constructionist approach to gender based on their studies of dimorphous gender attribution and categorisation practices is rarely referenced in the ethnomethodological literature. One reason may be that although they acknowledge that they are indebted to Garfinkel's suggestive questioning of the 'natural attitude' (or 'objective facts'), they "make no claim to be faithful to Garfinkel's particular intentions" (fn4, 19).[7] While they emphasise in their book that gender is a product of social interactions between members in everyday life (vii), Kessler and McKenna were not so much concerned with analysing actual language use in conversational interaction. Nevertheless, it is important to trace their model of gender since it has been influential on later theories, such as West & Zimmerman's.

Kessler and McKenna's (1978: vii) theoretical position (P2) is that "gender is a social construction, that a world of two 'sexes' is a result of the socially shared, taken-for-granted methods which members use to construct reality." Rather than assume the 'objective facts' of two and only two genders, they ask how do we 'do' gender attribution? They contend that not only is gender attribution far from a simple inspection process, but *"gender attribution forms the foundation for understanding other components of gender,* such as gender role (behaving like a female or male) and gender identity (feeling like a female or male)" (2, emphasis in the original). Here we see a trend in theorising that is picked up by scholars such as West and Zimmerman (1987), namely that categorisation and attribution form a foundation for the reproduction of gender as a structure or system.

Kessler and McKenna (1978) prefer to use 'gender' as a cover term, and thus they refuse to distinguish 'sex' as a separate domain; they refer instead to the 'gender differences' of male and female.[8] This is done so as to point out the social construction of all aspects of being male or female, yet this is not a *member's* orientation, and theoretically it is suspect. They are undoubtedly correct to suggest that the culture/biology distinction between gender and sex is problematic, but it is dubious to erase one of the terms as a solution. They have lost the opportunity to account for how, for example, discourses of gender produce sex as a category or how 'sex' is a discursive materialisation (Butler 1993b).

While Garfinkel's analysis is of the accomplishment of the 'natural attitude' of 'sex status' — what he calls "the cultural conception of a dichotomized sex composition" (1967: 117) — Kessler and McKenna (1978: 55, emphasis in the original) note from a feminist perspective that "he does not tell us how *female* and *male* are accomplished." Thus, they shift the focus from 'doing' sex status (or gender) to 'doing' more specifically male and female. They note that an asymmetry in practices is necessary if a woman is to convince others that she is one 'gender' (presumably female) and not another (male). What they do not say, taking an extra step, is that the accomplishment of male or female gender is most often bound up with heteronormativity. Although their recommendation that we 'discover' how persons 'do' sex difference is important, we should not forget the unnoticed doing of sexuality, particularly normative heterosexuality, that is interleaved with the doing of sex, sex difference and gender. One cannot be coherently 'gendered'— for instance, female and feminine — within a normative ideal of gender without also being heterosexual.

Performative practices and talk-in-interaction

This section briefly reviews the field of CA to consider how it conceives of performativity in members' activities. Although there has been antipathy amongst many conversation analysts towards analysing gender (it is often bracketed as a macro-structural variable), there have been isolated attempts to use conversation analysis in some form or another to analyse gendering practices. The review that follows enables us to appreciate in a later section one of the more sophisticated of these attempts, namely West and Zimmerman's model of 'doing' gender.

Harvey Sacks is considered to be one of the founders (along with Emanuel Schegloff and Gail Jefferson) of conversation analysis. The depth of his thinking has only recently come to light with the publication in the early 1990s of the bulk of his lectures from 1964 to 1972. At odds with the predominant de-politicised and sceptical position of CA, Sacks' original lectures are not lacking in examples and suggestive analyses of sexism- and racism-in-action, especially with regard to membership categorisation analysis. With regard to performativity, Sacks was keen to understand how particular practices 'do' particular actions or avoid them by making their absence unnoticeable.[9] In expanding on what he means by doing 'being ordinary', he explains that it "is the way somebody constitutes themselves, and, in effect, a job they do on themselves. They and the people around them may be coordinatively engaged in assuring that each of them are ordinary persons" (1995, II: 216). Echoing Garfinkel's understanding of accountability and reflexivity, Moerman and Sacks ([1971]/1988: 182) ask "what forms of social organisation get participants to occasions of talk to do the work of understanding the talk of others in the very ways and at the very times at which they demonstrably do that work?"

Schegloff has been heavily influenced by the work of Goffman, Garfinkel and Sacks, but his main contribution has been to bring to fruition the project originally conceived with Sacks that is now known as (sequential) CA. In several of his writings (for example, Schegloff 1987, 1991, 1992, 1996, 1997) and in various responses to criticisms (Schegloff 1998, 1999a, 1999b), Schegloff has carefully mapped out his version of CA, a version which is bound by certain methodological principles and which provides a 'technical' as opposed to a 'vernacular' analysis of members' conversational 'doings'. Schegloff (1996: 162) notes that no other sociological study "has yet provided a clear depiction and exemplar of how the prima facie, observable embodiment of sociality — action, activity, and conduct in interaction — as effectuated through the deployment of language and the body can be put at the centre of theorizing about the social and can be grounded and elaborated in detailed, empirical analysis of that conduct."

In his assessment of the place of defensible accounts of 'social structure' in CA, Schegloff (1991: 46) states his interest in "where talk amounts to action, where action projects consequences in a structure and texture of interaction which the talk is itself progressively embodying and realizing, and where the particulars of the talk inform what actions are being done and what sort of social scene is being constituted." Clearly, talk is seen as a reflexive performative practice, a 'doing' which effects actions and constitutes social scenes. Schegloff (1996) has laid out in detail his 'empirical account of action', which is basically a discovery procedure grounded in a particular social theory of conversational action, for which three distinct elements are needed. First, "the account requires a formulation of what action or actions are being accomplished, with compelling exemplifications in displays of data and analysis, including ways of 'testing' the claim via confrontation of problematic instances and apparent 'deviant cases'" (172). Second, a grounding of this formulation in the 'reality' of the participants is needed, which means that an analyst is required to demonstrate "that the interlocutors in the data being examined have understood the utterances (or other conduct) in question to be possibly doing the proposed action(s) or that they are oriented to that possibility" (172). Third, an explication and analysis of what it is about the observed talk or other conduct or the practices embodied in it, which "make the enactment of that talk/conduct possibly an instance of the proposed action, and makes it analyzable by the co-participants as an instance of that action... what about the production of that talk/conduct provided for its recognizability as such an action... this serves as part of the account of the utterance/action, *whether or not it was so understood by its recipient on any particular occasion*" (173, emphasis in the original). It is this third requirement that most closely draws upon Garfinkel's notions of accountability and reflexivity. Schegloff is at pains to counter what he sees as the 'interpretivist' or 'constructionist' treatment that valorises a recipient's understanding of an utterance as definitive of its import.[10] Thus, he argues that the analyst must carefully document not just the recipient's understanding of the import of an utterance, but on what basis one (the recipient) could form such an understanding.

With regard to the analysis of gender following these three methodological principles, Schegloff (1991) is careful to point out that he is *not* denying that persons are not, for example, male or female, *nor* that those aspects of society do not matter. What he would like to affirm is "the problem of *showing from the details of the talk or other conduct in the materials* that we are analyzing that those aspects of the scene are what the parties are oriented to. *For that is to show how the parties are embodying for one another the relevancies of the interaction and are thereby producing the social structure*" (51, emphasis in the original). In a recent paper, Schegloff (1997: 182) has given his seal of approval to a type of analysis which would elaborate "those forms of conduct by which persons 'do' gender, class or ethnicities of various sorts, and by which they may be shown to display and invoke participants' orientations to those features of the interactional context." This is a positive step forward when compared to the now dated position, argued in Schegloff (1991), that castigates the studies by West and Zimmerman (and others) in the 1970s because of their unjustified and politicised reification of gender 'roles' in empirical materials. West and Zimmerman's (1987) 'doing gender' thesis is discussed in the next section.

6.   West and Zimmerman's model of 'doing' gender

Thus far, I have laid out the basic principles of Butler's theory of performativity and have traced similar notions to performativity in ethnomethodology and CA. Both have sophisticated critiques of speech act theory as formulated by Austin and Searle. Both, in their own fashion, are non-mainstream and anti-assimilationist. In what other ways can we ascertain a theoretical convergence between performativity theory and CA? To answer this in a relevant and timely manner, I specifically examine 'gender performativity'. I trace its trajectory by introducing and re-reading the canonical model of 'doing' gender proposed by West and Zimmerman (1987). A consideration of its advantages leads to a more empirical account of the notion of 'performativity'. I also reflect on their proposed model extended to consider 'doing' *sexuality*, which I feel is justified since West and Fenstermaker (1995a) published later a more encompassing model of 'doing' difference in which they suggest that categorisation and accountability are intrinsic to the operation of many, if not all, social identities.

Working within the fields of feminism and CA, Candace West in collaboration with Don Zimmerman (1987) and later with Sarah Fenstermaker

(1995a) have broadened and politicised the CA methodology to cope with a feminist analysis of gendering practices in talk-in-interaction.[11] After critiquing the notion of gender as a role or a display, they propose a richer understanding of 'gender' (or 'difference') as an ongoing, interactional accomplishment. In order to proceed, West and Zimmerman (1987) define the three separate categories of 'sex', 'sex category' and 'gender'. Their positing of the concept of the intermediary 'sex category' (following the work of Goffman, Garfinkel, and Kessler and McKenna) gives a social constructionist dimension to 'sex'. By distinguishing 'sex category' from 'sex' they are able to posit a separate domain for the cultural manifestation of the moral order of two sexes, a domain in which the criteria of incumbency are purely social.

West and Zimmerman (1987) make a strong distinction between *performance* — the surface display of sex category, such as male/female — and *accountability*. 'Doing' gender consists of "managing such occasions so that, whatever the particulars, the outcome is seen and seeable in context as gender-appropriate or, as the case may be, gender-*inappropriate*, that is, accountable" (135). The key to their theory is that 'doing' gender renders the social arrangements based on sex category as normal and natural, that is, legitimate ways of organising social life. They claim that "insofar as sex category is used as a fundamental criterion for differentiation, doing gender is unavoidable" (145). It is unavoidable because of the social consequences of sex-category membership: the allocation of power and resources not only in the domestic, economic, and political domains but also in the broad arena of interpersonal relations. Thus, in virtually any situation, one's sex category can be relevant, and one's performance as an incumbent of that category (gender) can be subjected to evaluation. In sum, their model straddles two distinct orders of gender. On the one hand, gender is a practised phenomenon, which can only be addressed in terms of how participants themselves undertake the 'doing' of gender. On the other hand, gender exists as a structural inequality that is perpetuated and legitimated as an emergent phenomenon of social situations.

7. A comparison with Butler's theory of (gender) performativity

A sense for the conceptual overlap of Butler's formulation of gender performativity and West and Zimmerman's account of 'doing' gender can be seen in Butler's (1990: 25) assertion that gender proves to be performative because it constitutes the identity it purports to be, and "in this sense, gender is always a doing, though not a doing by a subject who might be said to preexist the deed." However, as Thorne (1995: 498) notes, Butler seems to be unaware of sociological analyses of the construction of gender, which predated her work by more than a decade. The following eight questions match the eight introduced earlier in this chapter to address the key areas for a comparison of Butler's theory of performativity and CA.

(1) Who are the 'members' or 'participants' who engage in (conversational) practices?

West and Zimmerman (1987: 126) are careful to point out that gender is an achieved property of situated conduct, an emergent feature of social situations. Rather than being a property of individuals, gender is both an outcome and a rationale for various social arrangements. Yet they claim that "the 'doing' of gender is undertaken by *women* and *men* whose competence as *members* of society is hostage to its production" (126, my emphasis). Notably, they use the expression "undertaken by women and men", which suggests problematically that 'women' and 'men' are already formed binary subjects before undertaking the task-at-hand. They also find a subject to act through the process of sex categorisation. Once one is categorised according to sex category (from displays and identifications), then one is accountable for engaging in conduct appropriate to (and as a member of) that category, so that one becomes a subject of that categorical discourse. However, the 'coherence' and 'continuity' of 'the person' are not logical or analytic features of personhood, but socially instituted and maintained norms of intelligibility (Butler 1990: 17). The work of producing the intelligibility of the 'self' as well as the 'social' is not often topicalised in conversation analysis.

Butler has firmly criticised any approach which wittingly or unwittingly places an intentional or constituting agent at the centre of a theory of performative action. Ethnomethodology in general cannot be so easily targeted since its conception of 'member' is neither intentional nor explicitly individual. Garfinkel and Sacks (1986: 163) proposed an alternative notion of the endogenous 'member', a notion which is often elided or misunderstood — it signifies *not* a person, but a mastery of natural language, in the sense that "persons, in that they are heard to be speaking a natural language, *somehow* are heard to be engaged in the objective production and objective display of commonsense knowledge of everyday activities as observable and reportable phenomena." Hilbert (1992: 193) argues that in ethnomethodology membership and members' methods are primary; in fact, there is little emphasis upon 'people' or 'individuals' or 'persons' as theoretic entities at all. In a phrasing strikingly similar to a post-structuralist emphasis on the dissolution of the enlightenment subject, he states that "individuality can be accomplished *only* through participation in these methods. Therefore the topic of ethnomethodology will *not* allow a study of individuals 'coming together to interact'" (194, my emphasis). Indeed, McHoul and Grace (1993: 29-31) contend that Garfinkel "rejected theories which give primacy to a sovereign or originary [conscious] subject", and he set out to describe the technical accomplishment of social objects.

Garfinkel topicalises subjectivity to some degree in his study of Agnes: she is the 'doer' of the accountable person, the self-same person that she has been all along. Yet Garfinkel's (1967: 181) discussion points to a paradox: 'she' is someone 'outside', not yet intelligible as a subject, who does; however, 'she' becomes a person with an identity by that doing. Butler's (1990: 142) anti-foundationalist argument is that there need not be a 'doer behind the deed', but that the 'doer' is "variably constructed in and through the deed". Thus, to 'do' is to render an activity morally accountable (by a doer) to a norm that is constituted in and through the accounting practices of everyday life. Nevertheless, we can ask if the analytical focus on norms in CA reifies the practices of certain 'members' as exemplars of members' methods. Also, because membership activity, which has a privileged neutral status (in the use of equalitarian terms such as 'resource', 'everyday', commonplace' and 'peer') before social power comes to operate, almost always produces/desires conformity to a moral social order, then a constitutive ambivalence at the core of membershipping itself, and thus for the very formation of the member as subject, is left unaddressed.

(2) Of what significance are the practices of 'co-participants' to the intelligibility and scope of actions?

We can find some similarity between West and Zimmerman's account of 'doing gender' and Butler's reworked account of gender as performativity. Gender is not a construction one chooses and puts on, it is an effect of a whole set of normative performances which regulate gender and sexual difference, and to which one is accountable. Nevertheless, for conversation analysis this is accomplished in *concert* with others — 'co-participants' — in social practices. This is clearly one of the strengths of CA. The theory of gender performativity, on the other hand, lacks a notion of constitutive audience or interaction, and so it can be charged with the same problem of reductionism as pertains to speech act theory.

(3) What role do categorisation practices play in the reproduction of gender?

West and Zimmerman base their claims about sex category on Garfinkel's original study of Agnes. In a recent reply to critics, West and Fenstermaker (1995b) acknowledge that this is the assumed basis for their hypothesis about the *omnirelevance* of sex category, in so far as sex categorisation provides others with an ever-available resource for interpreting actions.[12] Regardless of how a person views the situation or experience, a person is potentially categorisable in terms of a sex category, and this provides the possibility that the person may be held accountable for their actions as a member of that category. West and Zimmerman (1987: 136) trace their presumption that sex category is an omnirelevant concern to all actions to Garfinkel's (1967: 118) claim that 'sex status' for members is "an invariant but unnoticed background in the texture of relevances that compose the changing actual scenes of everyday life." They deduce that one is, therefore, at risk of gender assessment in virtually all activities. This appears to be a reverse argument to the one Sacks (1972) and Schegloff (1991) rehearse to demonstrate that because a person (or a particular noticing) is potentially describable (observable) using a number of different category sets, then the relevance of a particular category use (description or observation) needs to be demonstrated regardless of whether or not the category 'corresponds' in some way to the 'object' being described.

In an article which reviews their own work on interruptions in cross-sex conversations, West and Zimmerman (1985: 110) try to justify their claim that sex category was 'salient' in the interactions they studied because the distributional evidence suggests so, even though "sexual categorisation was not in any obvious manner 'built in' to the structure of the encounter." In a footnote, they contend that such categories as 'sex' are accountable features of persons in principle, and they loosely extrapolate that matters such as gender are 'noticeable' and 'salient' on all practical occasions (fn12, 114). They conclude that the asymmetries in the initiation of interruption that they 'discovered' in their data are *constitutive* of a power differential; they are a way of 'doing' power, "and to the extent that power is implicated in what it means to be a man vis-à-vis a woman, it is a way of 'doing' gender as well" (111). In one of the earliest papers to use a conversation analytic approach to gender in conversation, West and

Zimmerman (1977: 528) explain the asymmetries as "situationally induced attempts at dominance" by the male speaker, which are activated in some way by particular occasions and the talk within them. The asymmetry is an index of an underlying structure of settings that triggers the male to display dominance. What they seem to be arguing in the later article is that the asymmetries which are correlated with the 'salient' categories of 'male' and 'female' are, in fact, the endogenous means by which conduct is made accountable to those categories, thus reproducing those categories as 'salient'.

Although both sex category and gender are seen as social constructions, they do not propose, as Butler might, that gender reinstalls the sex categories of male and female as heteronormative binaries in order that gender be seen in terms of accountability to those sex categories. They assume that sex-category membership is a surface performance that one is accountable to. In a rather mechanical fashion, members perform (display) their respective sex categories, and in so doing keep in motion the oppressive institutions of gender that are conditional on recognisably sex-categorised subjects.[13] What is not so obvious from their theory is why accountability always results in a replica of a singular natural normative order of sex. Butler (1993a) argues that although one is forced to negotiate compulsory performances of hyperbolic versions of 'man' and 'woman', the compulsory character does *not* make them efficacious; they are haunted in the very anxious resignification of norms. If, as Speer (2001) points out in relation to hegemonic masculinity, categories are deployed and oriented to for a variety of interactional reasons, and often in contradictory ways, even in the same stretch of talk, then the stability of a 'patriarchal' social order consequent on such foundational categorisation practices would appear to be put in jeopardy.

(4) What status does context have in conversation analysis?

West and Fenstermaker (1995: 299) note that "the potential omnirelevance of sex category provides a *resource* for doing gender in the course of any activity." Thus, one aspect of the 'context' of an action is sex category, which one might characterise as a macro-level variable. They are not more explicit about the relation between action and context, but we can look at conversation analysis to see how it might be conceived. Given the locally occasioned nature of social action, actions are both context-shaped and context-renewing. Schegloff (1991) has argued, however, that it is misleading to think of context as a type of bridge between the micro and the macro. Context is not a structure external to and impinging on routine action from the outside. An analyst must show that context is relevant to the parties and is consequential for their activities because parties select and display moment-to-moment in their conduct which contextual particulars they are making relevant. We may see some parallel here with Butler (1997: fn23, 168), who suggests rather vaguely that social context comes to inhere in language.

(5) How is social order conceived and how is it reproduced by members' practices?

Butler (1997: 19) suggests that if 'social structure' is dependent upon its enunciation for its continuation, then it is at the site of enunciation that the question of its continuity is to be posed. How is social order conceived and how is it reproduced by members' practices? West and Fenstermaker (1995: 360) assert that "sex categorisation provides the resource for rendering actions accountable (for instance, as 'womanly' or 'manly') across different situations and different particulars of conduct." There are problems, however, with their model. For example, gender hierarchy is separated from the 'doing' of gender to the extent that a social structure is predicated on the successful instantiation of gender categorisation in everyday practices. Yet, if normative gender categorisation is a contingent performance, how can the solidity and stability of gender hierarchy be achieved?

Engaging in talk provides for the mutual sense of joint activity, and the sense of an action is negotiable and fundamentally social. Nevertheless, the social order is conceived in ethnomethodology and CA as a remarkably stable and homogeneous intersubjective realm. In a summary of the relevance of Garfinkel's study of Agnes, Heritage (1994: 229) concludes that the operation of accountability is stable for two reasons: "(1) The production of actions in full circumstantial detail that are recognizable and accountable within the relevant institutionalized framework of accounts, and (2) The maintenance of the accounting frameworks themselves in the face of 'entropic' tendencies deriving from 'discrepant' actions." Heritage claims that repair mechanisms and a 'core accounting framework' are at the root of the stability of a moral order. He suggests further that "if gender manifests itself as a density of minutiae, the latter are nonetheless stabilized both individually and collectively by the apparatus of moral accountability" (197). This may be true, but one cannot help but feel that West and Fenstermaker's (1995) claim for the invariance of accountability, and Garfinkel's (1967) exposition of the naturalness of 'normal sex', are a consequence of a general ahistoricity. Although particular practices of gender categorisation and accountability may be challenged, the lack of an historical or developmental account of how the 'natural attitude' and specific accounting practices developed means we are at a loss to explain or even conceive of social change. Some ethnomethodologists may be wary of importing a notion of 'change', but one cannot devote so much attention to the 'naturalness' (and hence, stability and invariance) of 'normality' without entertaining some conception of change as a necessary supplement to that of routine.

McHoul (1994: 115) provocatively suggests that "not all social/discursive practice actually *achieves* social order (let alone 'consensus') but that some instances ('situations', or collections or fragments of them) have such things as disorder, conflict, contradiction, struggle, antagonism (and so on) not merely as actional achievements but *as part of their taken-for-granted background and foundation*." Why is it inconceivable in ethnomethodology that members' situated production of an apparent social order is not only intrinsically vulnerable to fracture and subversion, but in fact is a site and stake in discursive struggles over legitimacy, subjecthood and 'the natural'? In accounting for one's conduct one may invoke a number of different 'discourses' in tension, but what status does the 'natural attitude' have in relation to that articulation of discourses? The 'natural attitude' (of sex status, for instance) could be seen as a discourse which constitutes naturalised social objects; nevertheless, we need to reconsider whether or not it is possible to have multiple 'natural attitudes' or versions in contradiction and tension — or at least sites of disruption to the 'natural attitude', where it is not operative or is less compulsive.

(6) In what ways is it possible to not reproduce the social order?

Thorne (1995: 498) points out that West and Fenstermaker (1995) emphasise the maintenance and reproduction of normative conceptions, but they neglect countervailing processes of resistance, conflict and change. West and Fenstermaker (1993: 157) insist that "doing gender does not always mean living up to normative conceptions of femininity or masculinity; what it means is rendering action *accountable* in these terms." So conduct itself does not have to conform to a normative order; it can diverge but still be accountable to a normative conception. What if there are competing conceptions of femininity or masculinity? Can one be partially accountable to several conceptions? With regard to the possibility of resistance, West and Fenstermaker (1995b: 510) have clarified that "since difference is 'done', there is both activity (including resistance) and agency at its foundation. Indeed, it is likely that resistance is as ubiquitous a feature of the shaping of inequality as the doing of difference itself." Sustained questioning of categorisation according to difference can not only weaken the accountability of conduct to existing categories, but it can also offer the possibility of a more widespread relaxation of accountability in general. This is a promising acknowledgement, but it is unclear how ethnomethodology and conversation analysis can provide us with the tools to analyse how resistance in practical activity is a feature of the shaping of inequality.

The regulative discourse of norm and deviance (or discrepancy) is invoked by Heritage (1984) to account for the reproduction of institutionalised gender relations. He does acknowledge, nevertheless, that naturalised core accounting frameworks are not so rigid and timeless as an ethnomethodological approach might sometimes suggest. For him, there are possibilities for gradual social change because of "the constitutive re-embedding of 'discrepant' activities within some new, normalising, but equally self-replicating accounting framework. The development of new frameworks of accounts is permanently possible through some *regrouping of the particulars which instance natural language categories*" (230, my emphasis). His example of the crisis of relations 'between the sexes' in Western societies is noteworthy; unfortunately, he articulates the 'crisis' using stereotypical phrases such as "relations between *the sexes*" and "ways of speaking and acting *associated* with gender relations" (231, my emphasis).

Rather than taking the endemic production of sex category (and the sex category dichotomy) as a sign of the stability of sex, why not read it as Butler (1993b: 2) does, as a 'forcible' materialisation that is (desperately) performed because bodies never quite comply with the norms of the 'natural attitude'? We also need to consider seriously whether we can ever *not* 'do' gender, or are we always, in all circumstances, every single body, the whole population, potentially accountable for our sexedness? In fact, that 'undoing' is what anti-assimilationist queer social movements have as a primary goal: to present and perform a deep disruption to accountability.

(7) Does the model of 'doing' gender fit with a constructionist perspective?

Collins (1995) has castigated West and Fenstermaker for a rehashing of social constructionist views of society in which ethnomethodology masquerades as new theory. Kessler and McKeena (1978) are explicitly social constructionist — in the sense that "social practices constitute givens which have consequences" (Michael 1996: 5) — but Garfinkel has taken a distance from constructionism. Indeed, Lynch (1993: 125) is adamant that we do not misunderstand the notion of 'local production' to mean some kind of nominalism or spatial particularism. In ethnomethodology, "the adjective *local* has little to do with subjectivity, perspectival viewpoints, particular interests, or small acts in restricted places. Instead, it refers to the heterogeneous grammars of activity through which familiar social objects are constituted." Lynch is also critical of versions of ethnomethodology that characterise vernacular accounts as naïvely realist. In such versions, in which a reality is 'talked into being' or constituted through mundane reason, "the 'actor' does not become the infamous 'cultural dope' but instead becomes a philosophically naïve agent who takes for granted a 'mundane world' that analysis recasts into a product of taken-for-granted 'social' practices" (152-3).

(8) How is gender theorised in relation to sexuality?

How does West & Zimmerman's theory cope with the complex relations between differences, particularly between gender and sexuality? In a short digression on the relationship between doing gender and a culture's prescription of 'obligatory heterosexuality', West and Zimmerman (1987: 144) claim that passing as heterosexual is achieved through the production of emphatic and unambiguous indicators of one's sex category. If one is to be ambiguous, then one is still accountable for one's categorical status, one's "normal, natural sexedness" (145). Thus, they assume that a gay man or lesbian would want to either pass or be 'ambiguous' — heterosexuality is the norm. But why, for instance, should a lesbian in the twenty-first century first have to establish "a categorical status as female"? In their model, sex categorisation precedes desire — one must be appropriately sexed before one can enter the interchange of desire. Also, it would appear that their notion of gender hierarchy presumes that gender is only made operative according to a heterosexual model. It may be more accurate to say that gender and sexuality cannot be separated out: doing gender reproduces heteronormativity, not only gender hierarchy. And 'doing' sexuality (or sexual harassment) may have a lot to do with reproducing gender hierarchy as well.

8. Un/doing' gender and sexuality in talk?

Clearly, conversation analysis stands out as an innovative empirical method-ology that 'discovers' practices integral to the 'performativity' of social cate-gories such as gender. However, despite the few engaging attempts to docu-ment practices of 'doing' sex and gender using ethnomethodological and con-versation analytic methods, this canonical work has its own problems regard-ing normativity, power, agency and subjectivity. From the perspective of Butler's theory of gender performativity they suffer from several maladies: a weak or absent theory of subjection and power; heteronormative assump-tions; the reproduction of conventional views on the transgression of gender; and a normalising appeal to the 'everyday' and a 'social order'. Nevertheless, we can see how Butler's elucidation of the reiterative nature of performativity matches to a degree with the local reflexivity and accountability of talk-in-interaction. We must, of course, take into account the competing attentions of ethnomethodology and performativity theory. Ethnomethodology is working against a structuralist/functionalist perspective in sociology that tends to regard the actor as a judgmental dope. Butler, on the other hand, is counter-ing both a deterministic linguistic constructivism and a voluntarism, and she opposes the latter by reminding us that discourse constitutes subjects, so that we do not have an essential identity prior to discourse.

In contrast to CA, performativity theory lacks a rich empirical account of action, and it has a weak conception of audience and reception. Therefore, we can also enquire as to the ways in which CA can inform Butler's approach and ask 'unmotivated' questions about agency, subjection, performativity and power. Parker and Sedgwick (1995b: 9) note that it is easy to find positive (normative interpellating) performatives, such as 'I dare you', but harder to find disinterpellations or negative performatives, such as 'Count me out' or 'Don't do it on my account'. Such performatives point to a potential crisis in every authority-wielding performative — it may fail. But how does one 'do' a negative performative, or even a 'deformative', and what does such a perfor-mative *do* in a conversational sequence? It may be more fruitful to think of performativities, comprising a diversity of constitutive practices and effects. A further issue is the relation between the poststructuralist notion of the reiter-ation of norms — a temporal relation of citationality — and the conversation analytic notion of the sequencing of structures of talk? If we are required to move away from the concept of an original and 'authentic' performative towards an understanding of performativity in which a performative act gains its force through the reiterative citation of an authoritative set of practices, then it is not yet clear how that citation is contingently negotiated and achieved in actual practice (see Campbell 1999). A revised approach would have to be suited to investigating how the reiteration of norms is achieved and made observable-reportable.

What evidence do we find, for example, that 'gender', 'heterosexuality' or 'queer' are relevancies for the participants? Or that they are proper glosses for the work the participants are doing? CA recommends that we avoid creating categorial identities/subjects who talk in categorical ways (for example, 'gay men talk this way'). Instead, look for local, reiterable, interactional practices that mediate, anchor and constitute the intelligibility and accountability of social orderings and cultural discourses. And, as far as possible, attend to the participants' perspective(s) as they construct accountably intelligible turns-at-talk and display an orientation to each other's turns. For instance, ask not 'Why is male sexuality inherently violent?' but 'What are the (conversational) occasions which lead some men to turn to aggressive sexual behaviour (and thus how they can be avoided or transformed)?' Ask not 'How do lesbians talk?', but 'How do participants talk such that their lesbianness is made salient and consequential for their activities?' Ask not 'How does a bisexual women pass as 'half straight', 'half lesbian'?' but 'How does an interlocutor actively construct (or resist) how a 'split self' is perceived when their gender/sexuality is ambiguous to others?'

Butler's reflections on the intrinsic fallibility of the performative suggest that we need to work on a *politics* of conversational action. In contrast to West and Zimmerman's original formulation of 'doing' gender, gender or sexuality can be *un*done, rather than repeatedly done. In ethnomethodological terms, one 'strategy' might be to deconstruct the operation of naturalisation such that the repair machinery of moral accountability no longer works in cases of 'deviancy' or 'discrepancy', or can no longer determine and demarcate 'normal' from 'deviant'. This may lead to a situation where a 'natural moral order' is challenged and secondary elaborations of accounting no longer repair and reinscribe a normative universe of binary sexes (see Heritage 1984). Another possibility would be to disalign with the 'sex/gender' system in talk in order to 'do' gender or sexuality ambivalently. Foucault (1984: 154) suggests that the notion of 'sex' made it possible "to group together, in an artificial unity, anatomical elements, biological functions, conducts, sensations, and pleasures." Sedgwick (1990, 1993b) has done most to follow on from this insight to unpack the alignments that normatively comprise sex, gender and sexuality. She attempts to deconstruct the constraining articulations of sexuality, yet each of her features of sexuality are themselves negotiated achievements. Her observation that we assume that everyone has a sexuality points to the necessity of describing the production of the very sense and scope of the naturalised categories and attributes of sex, gender and sexuality, and then to challenge them.

One might also 'do' *not* 'doing' gender in talk (Bornstein 1994). In this way we can still conceive of subversion and contestation as practical conversational activities with their locus within the space traced by hegemonic cultural expectations of gender. Stone (1991: 295) claims that "the transsexual currently occupies a position which is nowhere, which is outside the binary oppositions of gendered discourse", and that "for a transsexual, *as a transsexual*, to generate a true, effective and representative counterdiscourse is to speak from outside the boundaries of gender." Hausman (1995: 144) suggests, however, that transsexuals speak fully *within* the hegemonic cultural discourse on gender. A further possibility would be to degender or *not* 'do' gender at all (Lorber 1991, 2000). Or are we always, in all circumstances, every single body, the whole population, potentially acountable for our sexedness in talk? West and Fenstermaker (1993: 171) do admit that the accountability of "*particular* conduct" to sex category may be weakened by individuals who fail to live up to normative conceptions of gender, and that collective social movements may call into question "*particular* institutional practices" based on sex category, and so promote alternative practices. Transgenderism, a more encompassing political term, is about articulating a set of practices that attempt to transgress gender norms. If we take the view that talk as social practice is intimately connected to the production of gender relations, then we may expect both the destabilisation of talk practices and the disarticulation of gender relations to crisscross a transgender movement. Maybe it is in such a domain that we can not only learn of the congealed assumptions and presuppositions of a hegemonic perspective on gender and sexuality, but also explore from a CA perspective the sublime nature of alternative and subversive discursive practices operable in talk-in-interaction.

Notes

* Many of the ideas in this chapter were first presented at the *5th Finnish Seminar on Discourse Analysis*, 15-16 September 1995, Turku, Finland; at the *5th International Pragmatics Conference*, 4-9 July 1996, Mexico City; at the *11th Sociolinguistics Symposium*, 7-9 September 1996, Cardiff; at the *6th International Pragmatics Conference*, 19-24 July 1998, Reims, France; and at the *Talking Gender & Sexuality* symposium, 5-6 November

1999, Aalborg, Denmark. Thanks to the audiences at those venues for their helpful comments, and to James Haines for positive feedback on a very early draft.

1. Surprisingly, there is only a brief reference to Searle in Butler's (1988) article "Performative Acts and Gender Constitution", and no mention of Searle nor Austin in *Gender Trouble.*

2. Retrospectively, one of Goffman's insights can be seen as a precursor to the contemporary notion of gender performativity. In highlighting the tendency to see signs as expressive — what he calls the 'doctrine of natural expression' — Goffman (1987 [1976]) attempts to move away from a naturalising representational model of depiction/portrayal. In regard to natural expressions of gender, he elaborates further: "what the human nature of males and females really consists of, then, is a capacity to learn to provide and to read depictions of masculinity and femininity and a willingness to adhere to a schedule for presenting these pictures, and this capacity they have by virtue of being persons, not males or females. One might just as well say *there is no gender identity.* There is only a schedule for the *portrayal of gender*" (8, my emphasis).

3. It is surprising that Judith Butler does not cite Garfinkel, especially his study of Agnes, in her theory of gender performativity. An allusive link to Garfinkel and ethnomethodology can be found when she cites Kessler and McKenna (1978) in a footnote (Butler 1988: fn12, 528).

4. At other times in the text, Garfinkel refers instead to "the standpoint of an adult member of our society". We could conclude from this that to regard oneself as "normally sexed" is to be an "adult member of *our* society" (my emphasis). Just who makes up the "our" at this point is not clear.

5. Czyzewski (1994) points out the slippage between a notion of the (self)reflexivity of actors versus the richer ethnomethodological notion of the reflexivity of actions or accounts. He points to the importance of the notion of the reflexivity of accounts, even in recent ethnomethodological (and CA) texts which maintain such a notion despite their lack of explicit reference to it. He suggests that it is specified as a result of the analyses of, in a more contemporary phrasing, the 'local production of order' (167).

6. Garfinkel's study of Agnes contains a number of heterosexist presumptions. Denzin (1993: 210) argues that Garfinkel "produced a text that allowed him (and the reader) to see Agnes as an 'intersexed' person with male genitalia who managed to pass as a female." Garfinkel's text is part detective story and part melodrama, and through it Garfinkel gave a (heterosexual) masculine reading of Agnes' sexuality. More than this, he and his text can be seen as producing the sensefulness of conduct, behaviour and attitudes as accountable to a 'natural order' of (hetero)sexuality; for instance, of which kinds of sexed bodies can engage in what types of sexual act, and with which other sexed bodies. For instance, Garfinkel mentions obliquely that doctors and ancillary staff were constantly on the alert for so-called 'signs' of incipient homosexuality in their patient, and they would use such a sign to discount Agnes' self-representation as a woman. Thus, an alternative title for Garfinkel's chapter might well have been: 'The managed achievement of a normative notion of 'intersexuality' and the 'natural, normal sexedness' [qua 'heterosexuality'] of the observers by Agnes, Garfinkel and the medical/psychiatric professions'.

7. To illustrate the positive impact that Kessler and McKenna (1978) has had among persons they would categorise as 'proselytizing transsexuals' (125), we need look no further than Kate Bornstein's (1994) book *Gender Outlaw*, which is a provocative autobiographical transgender manifesto. In chapter six, entitled "Abandon your tedious search: the rulebook has been found!", Bornstein tells the reader that "the rules of gender are termed the 'natural attitude' of our culture (the real, objective facts) per Harold Garfinkel's (1967) *Studies in Ethnomethodology*." (45). Although Bornstein is mis-citing Garfinkel, since she is actually deploying the set of properties proposed by Kessler and McKenna (1978), it is noteworthy to see a burgeoning transgender movement developing out of the 'observations' of ethnomethodology.

8. Lundgren (2000: 59) contends that, despite their claims to the contrary, Kessler and McKenna reify a particular notion of 'sex' as pure, fixed and natural (as non-symbolic matter) in order to construe gender.

9. Sacks' (1995) studies can generate a wealth of inquiries into how the relevance of sexuality is established in practical activities. (i) How do people routinely establish the relevant conditions for noticing that something is *not* said? For example, noticing that a 'queer topic' was not broached or pursued, or noticing that someone was not included in a conversation because of their ascribed sexuality, or noticing that an interlocutor was presumed to be heterosexual for the purposes of the conversation at hand. (ii) How do people routinely undertake to not do something without its *absence* being noticed? For example, refusing a sexual invitation; not giving a second 'homophobic' assessment; or not disclosing one's 'marital status'. (iii) How do people methodically achieve recognizable conversational actions *without* paying some negative price associated with them? For example, disclosure of one's marginal 'queer' identity without anybody noticing (see Kitzinger this volume).

10. This position has implications for critical discussions of 'relevance' and 'participants' orientation' (see Stokoe and Smithson in this volume) in that it is all too easy to neglect, as do many conversation analysts, the third criteria as distinct from the second in Schegloff's list.

11. Although the 'doing' gender model was not published until 1987, it was first presented in a conference at least as early as 1977. Goffman (1977: fn4, 3) refers to such a presentation, and West and Zimmerman (1985) cite this earlier venue in the context of their work on interruptions in cross-sex conversations.

12. Schegloff (1999a: 566) does not believe that it has been adequately established that gender is *omni*-relevant in interaction. In contrast, West and Zimmerman (1987) argue that it is sex category, not gender, that is potentially omnirelevant. To say that "doing gender is unavoidable" means that on particular occasions 'doing gender' is being accountable as 'womanly' or 'manly'. Yet in West and Fenstermaker (1995: 18) they state that "gender is potentially omnirelevant to how we organise social life."

13. McElhinny (1995: 218) concurs that West and Zimmerman's account is "still closely linked to the dichotomous view of gender, which itself is derived from a kind of biological foundationalism that the rest of the work repudiates."

References

Ashmore, Malcolm. 1989 *The Reflexive Thesis*. London: University of Chicago Press.

Austin, John L. 1962 *How To Do Things with Words*. Oxford: Oxford University Press.

Bell, Vikki. 1999a "Performativity and belonging: An introduction". *Theory, Culture & Society* 16(2): 1-10.

Bell, Vikki. 1999b "On speech, race and melancholia: An interview with Judith Butler". *Theory, Culture & Society* 16(2): 163-174.

Benhabib, Seyla, Butler, Judith, Cornell, Drucilla and Fraser, Nancy (eds). 1995 *Feminist Contentions: A Philosophical Exchange*. London: Routledge.

Billig, Michael. 1999a "Whose terms? Whose ordinariness? Rhetoric and ideology in conversation analysis". *Discourse & Society* 10(4): 543-558.

Billig, Michael. 1999b "Conversation analysis and the claims of naivety". *Discourse & Society* 10(4): 572-576.

Bing, Janet M. and Bergvall, Victoria L. 1996 "The question of questions: Beyond binary thinking". In *Rethinking Language and Gender Research: Theory and Method*, V.L. Bergvall, J.M. Bing and A.F. Freed (eds), 1-30. London: Longman.

Bornstein, Kate. 1994 *Gender Outlaw*. London: Routledge.

Bourdieu, Pierre. 1977 *Outline of a Theory of Practice*. Cambridge: Cambridge University Press.

Bourdieu, Pierre. 1991 *Language and Symbolic Power*. Cambridge: Polity Press.

Bowers, John and Iwi, Kate. 1993 "The discursive construction of society". *Discourse & Society* 4(3): 357-393.

Butler, Judith. 1988 "Performative acts and gender constitution: An essay in phenomenology and feminist theory". *Theatre Journal* 49(1): 519-531.

Butler, Judith. 1990 *Gender Trouble: Feminism and the Subversion of Identity*. London: Routledge.

Butler, Judith. 1991 "Imitation and gender insubordination". In *Inside/Out: Lesbian Theories, Gay Theories*, D. Fuss (ed.), 13-31. New York: Routledge.

Butler, Judith. 1993a "Critically queer". *GLQ: A Journal of Lesbian and Gay Studies* 1: 17-32.

Butler, Judith. 1993b *Bodies That Matter*. London: Routledge.

Butler, Judith. 1995 "Burning acts: Injurious speech". In *Performativity and Performance*, A. Parker and E.K. Sedgwick (eds), 197-227. London: Routledge.

Butler, Judith. 1997 *Excitable Speech: A Politics of the Performative*. London: Routledge.

Butler, Judith. 1999a *Gender Trouble: Feminism and the Subversion of Identity (10th Anniversary Edition)*. London: Routledge.

Butler, Judith. 1999b "Never mind the bollocks: 2. Judith Butler on transsexuality". In *Reclaiming Genders: Transsexual Grammars at the Fin de Siecle*, K. More and S. Whittle (eds), 285-302. London: Cassell.

Cameron, Deborah. 1995 "Rethinking language and gender studies: Some issues for the 1990s". In *Language and Gender: Interdisciplinary Perspectives*, S. Mills (ed.), 31-44. London: Longman.

Cameron, Deborah. 1997a "Performing gender identity: Young men's talk and construction of heterosexual masculinity". In *Language and Masculinity*, S. Johnson and U. Meinhoff (eds), 47-64. Oxford: Blackwell.

Cameron, Deborah. 1997b "Theoretical debates in feminist linguistics: Questions of sex and gender". In *Gender and Discourse*, R. Wodak (ed.), 21-36. London: Sage.

Cameron, Deborah. 1998 "Gender, language and discourse: A review essay". *Signs* 23(4): 945-973.

Carlson, Marvin. 1996 *Performance: A Critical Introduction*. London: Routledge.

Collins, Patricia Hill. 1995 "On West & Fenstermaker's 'Doing difference'". *Gender & Society* 9(4): 491-494.

Czyzewski, Marek. 1994 "Reflexivity of actors versus reflexivity of accounts". *Theory, Culture & Society* 11: 161-168.

Denzin, Norman K. 1993 "Sexuality and gender: An interactionist/poststructuralist reading". In *Theory on Gender/Feminism on Theory*, P. England (ed.), 199-221. New York: Aldine de Gruyter.

Derrida, Jacques. 1977a "Signature, event, context". *Glyph* 1: 172-197.

Derrida, Jacques. 1977b "Limited Inc a b c.." *Glyph* 2: 162-254.

Esterberg, Kristin. 1996 "A certain swagger when I walk: Performing lesbian identity". In *Queer Theory/Sociology*, S. Seidman (ed.), 259-279. Oxford: Basil Blackwell.

Fishman, Pamela. 1978 "Interaction: The work women do". *Social Problems* 25: 397-406.

Foster, Susan Leigh. 1998 "Choreographies of gender". *Signs* 24(1): 1-33.

Foucault, Michel. 1972 *The Archaeology of Knowledge*. London: Tavistock.

Foucault, Michel. 1976 *The History of Sexuality, Volume One: An Introduction*. London: Penguin.

Foucault, Michel. 1984 "The order of discourse". In *Language and Politics*, M. Shapiro (ed.), 108-138. Oxford: Basil Blackwell.

Gardiner, Judith (ed.). 1995 *Provoking Agents: Gender and Agency in Theory and Practice*. Urbana: University of Illinois Press.

Garfinkel, Harold. 1967 *Studies in Ethnomethodology*. Cambridge: Polity Press.

Garfinkel, Harold and Sacks, Harvey. 1986 "On formal structures of practical action". In *Ethnomethodology and Studies of Work*, H. Garfinkel (ed.), 160-193. London: Routledge & Kegan Paul.

Goffman, Erving. 1959 *The Presentation of Self in Everyday Life*. New York: Anchor Books.

Goffman, Erving. 1977 "The arrangement between the sexes". *Theory & Society* 4: 301-332.

Goffman, Erving. 1987 [1976] "Gender display". In *Gender Advertisements*, 1-9. New York: Harper Torchbooks.

Hall, Kira. 1999 "Performativity". *Journal of Linguistic Anthropology* 9(1-2): 184-187.

Heritage, John. 1984 *Garfinkel and Ethnomethodology*. Cambridge: Polity Press.

Hilbert, Richard A. 1992 *The Classical Roots of Ethnomethodology*. Chapel Hill, London: University of North Carolina Press.

Hutchby, Ian. 1999 "Beyond agnosticism?: Conversation analysis and the sociological agenda". *Research on Language and Social Interaction* 32(1-2): 85-93.

Kessler, Suzanne and McKenna, Wendy. 1978 *Gender: An Ethnomethodological Approach*. Chicago: University of Chicago Press.

Kitzinger, Celia. 2000 "Doing feminist conversation analysis". *Feminism & Psychology* 10(2): 163-194.

Kulick, Don. 1999 "Language & gender/sexuality". From Language & Culture Mailing list: Online Symposium. <http://www.language-culture.org/archives/subs/kulick-don/index.html>. [Nov 17, 1999].

Kulick, Don. 2000 "Gay and lesbian language". *Annual Review of Anthropology* 29: 243-285.

Latour, Bruno. 2000 "When things strike back: A possible contribution of 'science studies' to the social sciences". *British Journal of Sociology* 51(1): 107-123.

Law, John. 1999 "After ANT: Complexity, naming and topology". In *Actor Network Theory and After*, J. Law and J. Hassard (eds), 1-14. Oxford: Blackwell.

Lee, Benjamin. 1997 *Talking Heads: Language, Metalanguage, and the Semiotics of Subjectivity*. Durham: Duke University Press.

Livia, Anna and Hall, Kira. 1997 "'It's a girl': Bringing performativity back to linguistics". In *Queerly Phrased: Language, Gender and Sexuality*, A. Livia and K. Hall (eds), 3-18. New York: Oxford University Press.

Lorber, Judith. 1987 "Introduction to special issue". *Gender & Society* 1: 123-124.

Lorber, Judith. 1991 "Dismantling Noah's ark". In *The Social Construction of Gender*, J. Lorber and S. Farrell (eds), 355-369. London: Sage.

Lorber, Judith. 2000 "Using gender to undo gender". *Feminist Theory* 1(1): 75-95.

Lynch, Michael. 1993 *Scientific Practice and Ordinary Action: Ethnomethodology and Social Studies of Science*. Cambridge: Cambridge University Press.

Lynch, Michael. 2000 "Against reflexivity as an academic virtue and source of privileged knowledge". *Theory, Culture & Society* 17(3): 26-54.

McElhinny, Bonnie S. 1995 "Challenging hegemonic masculinities: Female and male police officers handling domestic violence". In *Gender Articulated: Language and the Socially Constructed Self*, K. Hall and M. Bucholtz (eds), 217-243. New York: Routledge.

McHoul, Alec. 1994 "Towards a critical ethnomethodology". *Theory, Culture & Society* 11: 105-126.

McHoul, Alec and Grace, Wendy. 1993 *A Foucault Primer: Discourse, Power and the Subject*. Melbourne: Melbourne University Press.

Michael, Mike. 1996 *Constructing Identities: The Social, the Nonhuman and Change*. London: Sage.

Mills, Sara. 1997 *Discourse*. London: Routledge.

Moerman, Michael and Sacks, Harvey. 1988/[1971] "On 'understanding' in the analysis of natural conversation". In *Talking Culture*, M. Moerman (ed.), 180-186. Philadelphia: University of Pennsylvania Press.

Parker, Andrew and Sedgwick, Eve Kosofsky (eds). 1995a *Performativity and Performance*. London: Routledge.

Parker, Andrew and Sedgwick, Eve Kosofsky. 1995b "Introduction: Performativity and performance". In *Performativity and Performance*, A. Parker and E.K. Sedgwick (eds), 1-18. London: Routledge.

Sacks, Harvey. 1972 "An initial investigation of the usability of conversational data for doing sociology". In *Studies in Social Interaction*, D. Sudnow (ed.), 31-74. New York: Free Press.

Sacks, Harvey. 1995 *Lectures on Conversation: Volumes I and II*. Oxford: Basil Blackwell.

Schegloff, Emanuel A. 1984 "On some questions and ambiguities in conversation". In *Structures of Social Action: Studies in Conversation Analysis*, J.M. Atkinson and J. Heritage (eds), 28-52. Cambridge: Cambridge University Press.

Schegloff, Emanuel A. 1987 "Between micro and macro: Contexts and other connections". In *The Micro-Macro Link*, J. Alexander, B. Giesen, R. Munch and N. Smelser (eds), 207-234. Berkeley, CA: University of California Press.

Schegloff, Emanuel A. 1991 "Reflections on talk and social structure". In *Talk and Social Structure*, D. Boden and D. Zimmerman (eds), 44-70. Cambridge: Polity Press.

Schegloff, Emanuel A. 1992 "In another context". In *Rethinking Context: Language as an Interactive Phenomenon*, A. Duranti and C. Goodwin (eds), 191-227. Cambridge: Cambridge University Press.

Schegloff, Emanuel A. 1996 "Confirming allusions: An empirical account of action". *American Journal of Sociology* 102(1): 161-216.

Schegloff, Emanuel A. 1997 "Whose text? Whose context?" *Discourse & Society* 8(2): 165-187.

Schegloff, Emanuel A. 1998 "Reply to Wetherell". *Discourse & Society* 9(3): 413-416.

Schegloff, Emanuel A. 1999a "'Schegloff's texts' as 'Billig's data': A critical reply". *Discourse & Society* 10(4): 558-572.

Schegloff, Emanuel A. 1999b "Naivety vs. sophistication or discipline vs. self-indulgence: A rejoinder to Billig". *Discourse & Society* 10(4): 577-582.

Searle, John R. 1969 *Speech Acts: An Essay in the Philosophy of Language*. Cambridge: Cambridge University Press.

Searle, John R. 1977 "Reiterating the differences: A reply to Derrida". *Glyph* 1: 198-208.

Sedgwick, Eve Kosofsky. 1990 *The Epistemology of the Closet*. Berkeley, CA: University of California Press.

Sedgwick, Eve Kosofsky. 1993a "Queer performativity". *GLQ: A Journal of Lesbian and Gay Studies* 1: 1-16.

Sedgwick, Eve Kosofsky. 1993b *Tendencies*. Durham: Duke University Press.

Sedgwick, Eve Kosofsky. 1993c "Socratic raptures, Socratic ruptures: Notes toward queer performativity". In *English Inside and Out: The Places of Literary Criticism*, S. Gubar and J. Kamholtz (eds), 122-136. New York: Routledge.

Speer, Susan A. 2001 "Reconsidering the concept of hegemonic masculinity: Discursive psychology, conversation analysis and participants' orientations". *Feminism & Psychology* 11(1): 107-135.

Stokoe, Elizabeth H. and Smithson, Janet. 2001 "Making gender relevant: Conversation analysis and gender categories in interaction". *Discourse & Society* 12(2): 243-269.

Stone, Sandy. 1991 "The *empire* strikes back: A posttransexual manifesto". In *Body Guards: The Cultural Politics of Gender Ambiguity*, J. Epstein and K. Straub (eds), 280-304. London: Routledge.

Thorne, Barrie. 1995 "On West & Fenstermaker's 'Doing difference'". *Gender & Society* 9(4): 497-499.

Vasterling, Veronica. 1999 "Butler's sophisticated constructivism: A critical assessment". *Hypatia: A Journal of Feminist Philosophy* 14(3): 17-38.

West, Candace and Fenstermaker, Sarah. 1993 "Power, inequality, and the accomplishment of gender: An ethnomethodological view". In *Theory on Gender/Feminism on Theory*, P. England (ed.), 151-173. New York: Aldine de Gruyter.

West, Candace and Fenstermaker, Sarah. 1995a "Doing difference". *Gender & Society* 9(1): 8-37.

West, Candace and Fenstermaker, Sarah. 1995b "(Re)doing difference". *Gender & Society* 9(4): 506-513.

West, Candace and Zimmerman, Don. 1977 "Women's place in everyday talk: Reflections on parent-child interaction". *Social Problems* 24: 521-529.

West, Candace and Zimmerman, Don. 1985 "Gender, language and discourse". In *Handbook of Discourse Analysis, 4: Discourse Analysis in Society*, T.A.v. Dijk (ed.), 103-124. London: Academic Press.

West, Candace and Zimmerman, Don. 1987 "Doing gender". *Gender & Society* 1: 125-151.

Wetherell, Margaret. 1998 "Positioning and interpretative repertoires: Conversation analysis and post-structuralism in dialogue". *Discourse & Society* 9(3): 387-412.

Zimmerman, Don and West, Candace. 1975 "Sex roles, interruptions and silences in conversations". In *Language and Sex: Difference and Dominance*, B. Thorne and N. Henley (eds), 105-129. Rowley, M.A.: Newbury House.

CHAPTER 5

From performatives to practices

Judith Butler, discursive psychology and
the management of heterosexist talk[*]

Susan A. Speer & Jonathan Potter

1. Introduction

Judith Butler is a remarkable social theorist who has had a profound influence on the development of queer theory, and on our understanding of the relationship between sex, gender and desire. Her overall programme provides a framework for the "radical denaturalisation" of gender and heterosexuality (Jagose 1996: 125), drawing attention to the processes through which they are constituted and made to appear stable and natural. Butler's work represents a dense and complicated system of ideas, which, in part, reflects her ambitious combination of a variety of theoretical influences. However, it is also immensely challenging and illuminating.

We cannot possibly capture the subtleties and complexities of Butler's arguments here. However, what we do hope to do is to give the reader a flavour of her approach as it relates to some key themes in discursive psychology (DP). Part of Butler's programme involves a theorization and explication of the notions of discourse, hate speech, and performativity — something that DP and gender researchers would benefit from taking note of and engaging with more fully. However, from a discursive perspective, there are also some features of her work that are rather limited. In this chapter, we consider the implications for this strand of her work, of a DP, analytically based, action oriented approach to participants' practices (Edwards and Potter 1992, Potter and Wetherell 1987).

We begin by offering a brief overview of Butler's work. We then go on to describe in more detail some specifics of her approach. We highlight the similarities and differences between the theorisation of discourse, gender identity and prejudice in the work of Butler and DP, and set out the corresponding advantages of using a discursive approach. These centre on and around (i) DP's move from the abstract theorisation of discourse as a producer of gendered subjects, to the analytic exemplification of discourse as a social practice; (ii) DP's emphasis on the way gender identities are locally occasioned and action orientated, rather than the outcome or effect of decontextualised 'performatives' or 'reiterative' acts; (iii) DP's anti-cognitivist treatment of 'resistance' and 'agency'; and finally, (iv) DP's emphasis on the *in situ* production and local management of prejudice, or more specifically (what Butler and others term) 'hate speech', and its 'resignification' through irony. We illustrate these points with reference to three extracts of data which were drawn from a larger corpus developed as part of our work on the management of 'heterosexism' (Speer and Potter 2000).[1] We focus specifically on participants' *orientations* to heterosexism, thereby entering and extending a key debate at the intersection of feminism and conversation analysis (CA). In particular, we demonstrate how heterosexist talk – which may be regarded as just one form of hate speech, is managed, oriented to and resisted in specific contexts. We conclude by detailing some ways in which Butler and DP may be brought into a productive dialogue.

2.   Gender, heterosexuality and performativity

One of the central themes of this volume is the idea that gender and sexuality are mutually related to one another. These links are theorized most clearly in the work of Judith Butler. Butler argues that heterosexuality depends for its existence on the notion of two distinct genders. Therefore, heterosexuality is, like gender, a discursive production "an effect of the sex/gender system which purports merely to describe it" (Jagose 1996: 84). The concept of heterosexism is of particular interest in this chapter for two reasons. First, it represents just one way in which the "heterosexual matrix" (Butler 1990a) is maintained and reproduced. A fine-grained, discursive analysis of heterosexism in action can highlight the mechanisms through which heterosexuality and gender are made to seem normative, natural and inevitable. Second, an analysis of heterosexist talk allows us to provide an analytic exemplification of Butler's arguments concerning the problematics of (legal) definitions of 'hate speech'. In sum, heterosexism represents a particularly pertinent concept through which to consider the potential applicability of Butler's work to a (re)contextualised analysis of participants' practices.

In both *Gender Trouble* (1990a) and *Bodies That Matter* (1993) Butler elaborates on the discursive mechanisms through which gender is constituted. The distinctiveness of Butler's approach lies in her (re)conceptualisation of gender as a 'discursive practice' (1990a). Gender identity is "the stylised repetition of acts through time" (1990b: 271). It is "a performative accomplishment compelled by social sanction and taboo" (1990b: 271). Performative acts bear a resemblance to performances within theatrical contexts. However, the performance of gender does not embellish some authentic, original referent beneath it, nor is it wilful and deliberate. Instead, performative agency is both constrained and enabled through repetition, or the 'iterability' of signs.

The notion of iterability can be traced back to Derrida (1976) and the idea that discourse has a 'used again', 'citational' quality. Since discourse is not original, it will always escape the complete control of the intentional, speaking subject. For example, the midwife's statement "it's a girl" is a performative that works through this power of citation (Livia and Hall 1997: 11). In Butler's (1993: 232) terms, it "initiates the process by which a certain girling is compelled".

The citational nature of the utterance and the practices that produce gendered subjects do not just constrain an individual's behaviour, but provide space for resistance and transformation. Although, following Foucault, Butler (in Bell 1999: 165) argues that the subject "is constituted in and by discourse", she stresses that this is not a "unilateral" or "unnuanced" process, but is tenuous, vulnerable and subject to failure (164). The notion of iterability can help to account for this fluidity and unpredictability. The repetition that is central to the construction and maintenance of gender is always "repetition with a difference" (Lloyd 1999: 200). It is inevitable that each subsequent citation will diverge slightly from the previous one, and it is this which makes gender transformation possible. Having established this, the issue for Butler (in Bell 1999: 165) then becomes one of grasping precisely how it is that "a subject who is constituted in and by discourse" is able to "recite" the same discourse to another purpose, to "resignify" it and give it new meaning.

According to Butler, Foucault's account of subject constitution is "too unilateral" and "too unnuanced". Since he implies that the subject is simply "made" in a mechanistic fashion, he is unable to account for the "vulnerability" and "unpredictability" of identity construction (Butler, in Bell 1999: 164). Therefore, to provide a less one-sided and more 'nuanced' account that can explicate the processes through which resignification and resistance (in the form of drag, for example) might come about, Butler returns to psychoanalysis. By combining the notion of iterability with a theory of the 'psyche', Butler works to produce an account of gendered subject formation that captures a sense of both structure and agency, constraint and creativity.

3.   Hate speech

This concern to theorize both structure and agency – but at the level of the utterance – is taken forward in Butler's book, *Excitable Speech* (1997a). While we take issue with her discussion of decontextualised 'speech acts' that are insensitive to the local practices and activities of participants, it is here that Butler fleshes out her approach to discourse and hate speech.

Hate speech is a concept that has developed primarily in the U.S. context. According to Samuel Walker (1994: 8), "there is no universally agreed-on definition of hate speech." Traditionally used to refer to "any form of expression deemed offensive to any racial, religious, ethnic, or national group", it has, more recently, been widened in some U.S. campus speech codes to include gender, sexual preference, and a range of other categories (see Walker 1994: 8 and also Fish 1994). While there have been recent proposals to regulate hate speech on campuses and in the workplace, hate speech is more firmly protected constitutionally under the First Amendment (freedom of speech) than it is elsewhere in the world.

Butler, like many others, is sceptical of a law in which hateful *speech* (which is deemed distinct from 'action') is protected. Although hate speech is typically thought to refer to *explicitly uttered* verbal expressions of hatred toward minority groups (the insulting use of the words 'queer', 'dyke' and 'faggot', for example), what counts as hate speech is by no means straightforward. As Butler (1997a: 2) notes, it is not just the words but also the mode of address itself that may result in "linguistic injury". For Butler, the problem of defining hate speech is particularly acute in legal contexts, where it is a political and moral matter. Indeed, part of her concern in *Excitable Speech* is to consider the consequences of legal definitions of speech as action. For example, one way in which an instance of hate speech may be legislated against is to prove that it was not speech at all, but an action which incites violence or is harmful (thus the concept: 'fighting words' — see Fish 1994: 105). However, part of the difficulty for courts and jurors is in deciding what counts as 'just' speech, and what counts as an action. Therefore, Butler argues that any legislation based on attempts to separate speech from its effects is inherently problematic.[2]

Butler (1997a: 2) considers what it means to be "wounded" by language, and how we might identify "which words wound, which representations offend". Butler argues that the power to wound — to cause 'linguistic injury' or 'offence' — is not located in, or determined by the words themselves. Instead, according to Butler, which words wound will depend on the context or manner in which those words are deployed. It is, in DP terms, partly an *indexical* matter. However, she notes that one cannot change a word's meaning simply by manipulating the context: it does not follow that any word can wound given its appropriate deployment (1997a: 13). Some words seem to have a greater power to wound than others. Indeed, for Butler, it is the *failure* of certain words to wound which can help us to understand how we can change a word's meaning and use it in a critical way.

Just as Butler had used the notion of iterability to understand how gender can be resisted and 'resignified', in *Excitable Speech*, Butler (1997a: 13) uses the notion of iterability to explore "how the offensive utterance can be restaged". She asks, "how do we exploit" the 'ritual' or 'iterable' function of speech "in order to undermine it... what would it mean to restage it, take it, do something else with the ritual so that its revivability as a speech act is really seriously called into question" (Butler, in Bell 1999: 166).

Central to this endeavour is Butler's critique of Austin's (1962) notion of the illocutionary speech act. Austin had a tendency to treat the meaning of an utterance as bound up with the speech act and its grammatical organization. Following Derrida (1976), Butler argues that the iterable, open nature of the utterance means that meaning is not fixed but fluid. With each successive use, words take on a slightly different meaning, and come to be resignified. The very possibility of resignification undercuts the conflation of speech with its effect – the idea that the same word(s) will always produce the same outcome (McNay 1999: 178). It is this fluidity which, Butler (1997a: 15) suggests, makes it possible to theorise "how words might, through time, become disjoined from their power to injure and recontextualised in more affirmative modes". Terms such as 'queer', for example, "can be reclaimed, or 'returned' to the speaker in a different form", used to produce different, positive, or politically consequential effects (1997a: 14).[3] This problematises precisely the sort of rigid definitions of hate speech sought within legal contexts.

Butler argues that the theory of speech acts has some important legal and political consequences. Since no speech act (including violent and oppressive forms of hate speech) *necessarily* produces injury, then no simplistic conceptualisation of the speech act will produce a yardstick against which "the injuries of speech might be effectively adjudicated" (1997a: 15). According to Butler, it is this gap between speech and its effect — the idea that a word's meaning is iterable, 'resignifiable' and therefore at least partially shaped by its context of use — which allows for a theory of linguistic agency, and which "provides an alternative to the relentless search for legal remedy" (1997a: 15). From this perspective, it makes little sense to claim that certain words are *always* offensive and should be legislated against.

While Butler's theory of speech in general, and hate speech in particular, is sophisticated, rich and insightful, there are, nonetheless, several problems with her approach to discourse, gender identity and hate speech that we take issue with here. These can be illustrated most clearly via a comparison of some of Butler and DP's central tenets.

4. Discursive Psychology

DP is a constructionist approach that applies a combination of insights from the sociology of scientific knowledge, poststructuralism, ethnomethodology, and CA to *psychological* issues and concepts (Potter 1996b). However, it is a rapidly advancing field, and there are now a variety of approaches that claim the label 'discursive'. These vary in the extent to which they combine a poststructuralist and Foucauldian understanding of discourse, with an ethnomethodological and/or CA one. Therefore, each has a slightly different approach to the way discourse, gender and participant orientations (particularly their relation to ideology and 'macro contexts') may be understood (see, for example, the recent debate between Edley 2001, Speer 2001a, 2001b, and Wetherell and Edley 1999). The distinctiveness of the approach used in this chapter is that, in common with recent discourse work (Edwards 1997, Potter 1996a, Speer and Potter 2000), we adopt an approach that is more strongly influenced by CA in the Sacks (1995 [1992]) and Schegloff (1997) tradition. Indeed, it could be argued that there are more similarities than differences between DP and CA.

Like CA, DP is concerned with the *action orientation* and *sequential organization* of discourse. It pays considerable attention to the co-construction of the sense of an utterance across turns. Indeed, Derek Edwards (1995: 580) advocates for DP a form of analysis that takes from Sacks and CA the idea that there is "no hearable level of detail that may not be significant, or treated as significant by conversational participants". This includes exploring how participants use membership categories (such as 'girl' or 'woman') interactively (Edwards 1995, 1998, Stokoe 1998).

Although both approaches treat "reality as a members' phenomenon" (Widdicombe 1998: 195), unlike CA, DP is an explicitly *constructionist* approach to knowledge and reality. DP is concerned with the identification and analysis of ideological dilemmas (Billig *et al.* 1988), and with the rhetorical and argumentative organization of accounts (Billig 1996 [1987]). Ideological dilemmas are evident in the way participants attempt to manage dual concerns, or conflicting demands for accountability (how, as a heterosexual man, one might go about describing one's experience of a gay bar without seeming gay *or* homophobic, for example). Rhetorical analysis is concerned with the contextually sensitive relationship between different argumentative positions — which may or may not be organized sequentially. DP explores the way people's accounts are designed to counter actual or potential alternatives, and, in turn, to resist being countered.[4]

Both Butler and DP share some features in common, which can, in part, be traced back to their respective roots in poststructuralism. First, both are influenced by Austin's argument that utterances *do* things. For Butler this is captured in the notion of 'performativity', for DP, it is 'action'. Consequently, both view identity categories as resources with pragmatic efficacy, rather than an essential unity. Second, both share Derrida's critique of Austin's argument that the force of an utterance is under the intentional control of the speaker, and that serious (intended speech acts) can be separated from parasitic (unintended) speech acts (see Hepburn 1999, this volume). In Butler and (an anticognitivist) DP, the idea of an 'intentional' sovereign subject is dissolved. Third, they both view discourse as central to the construction of (gendered) identities. For Butler, this is a Foucauldian sense of construction, in which discourses (at least partially, and often only tenuously) constitute gendered subjects (Butler, in Bell 1999: 165). For DP (and CA) in contrast, it is an ethnomethodological or an 'endogenous' sense of construction ('endogenous' literally meaning "growing or originating from within" (*The Concise Oxford English Dictionary* 1995; see also Schegloff 1997). Discourses (like social contexts, structures and institutions) are not separate from identity, bearing down on it to determine or constrain (gendered) talk and behaviour. Rather, gender is 'endogenously' produced in and through discourse as a *social practice*.

Finally, both Butler and DP are anti-foundationalist: Butler (following Derrida and Foucault's stipulation that "categorising creates or constitutes that which it refers to" [Livia and Hall 1997: 8]), argues that there is no 'I' behind discourse (Butler 1993: 225), no referent preceding the moment of speech (Livia and Hall 1997: 9). Likewise, DP is anti-foundationalist – indeed – explicitly *relativist*, in the sense that, while it remains mute on matters of ontology, it treats what is real and not real, and matters of truth and falsity, as themselves discursively constructed and analysable accomplishments (Edwards, Ashmore and Potter 1995, Potter 1996a).

There are also a number of important differences between Butler and DP, which can be traced back to DP's roots in ethnomethodology and conversation analysis (CA). We deal with each in turn.

(i) Discourse: From performatives to practices

Butler is interested in the construction of gender through a performative re-iteration of acts. However, as Widdicombe and Wooffitt (1995: 28) have put it in relation to abstract theorizing elsewhere, such theories "are produced in isolation from the actual behaviour of those individuals whose... practices these theories are meant to illuminate". Therefore, Butler's notion of a politics of the performative has been criticized for remaining a purely "abstract account of subject formation" (McNay 1999: 178) that is "lacking in social specificity" (176). Her work on speech acts is, like Austin's, a theoretical abstraction, based on made-up, decontextualised examples or idealized typifications that are considered outside of their use in actual settings. While Butler talks about discourse, citation and iterability, her theorization of the processes underpinning the reiteration of gender is an abstract one, separated from features of interaction in specific contexts. Consequently, since Butler does not analyse 'real-life' accounts, there is no sense of a peopled world in which participants interact and speak with one another (see also McIlvenny's chapters in this volume). While her theory of hate-speech acknowledges the indexicality of discourse — how the same statements can perform a range of different actions, depending on the context in which they are deployed (to manage issues of identity, stake and responsibility, to justify one's actions, to make requests, invitations, compliments, blamings, and so on) — she does not translate her discussions about context sensitivity into an analysis of actual language use. Therefore, Butler, like Austin, does not provide an analytic programme for studying discourse practices. In contrast, DP provides the theoretical and methodological tools for just such a programme.

Discursive psychologists are not concerned with intangible, largely hypothetical performatives, but emphasize the primacy of interaction and participants' co-construction of orderliness and 'intelligibility'. In DP, talk is used to *do* things, it serves a function, and sense is built up sequentially, turn-by-turn. Thus, a focus on discourse practices in situated contexts is primary. Moreover, DP, like CA, is concerned to explicate the ways in which speakers display in each subsequent turn the sense they have attributed to a prior turn, and so on. DP therefore avoids producing theoretical abstractions that are isolated from features of talk in specific contexts, but is instead, an empirical, analytically grounded endeavour, which explicates and *validates* its claims using concrete examples taken from real life.

(ii) Identity, gender and participants' orientations

In DP, identity is not a feature of an individual's psychology, or something that may 'congeal' in recognizable, though albeit unfinal and tenuous forms through a process of performative re-citation. Instead, identity is reconceptualised as topic, and as something that is oriented to. In DP and CA, the (gendered) person is given the same status as institutions and other social structures. The person is not treated as having its own ontological status. Instead, identity descriptions (of oneself and others), identity categories and notions of gender are indexical, context sensitive resources. They are used to do business in interaction. For this reason, identity descriptions can *vary*, even within the course of one stretch of talk (see Potter and Wetherell 1987 and Speer 2001a). Likewise, the stability and coherence of gender may be worked up in talk to do business, and to do *moral* work. Part of what is interesting about the way speakers *do* gender, for example, may consist in the way they present it (and certain behaviours or "category bound activities" (Sacks 1995[1992])) as normative, thereby making gender morally *accountable* (Heritage 1984: 197).

By conceiving of gender identity, prejudice and so on as things which need explicating as *participants'* and not as *analysts'* concerns (see Schegloff 1997), discursive psychologists generally avoid imposing an agenda that is inattentive to the practices and understandings of the speakers it purports to analyse. In other words, analysis does not proceed with reference to the *analyst's theory* of what is important. Instead, DP treats the speakers' own construction of what is important and consequential as primary. Indeed, participants' orientations are key to understanding the differences between the more Foucauldian inspired, critical discourse analysis approach to identity associated with some forms of discursive psychology (for example, Wetherell and Edley 1999), and the more CA-inspired discursive approach to identity developed here (Speer 2001a).

According to Schegloff "one should take for analysis only those categories that people make relevant (or orient to) and which are procedurally consequential in their interactions" (Antaki and Widdicombe 1998: 4). Participants can be said to 'orient to' something when they treat it is as significant for, or pertinent to the interaction at hand (4-5). Thus, we can 'orient to' what you have said as if it were an invitation, an accusation, or as a joke. We can 'orient to' you as our sister, a teacher, or as a feminist, and so on (5). Since the requirement is that these orientations are analytically tractable, the conversation analyst — and the discursive psychologist who wants to remain faithful to CA principles – generally avoids relying on the analysts' prior assumptions about demographic and contextual features, such as participants' age, gender, sexual orientation, goals, and so on. They treat these things as (potentially) worked up and made relevant in the interaction, not as external determinants (see Widdicombe 1998). One of the goals of CA, and a DP informed by it, is to explicate the orientation of participants *to* those contexts.[5] Crucially, if gender and/or prejudice *are* relevant to the participants in an interaction, then they will be *oriented to*; that is, treated as significant or pertinent to the interaction as it proceeds (Antaki and Widdicombe 1998).[6]

(iii) Resistance and cognition

Butler is concerned to grasp the juncture at which resistance and the resignification of gendered meaning and hate speech is possible. In her attempt to provide a more even-handed account of subject constitution and resistance than that provided by Foucault, she returns to a notion of the psyche, the "internalisation" of norms, and "psychic excess" (see Butler, in Bell 1999: 164 and Butler 1997b). As Butler (1997b: 86) notes: "the psyche, which includes the unconscious… is precisely what exceeds the imprisoning effects of the discursive demand to inhabit a coherent identity to become a coherent subject." In other words, the unconscious works as a "destabilizing force" (McNay 1999: 175, 184), enabling agency and resistance. However, Butler is keen to note that the psyche is not separate from 'the social'. Instead, the psyche is "an effect of the interiorization of social norms" (McNay 1999: 176). In other words, the psyche and the social are contingently related to one another. They are not ontologically distinct and secure realms (the psyche cannot be conceived as pre-social, nor the social as extra-psychic [Butler 1997b: 19]).

While DP is also concerned to transcend the psyche/social (agency/determinism or creativity/constraint) dualism, it suggests a rather different way of proceeding. DP treats descriptions of the psyche, the unconscious and cognitive states, like descriptions of the (social) world, as things which are used in talk to do business (Edwards 1997, Potter and Edwards 2001). Consequently, resistance is not treated as the outcome or instantiation of agentive psychic and social processes made possible through the internalisation and displacement of constraining social norms. Instead, it is a discursive and *interactive*, action oriented accomplishment (see Widdicombe and Wooffitt 1995). For discursive psychologists, the 'causal locus' for resistance, as it were, is interaction, not cognition.

(iv) Hate speech and the management of prejudice

Butler's argument that it is at least partially an indexical matter whether the status of an utterance is derogatory or not (and that this problematises simplistic attempts to legislate around issues of hate speech) is compatible with the DP approach to prejudice and evaluation. However, her use of concepts such as 'linguistic injury' and 'offence' is rather more problematic. For example, these terms seem to imply a cognitivist account in which some speech is deemed to have psychological (and possibly also physical) effects that can be located in unitary 'individuals' – a position profoundly antithetical to post-structuralism and Butler's own form of anti-essentialism.

One anti-cognitivist route into dealing explicitly with such issues is provided by DP. In line with the critique of cognitivism set out above, within DP, prejudice is conceived not as some off-loading of pre-packaged, relatively stable, measurable attitudes emanating from within either the person's psyche or in 'wider' society. Instead, prejudicial attitudes and evaluations (like all attitudes and evaluations) are locally finessed, and constructed in talk to do business (Billig 1989, Edwards in press, Gill 1993, Potter 1998, Puchta and Potter in press, Wetherell and Potter 1992). In DP the 'effects' of prejudice are not located in, nor necessarily discernible from the overt 'reactions' or 'injuries' of the victim. Instead, potentially negative responses may be oriented to by those responsible for prejudice in interaction. Indeed, one of the features of such talk is that participants can be shown to be orienting to, or taking into account a range of possible 'uptakes' or effects as they speak, to "the possibility that the account might receive an unsympathetic or sceptical hearing" (Hutchby and Wooffitt 1998: 196). Again, one advantage of DP is that since it works with transcribed segments of data involving prejudice or hate speech *in action*, it can demonstrate precisely how prejudice is constructed, and reproduced on the page, along with its (interactional) effects and outcomes. Readers can then assess the validity of the analyst's claims, and reach their own independent conclusions.

5.   Speech acts, practices and orientations: Hate speech and heterosexism in action

In the analyses that follow, our concern is to illustrate some of these points of contrast between Butler and DP, using real-life materials from a range of settings. Our analytic task is to provide a discursive reformulation and *analytic demonstration* of the production and management of heterosexism, and the (interactional) mechanisms of resistance.

As we have seen, part of Butler's (1997a: 71ff) concern in *Excitable Speech* is to explore the consequences of legal definitions of 'injurious' speech and of hate speech as action, to determine what is at issue for legal practitioners in particular cases. By exploring whether participants themselves orient to their talk as heterosexist or problematic in some way, we hope to build on debates around the identification and constitution of Butler's concepts of 'acts' or 'performatives' of hate-speech (specifically, heterosexism) *in action* and the problematics associated with seeking legal remedy.

Butler has shown how defining hate speech from within a legal framework is no straightforward matter. We argue that this difficulty is not limited to theorists of jurisprudence. Indeed, we *demonstrate* that when we explore instances of heterosexism in action, it is rather difficult to identify an objective, concrete 'thing' called hate speech or heterosexism in participants' accounts that works in uniformly heterosexist and oppressive ways (indeed, on some occasions it is not clear whether our extracts qualify as explicit examples of hate speech in the traditionally defined sense of the term at all). Instead, we suggest that what counts as heterosexism and prejudice is precisely what is at issue for the participants. Therefore, rather than defining in advance of our analysis what counts as an instance of heterosexist talk, we explore what might count as an instance of heterosexism from a *participant's* perspective. We ask, can we understand the workings of heterosexism (and 'hate speech'), without resorting to interaction-external explanations or definitions?

We identify a range of ways in which participants construct, orient to, and work to deflect accusations of prejudice and potential counters. In doing so, we hope to provide a richer, analytically grounded understanding of some of

Butler's (and DP's) concepts, and open a productive dialogue between them.

The three extracts that we analyse below are taken from a larger corpus collected as part of a project exploring the constitution of gender and sexuality in talk about leisure (for more on this, see Speer 2000). They include data from a range of media and social scientific contexts, including an informal interview, a political talk show and a television documentary. While these extracts do not explicitly index purportedly 'hateful' words such as 'queer' 'dyke' or 'faggot' (excepting the ironic reference to 'poof' in Extract 3), this does not mean that the participants themselves do not *orient to* their talk as hateful or problematic in some way. Indeed, the extracts were chosen as representative of the range of ways in which participants can be said to orient to heterosexism in their talk. To oversimplify, these range from the rather *inexplicit* orientations associated with Brian Suter's management of an anti-gay agenda in Extract 1, through to the more *explicit* orientations exemplified in Ben's attempt to 'do being liberal' in Extract 2. Extract 3 represents an instance of resistance or resignification in practice, where the participants *exploit* het erosexist talk for another critical, subversive purpose. This sheds further light on the constitution of (orientations to) prejudice in the first two extracts.

Extract 1 is taken from BBC Television's *Question Time:* a British political question-and-answer panel show. We focus on the talk of one of the panellists, Brian Suter, a Scottish businessman who is well known publicly as someone who wishes to retain Section 28 — the clause in British law which bans teachers from "promoting" homosexuality as a "pretended family relationship" in schools.[7] Suter works to manage his remarks in a way that makes him, and his argument, appear rationally arrived at.

It is impossible to tell what the *effect* of his remarks might be, and the extent to which – to use Butler's terminology – they may have caused linguistic injury or offence. However, it is through the careful management and rhetorical design of his account that we 'find' as it were, Brian Suter's implicit orientation to possible uptakes and the *interactional* — as opposed to *psychological* — effects of his remarks. In this way, Suter works to pre-empt and deflect the potentially negative reaction that he takes to be engendered by his comments.

Extract 1 Question Time, BBC1, 11th May 2000
'David C': Studio audience member and questioner
'David D': The host

1 David C: I would like the panel to tell us, (.)
2   what they think the impact would be: (.)

3		↑on pupils ↓lives, (.)
4		when Section 28 gets ↓dropped.
5		(.)
6	David D:	If it does (.)
7		and when it does get dropped,
8		what will the impact ↑be?
9		Bri↑an ↑Suter
10		(0.8)
11	Brian S:	°Well° Section 28=
12		=we have to look at why
13		it came to being in the first ↓place.
14		(0.4)
15		It came into being in the first ↓place,
16		(0.4) because politically correct coun↓cils
17		(0.2) were putting material to children
18		in ↓schools,
19		(.) which parents found
20		completely unaccepta↓ble.
21		(0.2)
22		Material ↓like (.)
23		"Jenny lives with Eric and Martin"
24		(.)
25		And that's what started the whole process↓off.
26		(0.9)
27		The problem with Section 28 ↓is (0.2)
28		there's >a group o' people<
29		within the community (.)
30		who feel (.) it's an equality issue.
31		(1.0)
32		And the issue about equality ↓is,
33		(.) they're saying (.) that (.)
34		sexual equality is ↓right.(0.4)
35		And ↑we don't h:ave a problem with that
36		as par↓ent's (.)
37		for a↓dults.
38		(0.4)
39		The ↑problem here is (.)
40		we're talking about what we teach
41		our chil↓dren.
42		(.)

43	And so for <u>mo</u>st people in the coun↓try,
44	(.) it's not <u>s</u>een as an e<u>qua</u>lity issue,
45	(.) it's <u>s</u>een as a mo<u>ra</u>lity issue.
46	(0.6)
47	We have a law that <u>s</u>ays (0.4)
48	tha<u>t</u> a <u>m</u>an can only (.) marry one wo↑man. (.)
49	It dis<u>cri</u>minates (.) against people (.)
50	who would be: (0.6)
51	wanting to be pol↑ygamous.
52	(0.8)
53	It's <u>that</u> way because it's a <u>mo</u>ral issue:,
54	and the ↑law is <u>ba</u>cking up (0.2) a moral ca:se
55	(0.2)
56	and <u>that</u>'s what Section 28 is a↓bout.

There are at least three features of this extract which help us to understand why and how Suter constructs his justifications to retain Section 28 in the way that he does, and which provide evidence of his orientations to potential counters and (interactional) effects.

First, one of the most striking features of this extract from a DP perspective is how Suter works to avoid presenting his comments *as* views. This extract is almost entirely bereft of evaluative descriptions such as 'I think', or 'I feel', unqualified opinion statements, and so on. Suter does not answer the opening question on its own terms (indeed, the question is already asymmetrically weighted against the argument that Section 28 should and will be retained: "when Section 28 gets dropped" [line 4] and "If it does and when it does get dropped" [lines 6-7]). He does not talk about the *effects* of dropping Section 28, or what *he* 'thinks' as a 'panel member'. Indeed, he begins his answer using the qualifying word "well" (line 11), which indicates that his reply will be tailored to his own agenda. He proceeds to construct his own basis for legitimately adopting his particular position. He says, "we have to look at why it came into being in the first place" (lines 12-13). This initiates a detailed narrative which establishes the legitimacy and rationality of Suter's views. Note that he never gets to his *actual* views — whatever they may be. Instead this 'origin story', as it were, provides a readymade warrant for retaining it. The retention of the section is justified through the process of its own legislative existence.[8]

In considering the details of the narrative that follows, it is clear that despite having been asked a question about what he 'thinks', Suter manages his remarks in such a way that their content cannot be directly attributed to him — or at least not to him alone. He does not talk in the first person, but uses some careful footing (Clayman 1992) to defer accountability for the motivation to retain Section 28 onto a range of non-present others. He says, "parents found" (line 19), "a group o' people within the community who feel" (lines 28-30), "they're saying" (line 33) "for most people in the country" (line 43), "it's seen" (line 45), and "a law that says" (line 47). The implication is that Suter's cause is instigated from 'without' – from *factual* and *external* features of the world such as the improper actions of "politically correct" councils (line 16), not from some prejudice about 'gays' that emanates from within his psyche.

He refers to 'we' rather than 'I', which is something that people tend to do when speaking on behalf of an institution or community. This gives an apparent credibility to his argument, implying that others align with him, and that he is simply voicing their concerns (particularly those of "parents" – see lines 35-36 where this is made explicit, "*we* don't have a problem with that *as parents*" [our emphasis]). He says "we have to look" (line 12), "we don't have a problem with that" (line 35), and "we're talking about what we teach our children" (lines 40-41). In this way, Suter avoids mentioning his own views about lesbians and gay men. He situates himself as the helpful messenger rather than the lone bigot.

Second, by using a combination of repetition and pauses at the end of each clause, Suter works to demonstrate that he is constructing his response in a clear, ordered, and thoughtful manner. Note, in particular, the repetition of "it came into being in the first place" (lines 13 and 15); "it's an equality issue", "the issue about equality is", "an equality issue", "it's seen as a morality issue", "it's a moral issue" and "a moral case" (lines 30, 32, 44, 45, 53, 54); "the problem with Section 28 is", "we don't have a problem with that" and "the problem here is" (lines 27, 35 and 39); as well as "it's not seen as" and "it's seen as" (lines 44 and 45). Some of these repetitions form part of a contrast structure. Contrast structures are rhetorical formats used regularly in political speeches to generate applause (see Atkinson 1984 and Heritage and Greatbatch 1986). They contain first and second parts that are similar in length, wording, and structure. For example, in this extract there are at least two readily identifiable contrasts: first, "we don't have a problem with that as parents", "the problem here is we're talking about what we teach our children" (lines 35-36 and 39-41); and second, "it's not seen as an equality issue", "it's seen as a morality issue" (lines 44 and 45). Contrast structures work because the speaker contrasts one argument with another in such a way that their own position is seen to be favourable (Hutchby and Wooffitt 1998: 233). Indeed, Suter uses repetition and contrasts to demonstrate the importance of his message, to give force and a weighty credibility to the argument made, and thus a sense of its own facticity.

Third, the language of morality, and the appeal to parental concern and acceptability throughout this extract, work to construct the retention of Section 28 as motivated by culturally exalted values upheld in law, not by the hatred or prejudice of isolated individuals. So, we have several narrative characters: innocent "children in schools", "our children" (lines 17-18, 41); the "parents" who are concerned to protect them (lines 19, 36); comparatively bad characters such as "politically correct councils" who were "putting" gay literature to children in schools (line 16-17); the "group o' people within the community" (line 28-29) who see the issue in terms of equality rather than morality; and "polygamous" people who are, for Suter, justifiably discriminated against in law (line 51). Finally, Suter appeals to the law as the upholder and arbiter of morality. The law becomes an agent in its own right ("a law that says" – line 47), with the implication that since it discriminates against certain people who are immoral, then the law's own (superior) morality justifies its (discriminatory) existence, including the existence of Section 28.[9]

It is in this way that Suter works to justify the legitimacy of his political position. While heterosexism is not explicitly indexed anywhere in this account (he does not use openly derogatory or offensive language, and nobody shouts "you are being heterosexist!" or "that was a heterosexist comment!"), one could argue that Suter demonstrates what he *treats as* accountable and requiring care. While it is difficult to gauge whether he is successful (whatever 'success' may mean on these occasions), Suter nonetheless orients to and works to manage what he takes to be the possibly negative uptakes of his comments. He works to pre-empt and deflect such uptakes by constructing an account which is rhetorically robust, where no one individual can be held responsible for the claims made. The DP approach thus helps us to understand precisely how prejudice is made possible in relatively liberal contexts. It does so at a level of detail that would be obscured if we were to focus solely on abstract theorizations of speech acts divorced from their contexts of use.

While Suter's concern is to present (arguably prejudiced) arguments in a way that limits his personal accountability for them, in the next extract, the participants' concerns are rather different. Sue interviews a friend of hers called Ben – a man in his mid-twenties — in his home. In the moments preceding this sequence, Sue asks Ben if he has ever been to a gay club, and he describes a time he went with his girlfriend and some of her friends "coz she was intrigued". We join the interaction approximately halfway through the interview, at a point where Sue asks Ben if the man that he says "chatted him up" in a gay bar was "attractive".

Extract 2 SAS 27/12/97: B: 28

```
 1  Sue:    Was he attractive?
 2              (0.6)
 3  Ben:    Phh.
 4               (1.8)
 5          I s'pose he was reasonably well looking,
 6          ↑Yeah.
 7               (1.6)
 8          But you know it doesn't interest me,
 9          (.)
10          I'm definitely (0.8)
11          Not interest(h)ed(h) in(h) men(h).
12  Sue:    hhh.
13              (0.8)
14  Ben:    You know I think,
15          yeah some men as- as,
16          I'm sure it's the same for women (0.6)
17          find (.) other men–
18          think that other men–
19          "he looks really good".
20          (0.4) That's definite.
21          You know,
22          some men will deny that
23  Sue:    Mm
24  Ben:    but I know people who I think
25          "bloody-hell he's absolutely awesome (.)
26          figure, awesome".
27          You know.
28          (.)
29          Looks cool.
30          Totally and utterly.
31          Because I know I don't.
32          You know the- the- the Adonis type=
33  Sue:    =Mm=
34  Ben:    =physique and
```

35		(.)
36		whatever, you know
37	Sue:	Mm

Ben works to be seen as a liberal who is both heterosexual and non-heterosexist. While he does not produce, nor is he treated by Sue as having produced, what Butler and others might term an injurious or offensive speech act, it is nonetheless clear that Ben, like Suter in the previous extract, attends to the *possibility* that his remarks may be heard as prejudiced or troublesome in some way. Again, *what counts as* hate speech or prejudice is not just a concern for analysts, but is precisely what is at issue for the participants.

Indeed, there are a range of features of this extract that are interesting from a DP perspective. Unlike Suter in the previous extract, here Ben produces descriptions of his thoughts and feelings, his knowledge and his (sexual) interests. In each case, these are locally produced and finessed to manage the indexical demands of the interview situation. In this context, for example, Ben is clearly orienting to Sue's potential uptake and possibly also to the uptakes of any potential audience to the interview.[10] Ben's extended turn indicates that he treats what he says as accountable and delicate, and as raising issues that might have implications for his identity as a possibly gay and/or heterosexist person.

Sue's question about the man in the gay bar, "was he attractive?" (line 1), sets up a possible dilemma for Ben, or conflicting demands for accountability, which have implications for his (sexual) identity. Indeed, it could be said to trigger his sexual orientation into becoming relevant or at risk in the interview situation. On the one hand, if Ben answers "yes, he was attractive", then he may be held accountable for being gay himself, with the associated difficulties that such a 'coming out' may bring for the subsequent interaction (Kitzinger 2000, also this volume). On the other hand, if he responds "no, he was not attractive", he may be interpreted as anti-gay, or perhaps as someone who is in denial about his own sexuality. Either action, said immediately and without qualification, may indicate that Ben has already considered the attractiveness of this man, *prior* to being asked, with the associated, potentially problematic implications for his identity this may bring. It is important to note that these possibilities are not simply the analyst's speculation, but are oriented to by Ben, and are therefore tractable within the data, and in this case, within Ben's carefully crafted response. Ben manages these conflicting possibilities by constructing an identity as somebody who, at this moment, is neither gay nor homophobic, *nor* someone who ponders the issue of men's attractiveness on a routine basis.

Lines five onwards are particularly interesting for what they tell us about what Ben *treats as* accountable and relevant to his identity. First, Ben constructs his response in such a way that indicates he has not thought about whether the man in the gay bar was attractive or not *until now*. He pauses, demonstrates some difficulty with Sue's question ("Phh."), pauses again, and proceeds to say "I s'pose he was reasonably well looking, yeah" (line 5). This construction works to present Ben's views as not previously having been thought through or articulated. Since he has to construct an answer 'on the spot', Ben demonstrates that this is not something he has a readymade attitude or opinion about. The description "reasonably well looking" is interesting for its (productive) vagueness. While the word 'attractive' may indicate sexual interest or desire, "reasonably well looking", as a rather minimal, non-committal response, does not. The move from such vagueness to the upgraded specificity of "but you know it doesn't interest me" (with the "it" presumably meaning 'gay behaviour') (line 8) and "I'm definitely' not interested in men" (lines 10-11), may be motivated sequentially by the long 1.6 second pause (line 7). Indeed, the pause comes at a transition relevance place (Sacks, Schegloff and Jefferson 1974), but Sue does not come in. Ben treats Sue's non-response as evidence that his prior turn was insufficient, as requiring a further account. His response is interpolated with laughter, which diffuses the delicacy of the situation at the same time as orienting to it as such.

Having established that he is not gay, Ben works to deflect the possibility that his remarks may be interpreted as prejudiced (that he says he is not interested in men because he is homophobic, for example) *or* be taken as a sign that he is in denial about his own sexual identity. First, like Suter in Extract 1, he shifts footing, conceding that "some men" "think that other men – 'he looks really good'" (lines 15 onwards). The footing shift, along with the active voicing (Wooffitt 1992) allows Ben to defer accountability for his views about attractive men onto non-present others. Thus, he delicately manages his attempt at liberalism in a way that cannot be (mis)interpreted as deriving from his own peculiar male body-loving sensibilities. This view gains legitimacy through his reference to women (line 16) and through his claim that it is "definite" (line 20). These views are not peculiar to *him*, nor are they exclusively related to his gender. They are inclusive, applicable across the sexes (and thus also to Sue, the interviewer). Note that he repairs "find" to "think that other men 'he looks really good'" (lines 17-19). Not only is 'thinking' rather different from 'finding' — a subjective matter of opinion rather than an automated biological response associated with sexual attraction or desire — but looking "really good" is, like "reasonably well looking" on line five, rather vague in comparison to claiming that men are 'attractive'. The phrase "some men will deny that" (line 22) is marvellously robust, able to account for all possible circumstances: individuals who say other men are *not* good looking are in denial, while those who *do* think other men are good looking render Ben 'normal'.

Having ascertained this general rule, Ben upgrades the voicing of "he looks really good" to a 'blokish' "bloody-hell he's absolutely awesome figure, awesome" (line 25-26). The contrast in this upgrade, between what Ben voices "some men" as saying, and what he himself 'thinks', presents Ben as even more liberal than these others. Moreover, while this provides evidence that Ben is not averse to commenting on, and appreciating the looks of other men, it is, again, a carefully constructed description of the "cool" stature and god-like "physique" of certain men, and is not about their intrinsic sex appeal. Ben, therefore, positions himself as someone who is able to admire what other men look like, without finding them attractive in a homoerotic sense.

It is through this carefully managed accounting and identity work that Ben highlights (and at the same time constructs) the (commonly treated as) non-normative nature of the phenomena that he purports to be liberal about. In other words, his delicacy, and the *necessity* for management of issues around same-sex attraction, is evidence for the way homosexuality is treated as accountable and problematic in culture. Moreover, to the extent that Ben treats his comments as requiring work, and despite — or perhaps *because* of — Sue's minimal uptake, he treats homophobia (rather more explicitly than Suter) as relevant and something that requires orienting to at this moment.

So far we have considered two extracts in which the speakers orient to heterosexism in different ways. In the first extract, Suter sets about managing his anti-gay agenda in a way that makes it appear rationally arrived at, motivated by a community-based concern, rather than personal bigotry. In the second extract, Ben manages the difficulties associated with being asked if he finds a man "attractive" by constructing himself as liberal rather than anti-gay. Our analysis of both extracts demonstrates how heterosexism does not have to be explicitly or overtly indexed for it to be oriented to. Again, simplistic notions of speech acts, hate speech and their purported effects, cannot capture the subtleties of identity work and the interactional (rather than psychological) reasons for what is going on in these extracts.

Naming someone a 'poof' or a 'queen' need not always or necessarily be treated as heterosexist by the participants. As we have seen, Butler sets about exploring how it is that the speaker can reclaim words and use them for another purpose. The indexicality of language, or, in Butler's (1997a: 14) terms, the "open temporality" of the speech act, means that certain derogatory terms can be resignified and reclaimed for more positive, political purposes, in such contexts as rap music, political parody and satire. One of the advantages of DP is that it can capture those moments where resistance and resignification occur in practice, in real life situations. Unlike Butler, we do not treat resistance as (potentially) intrinsic to each performative re-citation. Nor do we treat it as something that is made possible by the *internalisation* and displacement of constraining social norms. Instead, we (re)theorise resistance as topic: as a discursive and interactive accomplishment that is constructed sequentially across turns (see Widdicombe and Wooffitt 1995).[11]

In the final extract, the concerns of the speakers are rather different. This extract is taken from *Gaytime TV Special* — a television documentary on the 1998 Gay Games in Amsterdam.[12] It is presented by Richard Fairbrass — an 'out' gay man – who is commenting on a football match between a gay and a straight team. Here, the participants use irony to problematise just the sorts of accounts Suter and Ben produce in Extracts 1 and 2. The speakers exploit and thereby ironize what they take to be a problematic heterosexist script, displaying their orientation *and* resistance to the normativity and futility of just such arguments.[13]

Extract 3: Gaytime TV Special: A Report on the Fifth Gay Games in Amsterdam (1998, September 5), BBC2: 4.

```
 1  Fairbrass:   This is a >really curious thing<.
 2                (.)
 3               You have erm (.) all these queens here (.)
 4               who: at any other time during the week,
 5               >would be< out clubbing and er,
 6               getting all their gear together and er,
 7               having a wonderful time and .hhh
 8               and >everything else<
 9               and being queens,
10               (.) and then you come here,
11               (.) and suddenly
12               football has turned everybody (.)
13               into a lager swilling ↑yob. (.)
14               I mean they just (.)
15               and they all sing the team songs
```

16   and they all-
17   they all start "GO ON MY SON"
18   and er y- you know it's j'st
19   where's it all ↑come from?
20   ((cameras cut to football match))
21 Man shouts: "It's a game for men not poofs"
22 Fairbrass: This heterosexuality
23   suddenly came out of nowhere.

Richard Fairbrass sets up a contrast between what he constructs as two seemingly incompatible scripts (Edwards 1994): the script for homosexuality, and the script for football playing. While "queens" ordinarily go out clubbing, "getting all their gear together", "having a wonderful time", and "everything else", and "being queens" (lines 3 9), footballers, on the other hand, are "lager swilling yob[s]", who "sing the team songs" and say things like "Go on my son" (lines 12-17). Together, these activities constitute "this heterosexuality" (line 22).

The irony (or the 'restaging of the ritual' in Butler's terms) comes in the juxtaposition of these two seemingly incompatible scripts, and in the ambiguity that Fairbrass indicates their juxtaposition engenders: "this is a really curious thing" and "where's it all come from?" (lines 1 and 19). In highlighting this incongruity, Fairbrass constructs this as a peculiar and accountable phenomenon: how can football turn queens – whom we typically associate with certain behaviours – into lager drinking heterosexuals? To emphasize the ridiculousness of this proposition, Fairbrass relies on the very script that he is working to subvert. He makes a mockery of stereotyping and category boundedness by playing up the implausibility in an extreme and scripted fashion, such that the implausibility itself appears ridiculous.

The interjection by the man on the sidelines shouting, "it's a game for men not poofs" (line 21), is rather neatly edited in by the producers of the programme at this particular moment in the sequence. It is juxtaposed within Fairbrass's narrative, coming clearly at the end of his rhetorical question (a transition relevance place), alongside images of gay footballers. The man's comments work *as* irony precisely because he seems to be working to make available the possibility that he is stereotyping gay men, or engaging in some form of sexual reductionism. Instead, however, his interjection, through its ironic placement, works to highlight the social construction of sexuality and the mechanisms through which heterosexuality comes to be seen as normative. Fairbrass' "this heterosexuality suddenly came out of nowhere" (lines 22-23) works to make *heterosexuality* and not homosexuality accountable —

which is precisely the opposite of what is typically held accountable in culture. The familiarity and repeatability (or iterable nature) of the script provides the framework for its own subversion, highlighting its normative but culturally constructed and problematic nature (for more on irony and prejudice, see Speer in press).

6. Judith Butler, Discursive Psychology, and the politics of conversation

We hope to have conveyed the distinctive features of a discursive approach as it can be applied to some of Butler's key concepts. Butler offers a theoretically sophisticated route into an analysis of gendered and prejudiced talk. What her approach lacks, however, is an examination of the *local accomplishment* of gendered and prejudiced actions in real-life situations. Instead of relying on abstract, idealized speculations about speech acts separated from their use in specific contexts, DP details the precise mechanisms through which certain forms of hate speech are constituted and managed in speakers' talk.

We argued that heterosexism is a particularly pertinent concept to explore in this respect, because, as Butler has shown, gender and sexuality are contingently related to one another. Heterosexism normalizes heterosexuality and buttresses a rigidly demarcated two gender system. Heterosexist *talk* relies on and invokes normative notions of gender and sexuality, policing their boundaries, consequently telling us much about the construction of both.

We have highlighted a number of ways in which heterosexist talk is oriented to and managed: in explicit orientations to liberal sentiments via a demonstration of the appreciation of other men's bodies; and in the presentation of an anti-gay agenda as rationally arrived at through an origin story narrative, careful footing and the discourse of community concern, care and responsibility. Finally, we have examined an instance of resistance or resignification in practice, which is achieved through the ironic juxtaposition of scripts.

One theme to come out of our analysis and which takes some of Butler's ideas in new directions, is that hate speech — and prejudice more generally — does not need to be explicit to be oriented to. Indeed, we demonstrated that what *counts as* prejudice is often precisely what is at issue for the participants, as they work to pre-empt and manage potentially negative uptakes. This is not a cognitivist approach to orientations and uptakes, where a person is understood to have been mentally or emotionally injured, offended or wounded. Within DP, such terms are themselves treated as available categories for descriptions and uptakes, which at any moment may be made relevant to the task at hand. Moreover, within DP, identities are not performatively constituted until they congeal in recognizable forms, their stability and coherence (however partial and tenuous) achieved through a process of re-citation. Instead, identity construction is topicalised as part of the business of interaction. Therefore, one's status as prejudiced, hateful or otherwise is constantly 'up for grabs'.

Likewise, while Butler discusses the problematics of legal definitions of speech as action, making reference to a variety of cases, we *demonstrate* the local instantiation of such problematics in actual talk. We build on and develop Butler's arguments by demonstrating how the status of talk as heterosexist, offensive or not, is not pre-determined, invariable and legislated in advance of the interaction (though of course it can be — for political or legal purposes [see Butler 1997a]), but is something that may or may not be treated as relevant on any given occasion and oriented to. Indeed, one of the most interesting features of Butler from a DP perspective, is her refusal to develop a legalistic yardstick against which to measure the injurious power of speech. Butler argues that words do not carry their meaning with them, but can be re-inscribed, and used in more positive ways. However, since she works at such a level of abstraction, the processes through which this re-inscription might come about remain largely unspecified. DP, in contrast, and as we have shown, *is* able to demonstrate precisely how this process operates, and how prejudiced talk can be ironized, inverted, and resisted on particular occasions, and in specific contexts.

We have explored how Butler and DP might be brought into a productive dialogue. Butler offers new ways of thinking about social psychological concepts, and new routes into an analysis of the politics of conversation. However, she fails to demonstrate the processes through which a coercive 'heteronormativity' — which so keenly binds us to restrictive notions of normative gender and sexuality – is constructed and maintained. DP provides an analytically tractable method for just such a project. Ultimately, we will be in a better position to identify, 'deconstruct' and 'disarm' hate speech (and other forms of prejudice), if we can chart the mechanisms of its constitution. It is likely that further exploration of Butler's ideas using DP will prove fruitful.

Notes

* We would like to thank Victoria Clarke, Paul McIlvenny and one anonymous reviewer for their comments on an earlier version of this chapter.

1. Heterosexism describes "a *diverse set of social practices* — from the linguistic to the physical. . covert and overt. . *in which the homo/hetero binary distinction is at work whereby heterosexuality is privileged"* (Plummer 1992: 19, emphasis in original).

2. In the United States there is considerable disagreement over which speech acts should be interpreted as speech and which as conduct in the legal sense (Butler 1997a: 20). Butler demonstrates how the State has used the distinction between speech and conduct strategically to further its own political interests. Thus, she says "arguments in favor of the collapse of the speech/conduct distinction tend to strengthen the case for state regulation and to suspend reference to the first Amendment. Arguments that insist that speech acts are speech rather than conduct, on the other hand, tend to work in favor of suspending state intervention" (1997a: 20). Butler illustrates this point with reference to three telling examples. In the Supreme Court case of R.A.V. v. St. Paul, the burning of a cross in front of a black family's house was interpreted as protected speech rather than speech and conduct. It communicated a message of inferiority but was not an act of discrimination (1997a: 20). Pornography, on the other hand, has been interpreted as both speech *and* conduct: it injures as it represents. This particular conceptualisation has, in turn, justified the growth of censorship laws. Butler suggests that this "ascription of such magical efficacy to words" is repeated in the context of the US military, where to 'come out' as lesbian or gay is treated as a homosexual *action*, and penalized accordingly (1997a: 21).

3. For further discussion of gender-based language reform see Ehrlich and King (1992) and McConnell-Ginet (1989).

4. While the analysis of ideological dilemmas and rhetoric is DP rather than CA, it is not incompatible with the focus on participant orientations developed here. For example, participants themselves orient to such dilemmas as relevant, and interact or account accordingly. Rhetorical analysis also shades into CA in its concern with the way members' talk may be designed to address what Hutchby and Wooffitt (1998: 196) call a "wider culturally based scepticism".

5. Cf. Wetherell and Edley's (1999) "synthetic approach", which, they say, enables them to join the "macro" ("top down") and "micro" ("bottom up") elements of context, and, in terms reminiscent of Marx's famous dictum, "to embrace the fact that people are, at the same time, both the products and the producers of language" (338), or "the master, and the slave, of discourse" (Edley and Wetherell 1997: 206, 1999: 182).

6. While Schegloff (1997) claims that gender does not have to be explicitly mentioned or 'indexed' (for instance, by using 'he', 'she', 'bloke', and so on) to be 'oriented to', there is some debate about what might count, analytically, as an inexplicit orientation (this is a complex set of issues taken up in more detail in this volume by Kitzinger and by Stokoe and Smithson).

7. As Kitzinger (1994: 128) says, this is "widely understood actively to endorse the removal of pro-gay literature from the shelves of public libraries, and the sacking of openly lesbian or gay teachers in schools".

8. This may provide a rather neat parallel with, and analytic exemplification of Butler's (1990a, 1993) arguments around performativity, and how a performative re-citation naturalizes a purportedly essential gender identity.

9. Cf. Butler's concern with the performativity of morality and the law in regulating hate speech (1997a: 43ff).

10. It is important to note that the presence of an interviewer in this extract means that it is possible to track a social science agenda through it. The interviewer, for example, structures the talk by making certain issues and identities relevant and not others. Likewise, in such contexts, the 'respondent' or 'interviewee' tends to orient to the research interview as relevant by speaking-as-a-generic-person who is keen to offer a suitably qualified response (as opposed to the type of unencumbered and spontaneous 'chat' that one might expect to find in more 'naturally occurring' materials) (see Potter and Wetherell 1995). Nonetheless, we would like to emphasise that we are treating these as natural materials in the specific sense that we are not privileging the actions and orientations of the researcher, but are instead treating her as an active implicated part of what is going on, whose actions and orientations are equally studiable for issues related to heterosexism. If the participants' institutionally structured status (as interviewer/interviewee) is relevant to the interaction, then, it will be oriented to.

11. A focus on sequentiality does not limit the analyst to exploring conversational turn-taking between two or more participants. Rather, it can be equally applied to the sequential organization of monologues, long stretches of narrative and the kind of extended one-person sequences that may be gathered from interviews, for example (see Wooffitt 1992, who applies a CA mentality to an analysis of the sequential organization of lengthy one-speaker accounts of paranormal experiences, and Hutchby and Wooffitt's 1998: 185ff discussion of monologic data).

12. This extract is rather different from the first two. For example, it is not an interactional encounter but a form of mediated speech that has been assembled through editing for public broadcast. However, this does not mean that it is any the less analysable *as* discourse, as talk-in-interaction. Indeed, the audience may be figured as a potential interlocutor, whose potential uptake or response needs to be taken into account by the current speaker. These potential uptakes can be encouraged or exploited by the programme makers by editing talk alongside visual imagery. This can create rhetorical contrasts which engender the audience's scepticism in the facticity of claims, as it does in this extract at line 21 (Pomerantz 1988/1989; see also note 11 on the analysis of monologues).

13. The process of ironization works in the opposite way to that of fact construction. Rather than attempting to reify descriptions as solid, literal and independent of the speaker, the process of ironization works to present those same descriptions as partial, invested, or the product of stake and interest (see Clift 1999 and D'hondt in this volume).

References

Antaki, Charles and Widdicombe, Sue (eds). 1998 *Identities in Talk*. London: Sage.
Atkinson, J. Maxwell. 1984 "Public speaking and audience responses: Some techniques for inviting applause". In *Structures of Social Action: Studies in Conversation Analysis*, J.M. Atkinson and J. Heritage (eds), 370-409. Cambridge: Cambridge University Press.

Austin, J.L. 1962 *How to Do Things With Words*. Oxford: Clarendon Press.

Bell, Vikki. 1999 "On speech, race and melancholia: An interview with Judith Butler". *Theory, Culture and Society* 16(2): 163-174.

Billig, Michael. 1989 "The argumentative nature of holding strong views: A case study". *European Journal of Social Psychology* 19: 203-223.

Billig, Michael. 1996 [1987] *Arguing and Thinking: A Rhetorical Approach to Social Psychology*. Cambridge: Cambridge University Press.

Billig, Michael, Condor, Susan, Edwards, Derek, Gane, Mike, Middleton, David and Radley, Alan. 1988 *Ideological Dilemmas: A Social Psychology of Everyday Thinking*. London: Sage.

Butler, Judith. 1990a *Gender Trouble: Feminism and the Subversion of Identity*. New York: Routledge.

Butler, Judith. 1990b "Performative acts and gender constitution: An essay in phenomenology and feminist theory". In *Performing Feminisms: Feminist Critical Theory and Theatre*, S-E. Case (ed.), 270-82. Baltimore: The Johns Hopkins University Press.

Butler, Judith. 1993 *Bodies That Matter: On the Discursive Limits of 'Sex'*. London: Routledge.

Butler, Judith. 1997a *Excitable Speech: A Politics of the Performative*. New York: Routledge.

Butler, Judith. 1997b *The Psychic Life of Power: Theories in Subjection*. Stanford, CA: Stanford University Press.

Clayman, Steve E. 1992 "Footing in the achievement of neutrality: The case of news-interview discourse". In *Talk at Work: Interaction in Institutional Settings*, P. Drew and J. Heritage (eds), 163-198. Cambridge: Cambridge University Press.

Clift, Rebecca. 1999 "Irony in conversation". *Language in Society* 28: 523-53.

Derrida, Jacques. 1976 *Of Grammatology*. Baltimore, MD: The Johns Hopkins University Press.

Edley, Nigel. 2001 "Conversation analysis, discursive psychology and the study of ideology: A response to Susan Speer". *Feminism & Psychology* 11(1): 136-140.

Edley, Nigel and Wetherell, Margaret. 1997 "Jockeying for position: The construction of masculine identities". *Discourse & Society* 8 (2): 203-17.

Edley, Nigel and Wetherell, Margaret. 1999 "Imagined futures: Young men's talk about fatherhood and domestic life". *British Journal of Social Psychology* 38: 181-94.

Edwards, Derek. 1994 "Script formulations: An analysis of event descriptions in conversation", *Journal of Language and Social Psychology* 13(2): 211-247.

Edwards, Derek. 1995 "Sacks and psychology". *Theory and Psychology* 5(3): 579-96.

Edwards, Derek. 1997 *Discourse and Cognition*. London: Sage.

Edwards, Derek. 1998 "The relevant thing about her: Social identity categories in use". In *Identities in Talk*, C. Antaki and S. Widdicombe (eds), 15-33. London: Sage.

Edwards, Derek. in press "Analyzing racial discourse: A view from discursive psychology". In *Analyzing Interviews on Racial Issues*, H. Van den Berg, H. Houtcoup, and M. Wetherell (eds). Cambridge: Cambridge University Press.

Edwards, Derek, Ashmore, Malcolm and Potter, Jonathan. 1995 "Death and furniture: The rhetoric, politics and theology of bottom line arguments against relativism". *History of the Human Sciences* 8 (2): 25-49.

Edwards, Derek and Potter, Jonathan. 1992 *Discursive Psychology*. London: Sage.

Ehrlich, Susan and King, Ruth. 1992 "Gender-based language reform and the social construction of meaning". *Discourse & Society* 3: 151-166.

Fish, Stanley. 1994 *There's No Such Thing as Free Speech... And It's a Good Thing Too.* Oxford: Oxford University Press.

Gill, Rosalind. 1993 "Justifying injustice: Broadcasters' accounts of inequality in radio". In *Discourse Analytic Research: Repertoires and Readings of Texts in Action*, E. Burman and I. Parker (eds), 75-93. London: Routledge.

Hepburn, Alexa. 1999 "Derrida and psychology: Deconstruction and its ab/uses in critical and discursive psychologies". *Theory and Psychology* 9(5): 639-665.

Heritage, John. 1984 *Garfinkel and Ethnomethodology.* Cambridge: Polity Press.

Heritage, John and Greatbatch, David. 1986 "Generating applause: A study of rhetoric and response at party political conferences". *American Journal of Sociology* 19: 110-57.

Hutchby, Ian and Wooffitt, Robin. 1998 *Conversation Analysis.* Cambridge: Polity.

Jagose, Annamarie. 1996 *Queer Theory: An Introduction.* New York: New York University Press

Kitzinger, Celia. 1994 "Anti-lesbian harassment". In *Rethinking Sexual Harassment*, C. Brant and Y.L. Too (eds), 125-147. London: Pluto Press.

Kitzinger, Celia. 2000 "Doing feminist conversation analysis". *Feminism & Psychology* 10(2): 163-193.

Livia, Anna and Hall, Kira. 1997 "'It's a girl!' Bringing performativity back to linguistics". In *Queerly Phrased: Language, Gender, and Sexuality*, A. Livia and K. Hall (eds), 3-18. New York: Oxford University Press.

Lloyd, Moya. 1999 "Performativity, parody, politics". *Theory, Culture and Society* 16(2): 195-213.

McConnell-Ginet, Sally. 1989 "The sexual (re)production of meaning: A discourse-based theory". In *Language, Gender and Professional Writing*, F. Frank and P. Treichler (eds), 35-50. New York: Modern Language Association.

McNay, Lois. 1999 "Subject, psyche and agency: The work of Judith Butler". *Theory, Culture and Society* 16(2): 175-193.

Plummer, Ken. 1992 "Speaking its name: Inventing a lesbian and gay studies". In *Modern Homosexualities: Fragments of Lesbian and Gay Experience*, K. Plummer (ed.), 3-25. London: Routledge.

Pomerantz, Anita. 1988/89 "Constructing skepticism: Four devices used to engender the audience's skepticism". *Research on Language and Social Interaction* 22: 293-314.

Potter, Jonathan. 1996a *Representing Reality: Discourse, Rhetoric and Social Construction.* London: Sage.

Potter, Jonathan. 1996b "Discourse analysis and constructionist approaches: Theoretical background". In *Handbook of Qualitative Research Methods for Psychology and the Social Sciences*, J.T.E. Richardson (ed.), 125-140. Leicester: BPS Books.

Potter, Jonathan. 1998 "Discursive social psychology: From attitudes to evaluative practices". *European Review of Social Psychology* 9: 233-266.

Potter, Jonathan and Edwards, Derek. 2001 "Sociolinguistics, cognitivism and discursive psychology". In *Sociolinguistics and Social Theory*, N. Coupland, S. Sarangi and C. Candlin (eds), 88-103. London: Longman.

Potter, Jonathan and Wetherell, Margaret. 1987 *Discourse and Social Psychology: Beyond Attitudes and Behaviour.* London: Sage.

Potter, Jonathan and Wetherell, Margaret. 1995 "Natural order: Why social psychologists should study (a constructed version of) natural language, and why they have not done so". *Journal of Language and Social Psychology* 14(1-2): 216-22.

Puchta, Claudia and Potter, Jonathan. in press "Manufacturing individual opinions: Market research focus groups and the discursive psychology of attitudes". *British Journal of Social Psychology.*

Sacks, Harvey. 1995 [1992] *Lectures on Conversation: Volumes I and II* (Edited by G. Jefferson). Oxford: Blackwell.

Sacks, Harvey, Schegloff, Emmanuel A. and Jefferson, Gail. 1974 "A simplest systematics for the organization of turn-taking for conversation". *Language* 50(4): 696-735.

Schegloff, Emmanuel A. 1997 "Whose text? Whose context?" *Discourse & Society* 8(2): 165-187.

Speer, Susan A. 2000 *Talking Gender and Sexuality: Conversations About Leisure.* Unpublished PhD Thesis. Loughborough University, UK.

Speer, Susan A. 2001a "Reconsidering the concept of hegemonic masculinity: Discursive psychology, conversation analysis and participants' orientations". *Feminism & Psychology* 11(1): 107-135.

Speer, Susan A. 2001b "'Participants' orientations, ideology, and the ontological status of hegemonic masculinity: A rejoinder to Nigel Edley". *Feminism & Psychology* 11(1): 141-144.

Speer, Susan A. in press "Sexist talk: Gender categories, participants' orientations and irony". *Journal of Sociolinguistics.*

Speer, Susan A. and Potter, Jonathan. 2000 "The management of heterosexist talk: Conversational resources and prejudiced claims". *Discourse & Society* 11(4): 543-572.

Stokoe, Elizabeth. 1998 "Talking about gender: The conversational construction of gender categories in academic discourse". *Discourse & Society* 9, 217-40.

The Concise Oxford English Dictionary. 1995 [Ninth Edition]. Oxford: Clarendon Press.

Walker, Samuel. 1994 *Hate Speech: The History of an American Controversy.* London: University of Nebraska Press.

Wetherell, Margaret and Edley, Nigel. 1999 "Negotiating hegemonic masculinity: Imaginary positions and psycho-discursive practices". *Feminism & Psychology* 9(3): 335-56.

Wetherell, Margaret and Potter, Jonathan. 1992 *Mapping the Language of Racism: Discourse and the Legitimation of Exploitation.* London: Harvester Wheatsheaf.

Widdicombe, Sue. 1998 "Identity as an analysts' and a participants' resource". In *Identities in Talk,* C. Antaki and S. Widdicombe (eds), 191-206. London: Sage.

Widdicombe, Sue and Wooffitt, Robin. 1995 *The Language of Youth Subcultures: Social Identity in Action.* London: Harvester Wheatsheaf.

Wooffitt, Robin. 1992 *Telling Tales of the Unexpected: The Organization of Factual Discourse.* London: Harvester Wheatsheaf.

CHAPTER 6

Negotiating gender identities and sexual agency in elderly couples' talk

Liisa Tainio

1. Introduction

The participants in conversational interaction can be described under a multitude of identity categories in respect to their gender, sexuality, age, ethnicity, nationality, occupation, and so on. However, the available categories are not necessarily oriented to by participants themselves in their interaction. Through mutual negotiations participants work up to certain identities during the talk-in-interaction by aligning to or resisting certain features of categories connected to specific identities (Antaki and Widdicombe 1998). Ethnomethodologists, particularly those informed by Harvey Sacks' work on membership categorisation, study identities in interaction by analysing the ways in which identities are used in talk, concentrating on the ways that people as speakers or recipients of talk understand the categories as relevant for the on-going situation also at the local level of the interactional organisation. Participants display their orientation to certain membership categories and social identities in their turns at talk in certain sequential contexts. The analyst should be aware of the subtle organisation of the talk by attending to the sequential analysis of the on-going talk-in-interaction, and also by attending to the linguistic organisation of the activities in which the participants are engaged (Schegloff 1997).

In this chapter I analyse the ways in which elderly couples display their discourse identities and social identities in informal, conversational interviews. The method used is ethnomethodological conversation analysis (see, for example, Sacks 1992, Heritage 1984). Firstly, I discuss the concepts of gender and heterosexuality in the light of the conversation analytic approach. Then I introduce my data, and move on to analysis. I analyse the participants' orientations to the discourse identities, such as speaker, recipient, addressee and overhearer (see, for example, Goodwin 1987, Greatbatch and Dingwall 1998). These identities also make visible some more institutional speaker roles — such as 'interviewer' and 'interviewee'. I treat discourse identities as a platform for 'macro' social identities that participants invoke within their turns at talk especially in the light of gender categorisation (Greatbatch and Dingwall 1998: 122). I investigate the actual language used by the interactants by focusing on syntactic and semantic choices that the participants make and align to in the course of the conversation. Finally, I discuss the meaning of these conversational practices in the light of the participants' identity work.

Although some of the practices that I investigate in my analysis are derived from the analysis of a larger data corpus (see Tainio 2000), I concentrate here on a single case. According to David Silverman (1999: 414-415), the "aesthetic" of the methodology of Harvey Sacks consists of, for example, the principles of "smallness" and "slowness". By 'slowness' Silverman means the methodological attitude that at first the question 'How' should be studied carefully, and only after having answered it we should go on to the question 'Why'. The term 'smallness' refers to the conversation analytic practice of focusing on small interactional sequences in order to show the range of meanings and perspectives constructed in them. In this chapter I follow the maxims of smallness and slowness by analysing in detail only one set of extracts from my data corpus that contain several interviews of elderly heterosexual couples living in the countryside in mid-western Finland. However, I also try to move from the question 'How' towards the question 'Why' by analysing the social identities the participants negotiate and orient to in the course of the conversation. In this respect my chapter offers an empirical contribution to the debate between conversation analysts and critical discourse analysts (see, for example, Schegloff 1997, Wetherell 1998, Billig and Schegloff 1999) by discussing further whether and how such concepts as gender, heterosexuality, and (sexual) agency can be taken into account in the studies of the sequential, grammatical and semantic aspects of talk-in-interaction.

There has also been discussion on the importance of taking into account doing, acting and agency as crucial parts of the identity-constructing process (see, for example, Roberts and Sarangi 1999: 229). In my analysis I show how the interactants align to, resist and reconstruct the gendered characteristics that are seen to be category-bound features of the participants as representatives of the category. However, not all of the features are brought into the conversation openly. Some of them are implicated so that it is possible for the recipients to draw conclusions about the participants on the basis of the 'inference-rich' categories in question. In doing this the interactants also elegantly exploit the syntactic and semantic possibilities available in language — which in my data is Finnish. The gendered aspects of the categories are brought into the conversation, for example by marking agency in different ways. In the grammar of Finnish there are several syntactic choices to mark agency. The participants make use of specific grammatical features that help constitute certain kinds of social agent in informal interaction as well as within a larger political process (see Duranti 1994). This is done by negotiating the roles of the participants as (heterosexual) actors in talking about the elderly couple's courtship memories that contain sexually oriented teasings. I focus especially on the local negotiation of the features of the category 'elderly woman'. The characteristics connected to membership categories may also present inferential problems which can provoke stereotypes that may be negotiated in the course of the conversation (see Widdicombe 1998: 53), as can be seen also in the analysis of the data presented here. Consistent with the conversation analytic approach, this chapter takes a stance that the social identities of the participants can best be studied through the activities of the interactants, in naturally occurring interactional settings where the work of category ascription, construction, and maintenance is observable and available for detailed analysis. I show how the more linguistic or discourse oriented approaches (for example, Duranti 1994, Mills 1995) can be applied to studies within the field of ethnomethodological conversation analysis. In addition, the chapter is a test of the usefulness of the conversation analytic perspective to feminist approaches to language use (see Kitzinger and Frith 1999).

2.   Social identities and gender categorisation

The social identities invoked by the participants in interaction are frequently connected to sex/gender, which seems to be one of the most likely candidates for an "omni-relevant" category in social interaction (see Sacks 1992a: 590-596, West and Zimmerman 1987). In my data the social identities made relevant in the interaction include 'male' and 'female', 'wife' and 'husband' and 'aged person'. These categories are seen in the light of Harvey Sacks' (1992a: 40-48) early work on membership categorisation devices. Membership categories are seen as inference-rich; that is, if a person is considered as a representative of a certain category, say 'wife', it is commonly inferred by recipients that she

— as a member of that category — has certain attributes and engages in certain category-bound activities, eg. 'being heterosexual', 'running a household' (Sacks 1992a: 179-181, Antaki and Widdicombe 1998: 3-4, Beloff 1993). What is assumed about the category can also be invoked as being relevant to the person and her activities in talk-in-interaction (Widdicombe 1998: 52-53). This is why I also analyse the ways participants handle the gendered aspects of the identity categories made relevant in the course of the conversation.

In this chapter I have chosen to analyse the talk of married couples. Therefore, I have assumed that as the men and women in my data talk as 'spouses', they, in their talk, also engage in displaying themselves as heterosexuals. Although there has been some conversation analytic work on the ways in which people talk as spouses either in everyday conversations (for example, Sacks 1992a: 690, 1992b: 437-443, Goodwin 1987, Lerner 1992, 1993) or in institutional settings such as relationship counselling (Edwards 1998) and divorce mediation (Greatbatch and Dingwall 1998), the display of heterosexuality has not usually been the focus of the analysis.

In conversation analysis and in other ethnomethodological approaches to interaction, it is common to use the analysts' own cultural knowledge as a resource for analysis in the same way that the participants use their cultural knowledge as a resource in their conduct (Antaki and Widdicombe 1998: 10). In his famous study of Agnes, an inter-sexed adolescent who had been born as a boy, Harold Garfinkel (1967) demonstrated that members of society — including Agnes herself — constructed their observations and behaviour according to the "natural attitude" toward sex status (see Heritage 1984: 180-198 for a summary and McIlvenny this volume for a critical review of Garfinkel's study of Agnes). The member's natural attitude consists of "real and objective facts", for example that there are only two natural and invariant sexes with no exceptions to be taken seriously, and that the fundamental criterion for one's sex are the nature of one's genitals (see Kessler and McKenna 1978: 112-115). In addition to these "facts", Agnes also highlighted several social category-bound features and activities to assure other people of her gender. The most important social evidence for her was to have a heterosexual boyfriend; that is, to prove that she too was a 'normal' heterosexual (Heritage 1984: 187). In other words, Agnes constructed her life in accordance with the members' overall orientation to heterosexuality, which some would call 'heterocentricity', 'compulsory heterosexuality', or 'heteronormativity' (see, for example, Kitzinger and Wilkinson 1993). In her case, she relied on an assumption that at least persons who are dating someone of the opposite sex are seen as heterosexual. The implied feature of heterosexuality in the "natural attitude" seems to predominate (Beloff 1993, McIlvenny this volume). Therefore, I see talk in and about heterosexual relationships as an important topic for studies focusing on the ways in which many people display their 'ordinariness' and achieve their status as 'normal' representatives of their gender in conversational interaction (Hollway 1995: 86-90).

3. Data

My data corpus consists of conversational interviews that were originally made for the purposes of dialectology.[1] The interviewers were to find old local people who had lived at the same place most of their lifetime and who therefore could speak the most 'pure' and traditional variety of the dialect in question. In order to catch the appropriate speech variant on the audiotape, the interviewers asked them, for example, about the old traditions, their former lifestyle and habits, and other kinds of memories they had.

The obvious consequence of the criteria for the selection of interviewees was that the dialect informants were old people. Their average age was 80 years, and, consequently, the couples that were interviewed had usually been married to each other for decades, some even for over 60 years (Yli-Paavola 1970: 35-37, 40.). This was one good reason for my decision to analyse these conversations, since I have been interested in the ways in which men and women speak as spouses (Tainio 2000) and in this data the interviewees are well rehearsed in the art of 'spouse talk'.

My analysis here arises partly from my earlier work on the conversational interviews of the elderly couples (Tainio 2000). The phenomenon of "spouse talk", or "couple's talk", was originally discussed by Harvey Sacks (1992a: 690, 437-443). He meant by "spouse talk" the kind of talk that makes relevant for the recipients that certain participants constitute a socially available and observable team — a (heterosexual) couple — whose members know each other very well, share mutual experiences and life history, and are able to anticipate their interactional reactions and even their inner states (Peräkylä 1995: 103-143). The spouses talk together, to each other and about each other with certain conversational practices that (re)establish and cement their partnership. Such practices include a word search addressed to the spouse as the knowing recipient (Goodwin 1987), completions of the spouse's turns (Lerner 1992), and collaborative story-telling sequences (Lerner 1992, Sacks 1992b:

437-443). Although the old couples negotiate and sometimes even quarrel about the details of the story-telling and about the most 'truthful' versions of their memories, the spouses usually demonstrate their relationship as a couple through agreement, by treating their separate experiences as common, and by agreeing for instance about the appropriate course of the conversation in a specific situation (Tainio 2000). However, the elderly spouses also recognise the right of spouses, as accepted in the community at large, to intrude on the other's right to their own private experiences when talking about each other or on behalf of each other. In the most extreme cases a spouse may act as an authority on the most personal, namely physical, experiences of the other spouse (Tainio 2000).

The data extract introduced below consists mainly of the couples' talk about their courtship memories, sexually oriented teasings and the reception of those teases. In the interviews of the old spouses the topics are usually quite 'decent', and therefore the extract analysed here is a little exceptional. However, this example is rich for the purposes of the study of gendered and sexualised social identities, and that is why I have chosen it. The interviewers are two young students, a man (MI) and a woman (FI), who are around 25 years old, and the interviewees are the wife (born 1888), who was 73 at the time of the interview, and her husband (born 1887). The conversation took place in 1961 at the couple's home in a small village in Reisjärvi. In the preceding talk the female interviewer has been asking about the husband's childhood. He has told that his father forced him to beggar in the neighbourhood. The lines 1-2 still belong to this topic, but quite soon the male interviewer starts to ask about something else.[2]

01	Husband:	siihen minä menin ku se oli niinku tutt:uin
		there I went because it was the most fami:liar
02		pai:kka mull:e niim minä menin siihen.=
		pla:ce for me: so I went there.=
03	FI:	=.jhoo=
		=.yeah=
04	Husband:	=joo:.
		=yea:.
05		(2.5)
06	Wife:	°mm:°,
07		(.)

08 Husband: annappas nyt tummu tul [la.
                okay now you go ahead gr[anma.
                                        [
09 Wife: [(m(h)hh)
                                        [
10 MI: [sittet te olitte
                                        then you were

11   yhtä aikaa sielä Savolassa.
                there at the same time at Savola.

12   (.)

13 Husband: joo.=sielä me oltii yhtä ai [kaa sitte=
                yea.=there we were toge[ther then=
                                        [
14 Wife: [°m(h)mhh°

15 Husband.   –palavelukse-ssa.
                =as live-in farm help.

16   (1.0) ((The wife laughs quietely))

17 Husband: tämä:n: ka[ns.
                with th:is [one here.
                           [
18 Wife: [°m(h)hh m(h) [hh°
                                         [
19 MI: [ja tyttöjä
                                         [and the girls

20   kiusat[tiin.
                were teased.
                      [
21 Wife: [m(h)h m(h)HH mhe mhe
                [mhee he mhehh mheh mheh he
                [
22 Husband: [no:: hohh
                well: hohh

23 Husband: <ei sunkaan   me kiusattu   vaan tytö:t
                <we certainly didn't tease but the girls teased

24   mei:tä>.
                 us.>

25 Wife: m(h)[hh m(h)hh m(h) m(h) m(h)
                     [

26 FI: [he hehh

27   (.)

28 MI: kuinkahan p(h)äin s(h)e nyt oli:, hhh
                 which way round was it, hhh (('who did the teasing?'))

29 Wife: m(h)[hh m(h)hh [m(h)hh m(h) m(h) m(h)
                     [[

30 FI: [ni(h)i hi [hhh
                     yea(h)i hi [hhh
                                 [

31 Husband: [mhehh

32   (.)

33 Husband: täyt-y+hän   0   s'tä   nyt vähä vastaan sitte
                must-SG3-PST+PRT it-PAR now a bit against then
                well one really had to chase them away as

34   hätistellä ku [ne   tul-i   ensin kii:ni.
                chase-INF as they come-PL3+PST first PRT 'stuck to'
                they grabbed us first.
                              [

35 (FI?):   [thi hi

36 Wife: ↓oi:: hyvä: isä h(h)h
                ↓oh:: my Go:d h(h)hh

37 FI: e he he [he hhh
                        [

38 Wife: [.h(h)hhh hhhh[hh
                                      [

39 FI: [°hi hi hi° hh

40   (0.4)

41 Wife: ↑jaa:, (.) 0 valavottaa 0   ett+ei 0 saa
                PRT   keep-SG3+PRE awake that+not can-SG3+PRE
                ↑I see, (.) keeps one awake so one can't

42		nukkua.
		sleep-INF
		sleep.

43		(.)
44	(Wife?):	↑m(h)h
45		(.)

46 Husband: ↓joo̲:[::.
             ↓ye̲a:[::.
                [

47 Wife: [°mm̲::°.

48   (1.0)

49 Husband: se+hän se̲ o̲li+kit   teiän   mi̲eli< a- asia hh
             it+PRT it be-SG3-PST+PRT your-PL favourite thing
             well that really was your favourite< th- thing hh

50   että **0** va̲lavott:aa **0**.
             that   keep-SG3+PRE/-INF awake
             that one was kept awake.

51 Wife: ↑@ja̲a::@ hhh
             ↑@aha̲a:@ hhh

52   (.)

53 FI: **hehehh**

54   (1.0)

55 Husband: .hhh ↓jo̲o:. hh
             .hhh ↓ye̲a:. hh

56   (1.2)

57 Wife: **m(h)**

58   (1.0)

59 MI: palijoko siel'o̲li renkiä.
             how many male workers did they have.

(Tape: SKNA 1229:2; Reisjärvi; A:102-114)

4.   Discourse identities as a basis for identity work

Although the interviews were meant to be informal and the situations every-day-like, there are some specific interviewing practices that the interviewers were advised to follow. For example, the longish pauses (for example, on line 5) are partly the consequence of the interviewers' attempts to give the interviewees as much time and space as possible. At the time of the recordings the interviewers were recommended, for example, not to respond verbally between their questions, not to give feedback by minimal responses, and not to interrupt in order to avoid any kind of overlapping talk (Yli-Paavola 1970: 35-53). In addition to that, the interviewers seem to act as 'orchestrators' of the interaction in other respects, too (see Greatbatch and Dingwall 1998: 125). The interviewees produce most of the responsive activities, such as answers to the questions posed by the interviewers (see lines 1-2).

In order to show the ways in which the participants invoke certain discourse and social identities in the course of the interaction, we have to take a closer look at the turn organisation. I start the analysis of the discourse identities by focusing on the husband's turn "okay now you go ahead granma" on line 8 and on the male-interviewer's turn "then you were there at the same time at Savola." on lines 10-11. With his turn the husband wants to change his role from the 'orchestrated' to the role of the 'orchestrator'; that is, he tries to get his wife to take a turn. However, the male-interviewer does not allow it, and hurries to ask a question addressed to them both: "then you were there" (line 10).[3] It has been demonstrated that in conversation it is common that the "speaker just prior to current speaker [will] be selected as next speaker", as formulated by Sacks, Schegloff and Jefferson (1974: 708). Here the husband — being the just prior speaker — also orients to this practice, and he responds to the interviewer's question on line 10.

The male interviewer demonstrates and reconstructs the division of the participant roles of the interviewer and the interviewee in his turn (lines 10-11). But in addition to this, by aligning to the common practice in conversational interaction (Sacks et al. 1974: 708), he also chooses the husband as the main speaker again, and the husband seems to agree with him. However, this may not be a coincidence. At the beginning of the twentieth century it was common that the researchers of Finnish dialects chose the male speakers as their informants. At that time the interviewers were advised to choose men as their interviewees since men were considered to be better informants because of their clearer and more logical way of talking, and because they were seen to have 'better' knowledge of the tradition than women (Nuolijärvi 1988: 134-138). Of course, at the time of this specific conversation (1961) the attitudes had changed a lot, and women were interviewed as frequently as men. However, in my data collection I still found some strategies of the interviewers that could be interpreted as gendered ones: for example, the interviewers usually took — either implicitly or explicitly — the husband's side when the spouses had disagreements about the appropriate topics or behaviour in the situation (Tainio 2000; see also footnote 4).

In his turn "okay now you go ahead granma" (on line 8) the husband orients to many kinds of identities. Firstly, although the interviewers were the main 'orchestrators' of the interviews, the spouses also frequently asked each other questions in order to clarify their memories to the interviewer. Sometimes the spouses even told each other to do something, for instance, to follow the 'rules' they thought to be an inevitable part of the interview (Tainio 2000). With his directive in line 8 the husband then orients both to his identity as an interviewee and to the identity of a spouse. Furthermore, the husband makes relevant the addressee's social identity as his spouse by establishing their partnership with this specific interactional activity (Schegloff 1997: 182). Secondly, the husband uses the address term "*tummu*" ('granma'). In my data the old spouses do not refer to each other by their first names. They talk to and about each other by using certain local varieties of the address terms 'granpa' or 'granma', address terms which invoke an identity connected to family. Furthermore, the use of the term 'granma' refers also to the identity of an old person, because among even slightly younger persons the spouses usually talk to and about each other by using their first names. So in sum, the husband's turn makes relevant the identities of a spouse-interviewee, of a husband, and of an old person. This is an example of the practice which Charles Goodwin (1987: 119) has formulated in the following way: "While discourse identities are invoked to specific actions within the conversation, they also make visible larger social identities that go beyond the talk itself."

5.   Gender and teasing

According to Paul Drew (1987: 220-221), participants in everyday conversation may show their intimate relationship by teasing each other, and even in more institutional settings participants may achieve an informal atmosphere through humorous teasings. One motivation for humorous teasings is to achieve laughing together, which can be seen as marking intimacy between the participants (Jefferson, Sacks and Schegloff 1987). In the interviews where my extract comes from, joint laughter was frequently pursued by the spouses teasing each other, though sometimes the interviewer also initiated the teases or was teased by the interviewees. Usually the informants oriented to their identity as interviewees by aligning to the mode of talk — for instance, talking nonseriously — initiated by the interviewer. This is what happens also in the data extract analysed here. The teasing sequence starts with the male interviewer's turn "and the girls were teased" (on lines 19-20), and the playfulness of the topic gets them to laugh together during the sequence. The teasing sequence is brought to its end after the participants, especially the spouses, have shown orientation to closing the topic (lines 51-58). Finally, the interviewer starts another and more 'serious' topic (line 59).

Because every activity and turn at talk in interaction routinely and publicly displays the participant's interpretation of the preceding turn(s), the turn starting the teasing sequence (on lines 19-20) can also be seen as a reaction to the previous activities. Just prior to the male interviewer's tease, the husband has responded (line 13-15) to the declarative question concerning the spouses' common past in the farmhouse called Savola (MI, lines 10-11). In his answer the husband uses the pronoun 'we' (in 'there we were together', line 13), and hence shows his orientation to talk also on behalf of his wife. After a pause and the wife's quiet laughter, he continues his previous turn and highlights the wife's role in the current participant framework (see, for example, Goodwin 1984). He shows her to be the target/referent of the talk by using a proximal demonstrative pronoun "*tämä*" ('this one here', line 17), which is a common (and non-offensive) way in Finnish to refer to a co-participant, and which rearranges the participant framework by marking the referent as being a ratified participant without being an addressee (Seppänen 1996: 167-173). Also, after his turn the wife reacts with small laugh particles (line 18). According to Drew, the teasers show with their teases that they have interpreted the preceding activities by the teased as overdoing something (Drew 1987: 232-243). The interviewer's utterance can then be seen as a reaction to the couple's (overdone) orientation to each other which they show with the laughters and with the rearrangement of the participation framework (on lines 13-18). That is, the interviewer sees them start a playful sequence when the interview is in progress. This gets further evidence when the wife starts to laugh in a more joyful manner and in quite a low register (line 21). Because of the laughters (lines 16 and 18) and the colour of the husband's voice (line 17), the interviewer may see the activities as somewhat 'improper' in this context (see Jefferson, Sacks and Schegloff 1987: 160). In any case, the spouses' mutual orientation to each other, initiated by the wife and highlighted by the husband during the sequence (lines 13-18), can easily be interpreted as marking their affection for each other — at least for this tiny moment. In this light, the male-interviewer's turn "and the girls were teased" seem to be an appropriate next to the spouses' 'overdoings', and in the light of the relationship between the interviewees it also seems to imply a slightly sexual tone or content.

By responding to the interviewer's turn (in lines 19-20), the husband takes the role of an addressee. However, in his turn the male interviewer seems to treat the wife as the target of his talk by using the noun 'girls'. In other words, in the formulation of his utterance the male interviewer seems to adopt the participant framework that was rearranged by the husband in his previous turn (line 17): the addressed one is the other male participant, and the target of the talk is the wife. The wife also seems to interpret the participant framework as described since she laughs (on line 21) even more joyfully and in a more louder voice than before. In other words, the participant framework is constructed by the two men as their mutual perspective. This is indicated also at the level of syntax of the men's utterances. In his turn, on line 13, the husband uses the verb form "*oltii(n)*" ('there we *were* together'), which can be used in two grammatical categories in colloquial Finnish: it can be used as marking passive voice, or as marking first person plural, especially when used with the personal pronoun itself, namely "*me*" ('we'). Although the husband uses in his turn the explicit personal pronoun with the verb form "*me ol-tii*" (be-PAS+PST) 'we were' and the male interviewer uses only the same verb form "*kiusat-tiin*" (tease-PAS+PST) 'was teased' without the personal pronoun, the male interviewer's turn offers a fluent syntactic continuation to the husband's turn: "*me oltiin*" + "*ja* ('and') *kiusattiin*" (on lines 13 and 20). So, the two men construct a mutual perspective which is arranged as a 'male perspective' with the help of the use of the word "girls" and by adopting the same participant framework with the help of the syntactic forms of the utterances.[4]

Teasing in interaction is always a potential face threatening activity: the teased one is presented in a humorous light, and the teaser gets to test, for example, her ability to receive the teasings 'po-faced', that is, with "some treatment of the humor of the tease, though usually combined with a po-faced component of rejection/correction" (Drew 1987: 225), or by non-seriously escalating the activity (Jefferson, Sacks and Schegloff 1987: 160-165). Studies of Finnish folklore have noted that formerly, also in the days of the couple's youth, it was common for the male workers of the farmhouse to test the female newcomers. For example, men used to present obscene riddles, and tell naughty jokes to the women or in the presence of the women. However, as many women have told afterwards, the most clever way to react to these sexual teasings was not to react at all but to stay po-faced. (Kaivola-Bregenhøj 1998: 201-202.) We find in this sequence of data that both of the women only laugh, hence they react 'appropriately' to the teasing. However, they do not react verbally. In this respect the participants seem to invoke the gendered cultural expectations; that is, the men tease, and the women remain silent.[5] But after a while, the wife starts to speak. Her contribution to the teasing sequence will be the focus of subsequent analysis.

6.   Transitivity choices and some characteristics of Finnish grammar

There have been many discourse oriented studies of spoken and especially written texts from a feminist point of view (see, for example, Lee 1992, Mills 1995). In particular, studies of written texts have used various linguistic approaches as the starting point for the analysis of the data. Studies of spoken interaction have recently used more 'conventional' linguistics as an important source for analysing the syntax and semantics of conversation (see for example, Duranti 1994, Helasvuo 1991, Sorjonen 1997). In my analysis, I apply results gained from research on (Finnish) syntax and semantics in order to analyse agency and the explicit and implicit identity work that participants are engaged in during their turns at talk. The main focus is the transitivity choices in the participants' utterances. With the help of a detailed analysis of the syntactic and semantic choices, it is possible uncover the subtle negotiations that participants do in the course of the interaction beneath the level of the more sequential conversational activities.

The transitivity choices of written and spoken texts have often been analysed in order to reveal the covert world view and the attitudes towards actors presented in texts (for instance, Lee 1992: 49-64, Mills 1995: 143-158). With the help of transitivity analysis it is possible to show how (social) actors are presented in the clauses as semantic agents — that is, as conscious actors that are able to control their actions — and how they are presented as experiencers who are unable to control their activities. It has also been shown that the roles of male and female actors may vary along these lines as well (see Mills 1995: 143-158). The semantic roles that are important for the present analysis are the 'agent', the independent actor and conscious controller of her activities, the 'target', the object of the agent's activities, and the 'experiencer', the one who acts but whose actions are not under her control (Tainio 1995).

In order to clarify the transitivity analysis below, I have to point out some grammatical features of Finnish. The Finnish passive is different from the passive in English. Firstly, the Finnish passive can also be formed with intransitive verbs. Secondly, the Finnish passive refers always to human actors This is such an essential feature of its meaning that the Finnish passive is sometimes called the Fourth person — and some would like to argue that there is no passive in Finnish at all (Shore 1988). Although the finite verbs in passive voice refer to human actors (in plural), the reference to the subject/actor(s) is left unspecified. Secondly, there is another phenomenon of the Finnish grammar (marked in the transcription with 0) that should be explained before going on with the analysis. For example, in the utterance "*täytyhän 0 s'tä nyt vähä vastaan sitte hätistellä*" ('well one really had to chase them away' [must-SG3-PST+PRT it-PAR now a bit against then chase-INF], line 33-34) the finite verb is in the third person singular form, but the grammatical subject is ellipted (although the translation covers it up). Sentences with this construction have no separate subject or other core constituent. This phenomenon is called a "missing person"-formula, or a zero person formula (Hakulinen 1987). Usually the sentences containing the zero person can be translated into English by using the generic pronouns 'you' or 'one' (Sorjonen 1997: 266). The zero person is a common phenomenon in Finnish syntax, which can also be seen in the amount of zero person-markings in the extract (on lines 33, 41, 50). In many respects the meaning and the functions of the zero person are similar to those of the Finnish passive voice. However, one of the differences is that although it is commonly used in generic clauses, the zero person always refers to a singular human being. In addition to this, it has been shown that the zero person very often refers to the speaker or writer of the utterance, especially in the sentences containing modal verbs (Hakulinen 1987: 144, 151).

7.   Negotiating agency

In my data, by their negotiations, the participants construct different kinds of social and cultural identities connected to the members' categories that the participants use in their conduct about themselves or about and to the recipients of the talk. They negotiate the identities of 'male' and 'female' in connection with the characteristics '(sexually) active/passive' in the light of their (heterosexual) memories, that is, if the 'male' is seen as (sexually) agentive and the 'female' as the target and the experiencer of the activities, which is the stereotypical scene (see Gilfoyle, Wilson and Brown 1993). In their talk the spouses seem to reconstruct the categories as less stereotypical by using the unquestioned authority that everybody has when talking on behalf of themselves (Widdicombe 1998). Furthermore, the participants also negotiate their identity as 'elderly'. Elderly people are usually seen as a sexually passive, but especially in the light of the wife's turns this common belief is challenged.

To begin the transitivity analysis, we look once more at the male interviewer's turn "and the girls were teased." ("*ja tyttöjä kiusattiin.*", on lines 19-20). In the semantics of the turn, "girls" is clearly in the role of an experiencer and a target. As mentioned earlier, the finite verb in the utterance is in the passive voice ("*kiusat-tiin*" (tease-PAS+PST)). Because of its voice the utterance thus implies agency to unspecified human actors. As explained earlier, the male interviewer aligns to the syntax of the previous turn of the husband's (line 13) by using the finite verb in passive voice. The implication is the mutual 'male perspective' that specifies the unnamed teasers as a male group that includes at least the husband. But in his response "we certainly didn't tease but the girls teased us" (on lines 22-24), the old man turns around the semantic roles of the genders, and thus also the participant roles in the scene of the past events. While continuing the teasing sequence, the husband formulates his turn as having a specific grammatical subject, the pronoun "we" that refers at least to the husband himself. Now "we" is set in the semantic role of an experiencer and a target, and the "girls" are seen as agents, the sexually active teasers. This is also true in the husband's next turn "well one really had to chase them away as they grabbed us first" (on lines 33-34), in which he escalates the non-serious statement (Jefferson et al. 1987: 162). Indeed, the (Finnish) formulation of the clause indicates that he might even be boasting. Here the girls, "they", are the agents.

However, although he seems to "chase the girls away", the husband presents himself as an experiencer, the one who acts as a victim of the external circumstances (lines 33-34). In his previous turn the husband refers directly to himself (line 23). Here (line 33) he uses the zero-person formulation, which is also sometimes used when referring to the speaker himself: "*täytyhän 0 s'tä nyt vähä vastaan sitte hätistellä*" ('well one really had to chase them away'). So, the verb "*täytyy*" ('have to') opens a place for the semantic role of an experiencer, for the 'I' who is seen as a victim of the external circumstances. Hence, the husband's utterance should be read as 'I had to chase them away'. So, in his turn the husband constructs himself as being in the position of an experiencer and a target, who is grabbed by the "girls". In other words, the husband is now finally stated personally and grammatically at the scene of the reminiscence. However, the place of the wife still remains only implied.

As in the preceding turns, the target of the utterance in the husband's turn analysed above is again the wife. The evidence for this interpretation comes from her activities. Namely, at this moment in the interaction, the wife finally starts to talk: after her assessment (line 36), and the joint laughter by her and the female interviewer (lines 37-39,) she develops the topic further on "*jaa. valavottaa ettei saa nukkua.*" ('I see. Keeps one awake so one can't sleep', on lines 41-42). The husband's turn is formulated as a playful accusation against the "girls". Because of the syntax and semantics of the husband's turn the accusation can be seen as nonserious and as addressed to his wife. In everyday conversation the accusations are usually followed by counter accusations or accounts (Dersley 1998). These are also the ways in which the wife's responses can be seen. In the beginning of her turn there is a delayed acknowledgement token *jaa*, which is frequently used as a receipt of news that anticipates subsequent disagreement or disbelief (Raevaara 2000: 187). However, the wife's tone of voice displays orientation to non-serious talk. Furthermore, the continuation of her turn refers quite openly to the sexual aspects of the current topic. However, the nature of the sexual aspects is covert in the syntax and semantics of her utterance; at which we take a closer look next.

As I mentioned above, in the transcription I have marked all the zero persons with 0. In the wife's response to the playful accusation (on line 41) there are as many as three 'missing persons': "*0 valavottaa 0 ett+ei 0 saa nukkua.*" ('0 keeps 0 awake so 0 can't sleep'). What is left unsaid is: (1) the agent: who is the one who does the keeping awake, (2) the target: who is the one who is been kept awake, and (3) the experiencer: who is the one who cannot sleep. For semantic reasons it is reasonable to interpret the two last zeros as having the same reference: the same person is the target as well as the experiencer. As I mentioned earlier, the zero person often refers to the producer of the utterance. In her turn there are then two opposing positions for the zero person — for the 'I': the position of the agent and that of the target/experiencer. Even if the wife is now — in the light of her syntactic choices in her utterance — for the first time more directly involved in the scene of the reminiscence, the character of her presence and her actions still remains unspecified.

In the light of the preceding analysis, the wife's turn and the 'missing persons' in it can be interpreted, depending on the sequential analysis, in two ways. If we take the wife's utterance as a counter-accusation, we should read her turn as: 'you keep me awake so I can't sleep'; where she is in the position of an experiencer/target. But if we take the wife's turn as a continuation of the recalled narrative or scene, and as an account of the latter sentence of the husband's preceding utterance ("as they grabbed us first", on lines 33-34), the wife's utterance should then be read as: 'I keep you awake so you can't sleep' — with the wife as the (missing) agent, and the husband as the (missing) target/experiencer. Neither the prosody nor the sequential position of the turn supports more strongly either of the two opposed interpretations. Both readings remain equally possible for the participants. In other words, the wife's formulation offers a solution to the negotiation over the sexual agencies: it is up to the participants to choose the more active or more passive role of the scene.

And finally, we should take a look at one more syntactic choice in the wife's utterance analysed above. The finite verbs in it are in the present tense while all the other verbs in the sequence are in the past tense, which is the main tense for narratives (Seppänen 1996: 156). However, researchers of story-telling have noticed that in the most important sequences, in the climax of the story, the teller may use the so-called historical or 'dramatic' present tense. It invites the recipients to enter into the events and into the atmosphere of the story (see Helasvuo 1991: 59.) Nevertheless, one function of the present tense is also to describe the state-of-affairs that are generic, reiterated, and relevant for the current moment (Hakulinen and Karlsson 1979: 246-248). In other words, the wife constructs an utterance that can be interpreted as a culmination of the sequence or as marking the action relevant for the moment, or, as both. So this utterance refers most directly to the spouses present because of the tense, and because of the zero persons that refer always to a singular actor and often to the producer of the utterance. Consequently, in terms of tense, the wife turns out to be the one who implies the sexual quality of the relationship of the spouses not only in the past but also in the present.

In his last turn of the teasing sequence the husband pursues the topic again: "*sehän se olikit teiän mieli asia että 0 valavottaa 0.*" ('well that really was your(PL) favourite thing that one was kept awake.', on lines 49-50). He talks to his wife directly now and shows it by using the address term "your", though again in plural form (see footnote 3) and in the past tense. At the end of his turn he repeats the same verb "*valavottaa*" ('to keep (one) awake') which again involves two zero persons as I have marked in the transcription. Again, it is difficult to say if the "you" (the 'girls' including the wife) should be interpreted in this utterance as the ones who keep the boys awake or as the ones who are kept awake. Although the "you" may be a more likely candidate for the agent of the causative verb 'valvottaa' than for the target of the action, we can conclude that, in his turn, the husband does not overtly resist the ambiguity of the agencies constructed by the wife in her previous turn.

In concluding the analysis, I want to argue that both in the wife's and in the husband's turns the identities of men and women, girls (and boys), and the present spouses can be attributed different kinds of agency, either agentive or more passive. Although the husband's turning away from the implication concerning their active sexuality at the current moment emerged in contrast with his wife's use of the present tense, the husband does build his turn on other elements of the wife's turn and her ambiguous transitivity choices in the current participation framework. The sequence is concluded with the result that the 'male perspective' available earlier has changed to the mutual perspective of the old spouses. The perspective of the spouses is now jointly reconstructed, and it goes against the stereotypes (see, for example, Gilfoyle, Wilson and Brown 1993) portrayed earlier in the sequence. In terms of agency, the gender identities — the (hetero)sexual female and male categories — are seen as being more open and flexible than the ones presented in the talk of the younger male interviewer at the beginning of the sequence analysed.

8.   Concluding remarks

In this chapter my aim has been to show with the help of the detailed analysis of the data what kind of "operative" identities (Sacks 1992b: 327) are represented in the course of the conversation, and how these identities are brought out, negotiated, accepted, and resisted. I have looked at the ways the participants responded to each other during the conversation, and how they negotiated the identities of the 'speaker', the 'receiver', the 'interviewer', the 'interviewee', the 'husband', the 'wife' and the 'old'. However, the focus of the chapter was the identities of 'male' and 'female' presented by the spouses in the light of agentivity and sexuality. By the subtle negotiations in their conversational activities as well as the syntax and semantics of their utterances, the spouses reconstructed presentations of (hetero)sexual identities, and they did this in the light of their current partnership.

In the data the male interviewer presents a stereotypical scheme of courtings between men and women, but in his response the husband changes the roles of the actors involved: he claims the girls to be the agents, and the men — "we" — are seen in the position of an experiencer and a target. However, the wife formulates her utterance in a way that still leaves unresolved the 'truth' about the gender of the agent as well as of the experiencer/target. In the utterances of the wife, the agency of the actors involved remains open in terms of the persons present or absent and the location of the actions in the past or present time of the telling (Helasvuo 1991: 57). At the end of the sequence, the husband aligns with the ambivalences of the wife's utterances. In the course of the topical sequence the perspective of the old couple became mutual.

One of the on-sight categorisations that the interviewees are vulnerable to in their interaction is their age (see Paoletti 1998). In many western societies, old people, and especially old women, are not usually considered in terms of an active sexuality. At least in Finland, in the tradition of sexual humour, a sexually active old woman is usually presented as the punch-line of the joke, as the element that offers the unexpected and humorous surprise for the recipients (Vakimo 1998: 308-310). However, in my data extract the identity displayed by the old woman and accepted by her husband included an orientation to (and favourable evaluation of) active (hetero)sexuality. Although the identity or the identities are frequently seen as fragmentary and flexible, by some postmodernists for example, the identities nevertheless still seem to matter to people, and identity politics is still a salient ground on which to contest political discourses. The negotiations over identities can be seen as a powerful means to reproduce political discourses, while at the same time they are necessary for the purposes of the politics of emancipation. However, the processes of stereotyping seem to freeze efforts to create the most appropriate and individual identities for participants. One of the resources to resist or make use of the stereotypes can be found in the resources of the grammar of interaction, which provides the means to negotiate the agentivities of the participants and the descriptions of their actions. It has been suggested that all the grammatical and syntactic formulations and choices in speech — especially those concerning agentivity — are potentially political choices (Duranti 1994). In this light the common, everyday, minimal negotiations about our identities concerning, for example, gender and sexuality in terms of agency, as in my data, are not as unimportant as they seem to be at first sight.

In this chapter I have used a line of analysis that draws upon different fields of studies. I have used conversation analysis as my starting point, and I have suggested that the analysis along the lines of CA is able to give and should give fair space also to other fields, such as more linguistically or discourse oriented as well as feminist approaches to language use. I have also claimed that in order to analyse the identities of the participants such as they emerge in the course of the conversational interaction, the analyst should take a look not only at the overall organisation of the interaction but also at the syntactic and semantic elements of the participants' utterances in their local contexts. With the help of the detailed analysis of talk in interaction on these terms, we have much better possibilities of also understanding the dynamic orientations that the participants themselves use in their continual negotiations of identities during the interaction.

Notes

1. The data comes from the Finnish Language Tape Archives of the Research Center for the Languages in Finland. The dialectologists audiotaped 15000 hours of colloquial speech variation; the task was to make recordings in every Finnish-speaking municipality in Finland and abroad. The interviews are by and large monological, but sometimes the researchers found it better to interview two or more persons at the same time: the result is about 1400 hours of conversational interviews that are appropriate material also for conversation analytic purposes. The recordings took place from the early 1950s until the late 1980s when the task was completed. For the purposes of my special interests (see also Tainio 2000) I selected 10.5 hours of conversational interviews taped between 1961 and 1981. My data consist of all the tapes that were made with married couples living in rural areas in Ostrobothnia, mid-western Finland (eleven couples altogether). I want to thank Erkki Lyytikäinen and Juhani Pallonen for their help with my data collection.

2. Additional transcription and glossing symbols are given below.

SG(1,2,3)	singular (1st, 2nd and 3rd person)
PL(1,2,3)	plural (1st, 2nd and 3rd person)
PAS	passive verb tense
IMP	imperative
PRE	present tense
PST	past tense
INF	infinitive
NEG	negation
PRT	particle
INE	case: inessive 'in'
PAR	case: partitive (partitiveness)
GEN	case: genitive (possession)
0	zero person

3. In Finnish there are different pronouns for 'you' in singular (sinä), and for 'you' in plural (te). Here the plural is used.

4. Here the mutual 'male perspective' was constructed by subtle negotiation of syntactic choices. In other kinds of negotiations the male perspective is much more obvious and

open. These include sequences where the male interviewer reacts to the female interviewee's queries of the appropriateness of her husband's topics. Usually, the MI disagrees
with her and supports his line of talk, as in the following three excerpts (to save space I
present here only English translations):

```
Husband:    . . there >are were< the kind of: poor people who had nothing s- so
            they (.) .hhh hh stayed like one night in one household,=
Wife:       =°maybe we won't now (.) talk about [it°
MI:                                             [oh yes it is, (.)
            [fine to talk (.) ab]out it,=sure.
Wife:       [I see,=is it so.   ]
Wife:       [I see.
Husband:    [yea. (.) .hh so that they stayed like one- one day
            and night and they were usually men . .
```

        (SKNA:13551:1; Ylihärmä; B:16-19)

```
Husband:    .hhh it is like [that nowadays.
Wife:                       [just talk about the things that (.) are asked from
            you:. (0.8) those were not the things you were he he he ask(h)ed
            [ab(h)out.
MI:         [it is okay,
            (.)
Wife:       I s(h)ee ha [ha
MI:                     [it is not so restricted what you (can talk about).
Wife:       .h(h) it is n(h)ot, he [he
MI:                                [no:,
```

(SKNA 8808:1; Kaustinen; A:160-168)

```
Husband:    . . I was at Ooström (.) as a littl- (1.0) I was wa:ndering there in
            the streets and,=
Wife:       =but do not explain it [so thoroughly=
MI:                                [well<
MI:         =[oh you may explain (      )]
Husband:    [then I found a job you know, ]
Wife:       mhe mhe
MI:         was- (.) did you get married at Kempele,
```

(SKNA 13894:2; Haapajärvi; B: 61-69)

In my larger data corpus I also found several occasions where the male interviewee or the
male interviewer sequentially deletes the turns of the female interviewee, and consequently
forms his subsequent turn as an appropriate next to the other male's prior turn (Tainio 2000).

5. Kaivola-Bregenhøj (1998) gives several examples in which men tease and women
remain silent in the earlier peasant culture in Finland. Nowadays, for example, Finnish
schoolgirls and schoolboys appear to follow the same schema (Anttila 1998). This gendered phenomenon seems to be observed widely across times and cultures; see, for example, Apte (1985: 67-81), Mulkay (1988: 120-151), Pizzini (1991) and Crawford (1995: 135,

147). According to these studies, humour is often linked to gender and gendered hierarchies in several kinds of communities. Usually those who have more status are the ones to tease and make jokes. Furthermore, the contents of sexual humour do not usually encourage women to engage in collaborative joking with men.

References

Antaki, Charles and Widdicombe, Sue. 1998 "Identity as an achievement and as a tool". In *Identities in Talk*, C. Antaki and S. Widdicombe (eds), 1-14. London: Sage.

Anttila, Anna. 1998 "Kiusasta kimppaan – tyttöjen ja poikien seurustelusuhteista" ["From teasing to togetherness – the relationship between girls and boys"]. In *Amor, Genus & Familia*, J. Pöysä and A.-L. Siikala (eds), 253-262. Helsinki: Suomalaisen Kirjallisuuden Seura.

Apte, Mahadev L. 1985 *Humor and Laughter. An Anthropological Approach*. Ithaca: Cornell University Press.

Beloff, Hannah. 1993 "On being ordinary". In *Heterosexuality. A Feminism & Psychology Reader*, S. Wilkinson and C. Kitzinger (eds), 39-41. London: Sage.

Billig, Michael and Schegloff, Emanuel A. 1999 "Critical discourse analysis and conversation analysis: An exchange between Michael Billig and Emanuel A. Schegloff". *Discourse & Society* 10(4): 543-582.

Crawford, Mary. 1995 *Talking Difference: On Gender and Language*. London: Sage.

Dersley, Ian. 1997 *Complaining and Arguing in Everyday Conversation*. Unpublished PhD Dissertation. University of York.

Drew, Paul. 1987 Po-faced receipts of teasing. *Linguistics* 25: 219-253.

Duranti, Alessandro. 1994 *From Grammar to Politics. Linguistic Anthropology in a Western Samoan Village*. Berkeley: University of California Press.

Edwards, Derek. 1998 "The relevant thing about her: Social identity categories in use". In *Identities in Talk*, C. Antaki and S. Widdicombe (eds), 15-33. London: Sage.

Garfinkel, Harold. 1967 *Studies in Ethnomethodology*. Englewood Cliffs, NJ: Prentice-Hall.

Gilfoyle, Jackie, Wilson, Jonathan and Brown. 1993 "Sex, organs, and audiotape: A discourse analytic approach to talking about heterosexual sex and relationships". In *Heterosexuality. A Feminism & Psychology Reader*, S. Wilkinson and C. Kitzinger (eds), 181-202. London: Sage.

Goodwin, Charles. 1984 "Notes on story structure and the organization of participation". In *Structures of Social Action. Studies in Conversation Analysis*, J.M. Atkinson and J. Heritage (eds), 225-246. Cambridge: Cambridge University Press.

Goodwin, Charles. 1987 "Forgetfulness as an interactive resource". *Social Psychology Quarterly* 50: 115-131.

Greatbatch, David and Dingwall, Robert. 1998 "Talk and identity in divorce mediation". In *Identities in Talk*, C. Antaki and S. Widdicombe (eds), 121-132. London: Sage.

Hakulinen, Auli. 1987 "Avoiding personal reference in Finnish". In *The Pragmatic Perspective*. Selected Papers from the 1985 International Pragmatic Conference, J. Verschueren and M. Bertucelli-Papi (eds), 140-153. Amsterdam: John Benjamins.

Hakulinen, Auli and Karlsson, Fred. 1979 *Nykysuomen Lauseoppia.* [The Syntax of Finnish.] Helsinki: Suomalaisen Kirjallisuuden Seura.

Helasvuo, Marja-Liisa. 1991 "Who said what? A study of tense variation in spoken Finnish narrative". In *Studies in Finnish Language and Culture.* Proceedings of the Fourth Conference on Finnish Studies in North America, M.J. Luthy (ed.), 57-61. Bloomington: Indiana University.

Heritage, John. 1984 *Garfinkel and Ethnomethodology.* Cambridge: Polity Press.

Hollway, Wendy. 1995 "Feminist discourse and women's heterosexual desire". In *Feminism and Discourse: Psychological Perspectives,* S. Wilkinson and C. Kitzinger (eds), 86-105. London: Sage.

Jefferson, Gail, Sacks, Harvey and Schegloff, Emanuel. 1987 "Notes on laughter in the pursuit of intimacy". In *Talk and Social Organisation,* G. Button and J.R.E. Lee (eds), 152-205. Clevendon: Multilingual Matters.

Kaivola-Bregenhøj, Annikki. 1998 "Pilako vai eroottinen viesti? — seksuaaliarvoitus on testi kuulijalle". ["A joke or a sexual message? — A sexual conundrum is a test for the recipient"]. In *Amor, Genus & Familia,* J. Pöysä and A.-L. Siikala (eds), 165-192. Helsinki: Suomalaisen Kirjallisuuden Seura.

Kessler, Suzanne and McKenna, Wendy. 1978 *Gender: An Ethnomethodological Approach.* Chicago: The University of Chicago Press.

Kitzinger, Celia and Frith, Hannah. 1999 "Just say no? The use of conversation analysis in developing a feminist perspective on sexual refusal". *Discourse & Society* 10(3): 293-316.

Kitzinger, Celia and Wilkinson, Sue. 1993 "Theorizing heterosexuality". In *Heterosexuality. A Feminism & Psychology Reader,* S. Wilkinson and C. Kitzinger (eds), 1-32. London: Sage.

Lee, David. 1992 *Competing Discourses: Perspective and Ideology in Language.* London: Longman.

Lerner, Gene H. 1992 "Assisted storytelling: Deploying shared knowledge as a practical matter". *Qualitative Sociology* 15: 247-271.

Lerner, Gene H. 1993 "Collectivities in action: Establishing the relevance of conjoined participation in conversation". *Text* 13: 213-245.

Mills, Sara. 1995 *Feminist Stylistics.* London: Routledge.

Mulkay, Michael. 1988 *On Humour: Its Nature and Its Place in Modern Society.* Cambridge: Polity Press.

Nuolijärvi, Pirkko. 1988 "Kielenulkoisten taustamuuttujien huomioon ottaminen 1800-luvun ja 1900-luvun alun murretutkimuksissa". ["How the extra-linguistic information was taken into account in the dialectology in 19th century and in the beginning of the 20th century".] In *Kieli 3* [Language 3], J. Kalliokoski, P. Leino and P. Pyhtilä (eds), 117-160. University of Helsinki: Department of Finnish Language.

Paoletti, Isabella. 1998 "Handling 'incoherence' according to the speaker's on-sight categorization". In *Identities in Talk,* C. Antaki and S. Widdicombe (eds), 171-190. London: Sage.

Peräkylä, Anssi. 1995 *AIDS Counselling: Institutional Interaction and Clinical Practice.* Cambridge: Cambridge University Press.

Pizzini, Franca. 1991 "Communication hierarchies in humour: Gender differences in the obstetrical/gynaecological setting". *Discourse & Society* 2(4): 477-488.

Raevaara, Liisa. 2000 *Potilaan Diagnoosiehdotukset Lääkärin Vastaanotolla*. [Patients' Candidate Diagnoses in the Medical Consultation. A Conversation Analytical Study of Patient's Institutional Tasks.] Helsinki: Suomalaisen Kirjallisuuden Seura.

Roberts, Celia and Sarangi, Srikant. 1999 "Introduction: Negotiating and legitimating roles and identities". In *Talk, Work and Institutional Order: Discourse in Medical, Mediation and Management Setting*, S. Sarangi and C. Roberts (eds), 227-236. Berlin: Mouton de Gruyter.

Sacks, Harvey. 1992 *Lectures on Conversation*. Vols. I (1992a) - II (1992b). Ed. G. Jefferson. Oxford: Blackwell.

Sacks, Harvey, Schegloff, Emanuel and Jefferson, Gail. 1974 "A simplest systematics for the organization of turn-taking for conversation". *Language* 50: 696-735.

Schegloff, Emanuel A. 1997 "Whose text? Whose context?" *Discourse & Society* 8(2): 165-187.

Schegloff, Emanuel A. and Billig, Michael. 1999 See Billig and Schegloff 1999.

Seppänen, Eeva-Leena. 1996 "Ways of referring to a knowing co-participant in Finnish conversation". In *SKY 1996. Yearbook of the Linguistic Association of Finland*, T. Haukioja, M-L. Helasvuo and E. Kärkkäinen (eds), 135-176. Helsinki: Suomen kielitieteellinen yhdistys.

Silverman, David. 1999 "Warriors or collaborators: Reworking methodological controversies in the study of institutional interaction". In *Talk, Work and Institutional Order: Discourse in Medical, Mediation and Management Setting*, S. Sarangi and C. Roberts (eds), 401-425. Berlin: Mouton de Gruyter.

Shore, Susanna. 1988 "On the so-called Finnish passive". *Word* 39: 151-176.

Sorjonen, Marja-Leena. 1997 *Recipient Activities: Particles nii(n) and joo as Responses in Finnish Conversations*. Unpublished PhD Dissertation. University of California, Los Angeles.

Tainio, Liisa. 1995 "The bodily self and the hollow self: Finnish everyday stories about the opposite sex". In *Cultural Performances*. Proceedings of the Third Berkeley Women and Language Conference, M. Bucholtz, A.C. Liang, L.A. Sutton and C. Hines (eds), 691-711. Berkeley: Berkeley WLG, University of California.

Tainio, Liisa. 2000 "Pariskuntapuhe ja kokemusten rajat". ["Couples' talk and the boundaries of experience".] *Virittäjä* 103(1): 23-45.

Vakimo, Sinikka. 1998 "'Vieläkö teillä tehdään yötöitä?' — vanhan naisen seksuaalisuuden kuva kaskuissa". ["'Are you still busy at nights?' — The image of the sexuality of old woman in jokes".] In *Amor, Genus & Familia*, J. Pöysä and A-L. Siikala (eds), 291-314. Helsinki: Suomalaisen Kirjallisuuden Seura.

West, Candace and Zimmerman, Don. 1987 "Doing gender". *Gender & Society* 1(2): 125-151.

Wetherell, Margaret. 1998 "Positioning and interpretative repertoires: Conversation analysis and post-structuralism in dialogue". *Discourse & Society* 9: 387-412.

Widdicombe, Sue. 1998 "'But you don't class yourself': The interactional management of category membership and nonmembership". In *Identities in Talk*, C. Antaki and S. Widdicombe (eds), 52-70. London: Sage.

Yli-Paavola, Jaakko. 1970 *Vuosikymmen Kielennauhoitusta: Suomen Kielen Nauhoitearkiston Toimintaa v. 1959-1968.* [A Decade of Taping Speech: The Activities of The Finnish Language Tape Archives in 1959-1968.] Tietolipas 60. Helsinki: Suomalaisen Kirjallisuuden Seura.

CHAPTER 7

Framing gender

Incongruous gendered identities in Dar es Salaam adolescents' talk

Sigurd D'hondt

1. Introduction

In this chapter, I analyse a short fragment of authentic conversational inter-action in Kiswahili, one which I accidentally recorded in the streets of a mid-dle class ('medium density') suburb of Dar es Salaam, Tanzania, in the spring of 1996. The fragment is drawn from a spontaneous, unforeseen meeting between three male adolescents. They are engaged in an exchange of com-ments about the alleged pregnancy (and possible abortion) of a teenage girl walking by inadvertently in front of the veranda where the three are having a conversation. Among the three participants we find N, my informant, and an acquaintance of his, here designated as E.[1] N accidentally bumped into E as he was strolling around in the vicinity of his parents' house, on his way to meet another acquaintance. E, who is trying to raise some extra income as a self-employed (moonshine) house-broker, is talking to a third party, F. The two are standing under the veranda of a shop, discussing the details of a vacant room that might suit one of E's candidate tenants. E is making a drawing in the sand with his toe. The entire encounter lasts no longer than two minutes and fifteen seconds. After about one minute, something unex-pected happens. While E is explaining to N what he and F are up to, a teenage girl living a few blocks away walks by in front of the veranda. The girl, who I shall refer to as 'Julie', immediately attracts E and F's attention. They greet her, upon which she is on her way again. After Julie has gone, a vivid discussion arises between E and F about whether or not she had an abortion recently. The peculiar thing about this part is that it contrasts differ-ent participant responses to mentioning the possibility of an abortion in their talk; the three young men are displaying different orientations to the issue, each of which entails its own distribution of gendered identities across the different parties involved. One participant, my informant N, formulates his stance *vis-à-vis* the abortion by casting himself as a 'Muslim'. Later in the course of the encounter, while two of the three participants (E and F) are working together towards a closing of the topic, N's friend E delivers a turn in which he advances the prospect of possible sexual intercourse with Julie as a warrant for their shared curiosity about the outcome of her pregnancy.

This chapter illustrates one way in which an investigation into N and E's contributions along the lines of conversation analysis (CA) could add to our understanding of how people perform gendered identities. The rich analytical apparatus that CA supplies promises a unique snapshot of the attribution of gender *in action*, of the *procedures* that are involved in devising and distributing gender identities in this single encounter. Both the contribution by my informant N and his interlocutor E's articulation of a heterosexual desire frame 'reality' in a particular way. The distribution of gender identities across the different parties in the encounter, including the 'talked about' party Julie, is an integral, constitutive, feature of this. Given its capacity to make explicit the forms of practical reasoning that inform our everyday activities, CA provides an opportunity to delineate *how* exactly and *by what means* each of these contributions calls its own specific set of gendered identities into being. CA is thus called upon to uncover how gender (and sex) are managed as integral features of a particular social arrangement. One of these arrangements, it turns out, concerns the enforcement of heterosexuality through policing gender identity. In the second contribution that will be analysed, a contextually embedded gender identity is made available through an articulation of heterosexual desire, in a way that in turn draws attention to the participants' onsight categorisability as 'Men' (thus securing at once the validity of heterosexuality as a norm and sex binarism). Here, a participant (E) orients to the apparent sex of himself and his two interlocutors (I shall return to the exact nature of this 'apparent sex' and 'on-sight categorisability' later on) as furnishing a sufficient ground for predicating that they share a sexual interest in the girl they have been talking about (and for publicly divulging such sexual interest as an icon of their virility). In this chapter, I shall refer to these procedures for making gender relevant *in a particular mode* as representing distinct 'interpretative repertoires'. In discursive psychology, the notion of 'interpretative repertoire' was introduced to underscore the socially distributed nature of the linguistic resources that people draw upon in construing accounts of events (Potter and Wetherell 1987). This chapter is also concerned with socially distributed procedures for sense-making, but its primary concern is not factual accounts but embodied identities. I shall therefore reformulate the notion of interpretative repertoire (fusing it with Goffman's 1974 notion of framing) as an aggregate of (tacit) argumentative practices that *frame* the identities of the participants to the encounter (including absent parties) in a socially recognisable way.

The specificity of this fragment also lies in the fact that it juxtaposes *two different* responses to the mentioning of abortion. In this case, the simultaneous mobilisation of two distinct 'interpretative repertoires' clearly presents a problem for one of the participants, as my informant N takes issue with E's display of sexual interest in Julie. The analysis offered below, however, not only accommodates the possibility that different interpretative repertoires articulate incompatible identities, it also explicates how the participants themselves *act upon* the inconsistency between different repertoires. The procedures for highlighting and resolving such inconsistencies will be elucidated in the second part of the analysis.

First of all, however, I would like to take a critical look at the way identity is customarily conceived of in CA. I argue that the narrow sequential conception of context that is currently in vogue in CA investigations of talk in institutional settings promotes a binary conception of identity that makes it unsuitable for the investigation of gender. To investigate gender, this overly restrictive conception of context ought to be expanded, so as to incorporate the participants' *argumentative* practices. In this way, it becomes possible to investigate *how* gender is framed as relevant to the understanding of talk.

2.   Argumentation and framing

The specific nature of gender obliges us to review some of the assumptions informing many currently fashionable CA approaches to uncovering situated enactments of identities. According to Bing and Bergvall (1996), much of language and gender research unwittingly perpetuates dichotomous conceptions of gender by assuming that masculinity and femininity comprise discrete, complementary categories which emanate directly from biological sex. Other authors in this volume have pointed out that, on the whole, CA scholars are reluctant to confront sex and gender issues directly. What could be the origins of CA's blind eye for gender? One possible explanation for this lack of interest could be that the single branch of CA that does explicitly cope with the identification of contextual elements which transcend the local organisation of talk — namely the analysis of talk in institutional settings (for example Boden and Zimmerman 1991, Drew and Heritage 1992) — seems to imply a similar, equally binary conception of identity. First of all, the analysis of talk in institutional settings is constrained by the requirement that the presumed relevance of a proposed contextual feature (or 'institutional' identity) must be grounded in a rigorous analysis of the details of the talk ('procedural consequentiality', see Schegloff 1991, 1992). Useful as Schegloff's injunction may be, when it comes to analysing talk in institutional settings (and identities that transcend the local organisation of talk in general) it brings along serious difficulties. These are partially due to an awkward synergy with what others have diagnosed as CA's impoverished notion of participant orientation. In a sweeping paper[2], Wetherell (1998: 404) criticises CA for its tenet that conversational materials "are adequately analysed when we have described the principal conversational activities and shown how participants' utterances contribute to and are occasioned by these activities". The range of contextual phenomena that participants presumably orient to is hereby artificially limited to the 'organisation of the conversational moment'. When it comes to analysing contextual features other than strictly local organisational identities like 'hearer', 'speaker' and so on, this narrow interpretation of participant context results in a very specific interpretation of procedural consequentiality. If the analyst focuses exclusively on sequential formatting, then the policy to ground characterisations of relevant context in the details of the talk automatically reduces the question of identity to a zero-sum game: either the stretch of talk under investigation *exhibits* the work-related (sequential) design features that are required, or it does *not*. In Schegloff's (1992: 117, emphasis in original) words, "[n]ot all talk at work is work talk. Further, sometimes the parties are not at all oriented to the relevance of the work setting and the related identifications of themselves. Sometimes, although they *are* oriented to its relevance, the setting does not directly contribute to the production of the talk; it is not procedurally consequential." CA practitioners themselves are hardly held back by these self-imposed restrictions. To identify the 'local rationalities' (ten Have 1999) that inform talk and activity in work-related settings, they advance a comparative perspective. First, it is assumed that the turn-taking system for 'everyday' or 'mundane' conversation furnishes the yardstick for rendering the institutional character of a stretch of talk recognisable. The participants call upon the normative expectations associated with mundane talk for displaying to one another in what sense their encounter qualifies as 'institutional': "By selectively reducing or otherwise transforming the full scope of conversational practices, concentrating on some and withholding others, participants can be seen to display an orientation to particular institutional contexts" (Hutchby and Wooffit 1998: 147). For the analyst, this comparative procedure provides an opportunity to pinpoint exactly those junctures at which participants enact an institutional identity, thus grounding the analysis firmly in the details of the talk (and fulfilling the requirement to demonstrate the 'procedural consequentiality' of the identity that is invoked) while at the same time staying well within the limits of CA's narrow sequential conception of context.[3]

In the domain of language and gender, the comparative route for demonstrating the procedural consequentiality of relevant contextual features would inevitably redirect us toward a re-assertion of gender dichotomies based on binary sex categories. One of the obstacles here appears to be that gender identity is qualitatively different from the work-related identities/tasks performed in institutional settings, since it is caught up in a radically different pattern of accountability. Instead of being attached to one particular 'social-structural locus' that can be unequivocally circumscribed, gender may be considered 'omni-relevant'. In principle, individuals can *on any occasion* be categorised on the basis of their perceptually available 'sex'; as a consequence, drawing attention to sex/gender constitutes a continually available resource for making sense of an action (see West and Fenstermaker 1995).[4] It is this elusive nature of gender — the fact it resists reduction to a single 'locus' unequivocally identifiable in a binary fashion — which defies analysis in comparative terms, confounding in particular the dichotomy between the 'mundane' and the 'institutional' on which the comparative version of CA is founded. Like 'age' and 'race', gender is rooted in an array of anatomical/physiological 'predispositions' that are perceptually available and which the individual (allegedly) carries along throughout the different realms and settings that social life is composed of. Let me clarify that in raising the issue of 'perceptual availability', I do not wish to revive received distinctions between 'sex' and 'gender', according to which sex forms part of 'nature' while gender belongs to the realm of 'culture'. It seems more accurate to conceive of these 'predispositions' and their perceptual availability as objects/features that are (re)produced and differentiated discursively, in the practice(s) of assembling a gendered identity. I shall return to this issue when I discuss Goffman's notion of framing.

To escape the pitfall of binarism, this restricted notion of 'relevant context' ought to be expanded. Wetherell's own work indicates one possible direction in which to proceed, namely by incorporating the *argumentative* practices of the participants, which she refers to as the 'argumentative texture' of a data set. In CA, there is another tradition, that of Membership Categorisation Analysis or MCA, which has paid attention extensively to 'argumentative' forms of practical reasoning (see the contributions by Sacks 1972a, 1972b, Jayyusi 1984, Watson 1994, plus the papers in Hester and Eglin 1997 and Antaki and Widdicombe 1998). MCA investigates the way in which participants classify/describe themselves and others, their respective actions, and the interrelationships between these descriptions and actions. In line with its underpinnings in ethnomethodology, MCA approaches these classifications and descriptions not in terms of abstract, inert schemata (of which they allegedly constitute a reflection) but as methodically accomplished activities of which the formal properties are made available in the talk itself, discernible to any competent member. For the investigation of these publicly available formal properties, MCA developed notions such as 'categorisation devices', 'category-bound activities', 'standardised relational pairs', etc. (for an overview, see, for example, the introduction to Hester and Eglin 1997). Zooming in on sequential and categorisation practices 'in a single take' (as Watson 1997 put it) constitutes a valid *modus operandi* for incorporating the argumentative texture of conversation into the analysis. This integrated form of CA investigates on a turn by turn basis *how* participants are oriented to by others as (gendered) persons, *on what grounds* (actions, attributes, etc.) such gendered categorisations are administered and the *formal procedures* that are put to use in that process. In this way, we can work toward a moment-by-moment account of the way the participants accomplish the transformation of 'gender' into a feature that is accountably relevant to the production and interpretation of their talk.

This 'argumentative turn' implies a thorough refashioning of the relationship between talk and identity. This relationship can no longer be conceived of in terms of a strict one-to-one correspondence (according to which 'talk' is interpreted as the sequential organisation of an encounter). Rather, we should imagine the link between the two as constituted in, or mediated by, argumentation. On occasion, as in the case below, this may result in an overt dispute over the sense of a previous utterance. Drawing argumentative practices into the analysis also prompts us to take into account (i) the possibility that an argumentative trajectory may topicalise contextual elements that are themselves of a non-discursive nature, and (ii) the possibility that different argumentative trajectories articulate contrasting, sometimes incommensurable, versions of what might at first sight appear to be a monolithic identity. At this point, I would like to refer to Goffman's (1974) multilayered conception of the social world as composed of different *frames*, emergent levels of reality that are superimposed onto one another, each superseding frame consisting of a transformation of a more primary level. For Goffman, the most basic frame is supplied by the physical environment in which interaction is taking place. Starting from this non-negotiable physical frame upwards, participants are free to negotiate superseding frames that elaborate lower ones, with the single proviso that these new frames should always be grounded in the adjacent lower frame. "Human life has a creative open-ended quality – but only at the 'upper end'" (Collins 1988: 62).

Respecifying this multilayered conception of social life from a conversation-analytic perspective, one could say that a stretch of talk inevitably makes salient (or 'frames') a specific portion of a more elementary frame as a contextual feature (say, an 'identity' or some other aspect of 'reality') that is accountably relevant to its own interpretation. Gendered talk, then, consists of utterances that frame elements of a lower frame, namely one's perceptually available 'anatomical' or 'physiological' sex, as relevant to their own understanding. That these predispositions are 'perceptually available' and belong to a 'lower' frame might be taken to mean that this frame is somehow 'more real' (thus raising suspicions that my discussion of the sex/gender nexus reinstalls biological essentialism). It should be kept in mind, however, that every categorisation of an individual, even those that are based on features which are perceptually available, is by definition a *discursive* act, a form of practical reasoning that is subject to public scrutiny. If 'on-sight' categorisations like 'man' and 'woman' are 'real', they are only so to the extent that they are treated as such (for example, by incorporating them within a judicious framework).

In contrast to the binary view of identity inscribed in the comparative approach, Goffman's multilayered conception of social life does not impose one single interpretation of a contextual feature like 'gender'. To the contrary, it fully accommodates the possibility (i) that 'higher' frames make salient the same portion of a 'lower' frame in various ways, and (ii) that on occasion the participants discover a conflict between two or more perceivably incompatible framings of the same lower frame items. In addition, it also provides ways for the participants to deal with and act upon such emerging conflicts.[5] In the fragment below, a conflict is revealed and subsequently resolved through the co-ordination of different frames, thus creatively exploiting the open-endedness of social reality 'at the upper end'. The disclosure of the inconsistency involves the *reification* of a categorical identity drawn from one frame ('Muslim'), and the identity in question is treated as existing independently from the practical context in/for which it was occasioned (Maynard and Wilson 1980). Resolving this inconsistency is done by re-framing the stretch of talk that appeared to be 'inconsistent' as *ironical* (Clift 1999). The details of these procedures will be elucidated in a later section. In spite of the relative weight it attaches to biological predispositions, the analysis outlined here avoids biological essentialism in that it respecifies the foundational role of these predispositions as a participants' phenomenon. To be sure, the anatomical/physiological predispositions of the participants, to the extent that they are perceptually available, do provide a resource (often) indispensable for performing a gendered identity (and in this sense, the analysis does not succumb to the tacit assumption that participants freely create society 'out of the blue', see Mehan 1991). However, the focal point of the analysis is the forms of practical reasoning that participants employ for transforming these predispositions into contextual features that are interactionally salient (thereby discursively reproducing both 'gender' and 'sex').

3. The fragment

Below, the second part of the encounter, the heated discussion that ensues after Julie's appearance together with the quarrel that precedes N's departure, is reproduced in its entirety. Those portions that are directly relevant to the analysis have been arrowed. The transcription system is based on that of Jefferson (see the appendix to this volume).[6]

088	E:	<u>we:</u> (.) ↑<u>huyu</u> si alikuwa na ↑<u>mi</u>:mba, (huyu).
		PRN2sg DEM1(sg) NEG 3sg-PST-be-FV with pregnancy DEM1(sg)
		hey you wasn't she pregnant, this one?
089		(.)
090	F:	mm?=
091	E:	=↑<u>huyu</u>, ha↑<u>kuwa</u> na <u>mi</u>mba, huyu.
		DEM1(sg) NEG.3sg-PST-be-FV with pregnancy DEM1(sg)
		this one, wasn't she pregnant, this one?
092		(0.5)

093   F: (alikuwa)   na   mimba,   huyu.
             3sg-PST-be-FV with pregnancy DEM1(sg)
             she was pregnant this one

094   (sasa hivi)   sionagi   kapangua.=
             now DEM1(pl) NEG.1sg-see-HAB-PRS 3sg.CNS-disarrange-FV
             but right now I can't see anything   she got rid of it

095   E: =ameshazaa?
             3sg-PERF-give_birth-FV
             has she already had the baby?

096   (1.0)

097   F: sijui   kama   ka↑zaa: au
             NEG.1sg-know-PRS whether 3sg.CNS-give_birth-FV or
             I don't know if she had the baby or

098   ka[pangua.
             3sg.CNS-disarrange-FV
             got rid of it
                [

099 E: [ka↑zaa   lini.
                 3sg.CNS-give_birth-FV when
                 when would she have had the baby?

100   hafu mbona anaonekana   [hana   dalili]
             then why 3sg-PRS-appear-FV NEG.3sg-have symptoms
             and why doesn't she seem to have any symptoms?
                                       [

101   F: [kapangua]   yule   naona.=
                                      3sg.CNS-disarrange-FV DEM2(sg) 1sg.PRS-
                                                                       see-FV
                                      she got rid of it, I see

102   E: =kapangua?=
             3sg.CNS-disarrange-FV
             she got rid of it?

103   F: =mm.=

104 → N: =↑hawa ↑mbona wanapenda   kuua   ua.
             DEM1(pl) why   3pl-PRS-like-fv INF-kill-FV REDUPL
             these (people), why do they like to kill and kill?

105 →   ↑vipi (hawa   yaani).=
         how   DEM1(pl) PRT
         what kind of people are they?

106   E: =eh?

107 → N: hawajui   (athari)   za kuua,   eh?
                                  (hatari)
             NEG-3pl-know-PRS (consequences) CN INF-kill-FV
                                  (dangers)
             they don't know the consequences of killing
             they don't know the dangers of killing

108   (1.0)

109 →   inabidi   siku uwekwe   muadhara,
         3sg-PRS-must day 3sg-call-PASS-SBJ (religious) gathering
          one day they ought to call a muadhara

110 →   uzungumziwe   kuua   tu.
         3sg-discuss-PASS-SBJ inf-kill-FV PRT
         to discuss the issue of killing

111   (0.5)

112   E: huyu   ↑mbona alikuwa   na   tumbo kubwa
             DEM1(sg) why   3sg-PST-be-FV with belly big
             this girl, why did she still have a big belly

113   juzi   juzi   hapa.
       day before yesterday REDUPL DEM1(loc)
       only a few days ago?

114   nasha[ngaa   leo   yuko ↑freshi, [ha↑lafu]
       1sg.PRS-be_amazed-FV today 3sg-be all right moreover
       I am amazed that she is all right now   and
             [[

115   N: [hh:: heh   [↑hih hih]

116   hh [h
          [

117   E: [dalili   ya ku↑zaa,   kweli ↑ile
             symptoms CN INF-give_birth-FV really PRT
             she really has the symptoms of delivering a baby

118   (1.0)

119   F: ku↑zaa,   hajazaa.   (.) kapangua.=
             INF-give_birth-FV NEG.3sg-PERF-give_birth-FV 3sg.CNS-disarrange-FV
             having a baby?   she didn't have a baby   she got rid of it

120   E: =a:u >kajifungua   mtoto< bahati ↑mbaya?
             or   3sg.CNS-give_birth-FV kid   luck   bad
             or did she have a miscarriage?

121   N: inaweze↑kan[a   vilevile]
             3sg-PRS-be_possible-FV   also
             that's also possible

                           [

122   F: [<labda ina]wezekana.>
                           maybe 3sg-PRS-be_possible-FV
                           maybe it's possible

123   (1.0)

124   ↑kama siyo bahati mbaya, basi kapangua   (**).
             if   NEG luck   bad   PRT 3sg.CNS-disarrange-FV
             if it is not a miscarriage then she got rid of it

125 → E: kama yupo   sa↑lama,   tuanze   u:pya.
             if   3sg-be good health   1pl-start-SBJ anew
             if she is all right   let us start all over

126   (1.5)

127 → N: kwani wewe: una::::   ↑vipi, si   una↑swali   wewe?
             CNJ PRN2sg 2sg-PRS- how   NEG 2sg-PRS-pray PRN2sg
             but you, you d-   how? don't you pray, you?

128 → E: eh?

129 → N: si   una↑swali   wewe.
             NEG 2sg-PRS-pray PRN2sg
             don't you pray, you?

130 → E: >sasa nataka   kuoa<
             now   1sg.PRS-want-FV INF-marry-FV
             this time I want to get married

131 → N: >aa:. unataka   kuoa.   s(h)awa sawa.
                   2sg-PRS-want-FV INF-marry-FV same same
                   you want to marry   all right then

132 →   a[salaam a<u>lei</u>(gh)kum<]
             peace be upon you
             [
133 → E: [heh heh <u>heh</u>:]

134   (.)

135 → N: ↑<u>hih hi</u>:h

136   (1.5)

137 → E: KA:ZI <u>KU</u>BWA BWANA.
             work big   mister
             a big job mister

138 → N: <u>SA:</u>WA BWANA.
             same   mister
             indeed mister

139   ((N walks away))

4. A multiplicity of interpretative repertoires (or, competing modes of framing gender)

As I anticipated in the opening paragraphs, it is possible to discern two distinct interpretative repertoires in the fragment quoted above, each of which frames the participants' anatomical/physiological predispositions in diverging ways. The first of these repertoires, discernible in lines N 104 to N 110, draws on religion, while the second one frames a 'reality' in terms of heterosexual desire.

'One day they ought to call a muadhara…'

In E 088, after Julie disappeared, E asks whether she wasn't pregnant. After a redo invitation (F 090), F confirms that Julie was indeed pregnant (in F 093) and adds that he 'can't see anything', so Julie must have had an abortion (F 094, to have an abortion is referred to by means of the slang expression *kupangua* 'to disarrange'). E then continues by asking whether Julie already delivered the baby, thus openly ignoring F's deduction that she must have had an abortion (E 095). F responds to E's question as if it were a challenge to his earlier deduction and states that he is unable to decide whether she delivered the baby or had an abortion (F 097/098). At this point, E inter-rupts, calling into question the likelihood of Julie indeed having delivered her baby and thus realigning himself with the position established in F 094 (E 099/100). In F 101, F reasserts his earlier position that she must have had an abortion (this time 'perspectivising' his assertion by means of the 'postscript' *naona* 'I see'), so it appears that finally a shared alignment on the issue of Julie's abortion has been secured. E's display of doubt in E 102 does not invalidate this. Since it was E who (in E 099/100) supplied the material that made F (in F 101) reassert his initial position, E's subsequent *kapangua?* 'she got rid of it?' (E 102) may be heard as soliciting an appraisal of these argu-ments rather than as yet another attack on F's position. Importantly, their talk constitutes E and F as people who are knowledgeable about Julie's past, namely the fact that she has been pregnant recently, which entitles them to appraise Julie's present appearance ('the absence of symptoms') in the light of that information.

Precisely at this point, when E and F appear to have reached a uniform alignment *vis-à-vis* the outcome of Julie's pregnancy, N takes the floor and exploits their 'conclusion' ('Julie must have had an abortion') to issue a contri-bution of his own (N 104). In the first line of his contribution, N orients to Julie as a token from a *collectivity* of people, designated by the 3rd person plural proximal demonstrative *hawa*, which is bound by their common desire to 'commit' abortion. The persistency of this desire is signalled by the reduplica-tion of the verb root (plus ending) -*ua*, a common technique for indicating repetition. Through this transformation of Julie into a representative specimen of people who 'don't mind' about abortion, N succeeds in producing a well placed contribution to the talk, at the same time carefully *avoiding to assume a position in the preceding exchange between E and F* (and hence avoiding to be seen as making a claim to the identities occasioned therein). Rather than indi-cating such an alignment, N 104 displays a different justification for its own occurrence: the question format conveys *amazement* over the fact that 'these people' (referred to as *hawa*) seem *enthusiastic* about having an abortion. Having an abortion is no longer referred to by means of the slang expression *kupangua* 'to disarrange' (as was the case in lines F 094, F 098, F 101 and E 102) but is unequivocally qualified as *kuua* 'to kill', a description that in turn makes plain the reasonableness of N's displayed amazement.

N's next utterance, N 107, explicitly characterises the 'killing' as 'conse-quential' (*athari* 'consequence') or as 'dangerous' (*hatari* 'danger').[7] Although this utterance may be heard as an additional question (by virtue of the try-marker *eh?*), it suggests an answer to the earlier question N 104: 'these people' are *ignorant* about the fact that abortion is consequential/dangerous. N 109/110, then, suggests a remedy for their ignorance: a *muadhara* should be called to explain the consequences of abortion to them. A *muadhara* is a public meeting held outside the mosque, usually on Friday evenings, where Muslims come together to receive instruction on religious issues.[8]

How does N's turn across N 104/N 110 frame the identities of the participants? To begin with, the utterances referred to cast their producer, N, unmistakably as a [Muslim].[9] An overt reference to Islam can be found in the suggestion that a *muadhara* should be called (N 109). The identity that is thereby instantiated retrospectively clarifies N's indignation over the act of abortion ventilated in N 104.[10] This reference to Islam elaborates the distribution of knowledge called into being by N as he develops an account for the erratic behaviour of 'these people'. In explaining the occurrence of abortion in terms of ignorance, N 107 construes a distinction between 'those who know' and 'those who do not know'. The very fact of accounting for other people's 'eagerness' to have an abortion in terms of knowing/not knowing automatically situates the one who does the accounting (that is, N) on the privileged side of 'those who know'.[11] The suggestion that a *muadhara* ought to be called to instruct those who are ignorant connects the 'knowing' position within this distribution of knowledge to the identity [Muslim].

The categorisation device that is at work here partitions individuals into [Muslims] and [ignorant people], and hence, Julie is categorised as belonging to the latter membership category.[12] This categorisation device does not topicalise or make relevant Julie's on-sight categorisability as a woman, but goes hand in hand with specific 'preparatory work' that downplays the relevance of Julie's on-sight categorisability. I already explained that the 3rd person plural demonstrative *hawa* (N 104) transforms Julie into a representative of an entire collectivity of people 'who like to kill and kill' – a class that is reflexively constituted through the use of that pro-term in combination with the attribution of an 'eagerness to kill' presumably shared by *all* members of the collectivity designated by that pro-term.[13] In attributing the occurrence of abortion to their alleged eagerness to kill, 'these people' are transformed into a *morally organised* collectivity, that is, a group "where the responsibility for the action of one member is morally [...] ascribable to the group as a whole" (Jayyusi 1984: 48).[14] 'These people' have abortions because that is what 'these people' are like. Any 'external' circumstances that might induce women like Julie to have an abortion (availability of contraception, economic pressures, not to forget the issue of *men*'s responsibilities) are thereby discarded as potential explanations. This 'decontextualising' effect can also be observed in the substitution of the gender-implicative *kupangua* 'to disarrange', slang for 'to have an abortion', by the 'general' description 'to kill', which shifts attention away from the gender-implicative description 'abortion'. The (tacit) categorisation (in lines N 107 to N 110) of the collectivity designated by *hawa* as [ignorant] (which accounts for their alleged 'eagerness to kill') continues this decontextualisation. Throughout these subsequent re-descriptions and categorisations, however, it remains clear that it is *abortion* that N is talking about, something which specifically pertains to members of the category [woman].

'If she is all right…'

A second repertoire that is identifiable in the data excerpt, drawing not on Islam but on heterosexual desire, surfaces near the projected end of E and F's joint attempt to establish what happened to Julie, in E 125. In this instance, the question of how identities are distributed across the different participants (and Julie) coincides to a great extent with a reconstruction of the recovery of the referents of the three 'pro-terms' in E's utterance: the bound subject morphemes *yu-* and *tu-* and the inchoative pro-verb *-anza* 'to start'.[15]

125	E:	kama **yu-po** salama,	**tu-anz-e**	upya.
		if 3sg-be good health	1pl-start-sbj	anew
		if she is all right	let us start anew	

The notion of a 'pro-term' refers to a class of items, including the morphosyntactic class of deictics but not confined to it, that have one feature in common: in order to establish what it stands for, the recipients must carry out an inspection of the surrounding expressions (and, one might add, of the extralinguistic environment of the talk). "In their use of […] pro-terms such as 'they' and 'do', members are aware that such pronominals may provide for the relevance of 'filling-in' activities of a retrospective-prospective kind; that is to say, the use of these pro-terms occasions 'consultative work', 'inspections', or 'operations'" (Watson 1987: 275). The goal of this 'consultative work' is to reconstruct the methodical basis for the selection of precisely this pro-term in this particular environment: the recipient must identify in the surrounding talk those features that allow the producer to use *this* pro-term as referring to someone in particular (at least, in the case of so-called person deixis).

The first part of our task, tracing down the referent of the 3rd person singular subject morpheme *yu-*, poses few problems. Kiswahili does not encode gender morphologically, but the 3sg *yu-* is straightforwardly redressable as referring to Julie, since she constituted the topic of the foregoing stretch of talk. The principle at work here is probably one of the most basic procedures for making sense of talk: tying a turn to the one which immediately precedes it.

Matters become increasingly complicated, unfortunately, as soon as we turn to the two remaining pro-terms, the first person plural deictic *tu-* and the inchoative pro-verb *-anza* 'to start'. In a stimulation recall interview after the recording, N repeatedly insisted that *tuanze upya* is to be understood as "let us (again) start make love to her until she (again) becomes pregnant", an interpretation that is consistent with the trajectory of subsequent contributions and that was later corroborated by the other respondents. *Tu-* would thus stand for the three male participants. What could be the procedural warrant the talk supplies for such an interpretation? Simply assuming that *tu-* stands for 'we men' because the producer of E 125 can be categorised as [man] on the basis of certain anatomical characteristics that happen to be perceptually available is untenable on methodological grounds.[16] For one thing, the observation that E and his two interlocutors are categorisable as [man] does not imply that *anything* E says or does is automatically said or done *in that capacity*. I am here merely reiterating a point that is made repeatedly throughout the CA literature (for example, in Schegloff 1992): namely, that if we invoke a contextual variable to explain a particular aspect of speech, in this case the choice of one pro-term over another, we must demonstrate in the details of the talk that the proposed feature was indeed relevant to the participants at the moment of speaking. The focal point of our analysis, therefore, is the procedures E employs for transforming the 'possible observation' that biologically speaking he is categorisable as [man] into a feature that is ostensibly salient to his selection of pro-terms in E 125. It is only by investigating the particulars of this process that we can elucidate the context-specific 'version' of masculinity encapsulated in E's expression of heterosexual desire.

First, let us attempt to find out what the inchoative pro-verb *-anza* refers to. To begin with, observe that E pictures himself as implicated in the resumption of 'something that has to do with a pregnancy'. Let us recall that the preceding stretch of talk was entirely devoted to the issue of whether or not Julie indeed had an abortion, which entails that at an earlier point, she must also have been pregnant. This, together with the fact that the producer of the utterance, who is obligatorily included in the aggregate of individuals designated by the 1pl deictic *tu-*, is on-sight categorisable as a [man], imposes severe restrictions on the range of possible interpretations of -*anza*. Uttered (i) in an environment where pregnancy-related matters are a relevant topic, and (ii) by a [man], the only way to make sense of a self-inclusive encouragement 'to start all over' is to interpret that encouragement as 'let us start all over *to make love*', sexual intercourse (ostensibly?) being the only phase in the biological course of a pregnancy which [men] contribute to actively. This interpretation of 'starting all over' as 'starting *to make love*' is further facilitated by the suggestion of a cyclical movement conveyed by the adverbial *upya* 'anew' and the conditional clause *kama yupo salama* 'if she is all right'. The adverbial (*upya* 'anew') suggests that at one point in time, the activity in question was interrupted, presumably as Julie became pregnant. The conditional clause (*kama yupo salama* 'if she is all right') pictures the projected resumption as facilitated by/conditional upon Julie's apparently successful recovery after her alleged pregnancy (and abortion), thus suggesting that Julie is now 'available' for a *new* pregnancy.

The picture of what the first person plural *tu-* refers to, however, is not yet complete solely on the basis of a description of the recovery operation triggered by -*anza*. Even though this contextually embedded interpretation of -*anza* as 'starting *to make love*' makes relevant the observation that one of the referents of *tu-* is a [man], there is still enough room for two contradictory interpretations of what this pro-term actually stands for. First of all, *tu-* can be interpreted *transitively*, designating a plurality of [men] including E:

(1)   let *us*, *[men]*, start all over to make love *to her*

Alternatively, *tu-* might be interpreted in a *reciprocal* sense, designating the speaker (E) plus Julie. This would result in the following interpretation:

(2)   let *us*, *Julie and me*, start all over to make love *to one another*

Observe that under this reciprocal interpretation, E 125 would be hearable as a proclamation by E that he is the one who made Julie pregnant the first time. The adverbial *upya* and the conditional *kama yupo salama* suggest (i) that E and Julie did have sexual intercourse in the remote past, (ii) but that this ceased when Julie became pregnant (see above), thus insinuating that Julie's alleged pregnancy was the result of those occasions of sexual intercourse.

To understand why this reciprocal interpretation was consistently rejected by N and by the other respondents, we must return to the sequence that utterance 125 is part of. F 124, the utterance that E's line 125 is a rejoinder to, accomplishes two tasks. First of all, utterance F 124 *formulates* what the foregoing stretch of talk accountably amounts to. In drawing together the two possible outcomes extractable from the foregoing discussion over Julie's alleged pregnancy by means of a construction of the format 'if not x then y' ('if Julie did not miscarry, then she must have had got rid of the baby'), F 124 offers a tentative 'conclusion' for that discussion. Also, insofar that it hearably proposes a candidate conclusion, F 124 may simultaneously be interpreted as initiating a *closure* of the foregoing stretch. Each of these tasks projects a range of sensible responses. Thus, a formulation makes relevant a token of appreciation by the recipient (Heritage and Watson 1979), while a proposal to terminate the foregoing activity implicates a demonstration of acceptance. It is against this backdrop of sequentially generated expectations that the participants work out the sense of E 125.

Keeping this in mind, let us recall that a reciprocal interpretation of E 125 would transform that utterance into some sort of public proclamation by E that he was the natural father of Julie's undelivered baby. E 125 would therefore be heard as an instance of 'boasting' or 'bragging'. This being the case, it is hard to conceive in what sense the reciprocal interpretation of E 125 could be heard as displaying an orientation to the sequential framework created by F 124 as characterised above. This is not so with the transitive interpretation of E 125, which unequivocally transforms that utterance into an encouragement addressed to himself and the two other participants in their capacity as [men]. First of all, by incorporating some kind of paraphrase of F's candidate conclusion ('if it is not a miscarriage then she got rid of it') in the conditional clause ('(If) Julie is all right'), 'transitive' E 125 orients to F's candidate conclusion as a valid ground for encouraging the others to participate in what he regards as the relevant next action ('to have sex with Julie'). E 125 may thus be heard as (i) *agreeing* with the candidate reading of the preceding talk that F puts forward in line 124, and as (ii) *collaborating* in the closing proposed by that utterance. Transitive E 125 may in addition be heard as elegantly formulating a (the?) reason *why* E, F, and N collectively participated in the previous discussion. If they indeed look forward to becoming a lover of Julie, then ascertaining what state she is in does constitute a matter of legitimate concern to them.

Here, our analysis finally takes us to the heart of the problem: the identities that are framed by E's articulation of heterosexual desire. We already know that the pro-term *tu-* appeals to N, E and F as members of the collectivity of [men]. The other parts of E 125 attribute to N, E and F a desire to have intercourse with Julie. This desire is reflexively imputed to *all* members of the category [man], since E 125 advances the prospect of heterosexual activity as the rationale explaining why the (male) participants present engaged in the previous discussion. In this process, the aggregate of individuals on-sight categorisable as [man] is oriented to as (and thereby transformed into) a morally organised collectivity (Jayyusi 1984, see also the previous section), since the (perceptually available) categorisation [man] is treated as providing the category feature accountably 'explaining' why E and F behaved the way they did. For the specific, context-embedded 'version' of [man] that is construed here, I propose the notation [man*desire for Julie].[17]

No such moral predisposition – a categorically bound penchant for sexual intercourse – is attributed to Julie. In this particular context ('making love'), the categories [man] and [woman] appear to make up what Sacks (1972b) refers to as a 'standardised relational pair', which means, among other things, that mentioning one category from the pair is sufficient basis for inferring the presence of the other (as is the case in this instance). For the moment, I shall refer to these paired categories as [male partner] and [female partner]. The derogatory character of utterance E 125 now seems to derive from the fact that Julie is *only* oriented to in her capacity as [female partner]. The only elements that warrant her eligibility as a suitable candidate for sexual intercourse is (i) the fact that she is a woman, and (ii) the observation that she recovered after the alleged abortion. It is this 'minimalist' orientation to Julie, which creatively exploits the topic 'abortion', which explains why she qualifies as a candidate [female partner] for the entire collectivity of [men].

5. Re-framing and the management of incompatibility

The preceding paragraphs have demonstrated that the question of whether or not Julie had an abortion elicits two different responses, represented by N 104/110 and E 125, each of which entails a distinctive distribution of identities among the participants (including the talked-about party, Julie). Each response displays a different orientation to the biological predispositions of the participants involved, and in that capacity they represent distinct frames that are 'nested' on top of an identical primary frame. The aim of this new section, then, is to investigate the extent to which the apparent incompatibility between these responses (and the interpretative repertoires they draw upon), each of which frames a different portion of 'reality' as relevant to the interpretation of the current encounter, constitutes a practical problem that the participants themselves (must) attend to. The procedures the participants use for disclosing and resolving this incompatibility have to do with the imposition and co-ordination of frames, thus fully exploiting the open-ended character of the 'upper end' of human experience. In N 127 and N 129, N re-frames E's articulation of heterosexual desire as uttered by someone who (on other occasions) appears to be a [Muslim]. In doing so, he draws upon the same discourse as the one that he made use of in N 104/N 110. This re-framing of E 125 is made possible by the reification of the identity [Muslim]. In E 130, then, E resolves the friction between the two frames by re-framing the current segment of talk, including the incident that occasioned the conflict, as 'ironical'.

Re-framing through reification

In line N 127 (repeated in N 129), N imputes to his interlocutor a specific kind of conduct, presumably accomplished by E on (a) remote occasion(s), which invites the interpretation 'ostensibly performed by a [Muslim]': prayer.[18] The grammatical format of the utterance conveys a perception of forthright incongruity between E's alleged participation in prayer on the one hand and what E declared in the prior turn on the other. This incongruity is imparted most vividly in the 'redone' segment of N 127, after N's self-initiated self-repair. The first item after the interruption, the interrogative pronoun *vipi* 'how', here used independently, counts as a display of amazement. The insertion (in the redone part) of the negative copula *si*, here used as question particle, transforms what was initially a 'straight' declarative into a question specifically designed for filling up a freshly emerged 'knowledge gap', thus suggesting an inconsistency between what E did in E 125 and certain elements of 'background knowledge' pertaining to E that N presumed to be valid. (The substance of N's repair, as made public in the redone segment of N 127, thus indicates what it is that N found lacking in his initial formulation: an expression of incongruity that is sufficiently strong.)

In this way, N 127 makes known that E's self-accredited identity [man*desire for Julie] does not match with another description of E, the activity-based categorisation [Muslim] made possible by his remote conduct 'participation in prayer'. In MCA-terms, the two categories [man*desire for Julie] and [Muslim] cannot validly apply to ('describe') the same individual at the same time.[19] As a result of this incompatibility, E is now caught in a trap. In the first half of the conversation (not reproduced in this chapter), E asserted forcefully that he does attend prayer in the mosque, responding to an accusation by N of recurring absence. At a later stage suddenly renouncing his participation in prayer is therefore not a valid option. The alternative that N 127 has in store for E is a reappraisal of the activity 'prayer'. We are facing an example of what Jayyusi (1984) called a 'category-occasioned transformation', in which the initial assessment of some activity is reappraised on the basis of the categorical identity of the individual who performs that activity. Importantly, N 127 does not question *that* E attended prayer. Rather, by raising E's participation immediately after an utterance in which E assumed the identity [man*desire for Julie] (and encouraged others too to engage in illicit sex), N is calling for a *reappraisal* of E's participation. If it can be shown that a person who on one occasion participates in an Islamic ritual, on another occasion assumes an identity blatantly incongruous with the identity [Muslim], then his/her participation in prayer is to be re-interpreted as the work of a [pretender]. The disjunction between [Muslim] and [pretender] coincides with that between 'truth' and 'appearance'.

In transforming E 125 into a demonstration of E's lack of integrity, N is simultaneously re-framing the current conversational moment. By inviting a re-appraisal of E's prayer, N in effect orients to E 125 as produced by a self-acclaimed member of the same [Muslim] identity that he himself put on in N 104/110. This re-framing of E 125, now, thrives on the *reification* of the identity [Muslim].

The notion of reification refers to an ensemble of situated practices that participants employ for separating objects and activities from the contexts of practical activity in/for which (and from the context-specific courses of conduct by which) these objects and identities were originally created (Maynard and Wilson 1980). In N's problematisation of E 125, reification takes place as N reinterprets E's *remote* behaviour (prayer), initially appraisable as 'performed by a [Muslim]', *on the basis of the identity E assumes 'on the spot', in the course of the preceding turn.* In this process, the categorical identity [Muslim] is accredited a relevance *beyond* the remote occasion of prayer, *beyond* the spatio-temporal confines of the event of going to the mosque itself. [Muslim] is lifted out of the biographical context of interaction in/for which E originally put on that identity and is instead oriented to as an abstract set of 'rules' that antedate practical activity and that individuals have to obey to. The individual is thus degraded to a *derivative* of this 'a priori' category, which possesses an autonomous existence. In displaying a sexual interest in Julie, then, E apparently violated one of the 'context-free' rules that define a [Muslim].

Re-framing through irony

E's response to this imposition of a new frame, which involved the reification of the identity [Muslim], exemplifies a second technique for the co-ordination of incompatible frames: *irony* (Clift 1999). In E 130, E does not contest *that* he is indeed a [Muslim], neither does he dismiss N's remark as irrelevant. Instead, he re-describes his desire to be Julie's partner in a way that is no longer incompatible with the identity [Muslim]: 'this time I want to marry'. However, E's avowal that he is keen on marrying Julie (which entails an *exclusive* sexual relationship) is also blatantly incongruous with the way E pictured himself in E 125, as one among *many* candidate [male partners] sharing an interest in Julie. For Clift (1999), such a (publicly available) incongruity between the content of nearly adjacent utterances may be seen as suggesting to the other interlocutors that E is only the animator/author of utterance E 130. The 'split' brought about by this shift in footing would then make discernible an 'outer' frame that surrounds the 'inner' meaning of what E is saying (which is manifestly untrue).[20] This suggestion of an 'outer' frame in turn invites the evaluation of the 'inside' with reference to a set of common assumptions (for example, that E 125 indeed constituted a violation of Islamic religious proscriptions). The function of the imposition of this frame, however, is not to offer a (self-)evaluation of his own behavioural transgression. Rather, in framing his answer to N's question in the 'ironical' fashion described here, E in turn re-frames the preceding segments, including E 125, as 'not to be taken seriously'. E transforms the encounter into an event in which the standard for evaluating what is said or done is no longer 'truth' but the measure of 'wit' or 'guile' displayed by the participants. The use of irony in E 130 thus lifts the entire current segment, presumably stretching back up to E 125, out of the stream of ordinary events, as it transforms the interactional here-and-now into a kind of 'vacuum' where the participants are temporarily allowed to clown around with the 'fixed' social world that otherwise regulates their behaviour 'from the outside'. This is accomplished, however, without ever calling into question (i) the validity of according a reifying treatment to the category [Muslim], and (ii) the principle of reification itself, namely the fact that the social world possesses an externally imposing character.

In his response (N 131/132), N reciprocates the split footing of E 130, thus perpetuating the suggestion of an outside frame. First, N issues the change-of-state token (Heritage 1984b) *aa:*, thus responding to E's ostensibly incongruous answer as containing 'real' new information. Next, N repeats E

130 and adds an evaluation component (*sawa sawa* 'all right'). Evaluation components after a change-of-state token mark the trajectory of the foregoing informing as 'completed' (Heritage 1984b). Finally, N produces the greeting *asalaam alei(gh)kum* 'peace be upon you'. Insofar as it is categorically bound to members of the category [Muslim], *asalaam alei(gh)kum*, delivered here with a distinctly Arabic-sounding guttural quality, can be heard as officially recognising that E indeed qualifies as a [Muslim]. The ironic character of this 'official' recognition can be inferred from the observation that it is not responded to by means of the appropriate second (*aleikum salaam*) but with laughter, both by E, in E 133, and by N himself, in N 135.

The last two utterances, E 137 and N 138, signify the participants' withdrawal from the split-footing pattern that characterised the two foregoing utterances. Unlike N's *asalaam alei(gh)kum*, E 137 (*kazi kubwa* 'a big job') is no longer directed solely towards the 'inner meaning' of the foregoing utterance. Rather, it sounds like a comment on the strictness of Islamic religious proscriptions. E 137 thus indicates (i) that E is no longer joking, and (ii) that he indeed wants to be considered an incumbent of the category [Muslim] (otherwise the strictness of religious proscriptions would not pose a problem).

6. Concluding remarks

In this chapter, CA was used to topicalise the argumentative practices through which the on-sight categorisability of certain individuals as incumbent of a particular sex category was framed as relevant to the understanding of a particular stretch of talk. In this way, we have avoided treating gender identity as a zero-sum game (as would be the case if we were to identify the construction of gender through a comparative analysis of the sequential practices of the individuals in question). As my analysis focuses on the argumentative practices through which the gendering of conduct is practically accomplished, it allows a conception of gendered identities as displaying a specific grasp of what it is to 'be' a man or woman in a particular situation. For example, in the section 'If she is all right ...' we saw that E's articulation of sexual desire imparted conversational relevance to the on-sight categorisability of himself and his two interlocutors F and N as [men], thus connecting [man] to sexual prowess and securing the operation of heterosexuality as a norm. This articulation of a heterosexual desire in turn provided a warrant for the interest these men showed in the well-being of a girl who (might have) had an abortion. It is in these situated practices of practical reasoning, the methods by which E accountably 'experiences' his maleness as a parameter which is relevant to this one occasion, that we can catch a glimpse of prevailing 'attitudes' and 'socio-cultural values' at the very moment they are 'shaping' E's behaviour. Unlike other qualitative research traditions, CA strongly objects against appropriating explicit statements of alleged 'values' (often gathered in rhetorical contexts that are radically different from the concrete sites of action that participants are routinely engaged in) as analytic *resources* for making sense of conduct. Instead they are treated, like other elements pertaining to social structure, as situated accomplishments, demonstrable features of the encounter whose transparency must be grounded in details of the participants' talk.

The analysis also demonstrated that different orientations to what is contextually relevant may exist side by side, and may sometimes even enter into direct competition with one another across sequentially adjacent turns. The identities that E draws upon in constructing his warrant for the curiosity he and his interlocutors displayed in Julie's recovery belong to one particular 'interpretative repertoire' (reinterpreted here as a socially shared way of distributing identities among different participants). As we have seen, the mention of the girl's abortion triggered a response that draws upon a different repertoire, one that frames the identities of the parties in terms of the categorisation device '[Muslim], [ignorant person]'. The analysis suggested that the implementation of this device involved specific work to downplay the relevance of Julie's on-sight categorisability as [woman] (see the section 'One day they ought to call a *muadhara*'). However, the analytic merits and potential of this 'argumentative' form of CA are not limited to identifying competing distributions of identities resorted to in the course of an encounter. In the section 'Re-framing and the management of incompatibility', I specifically addressed the procedures by which the various distributions of identities are *coordinated* that are discernible in the respective parties' responses *vis-à-vis* Julie's alleged abortion. Thus, we saw that one repertoire comprised an identity, [Muslim], that was treated as valid beyond the context in/for which E originally used it (that is, when he allegedly went to pray in the mosque). On the other hand, we observed that the identity that E assembled in his articulation of heterosexual desire, the 'version' of [man] that we elucidated in the section 'If she is all right ...', was relegated to the realm of carnival – a process in which E himself actively collaborated.

In her chapter in this collection, Kitzinger states that CA commits us to a view of the social world that conceives of its inhabitants as "agents actively engaged in methodical and sanctioned procedures for producing or resisting, colluding with or transgressing, the taken-for-granted social world." Incorporating elements from the work of Judith Butler, Speer and Potter, also in this volume, draw attention to the iterability of the sign as a possible starting point for inscribing new meanings into established discourses – for example, through the operation of *irony*. The incident reported in this chapter could be characterized as one such moment in a potentially endless sequence of resignifications, in which E and F are *in situ* (re)calibrating the positions which two interpretative repertoires assume *vis-à-vis* one another. How exactly this re-calibration comes to take on any political significance is, however, far from straightforward. It might well be the case, for example, that the distribution of identities that E drew upon in E 125 is perpetuated precisely *because of* the carnivalesque status E attributed to it in E 130. It goes without saying that we need more analyses, from comparable as well as from unrelated incidents, for such an analysis to be confirmed or refuted. It might also be worth considering, as Cameron (1996) insists, to what extent discursive struggles over gender mediate the participants' access to other highly valued resources, material or symbolic. For the moment, it appears that we have reached the limit of where the analysis of situated identity ascriptions and local rationalities of a singular moment may take us. For this other realm, where aggregates of singular (inter)actions coalesce to produce unintended consequences and other allegedly 'ideological' effects, lies beyond the horizon of what is intersubjectively available.

Notes

1. The recording (only audio) was made surreptitiously, with a small tape-recorder hidden under N's shirt. Afterwards, we solicited permission from the participants to use the materials thus obtained for research purposes.

2. In her paper, Wetherell criticised Schegloff (1997). Later on, she was joined by Billig (1999). The debate is discussed in the introduction to this volume and in Kitzinger's chapter.

3. It still remains to be empirically verified, of course, whether participants themselves indeed assess the presumed institutionality of the setting through the mirror of mundane interaction. Note, in this respect, that the standard argument in favour of the primacy of mundane conversation, viz. that mundane talk is the most ancient and pervasive form of human interaction and the primary vehicle of socialisation (eg. Heritage 1984a: 239), is of an entirely 'theoretical' nature (ie. it is grounded in the observation of circumstances *exter-*

nal to the concrete instance of talk itself). According to some authors (eg. Bjelic and Lynch 1992: 53ff, Lynch and Bogen 1994: 80, 1996: 283ff), this analytical strategy constitutes a violation of what they consider to be ethnomethodology's initial post-analytic commitment, viz. to explicate courses of action from 'within' the relevant community of practitioners.

4. Of course, it might well turn out that there are occasions on which participants are unable to raise gender as a relevant contextual variable. This 'unavailability' of gender, however, remains a matter of empirical verification that must be locally accounted for.

5. The description 'conflict' is warranted insofar as the incompatibility of discourses/frames constitutes a practical problem that the participants themselves act upon and try to solve. In Schegloff's (1984) terminology, the incompatibility of frames constitutes an 'empirical' problem, not a 'theoretical' one.

6.   The following abbreviations have been used for the interlinear morpheme translation:

1sg, 2sg, etc.	1st person singular subject marker, 2nd person singular subject marker, etc.
O1sg, O2sg, etc.	1st person singular object marker, 2nd person singular object marker, etc.
PRS	TAM-marker: present tense (TAM stands for 'tense/aspect/ modality'; in Kiswahili, there is no principled morphological distinction between expressions of tense, aspect, and/or modality)
PST	TAM-marker: past tense
CNS	TAM-marker: consecutive tense
PERF	TAM-marker: perfect aspect
HAB	TAM-marker: habitual aspect
INF	TAM-marker: infinitive mood
SBJ	TAM-marker: subjunctive mood
PASS	passive voice marker
NEG	negation marker
FV	final vowel (sometimes referred to as 'expletive verbal suffix')
PRN(1sg, 2sg, etc.)	independent pronoun (1st person singular, 2nd person singular, etc.)
DEM1(sg, pl)	proximal demonstrative pronoun (singular or plural)
DEM2(sg, pl)	medial demonstrative pronoun (singular or plural)
CN	connective pronoun
PRT	particle
REDUPL	reduplication

7. Because of the poor quality of the original tape, N and I were unable to decide which of the two hearings is correct.

8. Similar meetings are organised by (Evangelical) Christian groupings. In recent times, these meetings (from both sides) have been publicly denounced as one of the elements that play a role in the growing frictions between Muslims and Christians along the Tanzanian coast (Campbell 1999).

9. In this chapter, I adopt the convention of enclosing categorical identities between square brackets.

10. Inasmuch as the content of that identity is in turn elaborated by the antecedent display of indignation.

11. That N is on the side of 'those who know' is also evidenced by the fact that abortion is consistently referred to as *kuua* 'to kill'. The description 'to kill' is part of a discourse *about* people who commit an abortion and not part of the discourse produced *by* these people themselves. If 'they' themselves would refer to abortion as 'killing', they would presumably know that it is a sin.

12. The notion of 'membership categorisation device' (see Sacks 1972a, 1972b) stands for a collection of categories that conventionally go together (like '[mother], [father], [baby]' or '[Muslim], [Hindu], [Christian]'), plus the rules (or procedures) for their competent usage (like the consistency rule, see note 18). The MCD at work here vividly illustrates the intertwining of 'Islam' and 'knowledge'. It is particularly among Islamists (like N) that the concept of *jahiliyya* 'ignorance' has come to serve as a central factor in defining Islamic identity (see, for example, Rosander 1997).

13. The notion of 'pro-term' subsumes but is not confined to the morphosyntactic class of 'deictics'. The precise content of the notion 'pro-term' will be elaborated in the next section.

14. The transformation of an 'ordinary' collectivity into a morally organised one depends on what Jayyusi (1984: 49) refers to as "the operation of a transitivity of attributes [...]: whether, for some course of action or activity by a person who is a member of some collectivity, that 'collectivity' can be produced as an endogenous feature of that course of action."

15. An 'inchoative' verb profiles the incipient stage of an action or activity.

16. Perceptually available categorisations are discussed in Jayyusi (1984: 73ff).

17. One could furthermore argue – and this is the second sense in which *tu-* elaborates the perceptually available categorisation [man] – that the mere act of publicly *proclaiming* one's sexual interest may itself be perceived as emblematic of the category [man]. Articulating a heterosexual desire would then be heard as reflexively instantiating the categorical identity [man], *via* the viewer's maxim derived from the consistency rule (Sacks 1972a: 338). The 'version' of [man] that is designated by *tu-* would hence constitute an instance of what Matoesian (1998: 11, fn.10) refers to as a categorization that is "contingently and iconically embedded in [a] discursive [form] rather than merely occurring in overt descriptions of category-bound activities/competencies." In this sense, E 125 blurs the distinction McIlvenny (this volume) draws between token-reflexivity (P1) and 'appellation' (P3), since in this instance P3 draws on a token-reflexive form of performativity (the deictic *tu-*).

18. The rule at work here is one of the maxims derived from what Sacks (1972a) termed the 'consistency rule'. The consistency rule governs the co-selection of membership categories ('if two or more categories occur in close proximity, they should be interpreted, if possible, as belonging to the same device'). The viewer's maxim that is at work here regulates the co-selection of category-descriptors and action-descriptions ('if an action can be seen as being performed by a member of particular (contextually available) membership category, then see it that way'). Those actions that are conventionally associated with members of one specific category (and which may consequently generate a corresponding categorisation of the performer of that action) are referred to as 'category-bound activities'.

19. It could be argued (paraphrasing the viewer's maxim which Sacks (1972a) derived from the consistency rule; see the previous footnote) that N 127 calls into being a locally occasioned categorisation device, contrastively organised around the feature 'desire for illicit sexual intercourse', which divides members of the population into [Muslims] and [man*desire for Julie]. If an individual is simultaneously a member of two different membership categories (that is, if s/he is treated as such), these categories cannot be part of the same categorisation device.

20. The notion of 'footing' refers to the author role or 'participation status' a speaker assumes vis-à-vis the utterance s/he is producing. Goffman (1981: 144) distinguishes three different participation statuses: the *animator* is "the sounding box" who physically produces the utterance, while *author* stands for the person who drafted it (that is, the one "who has selected the sentiments that are being expressed and the words in which they are encoded") and *principal* for the one "whose position is established by the words that are spoken."

References

Antaki, Charles and Widdicombe, Sue (eds). 1998 *Identities in Talk*. London: Sage.

Billig, Michael. 1999 "Whose terms? Whose ordinariness? Rhetoric and ideology in conversation analysis". *Discourse & Society* 10(4): 543-558.

Bing, Janet M. and Bergvall, Victoria L. 1996 "The question of questions: Beyond binary thinking". In *Rethinking Language and Gender Research: Theory and Practice*, V. L. Bergvall, J. M. Bing and A. F. Freed (eds), 1-30. London: Longman.

Bjelic, Dusan and Lynch, Michael. 1992 "The work of a (scientific) demonstration: Respecifying Newton's and Goethe's theories of prismatic color". In *Text in Context: Contributions to Ethnomethodology*, G. Watson and R.M. Seiler (eds), 52-78. Newbury Park, CA: Sage.

Boden, Deirdre and Zimmerman, Don H. (eds). 1991 *Talk and Social Structure*. Cambridge: Polity Press.

Cameron, Deborah. 1996 "Theoretical debates in feminist linguistics: Questions of sex and gender". In *Gender and Discourse*, R. Wodak (ed.), 21-36. London: Sage.

Campbell, John. 1999 "Nationalism, ethnicity and religion: Fundamental conflicts and the politics of identity in Tanzania". *Nations and Nationalisms* 5(1): 105-125.

Clift, Rebecca. 1999 "Irony in conversation". *Language in Society* 28: 523-553.

Collins, Randall. 1988 "Theoretical continuities in Goffman's work". In *Exploring the Interaction Order*, P. Drew and A. Wootton (eds), 41-63. Cambridge: Polity Press.

Drew, Paul and John Heritage (eds). 1992 *Talk at Work: Interaction in Institutional Settings*. Cambridge: Cambridge University Press.

Goffman, Erving. 1974 *Frame Analysis*. New York: Harper & Row.

Goffman, Erving. 1981 "Footing". In *Forms of Talk*, 124-159. Philadelphia: University of Pennsylvania Press.

Have, Paul ten. 1999 *Doing Conversation Analysis: A Practical Guide*. London: Sage.

Heritage, John. 1984a *Garfinkel and Ethnomethodology*. Cambridge: Polity Press.

Heritage, John. 1984b "A change-of-state token and aspects of its sequential placement". In *Structures of Social Action: Studies in Conversation Analysis,* J.M. Atkinson and J. Heritage (eds), 299-345. Cambridge: Cambridge University Press.

Heritage, John and Watson, D.R. 1979 "Formulations as conversational objects". In *Everyday Language: Studies in Ethnomethodology,* G. Psathas (ed.), 123-162. New York: Irvington.

Hester, Stephen and Eglin, Peter (eds). 1997 *Culture in Action: Studies in Membership Categorisation Analysis.* Washington, DC: University Press of America.

Hutchby, Ian and Wooffitt, Robin. 1998 *Conversation Analysis: Principles, Practices and Applications.* Cambridge: Polity Press.

Jayyusi, Lena. 1984 *Categorisation and the Moral Order.* London: Routledge & Kegan Paul.

Lynch, Michael and Bogen, David. 1994 "Harvey Sacks' primitive natural science". *Theory, Culture & Society* 11: 65-104.

Lynch, Michael and Bogen, David. 1996 *The Spectacle of History: Speech, Text, and Memory at the Iran-Contra Hearings.* Durham, NC: Duke University Press.

Matoesian, Greg. 1998 "Discursive hegemony in the Kennedy Smith rape trial: Evidence of an age-graded allusion in expert testimony". *Pragmatics* 8(1): 3-19.

Maynard, Douglas W. and Wilson, Thomas P. 1980 "On the reification of social structure". *Current Perspectives in Social Theory* 1: 287-322.

Mehan, Hugh. 1991 "The school's work of sorting students". In D. Boden and D.H. Zimmerman (eds), 71-90.

Potter, Jonathan and Wetherell, Margaret. 1987 *Discourse and Social Psychology. Beyond Attitudes and Behaviour.* London: Sage.

Rosander, Eva Evers. 1997 "Introduction: The Islamization of 'tradition' and 'modernity'". In *African Islam and Islam in Africa: Encounters between Sufis and Islamists,* D. Westerlund and E.E. Rosander (eds), 1-27. London: Hurst & Co.

Sacks, Harvey. 1972a "On the analyzability of stories by children". In *Directions in Sociolinguistics: The Ethnography of Communication,* J. Gumperz and D. Hymes (eds), 325-45. New York: Holt, Rinehart & Winston.

Sacks, Harvey. 1972b "An initial investigation of the usability of conversational data for doing sociology". In *Studies in Social Interaction,* D. Sudnow (ed.), 31-74. New York: The Free Press.

Schegloff, Emanuel A. 1984 "On some questions and ambiguities in conversation". In *Structures of Social Action: Studies in Conversation Analysis,* J. M. Atkinson and J. Heritage (eds), 28-52. Cambridge: Cambridge University Press.

Schegloff, Emanuel A. 1991 "Reflections on talk and social structure". In D. Boden and D.H. Zimmerman (eds), 44-70.

Schegloff, Emanuel A. 1992 "On talk and its institutional occasions". In P. Drew and J. Heritage (eds), 101-34.

Schegloff, Emanuel A. 1997 "Whose text? Whose context? " *Discourse & Society* 8(2): 165-187.

Watson, Rodney. 1987 "Interdisciplinary considerations in the analysis of pro-terms". In *Talk and Social Organisation,* G. Button and J.R.E. Lee (eds), 261-289. Clevedon: Multilingual Matters.

Watson, Rodney. 1994 "Catégories, séquentialité et ordre social". *Raisons Pratiques* 5: 151-184.

Watson, Rodney. 1997 "Some general reflections on 'categorisation' and 'sequence' in the analysis of conversation". In S. Hester and P. Eglin (eds), 49-75.

West, Candace and Fenstermaker, Sarah. 1995 "(Re)doing difference". *Gender & Society* 9(4): 506-513.

Wetherell, Margaret. 1998 "Positioning and interpretative repertoires: Conversation analysis and post-structuralism in dialogue". *Discourse & Society* 9(3): 387-412.

CHAPTER 8

The repressed on parole

Gender categorisation, performativity and the unsaid in talkin' dirty jokes

Andrew Fish

In re-examining Harvey Sacks' (1995, II: 470-494) analysis of the telling of a dirty joke, I question his claim that the story told is categorisable by gender as female and by age as designed for twelve year old girls[1]. Close categorisation and sequential analysis of the pre-joke and post-joke talk shows that its footing (Goffman 1979) creates procedurally consequential ambiguities. The reason for these ambiguities is that Ken, the seventeen year old boy who tells the joke to his seventeen year old peers, introduces the joke as a story his little sister told him. This affects the reception of the joke, in that the recipients are caught between dealing with the joke per se, with Ken's sister as the 'original' teller, with Ken as the joke's situated teller or reporter, and with their own interaction as they speak. My analysis of Sacks' transcript leads to the conclusion that the talk of the recipients of the joke involves a policing of standard age and gender categorisations which constructs the tellers as naively transmitting a joke without understanding it. This categorisation is resisted by Ken's performance of a hyperbolic pastiche of the role thus constructed for the tellers. It is the boys' discursive production of their gendered selves — and Ken's pastiche in particular — that exemplify Judith Butler's (1997) multifaceted notion of performativity, whether as a 'reproduction' of normative gender roles or a form of resistance. However, like Speer and Potter (this volume), I believe that what Butler claims in theory is far better investigated in situated interaction by discursive analytic means and by ethnomethodological 'unmotivated looking'. The analysis performed in this article was, in fact, carried out before I had read Butler, and therefore constitutes direct support for her theories without drawing directly on them.

I claim that, whatever the merits or shortcomings of the joke per se, it is enrolled in the situated on-going production of the boys' identities in talk. The boys' talk is hearably performative of an adolescent-masculine, 'cool' gender identity. This involves a policing of gender norms in which categorisations of the joke and of the joke's original teller are produced to do local interactional business. The sequential and categorical anti-logic of the joke first constructs and then undermines normative heterosexist and sexist assumptions, and this construction and undermining re-emerge in the boys' talk about the joke and the little sister.

This connection between the joke and the boys' discussion leads me to a consideration of the *unsaid*. To categorise may be to shape the 'truth' about self and others, implicitly, by drawing on commonsense notions of the category and its predicates. Because the relationship between categories and their predicates is often subtle, contingent, contested, and under dynamic development in the sequentiality of conversation, each categorization involves the exclusion of potential meaning, which remains ever present at the margins of talk and may re-enter explicitly or tacitly in future turns. It is this phenomenon which, drawing on work by Billig (1999c), I call the *repressed on parole*.

Repression, as Michael Billig (1999c) has indicated, may be a discursive action rather than a deep mental event. I adopt and adapt the notion to suggest that categorisation may be a central way that such discursive repression occurs. In talk involving sex and gender, the categorisation both draws on and situatedly constructs a discursive formation which is, in a sense, both within the categorisation and external to it. The discursively repressed is absent-present. But the category does not, in itself, simply belong to a particular discourse; it is the particular situated way in which the category is used in the talk at hand that indexes a particular discourse and, importantly, an 'attitude' to that discourse. Members are not 'judgmental dopes': interactants will often be aware that the situated deployment of a category configures 'the world' in the shape that this particular discourse dictates, and equally aware that this is a version of 'the way things are' which, as Billig (1987, 1991) so valuably indicates, is a choice that counters other possible, unmentioned versions. Yet none of this need necessarily be made explicit in the data as participants orientate to it. It is the unsaid of the conversation; the exact sense in which presence and absence interact in situated talk. The unsaid does not just disappear: as a constant shadow at the margins of the said, it is a resource for inference, irony, playfulness and performance.

It is important to point out that of the multitude of things that are not said in any situation, 'the unsaid' as I use the term refers to pertinent absences that are created by the said. Such absences are essential to an understanding of the pre-joke and post-joke talk of the boys. The unsaid is a controversial idea in CA; however, my analysis aims to show that there is no way of understanding this particular conversation without including these pertinent absences. An examination of the unsaid will produce a radically different set of conclusions than those reached by Sacks.

Most chapters in this volume are, to varying degrees, indebted to the work of the late Harvey Sacks. As the founder of both Membership Categorisation Analysis (MCA) and Conversation Analysis (CA), Sacks left an enduring legacy of powerful procedures and principles that continue to inspire and guide the development of CA and MCA even today. It may therefore seem strange that this chapter submits a piece of excellent sequential analysis by Sacks to a critical, dissenting reading. Stranger still, this re-reading is itself largely informed by Sacks' work. Yet what is attempted here is not a deconstruction of the Sacksian legacy. What *is* being claimed is that Sacks' analysis of the telling of a dirty joke, both in lecture and article forms (Sacks 1974, 1978, 1995) contains puzzling lapses from Sacks' *own* principles. Importantly, these lapses arise from the separation of sequential and categorisation analysis and his failure to provide a fully situated categorisation analysis of the data. The result is a piece of theorising that mixes analysts' and members' concerns. Crucially, for the purposes of this volume, the fact that this occurs in connection with the treatment of gender (and age) categorisations is no random coincidence. Sacks' treatment of the dirty joke exemplifies the difficulty of *consistently* applying empirical methods to members' practices that may themselves be informed by the popular theories of common sense. Few areas of human experience are subject to more popular theorising than sex and gender identity.

One of the key tenets of CA and MCA as they have developed out of Garfinkel's (1967) ethnomethodology has been an insistence on the situated and occasioned nature of sequential and categorical phenomena in talk-in-interaction. At its best, Sacks' methodology involves an empirical, data driven analysis that resists the imposition of abstract theory. CA and MCA respect the particularity of human interactions. Strictly speaking, then, these ethnomethodologically inspired disciplines involve a principled refusal to deal with what is not empirically *present* in conversation, not hearably oriented to by the participants. If theorising is already reflected in talk involving sex and gender, however, it represents members' concerns which deserve attention. There is no problem when such theories are topics of conversation per se, but in many cases, I suspect, the categories and predicates of gender and sexuality can have effects that are not *directly* recordable at the surface of talk. To admit this, however, could be to enter the poststructuralist territory of Derridean absence and différance, Kristevian intertextuality and Foucauldian discursive formations, with the prospect of infinite regress into abstract theory.

A series of possible responses immediately presents itself. First, the membership categorisation analysis of sex and gender categories must be rigorously situated and combined with sequential analysis to follow how categorisations by *members* construct 'truths' and 'identities' in interaction. Second, we must be willing to acknowledge that talk does not always produce closure of 'meaning', but may actually depend on indeterminacy (McHoul 1994). That is, apparent indeterminacy present in transcripts of talk is not just a problem for analysts: it can be a members' resource in that talk. Third, we can then identify loci of indeterminacy, noteworthy absences, strange leaps and so on — apparent quirks in the sequential and categorical data that may signal an assumption by one or more participants that a wider discourse can be counted on to do implicit work. What is important, and so very difficult to accomplish, is that this looking remain 'unmotivated'; in other words, the analyst is not looking for 'gaps' that fit some pre-formed theory, but is simply responding to apparent indeterminacies in the data, for instance, with openness rather than attempting to close them down (McHoul 1994). Fourth, analysts must acknowledge that any further moves must involve the analyst's interpretations of members' interpretations. Purely empirical description can take us no further. Many CA and MCA purists will stop here, arguing reasonably that it is not their task to engage in explanatory activities. Hypotheses about members' interpretations occur on a different level of analysis. Fifth, a distinction must be continually observed between the analyst's theorising and what participants appear to be doing in the way of lay-theorising. This distinction can only be maintained by repeatedly returning to level one of descriptive analysis to 'cross-check' against the data. Finally, even after extensive testing, there can be no certainty that any such hypothesis actually reflects the complexity of what is happening in the interaction: all that can be established is that there is some degree of concordance between the data and the hypothesis. When the 'unsaid' is drawn into the analysis, there is no closure: indeterminacies in the talk are not resolved definitively for participants and any such closure through sophisticated, retrospective analysis would represent a degree of certainty unavailable to members in the ongoing interaction. What is produced is a 'story' about the event, and other analysts may produce other stories based on the same event, just as different participants may post-rationalise what happened in a conversation in contrasting ways. Indeterminacy is the locus of multiple meaning potential, but not of complete interpretative freedom. The unsaid is always formed by the said.

This way of working with the unsaid addresses some of the questions raised in recent controversies in CA. First, is it analytically defensible for analysts to deploy contextual knowledge that is not *explicitly* shown to be relevant as a members' concern in the data examined? (Schegloff 1991, 1997, 1998, 1999a, 1999b, Billig 1999a, 1999b, Wetherell 1998, Latour 1996, Stokoe and Smithson this volume, Kitzinger this volume). Second, and relatedly, does MCA have a place alongside, or even integrated with, the sequential analysis that is central to CA, or does it lead to 'wild' analysis and the import of analysts' concerns where practitioners should properly be attending to members' concerns? (Lepper 2000, Schegloff 1992a, Stokoe and Smithson this volume, D'hondt this volume – and the continuing debate on the 'ETHNO' electronic mailing list discussion forum). After all, although categorisations are deployed in specific ways *in situ*, they invoke, rely upon and inflect common-sense understandings that may or may not be 'common' to all members — including academic CA practitioners. Such assumptions of commonality are often precisely what are at issue for theorists of gender and sex. It is hardly surprising that such debates should emerge at a time when CA and MCA methodologies are being taken up to investigate non-essentialist notions of performativity and emergent identities as situated discursive constructions. Naturally, established practitioners are committed to maintaining the principled empirical attention to the data itself and to members' concerns that has made CA such a powerful force. On the other hand, it is hardly likely that participant members in conversations will *always* be aware (or make explicit an awareness) that their talk is potentially hearable as sexist or heterosexist, even if they sometimes do explicitly orientate to such issues, and they are even less likely to announce or orientate to the notion that they or their interactants are engaging in the discursive production of gendered identity. Part of the problem is definitional: when the phenomenon under investigation is contextual it is unnamed, but as soon as it is named it has become focal and is no longer contextual! Is the analysis of such phenomena then excluded within a CA framework?

Much depends on how narrowly we define such key terms as 'orientating to', 'context', 'demonstrable relevance', 'making relevant' and so on. For some researchers involved with issues of gender and sexuality, there is obviously something 'impoverished' and 'limiting' about current CA notions of what counts as orientation (Beach 2000, Kitzinger 2000, D'hondt this volume, Stokoe and Smithson this volume). Orientation surely involves more than explicit mention. Having provided an exemplary explanation of how the sequential, turn-by-turn unfolding action of talk provides situated public understandings and chances for repair, Heritage (1984: 260, my emphases) addresses this very issue:

> a second speaker's analysis of a prior is presented *indirectly* and must thus be *inferred*. As Goodwin and Goodwin have made the point, 'rather than presenting a naked analysis of the prior talk, next utterances characteristically transform that talk in some fashion — deal with it not in its own terms but rather in the way in which it is relevant to the projects of the subsequent speaker' (Goodwin and Goodwin 1982: 1). It is a commonplace that speakers may respond to earlier talk in ways which may blur, conceal or otherwise avoid displaying their true appreciation of its import. Similarly, speakers may avoid taking up and dealing with what they perfectly well know is accomplished or *implicated* by prior talk so as to influence the direction of the talk towards some desired objective. These occasions are common in talk and may be varyingly 'transparent' to analytic inspection. Some of their characteristic features can themselves be documented by means of comparative sequential analysis. But their existence serves to emphasize that *'official' treatments of talk occurring at the conversational surface are the starting point for interpretative and analytic work and cannot be treated simply as unproblematic representations of what the speakers' understandings or intentions in the talk consisted of.*

Schegloff (1997: 182) also concedes that category terms need no explicit mention for their relevance for members to be established and that "orientation to gender can be manifested without being explicitly named or mentioned". Elsewhere, however, Schegloff (1992b: 196) insists on the importance of the demonstrable relevance of context for participants, as opposed to academic analysts, and continues:

> If there are indefinitely many potentially relevant aspects of context and of personal or categorical identity which could have a bearing on some facet of, or occurrence in, interaction, and if the analyst must be concerned with what is relevant to the parties at the moment at which what is being analyzed occurred, and is procedurally consequential for what is being analyzed, then *the search for context properly begins with the talk or other conduct being analyzed* (197).

The procedure that I have proposed above and which I have attempted to use in preparing the analysis that follows takes its point of departure in the talk (the *said*). Here it examines the subtle kinds of 'orientation' through gaps and indeterminacies that Heritage indicates may be common in conversation, and from there moves to the wider context that these orientations presuppose and thus situatedly construct.

Whether or not Sacks followed his own principles in analysing the joke is a matter of little intrinsic interest. His analysis should, however, alert us to the danger of confusing our own gender theories, no matter how politically correct or intellectually well-founded they may be, with the object of analysis itself. Obviously, there is no such thing as a completely transparent, objective, empirical analysis, and mine is no exception. My own analysis of the participants' talk develops its own story about what adolescent boys do in groups, and this may feed back into the way I see their interaction unfolding. Since beginning the analysis, I have presented the data in various workshops and seminars. On several occasions this has engendered furious debate about what is happening in the talk. I take this as confirming my point: in addressing the kinds of indeterminacy likely to occur in talk involving gender categorisations, it is difficult for analysts to avoid the projection of their own gender 'theories' onto the object of analysis.

1. The joke[2]

```
 1  Ken:    You wanna hear muh-eh my sister told me a story last night.
 2  Roger:  I don' wanna hear it. But if you must.
 3              (0.7)
 4  Al:     What's purple en 'n island. Grape, Britain. That's w't iz
 5              si//ster-
 6  Ken:    No:. To stun me she says uh (0.8) There wz these three girls 'n
 7              they jis got married?
 8  Roger:  ehhh//hehh hhh hhh
 9  Ken:    A::nd uh
10  Roger:  Hey waita seco(h)nd.
11  Al:     [heh!
12  Roger:  [Drag th(h)at by ag(h)ai(h)n hehh // hehh
13  Ken:    There-
14  Ken:    There wz these three gi:rls. En they were all sisters. En they'd jis
15              got married tuh three brothers.
```

16 Roger: You better have a long talk with yer sister.
17 Ken: Waita waita // minute
18 Roger: Oh: // three brothers.
19 Al: eheh
20 Al: eh//heh!
21 Ken: A::nd uh, so
22 Al: The brothers of these sisters.
23 Ken: No they're different- mhh//hh
24 Al: heh
25 Ken: Y'know different families. // (No link-up.)
26 Roger: Th's clo:ser th'n before, // hhh
27 Ken: [So-
28 Al: [heh! hh hh
29   (0.7)
30 Ken: Quiet.
31 Al: hh hh // hhhh
32 Ken: So:, first'v all, that night, they're on their::: honeymoon the- uh
33   mother in law says- (to 'em) well why don'tcha all spen'th'night
34   here en then you c'n go on yer honeymoon in th'morning.
35   Th'firs'night, th'mother walks up t'the firs'door en she hears this
36   uuuuuuuuuhh! hh Second door is HHOOOHHH! Third door
37   there's NOthin'. She stands there fer about twunny five minutes
38   waitin' fer sump'n duh happen. — Nothin'.
39   (1.0)
40 Ken: Next morning she talks t'the firs' daughter en' she s'z — uh how
41   come yuh- how come y'went YAAA::: las' night'n daughter siz
42   well it tickled Mommy — second gi:rl, — How come yuh
43   screa:med. Oh: Mommy it hu:rts. — Third girl, walks up t'her.
44   (0.7) Why didn' y'say anything las'night. — W'you tol'me it wz
45   always impolite t'talk with my mouth full,
46   (1.5)
47 Ken: hh hyok hyok.
48   (0.5)
49 Ken: hyok
50   (2.5)
51 Al: HA-HA-HA-HA!
52 Ken: ehh heh heh // hehh
53 (Al):   hehhhehhheh hhh
54 Roger: Delayed rea:c//tio(h)n.
55 Al: hehh I hadtuh think abou//t it awhile y'know?

```
56  Roger:   hhh heh
57               (1.0)
58  Roger:   hehh hh hehh hhh You mea(h)n th(h)e dee(h)p (h)hidden
59               meaning there doesn' hitcha right awa-ay heh heh // hehhhh-
60               hhhh hehhhehh
61  Al:      hh hhh // hhh
62  (Dan):   (Yeh. I // guess so.)
63  Al:      What'e meant tuh say is the t- thet u:m
64               (0.5)
65  Roger:   Ki//nda got ps::ychological over//tones (to it).
66  Al:      (                    )
67  Ken:     Little sister's gittin' // older.
68  (Roger): hehh hh hehh
69  Ken:     ehheh heh That's w't I m(h)ean tih // say,
70  Dan:     Sounds like it,
71  Ken:     Fer twelve years old tellin' me- I didn' even // know-
72  Roger:   How do yuh know she's jis' not repeating what she heard'n
73               doesn'know wha//t it means.
74  Al:      She haftuh explain it to yuh Ke:n?
75  Ken:     Yeah she had to explain it to detail to me,
76               (0.5)
77  Al:      Okay, good. Gladju gotta sister thet knows // somethin'.
78  Ken:     hh hhh
79  Ken:     She told me she wz eatin' a hot dog,
80               (0.3)
81  Ken:     hh
82  Roger:   Wha'does that mean,
83  Ken:     hh hh
84  Al:      Yeah come // on. Explain // it to us, hnhh
85  Ken:     heh
86  Ken:     heh
87  Al:      Explai//:n,  explain everything you kno:w Ken,
88  Ken:     hhhh! Nuh I: D(h)ON'KNOW I j's' sai:d tha(h)t.
89  Al:      Explain everything.
```

(Sacks 1995, II: 470-472)

Sacks analyses the sequential economy of the joke, showing how, "for each point in it that is subsequent to some other point, an appreciation of that point turns on an appreciation of its position" (II: 473). Thus, the wedding night sequence of the mother's eavesdropping on three daughters behind three doors creates the 'puzzle' part of the 'puzzle-solution' sequence. Since the mother leads us through the story, we share her puzzlement at the third door. As the mother leaves the first and second doors after hearing sounds but waits at the third door, "Nothin'" (line 38) must refer to sound, and the silent third door presents the 'puzzle'. The 'solution' is provided in a parallel sequence in which the mother asks each girl, in the same order as she listened at their doors, the significance of the sounds heard. The solution is implied by the punchline.

Thus far Sacks' analysis seems unexceptionable. Problems arise, however, with Sacks' (1995, II: 478-482) argument that the joke is structured to hide the implausibility of the events narrated. As Mulkay (1988: 17-20) has argued, jokes thrive on implausibility. Whereas 'serious discourse' relies on the simplistic, exclusionary binary logic of truth and falsehood, humour relies on the contradictions that serious discourse strives to eradicate. Indeed, Sacks' transcript includes a 'weak' joke that flaunts its own implausibility ('What's purple and an island? Grape Britain'). Since islands are not purple, this is evidently not a request for information. Implausibility is the label of the joke, and recipients must not guess the solution before the punchline allows the pieces to snap into place. 'Grape Britain' illustrates the binary-defying nature of jokes perfectly. For the predicate 'purple' to obtain, the first word must be heard as 'grape': to be the name of an island, 'grape' must be heard as 'Great'. As *la langue* depends upon such systematic differences, we cannot afford to hear 'grape' as 'great', or 'great' as 'grape'. But in this joke we must. In defiance of the 'law', the object of categorisation is simultaneously forced to inhabit two mutually exclusive categories so that for a moment, and only in this context, this unsaid flickers to life. What *langue* denies, *parole* allows. The unsaid and unsayable can exist by virtue of the said as that most implausible of visitations: the repressed on *parole*.

Sacks' sequential analysis shows how the said carefully and economically creates a space for what I call 'the unsaid'. At the punchline, only one thought fits the space created by the sequential structure. The categories 'honeymoon', 'bedroom' and 'night' establish a 'cluster' in which sexual activities are to be expected. By cultural convention, the 'wedding night' device entails the predicate 'sexual intercourse', and, traditionally, the bride 'losing her virginity'. Since the mother is *listening* at bedroom doors, the laughter and screams from the first two daughters' rooms are designed to be heard as predicates of sexual activity and, by a simple binary, silence at the third door is hearable as 'lack of sexual activity'. Thus in the first two daughters' explanations ('Well it tickled, Mommy' and 'Oh, Mommy it hurts'), the word 'it' will also probably be taken to refer to sexual intercourse. 'Tickling' and 'hurting' are situatedly hearable as predicates of sexual intercourse, and most probably — again by tradition — of the loss of virginity. Of course, tickling and hurting on wedding nights need not necessarily refer to coitus or the loss of virginity: it is by the culturally conventional narrative of 'the wedding night' invoked in the 'gaps' by the sequentiality of the said that coitus is seen as happening.

In jokes the *recipient* must make a chain of inferences before the punchline is supplied. Although the 'said' of the joke creates spaces tailored for unavoidable inferences, they remain 'unsaid'. To 'get the joke' is to read the unsaid off the face of the said in the iteration of the myth of 'what we all know'. As Sacks notes, the joke hinges on the silence encountered at the third door. Since sexual activity *is* vocalisation in this joke, there has apparently been no sexual activity *at all* in the third room, and a solution may be expected to account for this. On this basis the third daughter's punchline response (line 44-45), "W'you tol'me it wz always impolite t'talk with my mouth full", restores the sexual line of thought, but whereas the innuendo has so far evoked stereotyped knowledge of the traditional 'deflowering' of the virgin, attention is now directed to her mouth.

Of course, the hearer might reasonably infer that the daughter was eating a snack, given that this injunction normally refers to eating. Here genre expectations play a vital role. The sexual expectations raised earlier in the joke make it obvious that the genre is 'the dirty joke', and a snack would be neither funny nor 'dirty'. To 'get' the joke and laugh, the recipient is thus forced into a 'double-take' on the punchline. Not talking with one's mouth full must be re-aligned with sexual activity to produce the inference and complete the joke. It is not just puerile embarrassment that produces laughter: 'There were three daughters who had sex on their wedding night: two had coitus and the other performed fellatio' is simply not funny. As Mulkay (1988) indicates in criticising Sacks' treatment of the joke, it is indirectness, the raising of inferences and their necessary and surprising re-adjustment without their being made explicit, that produces humour. Laughter is partly a public acknowledgement of having followed the unsaid to an unmentioned and unexpected conclusion, and to having shared an implicit train of thought with others. Sacks' sequential and categorisation analysis shows *how* the joke means, but fails to see what this has to do with humour and the unsaid.

It is not oral sex per se that is 'unmentionable', nor need we be ignorant of oral sex to be surprised by the punchline. The categorization device of the wedding night within the sequential elegance of the joke plays off cultural stereotypes to focus attention on the female genitals as the *exclusive* site of sexual experience, thus repressing awareness of other possibilities. Whereas language inevitably represses and channels meaning, humorous discourse represses meaning only to expose the repression reflexively. In this case, what is exposed is a stereotypical categorization of 'the-bride-on-her-wedding-night' as 'innocent' (that is, sexually inexperienced) and of interest primarily in terms of one anatomical site and one sexual possibility. The bride's function is thus discursively inscribed on her body in a culturally sanctioned operation that implicitly reduces her to the status of her (anatomical) sex. Stereotypical thinking and the resultant repressive production of the unsaid are demanded by the sequentiality and categorisations of the unfolding story (as analysed by Sacks) and exposed by the punchline. Obviously, this does not mean that this dirty joke queries heterosexism or masculinism — far from it. But the joke interpellates the recipient, male or female, to take up an absurdly simplifying categorization device and apply it, only to expose the simplicity of the style of thinking and speech it produces: much as drag or carnival can question the very natural order on which they are predicated.

2.   Sacks' gender and age categorisation of the joke

Sacks' categorisation of the joke as designed for and only of interest to twelve-year-old girls is triggered by Ken's announcement that he heard it from his twelve-year-old sister, and by evidence in his data that the boys are not amused. On this basis, Sacks develops the argument that the joke is an informational package for young adolescent females involving both sexual and non-sexual knowledge. The sisters marry the same night, according to Sacks (1995, II: 487), because teenage girls exist in 'packs', know that they are doomed to marry, and therefore fantasise about marrying in packs! In Sacks' words:

> I'd like to suggest that 12-year-old girls are perhaps in some way interested in sex and marriage and things like that, but I think it can be found that what they are rather more interested in is each other. That is to say, one of the really distinct features of that age group of girls is that they travel in packs, i.e., they have a group life among themselves. And when they fantasize about a future, one of the things they know in some way is that the future will involve the end of their travelling in packs, that being replaced by, e.g., that

they get married and end up in two two-person relationships, the other person being a male. Now, one of the things they do when they fantasy about the future is attempt ways to project their pack-travelling into that future. And one characteristic feature of such fantasy is that they get married together. That's about as far as they can go as a projectable aim because they know that having gotten married, they are now split up. Indeed their getting married together might in some not too bizarre way be about the only condition under which they could accept as interesting that they have to get married. That is to say, for a group travelling in packs together, that the marriage takes place in a pack is a way in which the future, of a marriage for each of them that splits the group apart, can be accommodated to their pleasure in their pack status. Notice again that in the joke the males play almost no part. They're introduced as a foil for the marriage and never appear again. So the event of the three sisters all getting married together can project a common fantasy that 12-year-old girls have (II: 487).

Whether Sacks' observations about little girls are accurate or not I would not presume to judge, preferring to leave such questions to colleagues with a past as pack animals, but their status as generalising theory far removed from the interaction is indubitable. Moreover, according to Sacks, as young girls are more related to their mothers than to men, the focus is the interaction between girls and their powerful, prying mothers (487). In a sense, then, the punchline of the joke is only 'dirty' as a cover in delivering the 'squelch' to the mother: her own teaching is turned back on her to show the limited applicability of her maxims (490-493). Sacks then concludes that the boys do not find the joke funny because they have not actually understood the special informational package for little girls embodied in this gendered and age-categorised joke (493-494).

Sacks' argument is a theoretical extension of his excellent sequential analysis that relies on questionable assumptions about the category 'twelve-year-old girls' and its supposed predicates. Apparently, little girls are a homogeneous group with identical reactions to sexuality, mothers, belonging and marriage. Neither argued nor proved, Sacks' generalisations are merely asserted as commonsense observations – as what any member would know. Importantly, there is nothing in the joke per se which demands Sacks' generalisations about little girls: it is Sacks' search for a reason for the *boys'* unamused response that leads to his categorisation of the joke and of the kind of little girl who supposedly tells it. Closer examination of the boys' interaction, however, will show that the boys orientate to the joke as *un*typical of little girls' jokes and that candidate explanations for their unamused response can be found within their interaction – without necessitating the analyst's imposition of his or her own categorisations on the joke or on 'girls'. If Sacks did indeed finally abandon MCA because it could produce 'wild' analyses, he might have found ample justification here in his own decontextualised and unsituated theorising. In imposing a package of predicates on the category 'twelve-year-old girls', Sacks does exactly what the dirty joke initially 'tricks' recipients into doing with the category 'brides-on-their-wedding-night'. So much more that could be said about 'brides' or 'little girls' is consigned to the unsaid by the very act of categorisation.

Since the original teller (in this connection) was a twelve year old girl, and the four principal actors in the joke are three daughters and their mother, Sacks' gender categorisation might initially seem reasonable. As Mulkay (1988: 130-31) points out, however, the joke reappears in Knott's (1985: 63) collection with the same core, but this time told from a male point of view. In this version, three young men seek shelter at a lonely farmhouse. The farmer demands that each man sleep with one of his three daughters. The rest of Knott's version is structured like Sacks' joke, with the same punchline, but the mother is replaced by the father. If the gender categorisation of the joke can be reversed by changing peripheral details, Sacks' implicit argument that this is *essentially* a female joke is weakened. Moreover, as Mulkay (1988: 129) points out, the joke is in fact transmitted to a boy (Ken) and then re-transmitted to his friends.

Even if Sacks is right in his assumptions about little girls, his claim (Sacks 1995: 486) that the joke contains an informational package uniquely designed for them is questionable. If the information concerns the relationship between mothers and daughters (487), the package must be empty because Sacks also claims that little girls *know* that mothers teach them maxims that are not universally valid (491). One cannot simultaneously claim that the joke is relevant to little girls because it appeals to shared experience *and* that the joke supplies the very same information that such experiences have given them. In fact, Sacks argues that the joke caters to the girls' need to know that their isolated experiences of the mismatch between the domain and scope of a rule's application are not uncommon (491-493). But in that case, it makes more sense to see the joke as a 'mention' of a common experience than as an 'informational package', and one might also ask what it is that restricts this anxiety to little girls. Perhaps, then, the package contains information about sexual behaviour. Sacks evokes the primal scene overheard at bedroom doors as a source of half-knowledge and anxiety for children (493). The packaged information may resolve such matters. Again, however, if recipients already know that other sexual activities than coitus exist, the informational value is minimal. On the other hand, without knowledge of oral sex, they would presumably be unable to 'unwrap' the package by making the connection between mouths and sexual activity.[3] Once again, it surely makes more sense to see the joke as a 'mention' of what is already known, or at least suspected. This leaves little girls (and boys!) in the same position as any other recipient, and once we see the joke as playing on the simultaneous, dialogic evocation and repression of so-called 'background knowledge', the narrow age and gender categorisation of the joke is inappropriate.

What leads Sacks to impose such dubious categorisations on his data? The answer lies in his *partial* appeal to the co-text of the joke's telling. Sacks accepts the boys' *situated* and implicit categorisation of the joke uncritically as *the* essential truth about the joke, and reifies it as an academic fiction by working backwards through commonsense to theory. This is not principled ethnomethodological indifference, for Sacks' seeks an explanation for the boys' reaction in his own theorising about jokes and little girls rather than in the detail of the boys' situated talk. It is to this talk that we must now turn.

3. Boyztalk: Precategorising the joke

If we re-examine the boys' talk, which Sacks draws upon but fails to analyse, it is immediately apparent that, quite apart from its intrinsic qualities, the joke is re-told as inappropriate for a twelve year old girl. In Ken's first turn in line 1, "You wanna hear…" can be heard as suggesting news value for the joke, or as a simple question (with 'do' elided). In either case, it is already presented as a joke with the history of its local 'origin' attached. The boys immediately begin to negotiate the likely value of jokes told by twelve year old girls. In line 2, Roger gives the dispreferred and flatly unmitigated response that he does not want to hear the joke, but self-repairs by reluctantly consenting. Roger's turn thus elegantly registers opposition *and* permission, putting the responsibility for continuing squarely on Ken's shoulders. As Al cites an example (in line 4) of the category of weak jokes ('Grape Britain') to be expected of Ken's sister, Ken seizes the floor at what is definitely not a transition relevance place (Sacks, Schegloff and Jefferson 1972: 12ff.), overlapping Al's contribution with an emphatic negation (line 6). Ken's "To <u>stun</u> me she says" (line 6) might imply an intention to shock or amaze on his sister's part, or simply to report the effect of the joke. This useful ambiguity allows Ken to arouse interest for the joke as potentially stunning without committing himself to this evaluation. Ken still has to battle for the floor as Roger and Al playfully sabotage the joke in its introductory phase by feigning misunderstandings.[4]

Before Ken tells the joke, then, the boys are positioning themselves in relation to the idea that a younger girl might be capable of telling a joke of interest to them. In other words, Sacks is mistaken in categorising the joke per se as only for adolescent girls on the basis of the boys' reactions: the categorisation is being negotiated by the boys *before* the joke has even been told. The joke is presented either as unusual enough to deserve retelling on its own merits or as revealing something unexpected about Ken's little sister, and he introduces the joke as designed to 'stun' him. As Roger clearly expresses his lack of enthusiasm, and Al provides an example of the category of joke that he believes little girls tell, this joke is already being dealt with in terms of a category-binary 'typical of little girls/atypical of little girls', and the boys' reactions on hearing it will later be negotiated in these terms – whatever the nature of the joke.

4.   Boyztalk: After the joke

The boys' reactions after the joke are difficult to judge, as their laughter and comments can be *read* as ironic or serious; here the limitations of transcription obscure exact tone of voice and non-verbal behaviour. Notably, only Al responds to Ken's laughter (line 47) as a cue to join in, but Al's emphatic laughter (line 51) may be a mocking parody. Roger maintains what might be hearable as a 'cool' distance at all times, and his turns comment on the reactions of others. First he comments on Al's 'delayed reaction' in line 54, and, when Al explains that he had to think about it awhile, Roger's subsequent turn (in lines 58-60) certainly sounds ironic ("hehh hh hehh hhh You mea(h)n th(h)e dee(h)p (h)hidden meaning there doesn' hitcha right awa-ay heh heh // hehh-hhhhhh hehhhehh"). This could be a comment on the joke, on Al's reaction, or on both. Roger did not laugh at the joke in the turn provided, but here he laughs at Al's reaction to his own 'delayed reaction' comment. His next turn on line 65 ("Ki//nda got ps::ychological over//tones (to it)") is a more sophisticated-sounding but equally uninformative version of Dan's characteristically flat and empty "Yeh. I // guess so" (line 62) and Al's incomplete "What'e meant tuh say is the t- thet u:m" (line 63). The boys are hearably marking time.

Ken's clear statement of the significance of the joke for him in line 67 ("Little sister's gittin' // older") might appear to be a response to Roger's preceding turn (line 65), but Ken's "That's w't I m(h)ean tih // say" in line 69 links it back to Al's incomplete turn (line 63) before Roger's, even giving the same emphasis to "m(h)ean" as Al gave to "meant". After Dan, in overlap with the end of Ken's turn, agrees with Ken's assessment, Ken expresses his amazement at a twelve year old telling him something of this nature and he admits his ignorance (line 71). What he did not know is lost, as Roger interrupts in line 72 to suggest that Ken's sister may not have understood the joke, but Al's question (line 74) ignores Roger's turn and instead connects back to pick up on the topic of Ken's ignorance in Ken's interrupted turn (line71). Ken and Al continue their sequence on this topic until, in line 79, Ken supplies a 'punchline' for the whole conversation in his 'hotdog' utterance.

A pattern thus emerges from the 'post-joke' interaction. Roger does not laugh at the joke in the turns immediately following the punchline, but supplies a comment including a laughter particle instead ("rea:c//tio(h)n"). As Mulkay notes, the laughter slot after a joke may be filled by commentary instead. Roger initially selects the topics in lines 54 and 58-60: first topicalising Al's delayed reaction, which could be seen as a 'dig' at Al or more obliquely at the joke, and then the joke itself ("dee(h)p (h)hidden meaning"), a topic he continues in his next turn ("psychological overtones"), thus ignoring Al's aborted attempt in line 63 to introduce the topic of Ken's intention in telling the joke. Until this point, Roger appears to have been setting the agenda, but now a sequence occurs in which Al and Ken respond to each other, 'skipping' Roger's contributions and thus tending to sideline him. Together, Ken and Al establish Ken's sister as the topic, and cooperate in negotiating the significance of the joke as re-categorising 'little sister' as 'getting older', with knowledge not expected of a twelve year old. Roger interrupts in line 72 and bluntly questions the significance of the joke as negotiated by Ken and Al, raising the possibility that Ken's sister may not have understood it.

Before Ken can supply the preferred second pair part of the adjacency pair initiated by Roger's question, Al gets in a question of his own in line 74 ("She haftuh explain it to yuh Ke:n?"), linking back to Ken's interrupted confession of ignorance in line 71. Ken answers Al immediately and directly ("Yeah she had to explain it to detail to me"). Al then seems to complete the sequence by acknowledging Ken's answer ("Okay, good. Gladju gotta sister thet knows // somethin'"), but Ken adds another turn that both addresses the sequence with

Al *and* provides the delayed second pair part to Roger's question. Ken says "She told me she wz eatin' a hot dog". Roger and Al then demand an account of the meaning of Ken's 'hot dog' turn, as well they might: is Ken seriously suggesting that neither he nor his sister 'got' the joke, is he providing a new obscenity in the form of a phallic hot dog to top the joke, or is he (non-seriously) making explicit what is implicit in Roger's and Al's questioning of his and his sister's understanding of the obscenity?

The sequence of turns leading to Ken's 'hotdog' remark is complex and ambiguous. Although Al's "She haftuh explain it to yuh Ke:n?" in line 74 is most readily hearable as a response to Ken's earlier unfinished confession of ignorance in line 71, it can also be heard as responding to Roger's last turn (lines 72-73), in that his sister's explaining the joke to him could be heard as evidence that his sister had understood the joke. In either case, Ken's accountability for having told the joke is at stake. If Ken has told them the joke to amuse them, their failure to laugh at it sincerely leaves Ken isolated. On the other hand, if the point is that the joke recategorises Ken's sister, Roger's last remark has just unmitigatedly challenged the point as negotiated by Al and Ken (that is, that his little sister is growing up), thus challenging Ken's credibility again. Finally, Al has suggested a way out for Ken, which, paradoxically, is the most damning of all. If his sister explained the joke to him, he can 'save' his 'alibi' for telling the joke, as this counters Roger's objection by showing his sister is growing up, but Ken must claim to have had the joke explained to him by a twelve year old girl – perhaps a difficult admission for a seventeen year old boy to make to his friends. Ken's answer, however, even retains the rather damning 'had to' and adds that she explained it in detail. Given the strangeness of Ken's 'confession' and the 0.5 second pause before Al's response, Al's "Okay, good" in line 77 can be heard as positive, ironic, noncommittal, or even as indeterminate. He makes no overt reference to the inference that Ken is less sexually sophisticated than his twelve year old sister, but the structure of Al's utterance makes such an inference hearable. He is not just glad that *Ken's sister* understood the *joke*: he is glad that Ken has *got* someone who understands *something* (at least). This might then be hearable as the dry ironic performance of an attempt to comfort Ken, to 'make the best of a bad thing': *I'm sad that you don't know anything, but I'm glad that you at least have a sister who understands something!*

Most of the utterances after the joke are equally indeterminate – for the analyst certainly, but perhaps also for the participants. Whereas I have implied that the boys' talk can be heard as somewhat aggressive, their interaction can also be heard as playful and ironic. Playful, ironic talk, like the joke, relies on not making 'play' explicit, but unlike the joke, there need be no final closure, no punchline, nor necessarily any laughter. In this particular conversation, the degree of seriousness or playfulness of any one turn is difficult to ascertain because other turns are equally indeterminate. The question here is whether everything that occurs is *present* at the moment of speech, and 'present' in the transcript in a form that third party analysts can retrieve. This rather Derridian question can be reduced to a more concrete, manageable and local form: does it not make a difference (or 'différance') to a reading of *this* interaction if we have seen similar patterns in other transcripts, involving the same participants, where the boys also 'put each other down' and yet seem to go on interacting reasonably amicably? This is not simply an analysts' concern, for it is precisely such a history of interaction that might affect how the boys hear each other's turns and respond to them. Yet the boys are hardly likely to orientate *explicitly* to this 'context' each time it is relevant to their talk, as it is embodied in the very pattern of their interaction. To put this another way, such previous interactions are only 'context' or 'history' insofar as analysts – of necessity – impose units of analysis on ongoing conversations. The necessary act of restricting analysis to an extract or even to a clearly bounded, complete conversation *constructs* some events as focal and present, and others as absent and contextual.

In Sacks' transcript of the telling of the dirty joke, however, the boys explicitly orientate to questions of playfulness, seriousness and even of interpretation in their demands for an explanation (lines 82-89) of Ken's hot dog turn. If we provisionally take Ken's turn ("She told me she wz eatin' a hot dog") in line 79 at face value, neither Ken nor his sister have understood the obscene point of the joke, and the negotiated point of telling it – that 'little sister's getting older' - is erased from the conversation as a patent misunderstanding. Worse still for Ken, he has then placed *himself as well as his sister* in the category that Roger has posited; the naive, unwitting transmitter of obscenities. Is this true? Pressurised to explain, Ken laughingly responds that he does not know (line 88): it was *just* something *he* said. This partly clarifies the situation: if it was just something he said, he has now changed its footing so that he takes responsibility for the utterance as an improvised fiction rather than as a true report of his sister's words. But why would Ken want to do that?

If Ken has been 'cornered' by his friends in an interactional situation where he must admit his own naivety, his 'hot dog' turn can be seen as the punchline in the joke of his own humiliation. By creating the fiction of his sister's misunderstanding and his own, he also creates an exaggerated version of Roger's hypothesis that Ken's sister transmitted the joke without understanding it, and exaggerates his own naivety so that not only did he need his younger sister's explanation, but he *still* has not understood the joke. Ken disarms his potential humiliation by hyperbole in a self-ironic, face-destructive move that can hardly be taken seriously, and is therefore 'safe'. At the same time, the possibility of an obscene hearing of 'hot dog' as phallic protects the utterance itself from closure.

To stop here, however, would be to impose a one-dimensional picture of teenage boys on the participants just as Sacks imposes simple gender and age categorisations on twelve year old girls and as the joke imposes on brides. If the boys' utterances can be heard either as serious or playful, the sequence leading to Ken's hot dog comment is particularly ambiguous: if Ken and Al are only *playing* with the idea that Ken needed the joke explained, then Ken's hot-dog punchline is simply a crowning moment of one-upmanship in a non-serious language game. To take the said at face value, ignoring the unsaid, would be to assume that participants lack reflexive awareness of the very categories by which, implicitly or explicitly, they construct others, each other, and themselves. An ethnomethodological respect for members' concerns should not reduce members to non-reflexive automatons in the grip of the categorisations to which they can be assigned, nor must it reduce their actions to simple 'instances' of interactional regularities. This is particularly evident when Ken performs his punchline. In 'confessing' his need for explanation, Ken retrospectively portrays himself as the sexually naive 'butt' of the joke. In offering the hot dog explanation, moreover, he constitutes himself and his sister as doubly sexually naive: implying that he still believes the incorrect, innocent explanation, he constructs himself momentarily as a parody of the identity category the boys' talk has been predicated upon. In that case, Ken's hot dog turn implicitly orientates to and indexes the role of the unsaid throughout the boys' talk after the joke. To put this another way, as it is impossible to account for this turn *without* turning to the unsaid, this rare moment of revelation makes apparent what can more easily be glossed over in other interactions. It is prima facie evidence that, as Heritage maintains, not everything is available at the surface of talk.

Ken's 'hot dog' punchline mirrors the logic of his sister's joke: as well as reflecting the mechanism it also *inverts* it, as words are inverted in mirrors. The tight sequential form of the 'three sisters' joke evokes the stereotypical categorisation of young brides on their wedding night, only to show the inadequacy of the stereotype through the 'mouth full' punchline. In commenting on the joke, the boys discuss the possibility of re-categorising Ken's sister as 'growing up', presumably as based on the predicate 'sexually knowing' consequent on her having told the joke. This re-categorisation of 'innocent girl' as 'sexual sophisticate' provides a striking parallel to the re-categorisation of the third bride involved in the 'obscene' understanding of the 'mouth full' punchline. In their post-joke talk, the boys use the same categorisational logic that the joke encourages and exploits to create the (dialogically repressed) unsaid that is glimpsed in the punchline. Ken's performance of the 'hot dog' explanation involves a multiple reversal. If the third bride's silence is indeed due to her eating a hot dog, her action departs from the sexual predicates stereotypically expected of the category 'bride-on-her-wedding-night', thus annulling the mechanism of the joke. The joke thereby becomes (fictionally) untellable, and Ken (fictionally) loses face by repeating it. His sister is (fictionally) re-recategorised as doubly naive, and, most tellingly of all, Ken (fictionally) joins her within this category, which the boys – and Harvey Sacks – would apparently like to reserve for little girls.

Ken's performance shows how the unsaid of the joke has continued beyond the boundaries of the joke's narrative into the boys' own stereotyped categorisation of the joke and of Ken's sister. By aligning himself with her, Ken parodies what they are inferring, and exposes what is at stake in their talk: the boys' own self-categorisation as sophisticated, knowing and coolly 'mature' seventeen year old boys – be it serious or ironically self-aware. Given that 'hot dog' might itself be heard as an obscene metaphor playing on the unsaid connections between food and sex in the joke, Ken's performance leaves his friends in a situation of radical uncertainty in which predicates such as 'naïve' or 'sophisticated' are inapplicable as simple binaries. In the face of such indeterminacy, any attempt by the others to categorise Ken or his sister is likely to reveal more about the categoriser than the categorised!

Ken's hot dog turn *might* be motivated by a desire to turn a seriously face-threatening situation into a joke, or by loyalty to his sister, but we cannot know. The point is that because talking with one's mouth full normally refers to eating, the 'hot dog' joke is already there in the unsaid of the joke as the innocent 'flip-side' of the obscene connection between mouth, talk, food and sex that completes the joke. The boys' talk uncritically adopts the official logic of the joke and with it the entire nexus of the said and the unsaid on which it depends. Like many improvised, occasioned witticisms, Ken's comment is probably not the result of genius or deep thought: it is waiting to be made in the mechanisms of constantly recurring dialogic repression that enable talk to occur at all (Billig 1999c). Ken claims that he cannot account for his last turn, that he does not know the meaning of his own words, and that he 'just said' something as though a force beyond him was laying claim to *his* mouth!

5.   Concluding remarks

I have attempted to show that Sacks imposes unwarranted age and gender cat-egorisations on the dirty joke – and, in the process and even more spectacu-larly, on 12-year-old girls. He does so partly because he uncritically adopts the boys' situated negotiation of the point and value of the joke, already cate-gorised as 'for twelve-year-old girls' before the boys hear it. Closer examina-tion reveals that what is at stake in the boys' talk may be their own identities, accountability and status, in relation to each other and to the situated cate-gorisations of females and juniors which help maintain the fragile identities of seventeen year old boys. Ken's sister and her joke are hostages in a negotiation of categories which uses them in doing very different interactional 'business' than is at first apparent. Sacks then embeds a few chosen features of the boys' categorisational work in his own academic fiction, which, while plausible and highly insightful, ignores the situated complexity of the categorisation and translates it into transcendental truths about little girls, their needs and their jokes.

My reading of the joke and the talk surrounding it presents another story, and possibly another fiction. I have tried to show that there are multiple and recursive indeterminacies in the boys' talk at practically every turn, and that ambiguities of meaning affect sequential, topical and categorisation analysis. I have attempted to recognise and honour a number of these ambiguities while pursuing my point that because both the joke and the talk surrounding it play off the unsaid, interpretation is inevitable for participating members and analysts alike. This is particularly apparent when interlocutors apparent-ly perform roles in the conversation with varying degrees of knowing self-irony. The resultant self-reflexive pastiche is particularly resistant to over-sim-plifications in the responses of co-participants and to the fictions which ana-lysts, however principled, are wont to impose on speech. Harvey Sacks is the most principled of analysts, but this particular instance reveals the dangers of assumptions about common sense and of the associated failure to carry out a full and integrated, *situated*, sequential and categorisation analysis that is also willing to approach the unsaid as constructed by the said.

Sacks' analysis of the dirty joke is atypical of his work in several ways. First, although it purports to be an analysis of the *telling* of a joke, the analytic object is the joke itself rather than the talk in which it occurs. The boys' talk is only drawn into the analysis in a perfunctory and superficial way as a point of departure for Sacks' theorising about the joke as an informational package for little girls. This means that what Sacks is doing here is applying sequential analysis to the joke as a semiotic object rather than to the interaction in which it is embedded. Having accomplished this rather successfully, Sacks then theorises the joke on the basis of the boys' unamused response, but he seeks an explanation in the joke itself and in some extraordinary generalisations about little girls, as pack animals for instance, rather than analysing the boys' talk-in-interaction, as he would normally do. Sacks (1995: 483-485) notes that jokes, unlike stories, belong to no-one. What he attempts to do, however, is a piece of sociological theorising which assigns this joke to a group (little girls) on the basis of its serious informational function. As McHoul (1996: vii-xxii and 3-60) has recently pointed out, however, the 'meaning' of a semiotic object may not be entirely intrinsic to it: what needs to be examined in some detail is the interaction at the frame between the semiotic object and its respective contexts or communities of production and reception. In a sense, this is what Sacks is attempting to do, but he subordinates the context of reception that is available for analysis (the boys' talk) to a context or community of production (little girls circulating risqué jokes for informational purposes) that is not available and must be invented. This in turn raises a further problem of footing and thus of (imagined) origins: the joke is no more the possession of Ken's little sister than it is Ken's. The 'intention' or serious function of a joke can only be fixed by an analytic fiction, since its origin is inaccessible, absent, and therefore, for all intents and purposes, non-existent. In this sense, jokes exemplify what Derrida (1982, see also Hepburn 1999) claims of all discourse: an origin is always absent where iteration re-circulates discourse so that meaning is always deferred – and always different. It is only by the imposition of an analytic fiction that this play of meaning can be shut down. For Sacks, members are front-line analysts, and in Sacks' transcript we have seen them in the process of negotiating the meaning of Ken's retelling of the joke that his sister passed on to him. The boys try to 'fix' the meaning of the event they are involved in by reference to what is absent (Ken's sister and her telling of the joke). Sacks follows them but theorises the function of the joke for little girls, and theorises little girls in general (both absent from the transcript). The insistence in CA and principled MCA practice on sticking to the data may not be foolproof, but it is the only known check to the misrecognition of absences as present origins. It is difficult enough for participants to resist the imposition of simplifying and generalising categories in ongoing talk, as many 'feminists', 'gay men' and 'lesbians' are only too aware, and this imposition on those who are not present is 'virtually' irresistible. Yet, as Ken's punchline attests, repression through categorisational simplifications also produces an unsaid — what Derrida might call 'the trace' — that haunts the said like a desire and may return to it as the repressed on *parole*.

A CA and MCA inspired approach to sex and gender in talk presents a challenging dilemma. On the one hand CA and other ethnomethodological approaches derive much of their strength from the refusal to speculate about what is not empirically present and consequential at the surface level of the said. On the other hand, sex and gender in talk involve stereotyped categorisations of self and others which are available for imposition, manipulation, play and performance without ever being stated. To ignore members' own sophisticated and ambiguous use of the unsaid as a resource for 'talkin' sex and gender' is to over-simplify and distort their talk in analytical fictions which re-transmit the stereotyped categories and clichéd thinking that we are presumably trying to counter.

Finally, and most importantly, this re-analysis of the re-telling of a dirty joke will hopefully have shown the provisionality and situatedness of categorisations and their predicates as contested constructions in ongoing interaction. The seemingly obligatory and monolithic sex and gender identity categories and predicates by which, or in denial of which, we live our lives (for instance, man/woman or gay/straight) are themselves binaries predicated at the tip of a hierarchy of underlying categorisations. Each categorisation is a constructive simplification, perhaps a way of 'doing being ordinary', or of doing being extraordinary in a way that is ordinarily recognisable (Sacks 1984, 1995). Each simplification into a binary (see Hepburn this volume) can produce a desire to retrieve the unsaid that the category denies, in subversive action, performance, or speech. In a sense, this might be the nature of desire. That, however, is a topic so large that it must await investigation in some 'other arena'.

Notes

1. It should be noted that Sacks himself did not publish the more speculative parts of his theorising about the joke. This re-analysis of his lectures on the subject is not an attack on Sacks' work: rather, it is 'intended' as an examination of some crucial issues attending categorisation, gender and theory. Sacks' lectures, never intended for this kind of scrutiny but preserved by a fortunate accident of history, are simply the occasion for my pointing out a danger inherent in analysis. In essence: if Sacks can do this in an unguarded moment, then anyone can!

2. This extract is reproduced exactly as it appeared in Sacks (1995, II: 470-472). The transcription conventions used by Sacks in the extract are a proto-form of what become the core set of conventions adopted by most conversation analysts, following Jefferson (see the transcription conventions appendix to this volume).

3. It is just possible that the sequential and categorical order of the joke is so tightly constructed that it might allow a leap from ignorance to enlightenment. However, this presupposes a categorisation of all little girls as sufficiently knowledgeable to follow the categorical and sequential logic evoking coitus in the body of the joke, and yet as sufficiently ignorant not to suspect the existence of fellatio. This is unlikely as a valid generalisation.

4. As Mulkay (1988: 58) has noted, such playful interruptions, feigned misunderstandings and attempts to take over the joke are standard features of the transition from serious discourse to the joke. They do not necessarily convey a particular attitude to the joke in question.

References

Beach, Wayne A. 2000 "Inviting collaborations in stories about a woman". *Language in Society* 29: 379-407.

Billig, Michael. 1987 *Arguing and Thinking: A Rhetorical Approach to Social Psychology.* Cambridge: Cambridge University Press.

Billig, Michael. (1991). *Ideology and Opinions: Studies in Rhetorical Psychology.* London: Sage.

Billig, Michael. 1999a "Whose terms? Whose ordinariness? Rhetoric and ideology in conversation analysis". *Discourse & Society* 10(4): 543-58.

Billig, Michael. 1999b "Conversation analysis and the claims of naivety". *Discourse & Society* 10(4): 572-576.

Billig, Michael. 1999c *Freudian Repression: Conversation Creating the Unconscious.* Cambridge: Cambridge University Press.

Butler, Judith. 1997 *Excitable Speech: A Politics of the Performative.* London, Routledge.

Derrida, Jacques. 1982 *Limited Inc.* Evanston, Illinois: Northwestern University Press.

Garfinkel, Harold. 1967 *Studies in Ethnomethodology.* Cambridge: Polity Press.

Gofman, Erving. 1979 "Footing". *Semiotica* 25(1/2): 1-29.

Hepburn, Alexa. 1999 "Derrida and psychology: Deconstruction and its ab/uses in critical and discursive psychologies". *Theory & Psychology* Vol. 9(5): 639-665.

Heritage, John. 1984 *Garfinkel and Ethnomethodology*. Cambridge: Polity Press.

Kitzinger, Celia. 2000 "Doing feminist conversation analysis". *Feminism and Psychology* 10(2): 163-193.

Knott, Blanche. 1985 *Outrageously Tasteless Jokes*. London: Arrow Books.

Latour, Bruno. 1986 "Will the last person to leave the social studies of science please turn on the tape-recorder?" *Social Studies of Science* 16: 541-548.

Lepper, Georgia. 2000 *Categories in Text and Talk*. London: Sage.

McHoul, Alec. 1994 "Towards a critical ethnomethodology". *Theory, Culture & Society* 11: 105-126.

McHoul, Alec. 1996 *Semiotic Investigations: Towards an Effective Semiotics*. Nebraska, University of Nebraska Press.

Mulkay, Michael. 1988 *On Humour: Its Nature and Its Place in Modern Society*. Cambridge, Polity Press.

Sacks, Harvey. 1974 "An analysis of the course of a joke's telling in conversation". In *Explorations in the Ethnography of Speaking*, R. Bauman and J. Sherzer (eds), 337-353. Cambridge: Cambridge University Press.

Sacks, Harvey. 1978 "Some technical considerations of a dirty joke". In *Studies in the Organisation of Conversational Interaction*, J. Schenkein (ed.), 249-270. London: Academic Press.

Sacks, Harvey. 1984 "On doing 'being ordinary'". In *Structures of Social Action: Studies in Conversation Analysis*, J. Atkinson and J. Heritage (eds), 513-529. Cambridge: Cambridge University Press.

Sacks, Harvey. 1995 *Lectures on Conversation*, vols I and II (edited by Gail Jefferson). Oxford: Blackwell.

Sacks, Harvey, Schegloff, Emanuel A. and Jefferson, Gail. 1978 "A simplest systematics for the organization of turn taking for conversation". In *Studies in the Organisation of Conversational Interaction*, J. Schenkein (ed.), 7-55. London: Academic Press.

Schegloff, Emanuel A. 1991 "Reflections on talk and social structure". In *Talk and Social Structure*, D. Boden and D. Zimmerman (eds), 44-70. Cambridge: Polity Press.

Schegloff, Emanuel A. 1992a "Introduction". In *Lectures on Conversation* (Vol. I, edited by Gail Jefferson), H. Sacks, ix-lxii. Oxford: Blackwell.

Schegloff, Emanuel A. 1992b "In another context". In *Rethinking Context: Language as an Interactive Phenomenon*, A. Duranti and C. Goodwin (eds), 191-227. Cambridge: Cambridge University Press.

Schegloff, Emanuel A. 1997 "Whose text? Whose context?" *Discourse & Society* 8(2): 165-187.

Schegloff, Emanuel A. 1998 "Reply to Wetherell". *Discourse & Society* 9(3): 413-416.

Schegloff, Emanuel A. 1999a "'Schegloff's texts' as 'Billig's data': A critical reply". *Discourse & Society* 10(4): 558-572.

Schegloff, Emanuel A. 1999b "Naivety vs. sophistication or discipline vs. self-indulgence: A rejoinder to Billig". *Discourse & Society* 10(4): 577-582.

Wetherell, Margaret. 1998 "Positioning and interpretative repertoires: Conversation analysis and post-structuralism in dialogue". *Discourse & Society* 9(3): 387-412.

CHAPTER 9

Figuring gender in teachers' talk about school bullying*

Alexa Hepburn

This chapter provides a detailed examination of interview talk with teachers, focusing on the ways that gender can be enrolled in making sense of and evaluating the seriousness of school bullying. It begins by setting out the theoretical tools drawn upon in the analysis. This involves a discussion of three elements of Derrida's work on deconstruction: his critique of *binary logic*, which highlights the role of oppositions and their accompanying evaluations; his development of *supplementary logic*, which shows that we need to move beyond simple binary contrasts towards an understanding of undecideability in order to appreciate the rhetorical work that texts can do; and his identification of the fundamental role of *figurative* language — metaphors, maxims and so on. These are issues that the analytic focus of discursive psychology does not attend to explicitly, but which provide useful tools in the subsequent analysis in this chapter.

A further three themes developed in discursive psychology will then be explored: firstly, *participants' enrolment of 'psychological' issues*, secondly, their *construction of 'factual' descriptions* with particular reference to variability and indexicality, and thirdly, their orientations to issues of *stake and accountability*. These themes will complement and supplement Derrida's post-structuralist insights into language. The chapter will then proceed with a close textual analysis of interviews conducted with Scottish secondary school teachers, designed to highlight the subtlety and complexity of a range of strategies for constructing and evaluating reported intimidation in line with traditional notions of gender.

To conclude, three broader features of the study will be discussed, with the aim of combining Derridean insights with discursive psychological and conversation analytic observations, leading us to a consideration of the importance of situated contexts and participants' orientations for the analytic understanding of 'subjective' terms. The first of these broad features is the fixity and oppositions that gendered talk can employ. Secondly, there is a discussion of the respecification of psychological notions of subjectivity, identity, desire and agency — as *participants' resources for action*. This, combined with a deconstructive perspective, allows us insights into the supplementary or 'undecideable' character of mental and gendered terms. The third theme relates to the contribution that this type of detailed study can make to issues of power relationships and social critique. For example, the various subtle discursive ways that bullying and intimidation can be linked to gender may have implications for young people's available ways of making sense of themselves, their relationships with each other and, hence, ultimately their appreciation of sexuality as a performative, rather than a predetermined, phenomenon.

1.   Derrida and deconstruction

Derrida (1976, 1978, 1982) argues that the operation of argument depends on its textuality: plays of oppositions, metaphors and tropes, spaces and absences. This chapter will briefly summarise and draw on three elements of Derrida's work: his critique of *binary logic*, his development of *supplementary logic*, and his identification of the fundamental role of *figuration* (see Hepburn 1999 for further elaboration of aspects of Derrida's work that are useful for textual analysis).

a) Binary logic

Derrida suggests that *binary logic* — which is central in arguments in which the outcome is dependent on sets of basic oppositions — is fundamental to the working of philosophical texts. For example, a text might set up a distinction between mental and physical, or male and female, and in doing so treat them as exclusive items in their own right. Moreover, such texts typically treat one pole of the opposition as having greater access to truth and reality. Derrida calls this assumption 'logocentrism', that is the metaphysical privilege of *presence* over *absence*. By privileging one opposition over another, the privileged term is thought to be present to us – its meaning is not contaminated by what it has excluded (the subordinated term). The reason that philosophers do this is simple – they want certainty (Derrida 1973: 53). Deconstructing an opposition is a process that shows how the privileged term *is* contaminated by the subordinated term. The terms have no fixed, universal meaning; they are always already 'undecideable'. Their essence is to be marked with a certain absence, not a full presence. So, to illustrate, 'male' may typically be associated with rationality, and 'female' with irrationality or emotionality. Employing these oppositions allows us to construct maleness in an evaluative way — for example, as giving us closer insights into truth and reality — with femaleness correspondingly characterised negatively by error and delusion. Deconstruction is not intended simply to criticise the operation of this kind of argumentation, which risks simply inverting the polarities, leaving us stuck with the same fixed categories and evaluations. Rather, deconstruction calls for *intervention* and *disruption* that interrogates both the hierarchisation of an opposition, as well as its very oppositionality (Bennington 2000).

In this sense Derrida's deconstructions are 'quasi-transcendental' – they aim to introduce absence via undecideables as the essential non-origins of meaning. The supplement is an example of an undecideable, *différance* is another. A transcendental enquiry, going back to Kant's *Critique of Pure Reason*, is an enquiry into the very condition of possibility of what is taken to be the 'empirical'. Derrida's analyses are quasi-transcendental in that they look for the conditions of possibility *and impossibility*: that is, the impossibility of the purity (the uncontaminated state of presence) of concepts (for example, the binary terms).

One outcome for this kind of analysis (or quasi-analysis, see following section) is that we start to recognise that simple contrasts cannot capture the complexity of argumentative effects. The signifying structures of texts, assuming for a moment that they are amenable to individuation, relate to what lies inside and outside of each other. Derrida introduces *the logic of supplementarity* to show their paradoxical relations, in that something defined as being complete, such as 'truth', is nevertheless completed by that which exceeds or threatens it, which is 'error'.

b) Supplementary logic

The term 'supplement' is taken from Rousseau, who saw it as an "inessential extra added to something complete in itself" (Arnason 1997: 3). Derrida introduces a 'double meaning' of the supplement. It was previously thought that, in the context of the opposition nature/convention, conventional ways of doing things are a supplement to the original, natural ways of doing things. The natural way of doing things, on this view, is *present* to us. Here, the supplement is something that simply adds to a pure presence that *ought* to be self-sufficient. However, Derrida recognises a second meaning: the supplement *supplies*. It supplies what is in fact (and in essence, again illustrating the quasi-transcendental aspect of Derrida's work) absent from what is supposed to be purely present and self-sufficient. Thus, origins, by their essence, are marked by absence, not presence. There is no 'natural' and thus 'stable' binary opposition (including the nature/convention opposition). Oppositions are always unstable, always and already. They are 'always already' marked by a certain 'conventional' way of using them.

Yet the supplement somehow exposes a lack of completeness. A signifier's supplementary character is therefore "the result of a lack which must be supplemented" (Derrida 1978: 290). If there is no centre or fixed point, then we are left with continual movement, a play between signifiers. This necessitates an emphasis on the *function* of language, rather than what it is assumed to *represent*. This development is something which structuralism could not deal with, stuck between seeing meaning emerging merely through a sign's differences from other signs, or through the reader's understanding in making the text coherent. This is a crucial insight if we want to conduct textual analysis of the type that this chapter seeks to develop. However, 'analysis' is a term with problematic metaphysical connotations – following Derrida's notion of the quasi-transcendental, we might develop the term 'quasi-analysis', as a way of showing that our analyses are seeking a primordial non-presence, they are escaping the metaphysical search for presence.

Thus, supplementarity means *both* to add to *and* to replace, and this type of double meaning is characteristic of Derrida's 'undecideables'. This strategy of *duplicity* invokes a kind of *double movement* whereby it is possible to operate within logocentrism, since there is no escape, while laying traps for it which it cannot deal with. *Différance*, for example, incorporates *both* difference *and* deferral, again alluding to the signifier's representation of presence in its absence. To oversimplify, the principle of undecideability is embraced, in that either/or binary logic is replaced by the 'logic of supplementarity' (Derrida 1976), which has a both/and, neither/nor construction: *différance* refers to both conceptuality and the possibility of non-conceptuality. "The supplement is neither a presence nor an absence. No ontology can think its operation" (Derrida 1976: 314). It then becomes possible to develop an understanding of the supplementary character of things assumed to be already complete. Hence, in introducing undecideables such as *différance* and the supplement, Derrida provides us with a way of thinking, accounting for and disrupting metaphysi-

cal foundations, without putting another foundation in their place. We therefore have a powerful tool in deconstruction — a way of undermining claims to
truth without ourselves having to argue from some fixed position. This also
provides us with a way into analysis; for example, in an earlier paper (Hepburn
2000b) I suggested that the utility of what is 'rational' and what is 'emotional'
for participants relies upon the supplementary character of rationality and
emotionality — both their presence and absence of meaning.

c) Figuration

This leads us to the focus on the fundamental role of *figuration* in Derrida's work,
and this also provides us with a glimpse into how Derrida applies these deconstructive terms. Traditional philosophical argumentation treats metaphors as an
imperfect alternative to clear reasoning using explicit, literal language. For
Derrida this binary distinction is unstable, in part because the very arguments
that separate literal and metaphorical discourse themselves utilise metaphors.
Metaphors are put into circulation by philosophy, and consequently:

> Simultaneously the first meaning and the first displacement are then forgot-
> ten. The metaphor is no longer noticed, and it is taken for the proper mean-
> ing. A double effacement. Philosophy would be this process of metaphoriza-
> tion which gets carried away in and of itself (Derrida 1982: 211).

The upshot is that our theoretical arguments can no longer rely on the distinction between words that name 'objects in the real world', and words (like
metaphors) that 'merely' relate to other words. Figurative language is not a
rhetorical cloak providing more attractive clothing for pure, logical argument;
rather, it is   the condition of argumentation. It is impossible to put forward an
argument that is purely literal; language is always already figurative. This reflects
the demise of the logocentric view of language, in which it somehow represents
the world. The status of metaphor as *derivative* can then be challenged, allowing the focus to shift towards the *function* of metaphor rather than seeing it as
an *a priori* and stand-alone category of language. Discursive psychologists also
seek to build upon this post-structuralist insight into language as non-repre-
sentational, especially with respect to the enrolment of psychological or 'mental' terms (for example, Edwards 1997, te Molder and Potter forthcoming).
    In the analysis of teachers' bullying talk that follows, I will draw on
Derridean insights to highlight features of the discourse that have been overlooked or underplayed in traditional content analysis, in Foucauldian inspired

discourse analysis, and in conversation analytic influenced discursive psychology (for earlier attempts, see Hepburn 1997, 2000b). However, the analysis will also draw on various discursive psychological ideas.

2.   Discursive psychology

In this chapter I am using discursive psychology (hereafter DP) to refer to a set of ideas and developments from discourse analysis and conversation analysis (CA) in psychology, first put together by Potter and Wetherell (1987) and Edwards and Potter (1992). It parallels deconstruction in its refusal to make a separation between rhetoric and logic (Billig 1987) and between rhetoric and description (Potter 1996a). Unlike deconstruction, DP works closely with conversational accounts, focusing on their orientation to action and the resources (metaphors, categories, commonplaces) they are constructed out of. There has been a growing interest in drawing on ideas from the perspective of conversation analysis (Atkinson and Heritage 1984, Drew 1995, Hutchby and Wooffitt 1998, Sacks 1992) and applying them to social and cognitive psychological issues (Antaki 1994, Edwards 1991, 1997, Edwards and Potter 1993).

I will now examine three aspects of DP that will be important for the subsequent analysis.

a) Talk about psychological issues

One important aspect is to examine how people talk or write about 'psychological' concerns. So I will examine the way reporting and accounting for events can employ 'subjectivity constructions', a term developed in a previous paper (Hepburn 2000b) to describe the work done by participants' constructions of various mental entities, inner distinctions and features of subjectivity. The study found that teachers employ features of subjectivity, such as accounts of 'personality', and cognitive notions of attention and memory to account for the sanctioning of some pupils rather than others. Another feature of the study was the teachers' construction of their own subjectivity as split. In some cases, they formulated a troubled, concerned mental 'executive' who is considering actions as they happen, and trying to act in the best way, but not always succeeding. This split neatly allowed teachers to sustain their moral accountability and yet concede that that they may, on occasion, have acted in a way that is understood as bullying by pupils. This work builds upon the existing discursive psychological approaches to the kinds of issues that traditional psychology studies, under headings such as event memory and causal attribution (Edwards and Potter 1992) and cognitive scripts (Edwards 1994, 1995).

b) 'Factual' descriptions — variability and indexicality

Another general focus has been the ways in which factual descriptions of all kinds are assembled and used, *on occasions, and for the occasions of their production* (Potter 1996), and this relates discursive psychology to conversation analysis. Discursive psychology is all about studying what people do with words — discursive actions — and, like CA work, this requires sensitivity to *indexicality* — the idea that the sense of particular terms and utterances is dependent on the sequences of interaction in which they are embedded, rather than on any self-evident meaning. This focus provides an empirically grounded study that can be used as a basis for theory and method in psychology. At the same time, discursive psychology introduces issues that are not explicitly confronted in CA. For example, *variability* across descriptions is one of the features of the extracts presented here, and is shown to be a useful resource in the analysis.

c) Stake and accountability

The final feature of interest is participants' orientations to stake and interest. When people attend to their own stake in actions they are attending to accountability: who or what is responsible for what they are saying? For example, one of the consequences of providing a different interactional footing for claims is to manage accountability: should the speaker be treated as responsible for their claim or are they quoting another person? (Goffman 1979, Levinson 1988, Potter 1996).

All these notions will be drawn on, along with the deconstructive notions discussed above, in the analysis of teachers' talk that follows. The analysis will focus on the way teachers manage a question about the existence and gendered nature of bullying in the school. The concern will be with the way teachers orient to and construct the world of gender and the school in their talk. This does not require the analyst to operate with any particular pre-defined notion of gender (see Hepburn 2000a for further discussion of this), rather attempts will be made to look at how descriptions of gender are assembled on and for the occasions of talk. Hence, from Derrida, we could suggest that whatever 'gender' (or any other category) is will be fundamentally undecideable. This suggests that gender can be continually re/constructed and attended to *in situ*, which is where discursive psychology and/or conversation analysis can come in, helping us to look at the specifics of how this gets done in interaction.

3. Analysing teachers' talk

The analysis is based on interviews with teachers from two coeducational East of Scotland secondary schools. These interviews were designed to be open-ended and conversational as is appropriate for discourse analysis and similar qualitative approaches (Potter and Mulkay 1985, Potter and Wetherell 1995). That is, the interviews did not attempt a formally neutralist stance to questions and answers as is common with survey interviews, but instead would fluidly follow topics and at times challenge participants' contributions. Such active interviewing is designed to produce a wider range of discursive resources than would be found in a survey interview. Interviews lasted up to an hour, and all participants were guaranteed anonymity and reminded that they could withdraw from the research at any time. The analysis makes no *a priori* distinction between the talk of the interviewer and interviewee. It focuses on the interaction as a joint product of both, considering them as equally concerned in the production of the talk.

Interviews focused on a range of issues to do with bullying, discipline and punishment. For the pupils, who were interviewed first, it focused on experiences of bullying, and ways of coping with it, as well as a discussion of their experiences with particular teachers, and with school in general. For the teachers the interviewer gave feedback from pupils' interviews, as well as a focus on experiences of bullying, gender differences, the role of teacher training in bullying management, problems resulting from stress, and ideas for improvements in school organisation. The element of the study reported here deals principally with the teachers' responses to questions about bullying as it relates to gender.

The analysis will be intensive, working with the orientations displayed in the unfolding of the sequence, rather than trying to provide general categories of interaction. Three sequences will be considered in detail. They were chosen for their explicit and detailed attendance to issues of gender differences in school bullying, and for their portrayal of many of the features found in other teachers' accounts.

Extract 1: Teacher C9: 512-565

1   Interviewer: In your experience have you fou:nd that (.)
2   boys bully more than girls?
3   Teacher: <u>Boys</u> are more (.) .hh on the who:le probably more
4   phy↑sical I suppose but then again tha-
5   >a:ctually since I came't <u>this</u> school I would have
6   said that before but<
7   Interviewer: [Yeah
8   Teacher: [.hh <u>here</u> (.) <u>no</u> (.)
9   Interviewer: yeah
10 Teacher: and the ↑girls are every bit as-as physical as
11   the boys (.)
12 Interviewer: [mm
13 Teacher: [in fact if <u>any</u>thing the girls probably are ↑worse (.)
14 Interviewer: mm
15 Teacher: you know? Because >they-they-they< <u>really do</u> (0.2)
16   they (.) <u>keep</u> things on lo:nger
17 Interviewer: yeah
18 Teacher: y'know >that's what I've noticed since I've
19   <u>been</u> here< it seems to be the girls that °are° (.)
20 Interviewer: d'ye find girls get more up<u>set</u> a↓bout bullying
21   °than boys mebbe or°
22 Teacher: Cert-eh- <u>younger</u> ones the cases I've had its
23   been m-it's more the <u>name</u> calling
24 Interviewer: yeah
25 Teacher: tha' up<u>sets them</u>
26 Interviewer: Yeah (.) [yeah
27 Teacher: [>rather than anything< .hhh (.) the (.)
28   bo::ys (.) it's em °there's only one or <u>two</u> of them that've
29   <u>come</u>° it's usually gi:rls come to you about-
30   about <u>verb</u>al bullying
31 Interviewer: Mmm
32 Teacher: The bo:ys it has to be something >really serious
33   like somebody's y'know threatened te<
34   .hhhh (0.4) <u>chop</u> their <u>head</u> off
35   [or anything y'know=
36 Interviewer: [hhahhahhahha°hha° .hhh
37 Teacher: =it's got te be something <u>phys</u>ical
38 Interviewer: [Yeah

39   Teacher: [before <u>they</u> think it's (.) a <u>pro:b</u>lem, (.)
40   Interviewer: Yeah
41   Teacher: but ↑boys won't <u>come</u> to you because somebody's called
42   them a <u>name</u>
43   Interviewer: Yeah
44   Teacher: because they don't (0.2)
45   Interviewer: [Yeah
46   Teacher: [think that that's (.) <u>right</u>
47   Interviewer: Yeah (.) [°yeah°
48   Teacher: [.hh e:m: >°which is unfor-° whereas the <u>girls</u><
49   e-a-in my °a-experience anyway w'd° tend to come about
50   ↑<u>s:ill</u>y ↑<u>triv</u>ial things (.)
51   Interviewer: Mm
52   Teacher: That they could <u>s:it</u> and s:ort out between them<u>s:elves</u>
53   Interviewer: M↑hm
54   Teacher: But you ↑<u>can't</u> say that <u>to</u> them y'↓know
55   because then they're never coming back
56   Interviewer: [huhhuhh
57   Teacher: [if there <u>was</u> something serious so
58   Interviewer: Yeah
59   Teacher: But ↑first time they come you sit them ↓all down
60   b-when y'know, (.) ye get the same three coming (.)
61   e-<u>week</u> after <u>week</u> ye know >b'cus <u>one</u>'s fallen out with the
62   the other b'cus of the colour of 'er shoes and the
63   colour of 'er ↑socks<
64   Interviewer: °oh good[ness heheheh°
65   Teacher: [.hhh ye <u>ha:ve</u> te- (0.2) y'know it gets te
66   the stage where ye're going "CUM(.hh)ON girls lets get
67   <u>ser</u>ious here ye know"

This extract occurred towards the end of the interview, after many of the main areas of school bullying had already been discussed, including the teacher's own experiences and difficulties in dealing with school bullying, along with discussion of feedback from pupil interviews.

Introducing gender categories

The first thing to note is the interviewer's question. This is both a request for a generalisation about gender differences — 'do boys bully more than girls?' — while suggesting it will come from experience — "In your experience have you fou:nd that" (line 1). This encourages participation since it suggests that the interviewee is expected to have an answer.

An obvious thing to note about the teacher's next turn is that she has no trouble orienting to these gender categories, although these are qualified and repaired, indicating some 'trouble' with the activity of discussing gender categories. She begins with the standard view that boys' bullying tends to be more 'physical', while girls' is more 'verbal'.

Fact construction

The teacher then constructs an opposing view, employing what Robin Wooffit (1992) has identified as 'at first I thought X, then I realised Y'. This pattern is typically employed when speakers are concerned to persuade us that their account is not a product of fantasy or imagination, but is a result of things that actually happened. Wooffitt draws on the work of Harvey Sacks (1984), who suggests that this pattern presents the speaker as having the kind of first thoughts that any normal person would have. So in lines 5-8 the teacher employs the following pattern: ">a:ctually since I came t'this school I would have said that before but< ... .hh here (.) no (.)". This constructs her account as based upon things that have happened in the real world, rather than her own imagination or prior knowledge.

As with Wooffitt's examples of people aiming to convince the interviewer that they had had a paranormal experience, this teacher is providing corroboration, or what Potter (1996a) would term 'stake inoculation', for her account, which runs counter to what 'normal' people might think. So while there may be concern about the way the initial interviewer's question sets up the gender categories, this initial enrolment of gender does not fully account for the teacher's elaborate orientation to them. The teacher goes on to recycle and reiterate her account with ">that's what I've noticed since I've been here<" (lines 18-19). By appealing to things that have been merely noticed, the teacher provides a nice epistemological warrant for the facticity of her account.

In contrast to the empirical noticings are the 'ye knows', appealing to what Derek Edwards would call common knowledge (Edwards and Mercer 1987). Rather than appealing to events that happened, they invite recipiency, appealing to things that we all know. These often occur at precisely the most troubling points (lines 15-18), where the generalisations about girls being worse are about to be made in lines 16 and 19.

Variability

What is striking about this extract is its variability. Discourse analysts have often emphasised that different forms of description will be tailored for their different contexts (indexicality and action orientation), and variability is the result of this. In this extract the teacher begins by constructing girls' bullying as "every bit as physical" (line 10)as boys, and indeed worse because they "keep things on longer" (line 16). Yet later on, it seems like the opposite scenario is being constructed.

From the interviewer's question in lines 20-21 — "d'ye find girls get more up<u>set</u> a↓bout bullying °than boys mebbe or°" — the teacher switches to characterising problems with female bullying as centred around 'name calling'. As always, this kind of variability starts to make more sense when we analyse the context. This requires that we explore some further features, namely oppositions and extremes, and figuration.

Oppositions and extremes

There are at least 3 binary oppositions employed in this extract. The obvious one introduced by the interviewer is boy-girl. A second is physical-verbal and a third is serious-trivial. What seems to happen after the initial account of female bullying as 'every bit as physical' yet worse, is that it gets constructed as verbal and trivial. This is done through two almost symmetrical *extreme case formulations* (ECF) (Edwards 2000).

The first of these is on lines 32-35 — "The bo:ys it has to be something >really serious like somebody's y'know threatened te< .hhhh (0.4) <u>chop</u> their <u>head</u> off or anything y'know=". We can hear this perhaps as a safe way of espousing a stereotyped view. By formulating something in such an extreme way, which elicited laughter from the interviewer, it signals caution, in the sense that this is an account that is obviously not linked to events in the real world, and so is not one that the teacher could be called to account for. At the same time it does build in the description of boys and the kind of bullying that they might engage in as 'something really serious'.

By contrast we have the second ECF, on lines 60-63 — "b-when y'know, (.) ye get the same three coming (.) e-<u>week</u> after <u>week</u> ye know >b'cus <u>one</u>'s fallen out with the other b'cus of the colour of 'er shoes and the colour of 'er –socks<". Once again we have a description that is ironically drawing attention to itself by being so extreme (Edwards 2000), again eliciting interviewer's laughter, while making the argument at the same time. What we can see, then, is that employing oppositions and ECFs attends to the delicate nature of making such stereotypically gendered and evaluative judgements, while simultaneously allowing us to make them. This can be linked to more deconstructive notions, in the sense that an opposition is always already in an unstable state, which is precisely what allows us to construct its stability. If an opposition is always already in a state of undecideability (the quasi-transcendental) then this calls for deconstruction – a quasi-analysis of the discourse(s) that have produced them as stable and transcendent.

Figuration

The Derridean point about the use of figurative language — for instance, the vivid imagery of head chopping and arguments about shoe and sock colours — is that it will not merely be a rhetorical fiction covering more serious concepts in language, rather it is responsible for much of its rhetorical force. The possibility of figurative language displays the impossibility of language that is 'purely' serious or factual. It is therefore possible to see this figurative language as capable of doing powerful work in making stereotypical judgements hearable and sayable. Also note the use of 'name calling' (lines 23 and 41-2) rather than, say, 'verbal abuse' or 'intimidation'. This provides further leverage for the 'boys as serious, girls as trivial' lining up of oppositions.

Having gone from spotting some initial variability in the way girls' bullying is constructed, to looking at what that variability is doing in context by fleshing it out with a whole set of features of the talk, we can move on to the other extracts for a similar detailed examination.

Extract 2: Teacher C3: 76-125

1   Interviewer: <u>look</u>ing at this gender difference then would you say that
2   boys bully ↑more than girls?
3   Teacher: yes I'd say a ↑different <u>kind</u> of bullying
4   would be on the go (.) girls' bullying
5   (0.2) em ((low whistle)) would <u>tend</u> to be less
6   physical but not exc<u>lu</u>sively so by any means,
7   Interviewer: mm
8   Teacher: em I ↑would say one of our fourth year
9   girls has been quite (.) em
10   (0.4) well >was hanging around this room at
11   lunch times and intervals< (.) and at ten to four

```
12                  was just waiting (.) until two or three other girls
13                  had gone because they had ↑threatened her,
14   Interviewer: yeah
15   Teacher:       and that was the issue I was ↑talk↓ing about
16   Interviewer: [°right°
17   Teacher:       [where the issue (0.2) i-it was over a boy
18                  (.) and this ↑other girl who was getting in with this boy
19                  (0.6) it's different from going out with ((smiley voice))
20   Interviewer: heh a wh(hh)ole new vocabulary
21   Teacher:       hh↑o:h absolutely (.)anyway (.) >there was no problem
22                  between these two girls< (.) it was all resolved
23   Interviewer: °mm°
24   Teacher:       but these ↑other girls had taken it upon themselves that
25                  they were gonna give her a doing for this=
26   Interviewer: =so it was a kind of physical thing.
27   Teacher:       it was physical yes (.) em but girls (.)↑girls
28                  bitch ↓more >to be honest< (.)
29                  and so th-there's a lot more of the verbal in making people
30                  unhappy and talking about people and saying cruel things=
31   Interviewer: [°mm°
32   Teacher:       [=I ↑don't think that is a sexist comment
33                  if you ↑think I'm saying all women are bitches
34                  it's ↑not thhat at hh↑a↓ll
35   Interviewer: Mmhm
36   Teacher:       but (0.4) IF somebody's going to bitch more
37                  it's more likely to be a girl
38                  (0.6) and it's ↑probably just that they have
39                  a better command of vocabulary
40                  th(hh)an g(hh)uys do em
41   Interviewer: mhm
42   Teacher:       and so ↑guys would be m:ore the direct threat
43                  (0.2) >and a ↑guy would be-would threaten someone else
44                  because he wants cigarettes or money
45                  or °something like that°<
46   Interviewer: °yeah°
47   Teacher:       it's not so much on something that's been done
48                  (.) or of something that's been said,
49   Interviewer: Right
50   Teacher:       Girls are much more into "you said this"
51                  (.) or "s:o and s:o told me this"
```

52 Interviewer: Yeah
53 Teacher: And <u>some</u>times you also get the sneaky thing about
54   somebody going up to someone and saying
55   "so and so said <u>this</u> about you"
56   and then they just sit back,
57   (.) and w(hh)atch this big th(hh)ing erupt
58 Interviewer: [Hehh
59 Teacher: [And it's not happened in <u>my</u> room,
60   (.) that I'm a<u>ware</u> anyway,
61   (.) but em I've heard an<u>oth</u>er teacher saying that,
62   (.) and we discovered that there was this con<u>tin</u>ual,
63   (0.2) this pupil would flare up
64   and explode at someone else and get into
65   hu:ge <u>trouble</u> for it because he had this
66   very short <u>tem</u>per that would just go up,
67   (0.4) and it turned out that there was
68   this ↑third person stirring it
69   >just ex<u>act</u>ly in those terms<
70   and would do this and would say the <u>com</u>ment,
71   (0.4) so boys can be sneaky and devious like that,
72 Interviewer: Mm
73 Teacher: but they're not so much concerned with,
74   (0.2) if ↑they say (.)
75   "so and so said <u>this</u> about you"
76   they just go "what you ↑on about"
77   or "what are you ↑saying"
78   girls will <u>talk</u> about it more and there's more
79   (.) impli<u>ca</u>tions a<u>long</u> with that
80   (.) and by the ↑same <u>to</u>ken because of the
81   <u>na</u>ture of things
82   (.) guys being more di<u>rect</u>
83   (.) >or I suppose more <u>sim</u>pler or whatever<
84 Interviewer: Yeah
85 Teacher: in a ↑flare up with <u>guys</u> it's ↑over ↓more <u>quick</u>ly
86   (.) with girls you have to <u>tell</u> them
87   or per<u>suade</u> them much more <u>read</u>ily
88   (0.2) and they ↑seem to hold <u>on</u>to things much
89   <u>lon</u>ger in those terms...

This was one of the longest interviews, and we are near the start; the participants have only discussed pupils and their different types of friendships in response to a question about whether the teacher himself had experienced any incidents of school bullying.

Introducing gender categories

Again, there is both a request for a generalisation about gender differences by the interviewer — "do boys bully more than girls?" — while again inviting participation — "would you say that" (line 1). Again the teacher has no trouble elaborating on these gender categories, which he himself had introduced. He also begins with the standard view, though again cautiously, that girls' bullying "would te:nd to be less physical but not exclusively so by any means" (lines 5-6).

Variability

A noticeable feature of this extract is its variability between different descriptions of bullying. The teacher begins with an account of female bullying that was 'physical' yet almost immediately switches to a description of female bullying as more 'verbal' (line 29), with male bullying being more 'direct' and utilitarian (lines 43-46). There is then a further account given of male bullying that was verbal — where there was a 'third person' stirring it up behind the scenes (lines 54-70). In this sense, this extract follows a similar level of *variability* to the previous one, in that the standard view is referred to, and then promptly undermined, only to reappear in full force later on. Again we have to examine what this variability is doing at the different points in the extract, which involves a consideration of similar themes to the previous extract.

Fact construction: Normalisation and active voicing

Gail Jefferson (1990) notes that in everyday conversation, lists are commonly delivered with three parts or items, since this is sufficient to indicate that we have instances that stand for something more general; hence, as Potter (1996) notes, they have a *normative* status. Speakers are seldom interrupted after the second part, even where they appear to be groping for a suitable term for the third part. And we often draw on 'generalized list completers' such as 'etcetera' or 'and that kind of thing'.

In this extract the teacher uses three-part lists to construct 'typical' features of 'girls' — "making people un<u>hap</u>py and <u>talk</u>ing about people and saying cruel <u>things</u>=" (lines 29-30) — and similarly to refer to 'the nature of things' with 'guys' "being more di<u>rect</u> (.) >or I suppose more <u>simp</u>ler or whatever"(lines 82-83). Also, they are used to construct male bullying as having a more practical utilitarian focus: "because he wants cig<u>arett</u>es or <u>mon</u>ey or °something like that°" (lines 44-45). Employing lists constructs and sufficiently exemplifies the normative nature of what 'guys' and 'girls' are like, and consequently of gender differences in bullying.

Wooffitt (1992) notes that when people produce accounts of extraordinary events they often establish the factuality of their claims through quoted speech, which he calls *active voicing*. Active voicing works through providing corroboration. By bringing in other voices, this proves that it is not just the speaker's judgements that are producing an account; it can therefore be heard as more objective and factual. In this extract, we have active voicing precisely at the point where we learn what 'girls' and 'guys' are like: "Girls are much more into '<u>you</u> said this' (.) or 's:o and s:o told me this'" (lines 50-51). And alternatively, with 'guys', "↑they say (.) 'so and so said <u>this</u> about you' they just go 'what you ↑on about' or 'what are you ↑saying'" (lines 74-77). So, as with the three-part lists, the active voicing appears at precisely those points where the teacher wants to lay claim to knowledge about the gendered nature of bullying, which of course he has been asked to do by the interviewer.

Oppositions and contrasts

In Extract 1, physical-verbal and serious-trivial oppositions were employed to distinguish between male and female bullying. Here in Extract 2, as well as being physical and serious, male bullying is also more practical — "a ↑guy would… threaten someone else because he wants cigarettes or money" (lines 43-44). Male bullying is also made simpler, more direct and is over more quickly, whereas "↑girls bitch ↓more" (lines 27-28) and "↑seem to hold onto things much longer" (lines 88-89). There is also variability in this account, in that the teacher gives two examples of bullying that run counter to the standard view. What are we to make of this?

According to Derrida, there is nothing intrinsically fixed about oppositions, yet owing to the tendency for one 'side' to be prioritised over the other, they can also play a part in producing a kind of fixity of interpretation. In this example, the fixity is built into how gender and bullying go together. Were they to appear in a philosophical text, these would be the kind of binary oppositions that Derrida would deconstruct. As they appear here, they can be heard as examples of both the supplementary and undecideable character of language, in that they display flexibility, and also they display the way that meanings can become fixed into producing certain versions of the world. Gender does not just come trouble-free as a category, because language does not work in this way. Instead, gender needs to be constantly re/constructed and attended to, which is what the participants here are doing. Hence, what is achieved by producing counter-examples is a reinforcement of the normative character of male bullying, which also attends to social science concerns, probably related to the interview context.

Figuration

As with Extract 1, it is possible to hear figurative language as being capable of doing powerful work in making stereotypical judgements hearable and sayable. An explosive metaphor is enrolled when 'guys' are described as bullying: "a ↑flare up with <u>guys</u>" (line 85) in which "this pupil would flare up and explode" (lines 63-64). This supports the general theme of male bullying as both more serious, yet over more quickly. It also manages agency: it is something that emerges like a chemical reaction from within the person. In common with all these internal/subjective explanations, this one also obviates any further need for explanation — this figurative account gives us all the resources we need to understand male bullying. On the other hand, "↑girls <u>bitch</u> ↓more" (lines 27-28) is a metaphor with potentially misogynist connotations that the teacher explicitly attends to (lines 32-34), despite returning throughout the extract to the standard notion that girls are more 'verbal' and more difficult to deal with and sort out.

The following extract occurred mid-way through the interview, after the issues of classroom control and feedback from pupil interviews had been discussed.

Extract 3: Teacher C2: 214-238

1	Teacher:	...what I've noticed <u>recently</u> and
2		>certainly at Chapelhill there is much more<
3		fema-aggression from <u>girls</u>
4	Interviewer:	yeah, that was one of my ↑questions, tra<u>ditio</u>nally bullying
5		is associated with <u>boys</u>=
6	Teacher:	=I mean the girls are attacking the boys

7		as <u>well</u> as girls
8		(0.2) and its in ex<u>ac</u>tly the same way as
9		↑boys used to do it
10		(0.2) em (.) tripping someone up (.)
11	Interviewer:	I found that in the <u>first</u> year classes quite often
12		the girls were much ↑bigger stronger and <u>tall</u>er
13		than the boys (.) and that there would often be-
14	Teacher:	and quite <u>loud</u>, so (0.2) possibly the sociologist
15		who said that it is society's re<u>ac</u>tion (.) er (0.4)
16		although I ↑<u>still</u> think that
17		on the whole girls conform <u>more</u>
18		because girls are morepeople group <u>ori</u>entated
19		(0.2) and boys work a lot more individua<u>list</u>ically
20		(0.4) parallel ↑lines generally
21		(.) they don't get into such close re↑lation↓ships
22	Interviewer:	yeah (.) yeah do you think that's more to do with
23		our views of masculinity and femi<u>nin</u>[ity=
24	Teacher:	[no
25	Interviewer:	=that <u>we've</u> imposed=
26	Teacher:	=I <u>do</u> think it (.) it is more
27		(0.4) perso<u>nal</u>ity thing
28		(.) and lots of girls and boys cross <u>over</u> of course=
29	Interviewer:	[°mm°
30	Teacher:	[=but at the ex<u>tremes</u> there's
31		>certainly at <u>one</u> extreme<
32		(.) <u>mas</u>culine characteristics,
33		(.) there are more <u>boys</u> in that,
34		(0.2) and the caring (.) soft (.) er,
35	Interviewer:	nurturant sort of?=
36	Teacher:	=yes nurturant <u>are</u> more dominant in the girls
37		(.) but as I say you get this big cross over…

Gender categories and variability

This extract differs from the previous two in that the teacher, rather than the interviewer, introduces the gendered nature of bullying. She does so in such a way as to suggest that there is more 'aggression' from 'girls', especially in this school. Once again the account contains variability in that the teacher starts off with a counter-example, and then goes on to reaffirm the standard view, suggesting that "girls conform <u>more</u> because girls are more people group <u>ori</u>-

entated" (lines 17-18). Again we can use this variability as a way into understanding how gender gets re/constructed. It seems then that despite being able to draw upon opposing constructions of gendered bullying, teachers are continually drawn back into the standard view. Here in Extract 3, we have a more explicit insight into one of the things that may be luring them back.

Subjectivity construction

When the interviewer asks whether the teacher's construction of the standard view might be "more to do with our views of masculinity and femi<u>nin</u>[ity... that <u>we've</u> imposed" (lines 22-25) the standard view is held in place via the notion of 'personality' (line 27). Claiming access to fixed aspects of internal categories is therefore a useful discursive strategy. Again we can see the usefulness of producing counter-examples — "lots of girls and boys cross <u>over</u> of course" (line 28) as a way of constructing the normative character of gender.

Fact construction

As we have seen, the use of 'personality' does useful subjectivity construction business for the participants. Being able to claim knowledge of inner features in general also gives our claims more of a factual status. To 'know' about 'inner' causal factors allows us to bypass 'external' causal factors, so our explanatory work is done. People are behaving this way because that is how they are made, not because that is what they are being encouraged to do by various environmental features. The former explanation entails a situation that we need to work around, while the latter entails more widespread, complicated and fundamental changes, for example, to everyday understandings and practices.

As with the previous extract, three-part lists can be found at exactly the points where constructions about the nature of girls and boys are being made. For example, the interviewer suggests that "I found that in the <u>first</u> year classes quite often the girls were much ↑bigger stronger and <u>tall</u>er than the boys" (lines 11-13). Also, "boys work a lot more individua<u>list</u>ically (0.4) parallel ↑lines generally (.) they don't get into such close re↑lation↓ships" (lines 19-21). Again a three-part list appears just at the point where the gendered nature of things is constructed. Perhaps this is providing a sense of sufficiency, the notion that one has completely characterised something, as well as indicating the normativity of gender. This in itself may be related to the interview situation — we are all trying to come across as knowledgeable in one way or another.

Figuration

As seen earlier, gender is constructed in this extract by building the metaphor of two binary 'extremes', which can be 'crossed over', but which nevertheless organise the way people are held in gendered categories. These 'extremes' are held in place internally through our 'personalities' — it is simply what we are like. Similarly, what boys are like can be described metaphorically in terms of 'parallel lines', conjuring up an image of 'isolated elements swimming in the same direction' to paraphrase a Damien Hirst title — the idea being that boys do not relate as closely to each other as girls do. This focus on figuration has been experimental, and the danger with this kind of analysis is in taking words and phrases as possessing some *a priori* or decontextualised meaning. The preliminary attempt here has been to develop a quasi-analytic focus, capable of dealing with figuration as a situated feature of talk.

4. Conclusions

This chapter has studied some general features of gendered accounts, and in the process many other interesting features of these accounts have been skated over. However the broader discursive strategies that have been found can be discussed in the light of their relationship to the theoretical perspectives that we started out with — Derrida's work and discursive psychology. The general focus is to take these findings and use them to build up a story (capable of being employed in the service of social criticism) of how gender can be made into, or oriented to as, something fixed.

DP's focus on accountability and variability across descriptions gives us a way of focusing on what talk is doing, and how versions of reality get produced. It is possible to examine the way the variability of these different accounts allows the flexible production of what constitutes gender and bullying, or at least orients to potential trouble in constructing them as fixed categories. We are also sensitised to the different discursive strategies that produce accounts as factual, such as extreme case formulations, three-part lists and active voicing. As we saw, these were useful precisely at the point that the gendered 'nature' of girls and boys was being built.

This study therefore not only supports the theoretical and analytical thrust of DP, but also illustrates the importance of not simply using internal subjective categories as part of our explanation. As the analysis showed, enrolling personality or other internal features as explanatory categories allows the explanation to stop — people behave this way because that is how they are, end of story. Similarly, analyses invoking cognitive categories entail that explanations focus on putative inner states (for example, the unconscious) of participants rather than on the interactional features of talk. Just as the teacher no longer needs to explain why girls are more 'caring' and 'soft' once 'personality' has been invoked as an explanation, so we, as analysts, no longer need to focus on the context and interactional features of talk — we can simply explain it with reference to participants' un/conscious motives or intentions, or simply 'what they are like'. Hence if we seek to ground our analytic claims in some kind of account invoking features of participants, it will be to the detriment of other analyses that will be more sensitive to the interactional and contextual features of talk. Potter (1998) makes this point in a more elaborate way, and Derrida (1982b) touches on these issues in his discussion of the speech-writing argument.

This also relates to what Derrida might term the supplementary character of psychological phenomena (Hepburn 2000b) — the sense in which the meaning of psychological terms is always undecideable, so attempting to describe definitively what is or is not the case psychologically becomes a futile exercise. Derrida also gives us a way into understanding how stories of gender can be made into something fixed. One feature of these accounts is the work done by *binary oppositions* — for instance, boy-girl, serious-trivial, physical-verbal, rational-emotional. These are used flexibly and cut across each other to produce an account that makes sense of, as well as provides evaluations of, gender differences in school bullying. Our ability to employ oppositions is useful in the sense that our accounts can be made more concrete — as Derrida notes, binary logic allows the reification/marginalisation and corresponding evaluation of one side of an opposition.

On the other hand, closer inspection of how these oppositions are actually used allows them to be seen as *flexible resources* rather than fixed categories, and this supports Derrida's call for a *logic of supplementarity*, involving an understanding of the essentially undecideable character of meaning. Philosophers and theorists tend to see language as static and representational, and therefore as something needing to be theorised and categorised in an abstract way. The categories we use to talk with therefore become frozen and decontextualized. Hence, the flexible ways that oppositions and contrasts get used in everyday talk is lost, and we need deconstruction to regain a sense of their undecideability. Therefore, within logocentric systems of meaning, within which we are irrevocably lodged, there is a move towards specifying or assuming the *presence* of meaning. To disrupt this, given that we need to work within the logocentric system, Derrida develops undecideable terms such as *différance*, the supplement, the trace, as a continual reminder of the impossibility of assuming meanings to be complete, self-evident, or simply present to human consciousness. Discursive psychology, with its focus on indexicality and the action-performing nature of both everyday talk and the psychological phenomena employed in that talk, allows us one way of staying analytically focused on these poststructuralist insights into language. Gender, and the psychological terms that often accompany gendered talk, are *participants' resources for action*.

A further feature of these accounts is the *figurative* work done by metaphors and tropes. Often these occur at precisely the point where the most fact constructional work is being done — in all three extracts they occur precisely at the point where fundamental features of girls and boys are being constructed. This supports Derrida's notion that metaphor is best seen as a resource rather than as a category of language that is derivative of more factual descriptions of the world. Such oppositions encourage us to see our 'realities' and 'cognitions' — key sites of gender construction — as simply present, not constructed in and through language.

This relates to the way that power relations can be read through the details of talk. Gender inequalities and fixed categories are constructed and oriented to through a variety of discursive resources – subjectivity constructions, oppositions, contrasts, metaphors, extreme formulations, lists and so on. It follows that the development of social critique entails the development of what Derrida might term a quasi-analytic approach – an approach to analysis that does not operate from any self-present meaning of issues such as gender, power and subjectivity. The various analytic approaches adopted throughout this volume each achieve or at least topicalise this shift in analytic focus to varying degrees. My feeling is that a thorough engagement with Derrida's work (for which there is insufficient space here) is necessary for further analytic innovation.

To summarise then it seems that when we want to make sense of our world, each other and ourselves, gender can be easily and flexibly enrolled in ways that make it into something fixed. This endless positing of foundations, and an endless commitment to metaphysical binaries, entails that our task must be to identify the discursive moves related to gendered constructions that attempt to place themselves beyond question. We need to recognise the economies of signification that occur in logocentric frameworks, which structure the reification, evaluation and marginalisation of terms such as male and female, and which can make our feelings and experiences seem prior to their textual construction.

Note

* I would like to thank Andrew Clark, Paul McIlvenny, Clare MacMartin, Jonathan Potter and anonymous referees for helpful comments on earlier drafts.

References

Antaki, Charles. 1994 *Explaining and Arguing: The Social Organization of Accounts*. London: Sage.
Arnason, D. E. 1997 "Derrida and deconstruction". [Online]. <http://130.179.92.25/Arnason_de/Derrida.html>.
Atkinson, John M. and Heritage, John C. (eds). 1984 *Structures of Social Action: Studies in Conversation Analysis*. Cambridge: Cambridge University Press.
Bennington, Geoffrey. 2000 *Interrupting Derrida*. London: Routledge.
Billig, Michael. 1987 *Arguing and Thinking: A Rhetorical Approach to Social Psychology*. Cambridge: Cambridge University Press.
Derrida, Jacques. 1973 *Speech and Phenomena and other Essays of Husserl's Theory of Signs*. Evanston: Northwestern University Press.
Derrida, Jacques. 1976 *Of Grammatology*. Baltimore: The Johns Hopkins University Press.
Derrida, Jacques. 1978 *Writing and Difference* [Trans.: Alan Bass]. London: Routledge & Kegan Paul.
Derrida, Jacques. 1982a "White mythology: Metaphor in the text of philosophy". In *Margins of Philosophy*, J. Derrida, 207-273. London: Harvester/Wheatsheaf.
Derrida, Jacques. 1982b "Signature, event, context". In *Margins of Philosophy*, J. Derrida, 307-330. Hemel Hempstead: Harvester Wheatsheaf.
Drew, Paul. 1995 "Conversation analysis". In *Rethinking Psychology, Volume 2: Alternative Methodologies*, J. Smith, R. Harré, L. van Langenhove and P. Stearns (eds), 64-79. London: Sage.
Edwards, Derek. 1991 "Categories are for talking: On the cognitive and discursive bases of categorization". *Theory and Psychology* 1(4): 515-542.
Edwards, Derek. 1994 "Script formulations: A study of event descriptions in conversation". *Journal of Language and Social Psychology* 13: 211-247.
Edwards, Derek. 1995 "Two to tango: Script formulations, dispositions, and rhetorical symmetry in relationship troubles talk". *Research on Language and Social Interaction* 28: 319-50.
Edwards, Derek. 1997 *Discourse and Cognition*. London: Sage.
Edwards, Derek. 2000 "Extreme case formulations: Softeners, investments and doing non-

literal". *Research on Language and Social Interaction* 33: 347-73.

Edwards, Derek and Mercer, Neil M. 1987 *Common Knowledge: The Development of Understanding in the Classroom.* London: Routledge.

Edwards, Derek and Potter, Jonathan. 1992 *Discursive Psychology.* London: Sage.

Edwards, Derek and Potter, Jonathan. 1993 "Language and causation: A discursive action model of description and attribution". *Psychological Review* 100: 23-41.

Goffman, Erving. 1979 "Footing". *Semiotica* 25: 1-29. (Reprinted in E. Goffman, 1981, *Forms of Talk.* Oxford: Basil Blackwell.)

Hepburn, Alexa. 1997 "Teachers and secondary school bullying: a postmodern discourse analysis". *Discourse and Society* 8: 27-49.

Hepburn, Alexa. 1999 "Derrida and psychology: Deconstruction and its ab/uses in critical and discursive psychologies". *Theory and Psychology* 9(5): 641-667.

Hepburn, Alexa. 2000a "On the alleged incompatibility between feminism and relativism". *Feminism and Psychology* 10(1): 91-106.

Hepburn, Alexa. 2000b "Power Lines: Derrida, discursive psychology, and the management of accusations of teacher bullying". *British Journal of Social Psychology* 39(4): 605-628.

Hutchby, Ian and Wooffitt, Robin. 1998 *Conversation Analysis: Principles, Practices and Applications.* Cambridge: Polity.

Jefferson, Gail. 1990 "List construction as a task and resource". In *Interaction Competence,* G. Psathas (ed), 63-92. Lanham, MD: University Press of America.

Levinson, Stephen C. 1988 "Putting linguistics on a proper footing: explorations in Goffman's concepts of participation". In *Erving Goffman: Studies in the Interactional Order,* P. Drew and A. Wootton (eds), 161-289. Cambridge: Polity.

te Molder, Hedwig and Potter, Jonathan (eds). forthcoming *Talk and Cognition: Discourse, Cognition and Social Interaction.* Cambridge: Cambridge University Press.

Potter, Jonathan. 1996 *Representing Reality: Discourse, Rhetoric and Social Construction.* London: Sage.

Potter, Jonathan. 1998 "Cognition as context (whose cognition?)". *Research on Language and Social Interaction* 31: 29-44.

Potter, Jonathan and Mulkay, Michael. 1985 "Scientists' interview talk: Interviews as a technique for revealing participants' interpretative practices". In *The Research Interview: Uses and Approaches,* M. Brenner, J. Brown and D. Canter (eds), 247-271. London: Academic Press.

Potter, Jonathan and Wetherell, Margaret. 1987 *Discourse and Social Psychology: Beyond Attitudes and Behaviour.* London: Sage.

Potter, Jonathan and Wetherell, Margaret. 1995 "Discourse analysis". In *Rethinking Methods in Psychology,* J. Smith, R. Harré and L. van Langenhove (eds), 80-92. London: Sage.

Sacks, Harvey. 1984 "On doing 'being ordinary'". In *Structures of Social Action: Studies in Conversation Analysis,* J.M. Atkinson and J. Heritage (eds) , 413-429. Cambridge: Cambridge University Press.

Sacks, Harvey. 1992 *Lectures on Conversation.* Vols. I & II (edited by G. Jefferson). Oxford: Blackwell.

Wooffitt, Robin. 1992 *Telling Tales of the Unexpected: The Organization of Factual Discourse.* Hemel Hempstead: Harvester Wheatsheaf.

CHAPTER 10

"I'm still not sure she's a she"

Textual talk and typed bodies in online interaction

Jenny Sundén

mira enters with the sound of chimes.
Jenny waves to mira
mira curtsies.
mira asks, "Is there a particular thing I am supposed to discuss?"
Jenny smiles
Yazmine gestures to Jenny.
mira clambers to sit on the side of the boulder nearest the fire.
You say, "Yazmine here thought you would be a good person for me to talk
    to... i'm Jenny, as you can see, and i'm looking at the way people present
    themselves in text-based VR for my doctoral thesis..."
mira nods.
mira says, "ah"
Yazmine [to mira]: "I thought she'd want to speak to you because of all the
    mystery you surround yourself with"
You say, "i'm especially interested in the way gender works in spaces like this..."
mira nods.
Jenny nods
mira says, "Gender doesn't seem to work very well at all"

Created through a few strings of text, occupying almost no disk space, this excerpt is taken from a conversation in a text-based online world, or MUD (here referred to as WaterMOO), that I have been visiting for two years.[1] In the midst of my 'fieldwork', a character named Yazmine invited me to her virtual home to tell me a story about another female character in the MOO: mira. The peculiar thing about mira is that she is referred to as an 'it' by other WaterMOOers:

You ask, "mira, you said?"
Yazmine nods.
Yazmine says, "I'll leave a note for it to contact you or something"
You say, "sounds pretty womanly to me..."
Yazmine nods.
Yazmine says, "That's one of its female morphs"
Yazmine says, "Most of its morphs are female, as well"
You say, "that would be great.. i'll look for it too"

In this passage, Yazmine tells me that she will leave a note for *it* to contact me, which left me wondering why a female character is not referred to as a 'she' (in particular if the typist of this character chooses to let her curtsy on her entry, which is in Western culture a clear way of 'doing femininity'). Yazmine explains that the female sounding name 'mira' is an index that this particular 'morph' happens to be female. Morph, as in *morphology*, refers to the possibility of online shape shifting, of moving between different characters that belong to the same typist. In the excerpt that introduces this chapter, I express a wish to find out how 'gender' works online, and I get the reply from mira that: "Gender doesn't seem to work very well at all". The purpose of this chapter is to explore statements like this one, to investigate the connections between what I call textual talk and typed bodies, in particular along the dimensions of gender and sexuality.

As opposed to previous research in the intersection of discourse, gender, and online spaces (for example, Bruckman 1992, Cherny 1994, Hall 1996, Herring 1993, 1996, Kramarae and Taylor 1993, McRae 1996, Reid 1994, Stone 1995 and Turkle 1995), I do not view online activities as exclusively liberating and subversive, nor as automatic reproductions of gender inequalities and stereotypes locked up in language. Instead, I see online performances as something exceedingly transgressive in the sense that they take place in the intricate borderland between typists and online characters, writing and speaking, the 'real' and the fictional, physicality and imagination. They are processes of meaning-making in which textually speaking subjects come to signify in a sense that is neither 'false' (disconnected from the 'real') nor 'true' ('unmediated' copies of 'reality'), but rather typed-in enactments of cultures with diffuse points of origin. The question is no longer about whose perspective is being reproduced in cyberspace, but rather a matter of discerning what type of perspectives are taking shape in the wires, to carry out an analysis that performs a similar walk on the virtual tightrope as the activities it aims to capture.

The excerpts used in this chapter can be seen as collaboratively typed-in stories about gender and sexuality circulating in WaterMOO. Instead of narrowly focusing on individual turns, ripped out of context to represent subjective perspectives, longer passages are taken here as points of departure in an attempt to culturally situate these texts, as well as to show how textual talk constitutes (online) bodies and render them meaningful. Excerpts are not understood as representing true or false accounts of (virtual) reality, but as displays of co-authored perspectives of sexed and gendered bodies. The analytical emphasis is not primarily on the activity of 'doing' gender and sexuality (for example, Bergvall 1996, Cameron 1997) in online textual talk, but rather on participants' textual talk 'about' these matters (see Stokoe 1998) together with me, as a researcher. But instead of trying to analytically separate the process of 'doing' from the activity 'talking about', I would instead suggest that talking about could be seen as a way of doing. Stories always do something. They are never just there, as passive comments or meta-accounts of something more 'real', but rather they actively (re)configure this reality.

This exposé opens with a brief background to MUDs and MUDding, including a short cut to the practical construction of textual talk. Secondly, the notion of textual talk, as well as various connections between language, bodies, and text-based online spaces, will be framed theoretically. Finally, excerpts of textual talk in WaterMOO that explicitly focus on performances of gender and sexuality will be explored.

1.   MUDs and typed-in interaction

A MUD (Multi User Dungeon) was originally an offspring of traditional role-playing and text-adventure computer games, a virtual world in which Internet users could get together and play. Today, many MUDs are still closely related to the original system, while other MUDs, sometimes called social MUDs, provide spaces for a kind of role-playing more related to improvisational theatre. A MUD can be described as an ongoing, collaboratively written, online performance. It consists of the writing of scenery, characters, movement, dialogues and action. MUD performances are always grounded in a complex interplay between typing and responses/initiations from the MUD program (special software that runs on a server to which the participants connect through a client, such as telnet). The MUD program gives the participants a hypertext geography of thousands of inter-linked 'rooms' that are available to navigate, explore, and inhabit. Each participant creates and performs a textual character, an electronic *persona*, which against the background of this written landscape encounters and interacts with others. The written dialogue grows out of the 'spoken' present, since there is no difference in this context between text and gesture, writing and acting. When I, for example, produce the line "Jenny waves to mira", this is simultaneously the textual description of the action *and* the actual performance of the action itself. In contrast to its role-playing game oriented ancestors, WaterMOO belongs to the category of social MUDs, providing its participants with a relatively open social space with the primary purpose of hanging out and socializing.[2]

MUD performances are always grounded in a complex interplay between writing and computer code (Aarseth 1997: 103-105). The two most common commands used in MUD conversations are <say> and <emote>. When I type "say sounds pretty womanly to me..." the line "You say, 'sounds pretty womanly to me...'" is produced on my screen. Other persons present, with characters in the same textual room as me, will instead read "Jenny says, 'sounds pretty womanly to me...'" The program takes care automatically of changes in pronouns. When I instead use <emote> and type "emote smiles", everybody in the room will read "Jenny smiles". The command <say> logically realizes speech, and <emote> precedes nonverbal actions. Moreover, it is possible for characters to <whisper> privately, <page> each other from a distance, interact with programmed parts of the scenery, and enter and leave rooms with personal, pre-written messages, such as: "mira enters with the sound of chimes". Lynn Cherny (1999: 41) points out that: "In a MOO, all characters are technically objects, just like all scenery and all props. This means that they can be programmed and interacted with in various automated ways." Interaction in a MUD is thus an interweaving of spontaneous typing, pre-written messages, and automatic responses from the MUD program (ie. the server software that everybody who is connected to the MUD interacts with).

It is worth noticing that the MUD program makes a grammatical distinction between <say> and <emote> in relation to the creator of the text, since the command <say> uses 'you', whereas <emote> uses the third person (in this case 'Jenny'):

> You say, "i'm especially interested in the way gender works in spaces like this..."
> Jenny smiles

This linguistic differentiation creates a closeness for the typist to the words 'spoken', whereas a certain distance is introduced in relation to nonverbal gestures. As if to suggest a stronger identification between the typist and the textual 'I' in typed talk, the use of 'you' almost renders the character transparent. When the words "you say" appear in front of you on the screen, this makes almost invisible the fact that you are performing a character in an online world. "You say" seems to pretty straightforwardly indicate that the one who is talking is you, the typist. In contrast, nonverbal acts seem more closely tied to the character through the use of a distancing third person. As soon as the textual body moves instead of speaks, a gap between typist and character is created. In this sense, "Jenny smiles" may work as an active reminder of the different layers involved in textual talk, where 'you' the typist is one layer, and 'Jenny' the character is another, and that these subjectivities are linked to and confused with each other in intricate ways. While constantly being mixed in the course of speech and movement, this interplay between narrow identification, and more distant contemplation, illustrates how the (philosophical) dilemma of locating 'agency' in online practices is grounded already in the interaction between typed-in commands and the MUD program.

2. Textual talk

Online dialogues take place in a rarely acknowledged borderland between talk and text, where the ephemerality of talk is tied down by the textual practices of inscription. Most researchers have looked at MUD practices from the perspective of social interaction (Cherny 1995, 1999, Kendall 1998 and Reid 1994, 1995). Elizabeth Reid (1995: 171) points out that:

> Interaction on a MUD is, after all, interactive, synchronous and ephemeral. Although sessions may be recorded using computer programs designed for this purpose, MUD interaction is not enacted to be read but to be experienced. As would spoken interaction, virtual interaction loses meaning when transposed to a computer file and reread. The pauses, breaks, disjunctions, speed and timing of virtual conversations are lost in such transposition, and such factors are a crucial signifier of meaning and context.

As with spoken dialogues, online conversations exist in the moment when they develop, and then they dissolve. They do not take place with the *primary* purpose of being recorded, but to be performed and interpreted in the here and now. On the other hand, 'readings' of online sessions are not only a possibility, but a necessity to realize an analytical perspective. Espen J. Aarseth (1997: 13) states that "life in the MUD is literary, relying on purely textual strategies", and he draws attention to the fact that almost no research on MUD as literary phenomenon has yet been done. In a critique of Reid, Aarseth points out that the argument about how "virtual interaction loses meaning when transposed to a computer file", and how "the pauses, breaks, disjunctions, speed and timing of virtual conversations are lost in such transposition", parallels the ancient romanticization of 'presence' and of the spoken word as the primary carrier of meaning (cf. Derrida 1976, and his critique of logocentrism). Aarseth further argues that this elevation of contemporaneity is particularly out of place in discussions of MUDs, since MUD dialogues are brilliant examples of how much meaning written words can embrace. I agree with Aarseth in his argument that MUD sessions, no matter how fluid, can be fruitfully regarded as 'texts', composed of written words, based entirely on the activity of reading and writing. If MUD practices are regarded as 'texts', the necessary detour of mediation in all communication (see Ricoeur 1991) becomes particularly clear.

But instead of regarding MUD conversations as either 'text' *or* 'talk', I would like to propose an alternative path within the domain of what I call *textual talk*. In conversation analysis, there has been a growing discussion of 'texts' as situated productions and receptions (McHoul 1987, Mulkay 1985, 1986), as an attempt to view texts as a place for dialogues, existing both within a single text ('fictional dialogues') and between texts (intertextuality). McHoul (1987: 87-88) takes this argument one step further:

> Ironically, while ethnomethodology and conversation analysis rely upon a world in which 'actual people' interact, a theory of what is to count as 'actual' is never stated – it remains an unexplicated commonsense resource. Somehow, we are expected to know – and we are expected to know that the category 'naturally' excludes the fictional. [...] In a parallel way we could say, after Derrida, that fictional talk is also an equally 'actual' happening insofar as it constitutes a trace of a culture's iteration machinery; that, in fact, 'the actual' is no longer a defensible category.

Following this line of thought, a MUD appears to be an ideal site for a conversation analysis with the ambition to challenge any clear division between the language of 'artifice' and that of 'real life', as well as that between the written and the spoken word. The inhabitants of WaterMOO would never agree that they are not in a crucial sense meeting 'actual people' in this online world, no matter if face-to-face is replaced with face-to-screen, speaking and listening with writing and reading, and physical touch with textual imagination. At the same time, the inherent instability of the category 'actual' or 'real' is clearly expressed in online textual talk, since these conversations constantly move between a mode of everyday socializing and a type of fiction writing (even if this online 'fiction' might be alluringly realistic). This floating distinction between 'world' and 'text' has, as will become clear, the most interesting consequences for the participants' textual talk about (online) embodiment, in particular along the dimensions of gender and sexuality.

3.   'Real' sex and 'virtual' gender?

Not surprisingly, feminist theorists with an interest in the relation between language and gender saw early on the great research potential in text-only online environments. In these textual spaces, language and gender are not only mutually constituted, but inevitably the same thing, since language is the only thing there is. Or so it seems. Typically, there are two versions of the language/gender discussion in online research, both organized around a separation between a 'real' physical body and its 'virtual' gender (where gender is understood as the textual figuration online, while sex is firmly anchored in the material body left in physical reality).

On one hand, there is a kind of postmodern utopianism in which online bodies are constituted through a dramatic divorce from every cultural implication of material bodies in virtual space (Plant 1997, Reid 1994). Within this perspective, the virtual body moves freely through the online landscape, effortlessly performing subversive gender positions (see Bruckman 1992 on 'gender swapping'). Gender is turned into 'pure' fiction, completely disconnected from the limits of the 'real', and most obviously from the limits of language. Through a peculiar move that conceals its intimate connections with ideologies and the meaning of matter, language is made both transparent and immaterial.

Elizabeth Reid (1994: under "Identity and the Cyborg Body") claims that in text-based online worlds "with the body freed from the physical, it completely enters the realm of the symbol. It becomes an entity of pure meaning, but is simultaneously meaningless, stripped of any fixed referent." In Reid's interpretation, the separation between 'virtual' and 'real' has gone so far as to completely disengage the former from the latter. Virtual space appears to be a place where textual bodies, freely and imaginatively, are being written with a fluidity that does not seem to have any limits. It even seems as if the physical body ceases to exist, or dies, when "the body freed from the physical [...] completely enters the realm of symbol." The question is how this symbolic entity can be "an entity of pure meaning" and "simultaneously meaningless, stripped of any fixed referent." This "fixed referent" is most likely the physical body that here is being left behind. How can one claim that these texts are disengaged from a culture that, somehow exclusively, belongs to the material world, and at the same time they are said to exist in a purely symbolic realm? How could they mean anything outside of, and beyond, everything that is not part of life as it is lived online? This further implies that the boundaries between online and the material realities in some sense are absolute, without leakages, as if the online culture actually is a "culture of no culture" (Haraway 1997: 23), where bodies are performed under the illusion of transparency.[3]

On the other hand, there is a discussion that almost inverts this argument. Instead of claiming full freedom of language-made online bodies, several theorists have criticized this view for ignoring the ways in which gender inequalities are far from erased when we go online, but rather reproduced, and possibly even fortified (Hall 1996, Herring 1993, 1996, Kramarae and Taylor 1993). They argue (as have 'off-line' linguists!) that men and women have different communicative strategies online, and that this communication is both male-dominated and male-oriented. Male participants are said to accomplish this by "ignoring the topics which women introduce, producing conversational floors based on hierarchy instead of collaboration, dismissing women's responses as irrelevant, and contributing a much higher percentage of the total number of postings and text produced" (Hall 1996: 154). While certainly being most valuable for pointing out that online worlds are not separated from discourses of gender difference and sexism, these analyses reproduce the problematic idea of language as something gendered (or rather, sexed); that inequalities produced in and through language are somehow biologically grounded in sex differences.

This understanding of language and gender seems particularly out of place in online environments, since the sex of the typist, of the physical body at the keyboard, is literally an ambiguous matter. In Amy Bruckman's classical article "Gender Swapping on the Internet" (1992), online characters are paradoxically reduced to mere reflections of the sexed and gendered realities of their typists: "*Female characters* are often besieged with attention [...] Unwanted attention and sexual advances create an uncomfortable atmosphere for *women* in MUDs, just as they do in real life" (under "III. A Public Debate About Gender", my emphasis). This suggests that female characters are actually manoeuvred by women, and that these women are confronting the same problems online as they do in their everyday life. Even though this sometimes is the case, my point is that in reducing online practices to straightforward effects of (an unknown) physical reality, language is not only essentialized, but this time without any knowledge of the essence! To collapse female characters into the category of 'women' oversimplifies the relation between the world of the character and that of the typist, and ultimately makes investigations of differences (and not only similarities) between these realms impossible.

4. Performing @gender

I would instead argue for a perspective on typed bodies which is not limited to one side of the real/virtual divide, but which complicates this distinction (Sundén 2001). This understanding is the fruit of a long-term participation in everyday practices in WaterMOO, in which clear distinctions between 'real' and 'virtual' are both articulated and contested. It is a perspective that does not believe in the 'real' as an underlying truth, nor dismisses the 'virtual' as a mysteriously disengaged fiction, but that is rather interested in how participants' understandings of 'real' and 'virtual' are typed into being through textual enactments of sexed and gendered bodies. It is an attempt to explore how people handle an online borderland where they meet without seeing each other, how bodies come to matter, textually as well as materially, through online textual talk. As such, this approach focuses on the *performative* dimension of language and embodiment.

This online performativity is clearly illustrated in the use of the @gender command. To become an inhabitant in a MUD, you must create a character. A character consists of a name, a textual description, and an @gender. The name of the character chosen by the user appears in the interaction whenever the character is actively invoked or interpellated, the user-entered description is available to other participants through the <look> command, and the 'gender' attribute is most obviously revealed through the automatic use of the appropriate @gender pronoun by the MUD program. Choosing an @gender is more complicated than it first might appear. In WaterMOO, the following choices are available: 'male', 'female', 'neuter', 'either', 'Spivak', 'splat', 'plural', 'egotistical', 'royal' and '2nd'. Characters @gendered something else than 'female' or 'male' are (in this particular MUD) rare. The @gender command, by producing the effects it names, could fruitfully be compared to what John

L. Austin (1962) designates a 'performative'. This concept "is derived, of course, from 'perform', the usual verb with the noun 'action': it indicates that the issuing of the utterance is the performing of an action – it is not normally thought of as just saying something" (6-7).

The notion of 'performativity' has further been remodelled and used by queer theorists, such as Judith Butler (1990, 1993), with the purpose of showing that there is no pre-existing, biological sex on which gender acts as a cultural imprint. Rather, sexed and gendered bodies are materialized through a series of re-iterated acts in language. Materiality is viewed as the effect of various power relations, which is why bodies would not make sense, would be unthinkable, outside the normative practices that give them their meaning. This argument is particularly fitting in relation to the @gendering of MOO characters, by which the constitution of bodies through repetitive, stylized language acts takes place. Textual bodies exist only as language, and as such inhabit a symbolic universe, temporarily released from the physical reality of their typists. Simultaneously, these online bodies can never be completely released from the material and cultural conditions in which they are grounded, nor from those discourses of the gendered body that render them meaningful.

By deconstructing not only gender but sex itself, Butler's theories of gender performativity are for several reasons very useful in formulating an alternative framework for a study of online bodies. Butler's notion of gender performativity goes against the idea of boundless gender play, freed from every constraint of the meanings always already embedded in the body. In her theory, there is no subject who decides its gender, but the subject is, rather, partly constituted through gender. One reason to apply Butler's ideas to online worlds is to demonstrate how the construction and enactments of characters can never be as conscious and free as it might seem. The performance of a character can never be regarded as disconnected from dominating discourses surrounding sex and gender. Seemingly disconnected from the material world behind them, online bodies ultimately depend on the materiality of computers, computer networks, and not least embodied human beings. This complex dialectics between textual talk and the materiality of physical bodies and technologies is constantly actualized in typed-in interactions in WaterMOO.

5. "I'm still not sure she's a she"

> mira says, "Gender doesn't seem to work very well at all"
> You ask, "doesn't seem to work?"
> mira says, "That is why I never let anyone be sure of mine"
> mira shrugs.
> mira says, "People treat you differently if they think you are female or if they think you're male."
> You ask, "how long have you been doing that??"
> mira asks, "Isn't it better to make them just treat you as you?"
> mira grins.
> You say, "of course it is"
> mira says, "Well, I have been physically ambiguous for as long as I can remember."
> Yazmine [to Jenny]: "I met her, and I'm still not sure she's a she."
> mira grins.
> mira says, "I do it in real life as well"
> mira says, "Although of course it's easier in moos"
> Jenny nods.
> mira says, "It's a little funny. People on MOOs are more demanding about knowing what you are than people are in real life"
> You ask, "but why did you set your gender to female then??"
> mira says, "Which is rather stupid considering that it means more there"
> You say, "that is very silly, i agree"
> mira says, "My gender is set to female because this character is female"

In this excerpt, mira, who is @gendered 'female', explains that people (online) treat each other differently depending on whether or not they think the person they meet is male or female (in 'real' life), and asks: "Isn't it better to make them just treat you as you?" The wish to be treated 'as oneself' seems to parallel the ancient desire to leave the body behind and inhabit a disembodied universe, which according to several theorists now is being remapped onto virtual worlds (Balsamo 1996: 116-132, Hayles 1996, 1999, and Stone 1991). To mira, this longing for an existence in relation to which the body no longer matters is rendered accountable in terms of her physical ambiguity ("I have been physically ambiguous for as long as I can remember"). At this point, it is very difficult, if not impossible to tell whether this physical ambiguity refers to mira's typist or the online character (or both!). The uncertain distinction between 'real' and 'virtual' gets increasingly complicated throughout the excerpt, and culminates in Yazmines' line: "I met her, and I'm still not sure she's a she".

In MOO discourse, participants certainly say that they 'meet' in the MOO, no matter if these encounters are purely textual affairs. In this case, however, "I met her, and I'm still not sure she's a she" rather seems to indicate that these typists have met face-to-face, but that the additional resources available in face-to-face encounters (physical body, voice etc.) did not clarify much. What captures my attention is the use of pronouns. Mira is suddenly referred to not as an 'it', but as a 'she', even if the status of this 'she' remains unclear. "I'm still not sure she's a she" is of course a wonderful contradiction of terms, since it is most unlikely that one would be uncertain about a 'she' being a 'she' when a linguistic determination of sex has already been made. More importantly, this (Freudian) slip at the keyboard shows how hard it is to rest within a gender neutral discourse in discussions of uncertain bodies. On the other hand, "I'm still not sure she's a she" can also be a perfectly logical way in typed-in interaction to account for the multiple selves involved in MOO discourse, where the first 'she' corresponds with the female character mira, whereas the uncertainty of the second 'she' is directed toward the physical ambiguity of the typist.

Similarly to a novel, WaterMOO provides its inhabitants with a fictive world open to play and imagination. But apart from being textual in this 'literary' sense, MOO dialogues are literally technological extensions of the physical bodies of the participants, which make them an intimate part of a networked social space quite different from the imaginary worlds of novels. Within this blend of fantasy and everyday socializing, the question of 'gender' (or rather sex) appears to be a burning one. In sympathy with Donna Haraway's (1991) notion of the cyborg, WaterMOOers are certainly fusions of mechanical and organic parts in being both embodied typists and computerized, textual characters. But instead of embracing Haraway's hopes and desires related to uncertain and sometimes contradictory subjectivities whose significations are not determined by categorizations such as human and machine, man and woman, textual talk in WaterMOO is rather concerned with the reinscription of these categories. Following mira's lines throughout the conversation above, this text points toward a general obsession with sex and gender. At the same time, mira wants people to stop thinking about these categories and to start treating one another as (supposedly sexless) persons. A wish to liberate ourselves from the limits of sex is here repeatedly turned into discussions of these limits as inescapable.

Samantha Holland (1995), in her work on body and gender in cyborg cinema, addresses the question of what it means to be human in an era when the boundaries between humans and machines are becoming increasingly blurred. She finds that cyborgs in films such as *Terminator* and *Eve of Destruction* not only have bodies, but that these bodies are highly gendered. She further points out that the fears related to technology in the cyborg film are the fears of being replaced by, or actually becoming, a machine. In this becoming, which refers to a cyborg future in which bodies no longer need an organic foundation, the biologically engraved body is at risk of disappearing, and with it the notion of biologically grounded difference. In fighting this double fear, the fear of not only losing the category 'human', but with it the category 'sex', cyborg bodies are hyper-gendered, so as to ensure that sex differences remain even in a world populated by post-humans (Holland 1995). In WaterMOO, consistent constructions of textual sex as either male or female (through the @gender command as well as the conversational use of 's/he' and 'her/him') could be understood in a similar way. In a world where you cannot be sure of whether the person you are meeting is a man or a woman (in the flesh), or even if it is a *person*, one way to deal with this insecurity is to textually re-inscribe familiar categories on the level of sex and gender, to insist on a system of recognizable differences (Bassett 1997, Kendall 1996, 1998, O'Brien 1999, and Slater 1998).

In the midst of the above conversation, a third character, Taxidriver, enters "A Cave":

> Taxidriver politely knocks on the entrance to A Cave. You get the impression that he would like to come in.
> A black fog rolls in from everywhere, and obscures your sight. When it finally dissipates, you see Taxidriver standing nearby.
> Yazmine says, "What a party today."
> mira nods.
> Jenny smiles
> Taxidriver bows to all, and sundry
> mira says to Taxidriver, "How do you feel about not knowing my gender?"
> [...]
> Taxidriver says, "Well, from a relational point of view, it causes a bit of difficulty, because normally people relate to people by gender among other things."
> Jenny nods
> Taxidriver says, "Translation to English: It bugs me and my pronouns"
> Jenny thinks Taxi sounds very professional

mira . o O (that is something I tend to try to avoid)
mira laughs.
mira says to Taxidriver, "I hear that I have become "it""
Taxidriver [to mira]: "I dislike calling you an "it." But it's the only fitting
    pronoun I know."
Jenny chuckles
You say, "could have been worse."
Taxidriver says, "I mean, if I say "she" or "he" I could be wrong, and it's
    misleading to myself to fit one of them to you. Else if/when I find out
    the truth, I could be disappointed."
Jenny hmmms
mira hmms, as well.
Taxidriver hmms.
    [...]
Taxidriver [to Jenny]: "Well, I know mira from powermoo. mira's character
    there has both female, and male morphs. So, if she had stayed to one
    gender or the other, I'd relate to mira as one or the other."
Jenny [to Taxidriver]: "but here – in the WaterMOO context – she's female...
    even if *it* doesn't wanna reveal its "true" gender..."
Taxidriver [to Jenny]: "Of course, all the intellectual stuff aside, I'm curious
    as he** to find out mira's true nature ;)"
Taxidriver doesn't relate to mira in the "WaterMOO" context.

In this passage, mira is returned to the position of an 'it', even if Taxidriver elo-
quently articulates the dilemma this puts him in: "It bugs me and my pronouns". The paradoxical tension between mira's reputation of being an 'it', and
the fact that the character mira is @gendered 'female', is significantly explored.
On one hand, the mystery surrounding mira does not seem to have much to
do with the online character, but rather with the person behind the text who
refuses to answer the question, "are you male or female?"[4] This becomes particularly clear when Taxidriver says, "I mean, if I say 'she' or 'he' I could be
wrong, and it's misleading to myself to fit one of them to you. Else if/when I
find out the truth, I could be disappointed." Here, the online character mira
seems to become almost transparent. What matters is the 'true' body of mira's
typist, regardless of the fact that the character mira is female. But in the next
moment, a few lines further down, the online body is instead saturated with
meaning: "Well, I know mira from powermoo. mira's character there has both
female, and male morphs. So, if she had stayed to one gender or the other, I'd
relate to mira as one or the other". Here, the typist of Taxidriver goes explicit-

ly out of character by referring to another game, "powermoo", where s/he has met the character mira. "So, if she had stayed to one gender or the other, I'd relate to mira as one or the other" indicates that a certain degree of consistency in the online performance is needed, in order for its integrity not to be questioned. As long as the character is convincingly coherent, and consistently written as either male or female, the issue of an underlying 'truth' might never be called into question.

This raises some interesting questions related to the possibility of online 'cross-dressing'. Brenda Danet (1996: under "Language, writing and the performance of gender: Some questions for research") notes that "at least on the face of it, virtual cross-dressing should be much easier than real-life (RL) cross-dressing [...] [but] textual passing may be more difficult than appears at first glance."[5] In spaces where language literally substitutes for the 'real', the notion of cross-dressing is intimately connected to not only the way bodies can be read *as* texts, but actually to the way bodies *become* text. 'Passing' is further turned into a textual practice, a matter of being able to uphold, textually, the illusion of stable gender identities.

Marjorie Garber (1993) investigates how cultural discourses of transvestites and transsexuals reveal fundamental asymmetries between definitions of 'male' and 'female'. She points out how transvestites (as opposed to *female* transvestites!), even though they dress up as women, paradoxically, still manifest their male subjectivity: "Their wives will address them as 'Donna' or 'Jeanne' or whatever, when they are wearing women's clothes. Yet this is clearly not 'female subjectivity,' even though it goes by women's names. It is a man's idea of what 'a woman' is: it is male subjectivity in drag" (324).

In a similar fashion, characters with names like "Sexy_Babe" and "sugarpie" can easily be found in MUDs. Typically, these 'women' carry descriptions that point in the direction of 'woman', but perhaps without convincingly reaching this destination. These texts could without much effort be read as male fantasies about women, or as male subjectivities in drag. But to do this kind of reading would be to re-establish the essentializing view of language I have intended to criticize. It would be to re-connect language to gender, to insist that language is grounded in and determined by gender differences. Moreover, the act of cross-dressing relies on the knowledge of the underlying sex, no matter how unstable. It depends on a complex interplay between gazes and physical bodies, on the activities of looking at and being seen, on the power of the visible as well as the unspoken. According to Butler (1990: 137-141), drag has the potential to denaturalize and disrupt the notion of an 'original' gender, since the distinction between the material and the imaginary, between the physical body of the performer and the gender being performed, is put into question. Parody, in this sense, has the power to unveil the constructed nature of gender, and ultimately that of sex itself. But, again, this presupposes the visibility of the physical. It therefore seems very problematic to fruitfully apply a concept like cross-dressing to language-made gender performances in online worlds. Otherwise, how could the 'naturalness' of sex and gender in any sense be challenged if what we see only takes place at the 'surface level' of parody (the textual performance and not the typist's body)? This would, by definition, be no parody at all.

To return to the above excerpt, the difficulty to stay within a gender neutral discourse when discussing mira, without being carried away by the inert dichotomy dividing humanity in two, is apparent in some of Taxidriver's formulations: "So, if *she* had stayed to one gender or the other, I'd relate to mira as one or the other" (my emphasis). In statements like this, mira's typist is no longer understood as positionless, but more or less consciously interpreted as a (physical) woman. In Taxidriver's concluding comment, this belief, or wish, is made even more explicit: "Of course, all the intellectual stuff aside, I'm curious as he** to find out mira's true nature ;)". In his capacity as a male character, Taxidriver here seems to express a desire to find out whether this textual female is a woman for *real*, thus actualizing what could be called a *heterotextual* male perspective. 'Heterotextuality', obviously a fusion of heterosexuality and textuality, seems to be an always present reality in the MOO. No matter who the typists are, the relationships between these textual men and women are regulated by a heteronormative online system. The construction of WaterMOO as a heterotextual space might not be grounded in frequent, explicit references to heterosexuality (even though this occasionally occurs). Rather, silences and absences of alternatives to male/female sexual desires speak for themselves. Through their nonexistence, these voids of unformulated desires create a powerful normative framework in which WaterMOO relationships and fantasies are played out.

6. "Sexual but sexless"

> Jenny [to Taxidriver]: "so.... what's your image of mira?"
> Jenny [to Taxidriver]: "as a 'person'..."
> Taxidriver says, "Good question."
> Jenny smiles

Taxidriver [to Jenny]: "Do you read Clive Barker at all?"
mira chuckles.
You say, "i'm afraid i don't..."
Taxidriver says, "Ah well."
You say, "would i understand this better if i did? :)"
Taxidriver says, "The best image I could compare mira to, would be the
      mystif, in Clive Barker's Imajica"
      [...]
Taxidriver says, "The literary character is a mystif, named Pie'oh'Pah."
Jenny is listening carefully
Taxidriver says, "A mystif is a special being, rarely born, but very magical."
Taxidriver says, "And also a very sexual being, Although, it has no sex."
Jenny nods
You say, "interesting..."
Taxidriver says, "It's appearance differs for anyome looking at it."
You ask, "it has really no sex.... or is it just different?"
Taxidriver says, "Er anyone"
Taxidriver says, "It's all sexes, and none."
You say, "fascinating"
Taxidriver says, "It's sex depends on the person looking at it. For me, it
      could be a woman. For you, a man."
Taxidriver says, "Whatever person you would most desire, that's what it
      looks like."
Taxidriver says, "And it's appearance could change, even to you... because
      your desires could change"
Jenny nods
Taxidriver says, "I thought it quite fitting, since mira is sexual, but sexless...
      to me anyway."
You say, "very fitting... although i've never met mira before"
Taxidriver says, "Neither have I ;)"

Taxidriver starts by comparing mira with a literary character: "A mystif is a
special being, rarely born, but very magical. [...] And also a very sexual being,
Although, it has no sex. [...] It's all sexes, and none. [...] It's sex depends on the
person looking at it. For me, it could be a woman. For you, a man. [...]
Whatever person you would most desire, that's what it looks like. [...] And it's
appearance could change, even to you... because your desires could change
[...] I thought it quite fitting, since mira is sexual, but sexless... to me anyway."
In this excerpt, a distinction is made between having a sex and being 'sexual'.
Taxidriver's comparison of mira with a "mystif" disconnects sexual desire

from a body with a certain sex. 'Desire' is here textualized as something constantly shifting, which appears in the shape and flavour of others' sexual longings. mira and 'its' other male and female morphs interestingly correspond to this idea of polymorphous sexuality and shape shifting. At the same time, the uneasiness related to 'plural' beings in the MOO turns this potential space for multiple desires into something safely unified and 'sex-neutral', projected onto the body of the typist. This move from multiplicity to unity makes mira "sexual, but sexless".

In all of these excerpts, the ambiguity related to the issue of 'agency' is striking. Who is talking? Where is 'it' (who is talking) located? In the above excerpt, this becomes evident when I tell Taxidriver that I have never met mira before, and he answers, "Neither have I ;)", which with a hint of irony produces a difference between textual and 'fully fleshed' encounters. Lynn Cherny (1999: 42) identifies the complexity of the relationship between the 'real' person and the character as one that contains both identification and distinction, but concludes that:

> Generally, it is not a question of pretended or playful identification when a user describes something that happened to her character as something that happened to her: her character is her in the context of the virtual world, and there simply aren't enough pronouns in English to differentiate between the selves involved.

This approach seems reasonable in relation to her purposes, since her primary interest is in how 'speech' in a social MUD constitutes notions of community. In analyzing MUD practices as a *register* – a particular linguistic repertoire – Cherny explores how communicative elements at a micro-level, such as turn-taking, back channels, and non-verbal expressions create and confirm insider status. In her exposé of speech patterns in a MUD, the differences between MUD dialogues and face-to-face interactions are richly illustrated, but her discussion never quite complicates the relation between user and character. In fact, this relation has been very little explored in MUD research, but as these WaterMOO excerpts suggest, there is an intense dialectics between different levels of embodied subjectivity and the construction of textual talk.

Throughout these excerpts, it becomes clear that the relation between typist and character is a complex one, consisting of mediations between textual and physical realities. The MOO character mira is (unproblematically) @gendered 'female', but is also accompanied by a whole set of other textual beings (morphs), some of them male but most of them female, which belong to the same typist. This inconsistency in the online performance obviously makes room for suspicions regarding the sex of the typist, which might never have occurred if s/he had merely performed, for example, coherent and believable female characters. WaterMOO is an imaginary space, open to creative writing and textual pleasure. But when it comes to constructions of sex and gender, the demand for realism is striking. It is as if the online 'fiction' is suddenly too thin to embrace performances with uncertain or contradictory relationships to their embodied creators. At the point where textual playfulness intersects with @gender, non-realistic aspects of an imaginative universe suddenly have to give in to a discourse based on naturalistic sex/gender incarnations. On the other hand, this means that if the online fiction is convincing enough, it might never be questioned. No matter if gender practices in online worlds typically follow 'conventional', even exaggerated gender codes, the demand for coherence (rather than correspondence) potentially creates space for a more subtle textual drag not immediately visible on the written surface. Or rather, this would be an example of online 'passing', since the sex/gender fiction would pass unnoticed. But, then again, since it passes unnoticed it will lack subversive potential. The act of textual passing might be subversive for the individual typist, but it will have a very limited power over the demand for gender realism and heterotextuality in the MOO.

7. Concluding comments

Instead of claiming that online everything can be different, or that online everything is the way it has always been, I argue for a perspective on textual talk and typed bodies that problematizes any simple real/virtual distinction. In transferring only 'gender' to discussions of online circumstances, the classical distinction between biological sex and cultural gender as immutable properties is repeated, and possibly fortified. As opposed to this translation of the sex/gender dichotomy onto virtual worlds, I argue that not only gender, but also sex, is being written online, even though sex in this case must be understood as immaterial. It is preferable to understand online bodies (as well as material bodies) as both sexed and gendered, but not in a sense that makes sex a passive, natural foundation on which gender is culturally inscribed (see Butler 1993). When the sexed body is viewed instead as an active materiality, as a site for political, social and cultural struggle, the body is no longer opposed to culture, but is itself a cultural product. This approach does not reduce sex to essence, nor does it ignore its material existence.

In a similar manner, the writing and meaning of messages appearing in online textual talk, what could be called *virtual gender* (O'Farrell and Vallone 1999) is intimately related to the specificity of *virtual sex*, constituted through the @gender command. 'Sex' in this case is not primarily grounded in the physical body, but takes on a linguistic existence intimately related to the (material) logic of computer code (Zdenek 1999). Even if it is easier to see that virtual sex, compared to material sex, is not something outside of and beyond processes of inscription (since it, literally, has to be inscribed), it is important to point out that the @gender command serves as an underlying, material structure in bodily practices in MUDs not reducible to the construction of other texts/utterances. While being an intimate part of the code of the MUD program itself, automatically determining the pronouns being used in textual talk, the @gender command comes as close as one can possibly get to a material existence of immaterial bodies.

This approach to online embodiment, in questioning the distinction between the textual and the material, is closely related to my understanding of the complicated dance between typist and character in textual talk. The study of textual talk aims at exploring the complex *doubleness* of online practices, constituted through constant translations and mediations between the embodied self and the textual 'I'. Conversational journeys within and between these 'locations' invite both playfulness and anxiety. But, as the excerpts in this chapter have shown, anxiety, or at least a fairly demanding curiosity, dominates textual talk about (online) bodies. Among participants there is (not surprisingly) a never yielding awareness of the necessary (wo)man/machine-parts involved in the making and interpretation of an online world like WaterMOO. What they meet is not only language and technology, but *people*. If within technoromantic discourses (Coyne 1999), cyberspace is a liberating playground for disembodied minds, textual talk in WaterMOO shows how hard it is to get released from a world where the sexed and gendered body is a cultural foundation. The insecurity tied to the state of not knowing how character and typist are related in terms of sex and gender, creates conversational strategies to counter, maybe not the absence, but the *invisible presence* of physical bodies in online encounters. The body of the other is still there, on the far side of the screen, but it cannot be reached, looked at or touched – other than through typing textual talk.

Notes

1. Names of characters have been changed throughout this text to protect the online identities of participants. In addition, all typing errors have been left uncorrected.

2. MOO, or MUD Object Oriented, refers to the use of object oriented programming in these worlds. A MOO is one of several other MUD subcategories. For excellent introductions to MUDs and MUDding, see Turkle (1995), and Reid (1994).

3. Donna Haraway (1997: 23) argues that "no one exists in a culture of no culture, including the critics and prophets as well as the technicians. We might profitably learn to doubt our fears and certainties of disasters as much as our dreams of progress. We might learn to live without the bracing discourses of salvation history. We exist in a sea of powerful stories: They are the condition of finite rationality and personal and collective life histories. There is no way out of stories; but [...] there are many possible structures, not to mention contents, of narration. Changing the stories, in both material and semiotic senses, is a modest intervention worth making." Even if women and other marginalized groups might go to great lengths in their attempts to erase themselves, to be temporarily accepted as a part of "the culture of no culture", this will only serve those whose power is dependent on the maintenance of the illusion of transparency. Haraway shows how this striving constructs a notion of 'objectivity' that remains to stand in the way of a more self-critical position committed to partial and situated knowledges.

4. In her essay "'Are you male or female?' Gender performances on muds", Kendall (1998) shows how the question "are you male or female?" is common enough to circulate as a joke among experienced MUD participants.

5. In the revised version of this article, Danet (1998), this phrase is slightly reformulated: "At least on the face of it, textual cross-dressing should be much easier than the RL variety. Nonetheless, it may be much more difficult than appears at first glance" (145). For my purposes, I chose the online version that included a reference to 'textual passing'.

References

Aarseth, Espen J. 1997 *Cybertext: Perspectives on Ergodic Literature*. Baltimore: The Johns Hopkins University Press.
Austin, John L. 1962 *How To Do Things With Words*. Urmson, J. O. and Sbisà, Marina (eds) Cambridge, Mass.: Harvard University Press.
Balsamo, Anne. 1996 *Technologies of the Gendered Body: Reading Cyborg Women*. London: Duke University Press.
Bassett, Caroline. 1997 "Virtually gendered: Life in an online world". In *The Subcultures Reader*, K. Gelder and S. Thornton (eds), 537-551. London: Routledge.
Bergvall, Victoria L. 1996 "Constructing and enacting gender through discourse: Negotiating multiple roles as female engineering students". In *Rethinking Language and Gender Research: Theory and Practice*, V.L. Bergvall, J.M. Bing, and A.F. Freed (eds), 173-201. London: Longman.

Bruckman, Amy. 1992 "Gender swapping on the Internet". [Online]. Available: <http://www.cc.gatech.edu/fac/Amy.Bruckman/papers/index.html#INET>. [Date accessed: Dec 12, 1998].

Butler, Judith. 1990 *Gender Trouble: Feminism and the Subversion of Identity*. London: Routledge.

Butler, Judith. 1993 *Bodies that Matter: On the Discursive Limits of 'Sex'*. London: Routledge.

Cameron, Deborah. 1997 "Performing gender identity: Young men's talk and the construction of heterosexual masculinity". In *Language and Masculinity*, S. Johnson and U. Meinhof (eds), 47-64. Oxford: Blackwell.

Cherny, Lynn. 1994 "Gender differences in text-based virtual reality". [Online]. Available: <http://www.research.att.com/~cherny/genderMOO.html>. [Date accessed: Dec 12, 1998].

Cherny, Lynn. 1995 "'Objectifying' the body in the discourse of an object-oriented MUD". [Online]. Available: <http://acorn.grove.iup.edu/en/workdays/toc.html>. [Date accessed: Jan 17, 2000].

Cherny, Lynn. 1999 *Conversation and Community: Chat in a Virtual World*. Stanford: CSLI Publications.

Coyne, Richard. 1999 *Technoromanticism: Digital Narrative, Holism, and the Romance of the Real*. Cambridge, Mass.: The MIT Press.

Danet, Brenda. 1996 "Text as mask: Gender and identity on the Internet". [Online]. Available: <http://atar.mscc.huji.ac.il/~msdanet/mask.html>. [Date accessed: Dec 12, 1998].

Danet, Brenda. 1998 "Text as mask: Gender, play, and performance on the Internet". In *Cybersociety 2.0: Revisiting Computer-Mediated Communication and Community*, S. Jones (ed.), 129-158. London: Sage.

Derrida, Jacques. 1976 *Of Grammatology*. Baltimore: The Johns Hopkins University Press.

Garber, Marjorie. 1993 "Spare parts: The surgical construction of gender". In *The Lesbian and Gay Studies Reader*, H. Abelove, M.A. Barale and D.M. Halperin (eds), 321-336. New York: Routledge.

Hall, Kira. 1996 "Cyberfeminism". In *Computer-Mediated Communication: Linguistic, Social and Cross-Cultural Perspectives*, S. Herring (ed.), 147-170. Amsterdam: John Benjamins.

Haraway, Donna. 1991 *Simians, Cyborgs and Women: The Reinvention of Nature*. New York: Routledge.

Haraway, Donna. 1997 *Modest_Witness@Second_Millennium: FemaleMan©_Meets_OncoMouse™*. London: Routledge.

Hayles, Katherine N. 1996 "Embodied virtuality: Or how to put bodies back into the picture". In *Immersed in Technology: Art and Virtual Environments*, A. Moser and D. MacLeod (eds), 1-28. Cambridge, Mass.: The MIT Press.

Hayles, Katherine N. 1999 *How We Became Posthuman: Virtual Bodies in Cybernetics, Literature, and Informatics*. Chicago: The University of Chicago Press.

Herring, Susan. 1993 "Gender and democracy in computer-mediated communication". *Electronic Journal of Communication* 3(2).

Herring, Susan. 1996 "Two variants of an electronic message schema". In *Computer-Mediated Communication: Linguistic, Social and Cross-Cultural Perspectives*, S. Herring, (ed.), 81-106. Amsterdam: John Benjamins.

Holland, Samantha. 1995 "Descartes Goes to Hollywood: Mind, body and gender in contemporary cyborg cinema". In *Cyberspace, Cyberbodies, Cyberpunk: Cultures of Technological Embodiment*, M. Featherstone and R. Burrows (eds), 157-174. London: Sage.

Kendall, Lori. 1996 "MUDder? I hardly know 'er! Adventures of a feminist MUDder". In *Wired Women*, L. Cherny and E.R. Weise (eds), 207-223. Seattle: Seal Press.

Kendall, Lori. 1998 "'Are you male or female?' Gender performances on Muds". In *Everyday Inequalities: Critical Inquiries*, J. O'Brien and J.A. Howard (eds), 131-153. Oxford: Blackwell.

Kramarae, Cheris and Taylor, H. Jeanie. 1993 "Women and men on electronic networks: A conversation or a monologue?" In *Women, Information Technology, + Scholarship*, H.J. Taylor, C. Kramarae and M. Ebben (eds), 52-61. Urbana: University of Illinois Press.

McHoul, Alec. 1987 "An initial investigation of the usability of fictional conversation for doing conversation analysis". *Semiotica* 67(1/2): 83-104.

McRae, Shannon. 1996 "Coming apart at the seams: sex, text and the virtual body". In *Wired Women*, L. Cherny and E.R. Weise (eds), 242-264. Seattle: Seal Press.

Mulkay, Michael. 1985 "Agreement and disagreement in conversations and letters". *Text* 5(3): 201-227.

Mulkay, Michael. 1986 "Conversations and texts". *Human Studies* 9: 303-321.

O'Brien, Jodi. 1999 "Writing in the body: Gender (re)production in online interaction". In *Communities in Cyberspace*, M.A. Smith and P. Kollock (eds), 76-104. London: Routledge.

O'Farrell, Mary Ann and Vallone, Lynne (eds). 1999 *Virtual Gender: Fantasies of Subjectivity and Embodiment*. Ann Arbor: University of Michigan Press.

Plant, Sadie. 1997 *Zeros + Ones: Digital Women + The New Technoculture*. New York: Doubleday.

Reid, Elizabeth. 1994 "Cultural formations in text-based virtual realities". [Online]. Available: <http://people.we.mediaone.net/elizrs/cult-form.html>. [Date accessed: Dec 12, 1998].

Reid, Elizabeth. 1995 "Virtual worlds: Culture and imagination". In *Cybersociety: Computer Mediated Communications and Community*, S. Jones (ed.), 164-183. London: Sage.

Ricoeur, Paul. 1991 *From Text to Action: Essays in Hermeneutics II*. London: Athlone.

Slater, Don. 1998 "Trading sexpics on IRC: Embodiment and authenticity on the Internet". *Body and Society* 4(4): 91-117.

Stokoe, Elizabeth H. 1998 "Talking about gender: The conversational construction of gender categories in academic discourse". *Discourse & Society* 9(2): 217-240.

Stone, Allucquère Rosanne. 1991 "Will the real body please stand up? Boundary stories about virtual cultures". In *Cyberspace: First Steps*, M. Benedikt (ed.), 81-118. Cambridge, Mass.: The MIT Press.

Stone, Allucquère Rosanne. 1995 *The War of Desire and Technology at the Close of the Mechanical Age*. Cambridge, Mass.: The MIT Press.

Sundén, Jenny. 2001 "What happened to difference in cyberspace? The (re)turn of the she-cyborg". *Feminist Media Studies* 1(2): 215-232.

Turkle, Sherry. 1995 *Life on the Screen: Identity in the Age of Internet.* New York: Simon and Schuster.

Zdenek, Sean. 1999 "Rising up from the MUD: Inscribing gender in software design". *Discourse & Society* 10(3): 379-409.

Biographical details

Sigurd D'hondt obtained an MA in African Studies at the University of Ghent (Belgium). In 2001, he received a PhD in linguistics from the University of Antwerp (also in Belgium). His research interests include Kiswahili, conversation analysis, membership categorisation, and political communication.

address
IPrA Research Centre, University of Antwerp (GER),
Universiteitsplein 1, B-2610 Wilrijk, Belgium.
E-mail address: <sdhondt@uia.ua.ac.be>.

Andrew Fish is a final year, staff-salaried PhD student at Aalborg University. He is a recent convert to ethnomethodological principles, having taught English literature and literary theory at Danish universities for the last eleven years. His current research attempts to apply the insights gained from CA, MCA and discursive psychology to the analysis of dialogue in fiction.

address
Department of Languages and Intercultural Studies, Aalborg University,
Kroghstraede 3, Aalborg, DK-9220, Denmark.
E-mail address: <fish@sprog.auc.dk>.

Alexa Hepburn is a Senior Lecturer in Psychology at Nottingham Trent University. She has published on school bullying, feminist theory, the use of deconstruction in psychology, and discursive psychology. She has just completed her first book, *An Introduction to Critical Social Psychology*, for Sage, and is currently researching interaction in calls to the NSPCC child protection helpline, for which she has been awarded a Leverhulme Fellowship.

address
Psychology Division, School of Social Sciences, Nottingham Trent University,
Burton Street, Nottingham, NG1 4BU.
E-mail address: <alexa.hepburn@ntu.ac.uk>.

Celia Kitzinger is Professor of Conversation Analysis, Gender and Sexuality in the Sociology Department at the University of York, UK. She has published ten books and around a hundred articles and chapters on issues relating to gender and sexuality, including *The Social Construction of Lesbianism* (Sage, 1987), *Changing Our Minds* (New York University Press, 1995, with Rachel Perkins), *Heterosexuality* (Sage, 1995, with Sue Wilkinson) and *Lesbian and Gay Psychology* (Blackwell, 2001, with Adrian Coyle).

address
Department of Sociology, University of York,
Heslington, York YO10 5DD, UK.
E-mail address: <celia_kitzinger@yahoo.com>.

Paul McIlvenny is an Associate Professor in the Department of Languages and Intercultural Studies at Aalborg University, Denmark. After his PhD training at Edinburgh University, Scotland, he relocated east to Scandinavia and has taught at universities in Finland, Sweden and Denmark. Since 1998 he has worked at Aalborg University. He has researched and published on computer-mediated communication, sign language talk, stand-up comedy, popular public discourse and heckling at Speakers' Corner, disability and masculinity in autobiographical comics, and heteronormativity in the new media and in intercultural encounters. He currently dabbles in the queer politics of posthuman practices and CA in/on the margins.

address
Department of Languages and Intercultural Studies, Aalborg University,
Kroghstraede 3, Aalborg, DK-9220, Denmark.
E-mail address: <paul@sprog.auc.dk>.

Jonathan Potter is Professor of Discourse Analysis at Loughborough University. After a BA in Psychology, an MA in Philosophy and a PhD in Sociology, he taught statistics in the Psychology Department at St Andrews University. Since 1988 he has worked in the Social Sciences Department at Loughborough. He has studied scientific argumentation, descriptions of crowd disorder, current affairs television, racism, and relationship counselling. His books include: *Mapping the Language of Racism* (Columbia University Press, 1992, with Margaret Wetherell); and *Discursive Psychology* (Sage, 1992, with Derek Edwards). In his most recent book (*Representing Reality*, Sage, 1996) he attempts to provide a systematic overview, integration and critique of constructionist research. He is co-editor of the journal *Theory and Psychology*.

address
Department of Social Sciences, Loughborough University,
Loughborough LE11 3TU, UK.
E-mail address: <j.a.potter@lboro.ac.uk>.

Janet Smithson is a Research Fellow in the Department of Psychology and Speech Pathology at Manchester Metropolitan University. Current research includes the reconciliation of future work and family for young people in Europe, the effects of workplace change on individuals and families, and discourses about gender.

address
Department of Psychology and Speech Pathology,
Manchester Metropolitan University,
Elizabeth Gaskell Campus, Hathersage Rd, Manchester, M13 0JA, UK.
E-mail address: <j.smithson@mmu.ac.uk>.

Susan A. Speer is a Lecturer in Sociology at Brunel University. She gained her PhD *Talking Gender and Sexuality: Conversations About Leisure* from the Department of Social Sciences, Loughborough University. She has published an article on heterosexism (with Jonathan Potter) in *Discourse & Society* 11(4), an article on masculinity (and a rejoinder to Nigel Edley) in *Feminism & Psychology* 11(1), and is currently writing a book on *Feminism, Discourse and Conversation* (Routledge).

address
Department of Human Sciences, Brunel University,
Uxbridge, Middlesex UB8 3PH, UK.
E-mail address: <Susan.Speer@Brunel.ac.uk>.

Elizabeth H. Stokoe is a Senior Lecturer in Social Psychology at University College Worcester. Her research interests include ethnomethodological and discursive approaches to gender and discourse, the organisation of tutorial talk, and issues around neighbour relationships.

address
Department of Psychology, University College Worcester,
Henwick Grove, Worcester WR2 6AJ, UK.
E-mail address: <e.stokoe@worc.ac.uk>.

Jenny Sundén is a PhD student in the Department of Communication Studies (Tema Kommunikation) at Linköping University. She is teaching in the field of media and cultural studies, and is part of the research group "Digital Borderlands" funded by the Swedish Research Council for the Humanities and Social Sciences (HSFR). Her dissertation in Spring 2002 focuses on textuality and embodiment in MUDs (text-based online worlds) and is entitled *Material Virtualities: Approaching Online Textual Embodiment*.

address
Department of Communication Studies (Tema Kommunikation),
Linköping University, SE-581 83 Linköping, Sweden.
E-mail address: <jensu@tema.liu.se>.

Liisa Tainio is currently working in the Department of Finnish at the University of Helsinki. She is interested in conversation analysis, text analysis and women studies. She has studied the gendered aspects of Finnish everyday conversations, interruptions, everyday stories, spouse talk, and elderly people's talk. She has also studied Finnish self-help books for relationships, and, for example, postcards. She is interested in the role of grammar and syntax in the conversation analytic approach.

address
Department of Finnish,
P.O. Box 3, FIN-00014 University of Helsinki, Finland.
E-mail address: <Liisa.Tainio@Helsinki.Fi>.

Index

In the PRAGMATICS AND BEYOND NEW SERIES the following titles have been published thus far or are scheduled for publication:

1. WALTER, Bettyruth: *The Jury Summation as Speech Genre: An Ethnographic Study of What it Means to Those who Use it.* Amsterdam/Philadelphia, 1988.
2. BARTON, Ellen: *Nonsentential Constituents: A Theory of Grammatical Structure and Pragmatic Interpretation.* Amsterdam/Philadelphia, 1990.
3. OLEKSY, Wieslaw (ed.): *Contrastive Pragmatics.* Amsterdam/Philadelphia, 1989.
4. RAFFLER-ENGEL, Walburga von (ed.): *Doctor-Patient Interaction.* Amsterdam/Philadelphia, 1989.
5. THELIN, Nils B. (ed.): *Verbal Aspect in Discourse.* Amsterdam/Philadelphia, 1990.
6. VERSCHUEREN, Jef (ed.): *Selected Papers from the 1987 International Pragmatics Conference. Vol. I: Pragmatics at Issue. Vol. II: Levels of Linguistic Adaptation. Vol. III: The Pragmatics of Intercultural and International Communication* (ed. with Jan Blommaert). Amsterdam/Philadelphia, 1991.
7. LINDENFELD, Jacqueline: *Speech and Sociability at French Urban Market Places.* Amsterdam/Philadelphia, 1990.
8. YOUNG, Lynne: *Language as Behaviour, Language as Code: A Study of Academic English.* Amsterdam/Philadelphia, 1990.
9. LUKE, Kang-Kwong: *Utterance Particles in Cantonese Conversation.* Amsterdam/Philadelphia, 1990.
10. MURRAY, Denise E.: *Conversation for Action. The computer terminal as medium of communication.* Amsterdam/Philadelphia, 1991.
11. LUONG, Hy V.: *Discursive Practices and Linguistic Meanings. The Vietnamese system of person reference.* Amsterdam/Philadelphia, 1990.
12. ABRAHAM, Werner (ed.): *Discourse Particles. Descriptive and theoretical investigations on the logical, syntactic and pragmatic properties of discourse particles in German.* Amsterdam/Philadelphia, 1991.
13. NUYTS, Jan, A. Machtelt BOLKESTEIN and Co VET (eds): *Layers and Levels of Representation in Language Theory: a functional view.* Amsterdam/Philadelphia, 1990.
14. SCHWARTZ, Ursula: *Young Children's Dyadic Pretend Play.* Amsterdam/Philadelphia, 1991.
15. KOMTER, Martha: *Conflict and Cooperation in Job Interviews.* Amsterdam/Philadelphia, 1991.
16. MANN, William C. and Sandra A. THOMPSON (eds): *Discourse Description: Diverse Linguistic Analyses of a Fund-Raising Text.* Amsterdam/Philadelphia, 1992.
17. PIÉRAUT-LE BONNIEC, Gilberte and Marlene DOLITSKY (eds): *Language Bases ... Discourse Bases.* Amsterdam/Philadelphia, 1991.
18. JOHNSTONE, Barbara: *Repetition in Arabic Discourse. Paradigms, syntagms and the ecology of language.* Amsterdam/Philadelphia, 1991.
19. BAKER, Carolyn D. and Allan LUKE (eds): *Towards a Critical Sociology of Reading Pedagogy. Papers of the XII World Congress on Reading.* Amsterdam/Philadelphia, 1991.
20. NUYTS, Jan: *Aspects of a Cognitive-Pragmatic Theory of Language. On cognition, functionalism, and grammar.* Amsterdam/Philadelphia, 1992.
21. SEARLE, John R. et al.: *(On) Searle on Conversation.* Compiled and introduced by Herman Parret and Jef Verschueren. Amsterdam/Philadelphia, 1992.

22. AUER, Peter and Aldo Di LUZIO (eds): *The Contextualization of Language*. Amsterdam/Philadelphia, 1992.
23. FORTESCUE, Michael, Peter HARDER and Lars KRISTOFFERSEN (eds): *Layered Structure and Reference in a Functional Perspective. Papers from the Functional Grammar Conference, Copenhagen, 1990*. Amsterdam/Philadelphia, 1992.
24. MAYNARD, Senko K.: *Discourse Modality: Subjectivity, Emotion and Voice in the Japanese Language*. Amsterdam/Philadelphia, 1993.
25. COUPER-KUHLEN, Elizabeth: *English Speech Rhythm. Form and function in everyday verbal interaction*. Amsterdam/Philadelphia, 1993.
26. STYGALL, Gail: Trial Language. *A study in differential discourse processing*. Amsterdam/Philadelphia, 1994.
27. SUTER, Hans Jürg: *The Wedding Report: A Prototypical Approach to the Study of Traditional Text Types*. Amsterdam/Philadelphia, 1993.
28. VAN DE WALLE, Lieve: *Pragmatics and Classical Sanskrit*. Amsterdam/Philadelphia, 1993.
29. BARSKY, Robert F.: *Constructing a Productive Other: Discourse theory and the convention refugee hearing*. Amsterdam/Philadelphia, 1994.
30. WORTHAM, Stanton E.F.: *Acting Out Participant Examples in the Classroom*. Amsterdam/Philadelphia, 1994.
31. WILDGEN, Wolfgang: *Process, Image and Meaning. A realistic model of the meanings of sentences and narrative texts*. Amsterdam/Philadelphia, 1994.
32. SHIBATANI, Masayoshi and Sandra A. THOMPSON (eds): *Essays in Semantics and Pragmatics*. Amsterdam/Philadelphia, 1995.
33. GOOSSENS, Louis, Paul PAUWELS, Brygida RUDZKA-OSTYN, Anne-Marie SIMON-VANDENBERGEN and Johan VANPARYS: *By Word of Mouth. Metaphor, metonymy and linguistic action in a cognitive perspective*. Amsterdam/Philadelphia, 1995.
34. BARBE, Katharina: Irony in Context. Amsterdam/Philadelphia, 1995.
35. JUCKER, Andreas H. (ed.): *Historical Pragmatics. Pragmatic developments in the history of English*. Amsterdam/Philadelphia, 1995.
36. CHILTON, Paul, Mikhail V. ILYIN and Jacob MEY: *Political Discourse in Transition in Eastern and Western Europe (1989-1991)*. Amsterdam/Philadelphia, 1998.
37. CARSTON, Robyn and Seiji UCHIDA (eds): *Relevance Theory. Applications and implications*. Amsterdam/Philadelphia, 1998.
38. FRETHEIM, Thorstein and Jeanette K. GUNDEL (eds): *Reference and Referent Accessibility*. Amsterdam/Philadelphia, 1996.
39. HERRING, Susan (ed.): *Computer-Mediated Communication. Linguistic, social, and cross-cultural perspectives*. Amsterdam/Philadelphia, 1996.
40. DIAMOND, Julie: *Status and Power in Verbal Interaction. A study of discourse in a close-knit social network*. Amsterdam/Philadelphia, 1996.
41. VENTOLA, Eija and Anna MAURANEN, (eds): *Academic Writing. Intercultural and textual issues*. Amsterdam/Philadelphia, 1996.
42. WODAK, Ruth and Helga KOTTHOFF (eds): *Communicating Gender in Context*. Amsterdam/Philadelphia, 1997.
43. JANSSEN, Theo A.J.M. and Wim van der WURFF (eds): *Reported Speech. Forms and functions of the verb*. Amsterdam/Philadelphia, 1996.

44. BARGIELA-CHIAPPINI, Francesca and Sandra J. HARRIS: *Managing Language. The discourse of corporate meetings.* Amsterdam/Philadelphia, 1997.
45. PALTRIDGE, Brian: *Genre, Frames and Writing in Research Settings.* Amsterdam/Philadelphia, 1997.
46. GEORGAKOPOULOU, Alexandra: *Narrative Performances. A study of Modern Greek storytelling.* Amsterdam/Philadelphia, 1997.
47. CHESTERMAN, Andrew: *Contrastive Functional Analysis.* Amsterdam/Philadelphia, 1998.
48. KAMIO, Akio: *Territory of Information.* Amsterdam/Philadelphia, 1997.
49. KURZON, Dennis: *Discourse of Silence.* Amsterdam/Philadelphia, 1998.
50. GRENOBLE, Lenore: *Deixis and Information Packaging in Russian Discourse.* Amsterdam/Philadelphia, 1998.
51. BOULIMA, Jamila: *Negotiated Interaction in Target Language Classroom Discourse.* Amsterdam/Philadelphia, 1999.
52. GILLIS, Steven and Annick DE HOUWER (eds): *The Acquisition of Dutch.* Amsterdam/Philadelphia, 1998.
53. MOSEGAARD HANSEN, Maj-Britt: *The Function of Discourse Particles. A study with special reference to spoken standard French.* Amsterdam/Philadelphia, 1998.
54. HYLAND, Ken: *Hedging in Scientific Research Articles.* Amsterdam/Philadelphia, 1998.
55. ALLWOOD, Jens and Peter Gärdenfors (eds): *Cognitive Semantics. Meaning and cognition.* Amsterdam/Philadelphia, 1999.
56. TANAKA, Hiroko: *Language, Culture and Social Interaction. Turn-taking in Japanese and Anglo-American English.* Amsterdam/Philadelphia, 1999.
57 JUCKER, Andreas H. and Yael ZIV (eds): *Discourse Markers. Descriptions and theory.* Amsterdam/Philadelphia, 1998.
58. ROUCHOTA, Villy and Andreas H. JUCKER (eds): *Current Issues in Relevance Theory.* Amsterdam/Philadelphia, 1998.
59. KAMIO, Akio and Ken-ichi TAKAMI (eds): *Function and Structure. In honor of Susumu Kuno.* 1999.
60. JACOBS, Geert: *Preformulating the News. An analysis of the metapragmatics of press releases.* 1999.
61. MILLS, Margaret H. (ed.): *Slavic Gender Linguistics.* 1999.
62. TZANNE, Angeliki: *Talking at Cross-Purposes. The dynamics of miscommunication.* 2000.
63. BUBLITZ, Wolfram, Uta LENK and Eija VENTOLA (eds.): *Coherence in Spoken and Written Discourse. How to create it and how to describe it.Selected papers from the International Workshop on Coherence, Augsburg, 24-27 April 1997.* 1999.
64. SVENNEVIG, Jan: *Getting Acquainted in Conversation. A study of initial interactions.* 1999.
65. COOREN, François: *The Organizing Dimension of Communication.* 2000.
66. JUCKER, Andreas H., Gerd FRITZ and Franz LEBSANFT (eds.): *Historical Dialogue Analysis.* 1999.
67. TAAVITSAINEN, Irma, Gunnel MELCHERS and Päivi PAHTA (eds.): *Dimensions of Writing in Nonstandard English.* 1999.
68. ARNOVICK, Leslie: *Diachronic Pragmatics. Seven case studies in English illocutionary development.* 1999.

69. NOH, Eun-Ju: *The Semantics and Pragmatics of Metarepresentation in English. A relevance-theoretic account.* 2000.
70. SORJONEN, Marja-Leena: *Responding in Conversation. A study of response particles in Finnish.* 2001.
71. GÓMEZ-GONZÁLEZ, María Ángeles: *The Theme-Topic Interface. Evidence from English.* 2001.
72. MARMARIDOU, Sophia S.A.: *Pragmatic Meaning and Cognition.* 2000.
73. HESTER, Stephen and David FRANCIS (eds.): *Local Educational Order. Ethnomethodological studies of knowledge in action.* 2000.
74. TROSBORG, Anna (ed.): *Analysing Professional Genres.* 2000.
75. PILKINGTON, Adrian: *Poetic Effects. A relevance theory perspective.* 2000.
76. MATSUI, Tomoko: *Bridging and Relevance.* 2000.
77. VANDERVEKEN, Daniel and Susumu KUBO (eds.): *Essays in Speech Act Theory.* 2002.
78. SELL, Roger D. : *Literature as Communication. The foundations of mediating criticism.* 2000.
79. ANDERSEN, Gisle and Thorstein FRETHEIM (eds.): *Pragmatic Markers and Propositional Attitude.* 2000.
80. UNGERER, Friedrich (ed.): *English Media Texts – Past and Present. Language and textual structure.* 2000.
81. DI LUZIO, Aldo, Susanne GÜNTHNER and Franca ORLETTI (eds.): *Culture in Communication. Analyses of intercultural situations.* 2001.
82. KHALIL, Esam N.: *Grounding in English and Arabic News Discourse.* 2000.
83. MÁRQUEZ REITER, Rosina: *Linguistic Politeness in Britain and Uruguay. A contrastive study of requests and apologies.* 2000.
84. ANDERSEN, Gisle: *Pragmatic Markers and Sociolinguistic Variation. A relevance-theoretic approach to the language of adolescents.* 2001.
85. COLLINS, Daniel E.: *Reanimated Voices. Speech reporting in a historical-pragmatic perspective.* 2001.
86. IFANTIDOU, Elly: *Evidentials and Relevance.* 2001.
87. MUSHIN, Ilana: *Evidentiality and Epistemological Stance. Narrative retelling.* 2001.
88. BAYRAKTAROĞLU, Arın and Maria SIFIANOU (eds.): *Linguistic Politeness Across Boundaries. The case of Greek and Turkish.* 2001.
89. ITAKURA, Hiroko: *Conversational Dominance and Gender. A study of Japanese speakers in first and second language contexts.* 2001.
90. KENESEI, István and Robert M. HARNISH (eds.): *Perspectives on Semantics, Pragmatics, and Discourse. A Festschrift for Ferenc Kiefer.* 2001.
91. GROSS, Joan: *Speaking in Other Voices. An ethnography of Walloon puppet theaters.* 2001.
92. GARDNER, Rod: *When Listeners Talk. Response tokens and listener stance.* 2001.
93. BARON, Bettina and Helga KOTTHOFF (eds.): *Gender in Interaction. Perspectives on femininity and masculinity in ethnography and discourse.* 2002
94. McILVENNY, Paul (ed.): *Talking Gender and Sexuality.* 2002.
95. FITZMAURICE, Susan M.: *The Familiar Letter in Early Modern English. A pragmatic approach.* n.y.p.
96. HAVERKATE, Henk: *The Syntax, Semantics and Pragmatics of Spanish Mood.* n.y.p.

97. MAYNARD, Senko K.: *Linguistic Emotivity. Centrality of place, the topic-comment dynamic, and an ideology of Pathos in Japanese discourse.* n.y.p.
98. DUSZAK, Anna (ed.): *Us and Others. Social identities across languages, discourses and cultures.* n.y.p.
99. JASZCZOLT, K.M. and Ken TURNER (eds.): *Meaning Through Language Contrast. Volume 1.* n.y.p.
100. JASZCZOLT, K.M. and Ken TURNER (eds.): *Meaning Through Language Contrast. Volume 2.* n.y.p.
101. LUKE, Kang Kwong and Theodossia-Soula PAVLIDOU (eds.): *Telephone Calls. Unity and diversity in conversational structure across languages and cultures.* n.y.p.
102. LEAFGREN, John: *Degrees of Explicitness. Information structure and the packaging of Bulgarian subjects and objects.* n.y.p.
103. FETZER, Anita and Christiane MEIERKORD (eds.): *Rethinking Sequentiality. Linguistics meets conversational interaction.* n.y.p.
104. BEECHING, Kate: *Gender, Politeness and Pragmatic Particles in French.* n.y.p.

STREAMING:
TWO YEARS LATER

STREAMING: TWO YEARS LATER

A follow-up of a group of pupils who attended streamed and non-streamed junior schools

Elsa Ferri
Research officer, NFER

National Foundation
for Educational
Research in
England and Wales

Published by the National Foundation for Educational Research
in England and Wales

Registered Office: The Mere, Upton Park, Slough, Bucks, SL1 2QD
London Office: 79 Wimpole Street, London, W1M 8EA

Book Publishing Division: 2 Jennings Buildings, Thames Avenue,
Windsor, Berks, SL4 1QS

First Published 1971

SBN   901225   55   X

Cover design by
PETER GAULD, FSIA

Printed in Great Britain by
KING, THORNE & STACE LTD., SCHOOL ROAD, HOVE, SUSSEX   BN3 5JE

Acknowledgements

I GRATEFULLY acknowledge the help and co-operation from the heads, teachers and pupils of the schools involved in the study.

I should like to express my thanks to Dr. Joan C. Barker Lunn for her helpful advice and comments throughout the project. My thanks are also due to Dr. D. A. Pidgeon, Dr. S. Wiseman, Mrs. E. Britton and Mr. A. Brimer for reading and commenting on the report, to Miss Lois Wilson, who was secretary to the project, and to Miss Wendy Fader of the NFER's statistics department.

The research was supported by a grant from the Department of Education and Science.

Contents

7

Contents

List of Tables

List of Tables

List of Tables

CHAPTER ONE

Introduction

THE study reported here follows up the school careers of a group of children who had taken part in an earlier investigation into the effects of streaming and non-streaming in junior schools.[1] The broad aims of the previous study were to examine the effects of different types of school organization on the personality, social and intellectual development of junior school pupils. The main feature of the research was a longitudinal study of approximately 5,500 children in 36 matched pairs of streamed and non-streamed schools. Annual assessments were made of pupils' performance in the various cognitive and non-cognitive areas under investigation.

One of the major findings of the research concerned the importance of the teacher in addition to—or, in some cases, as opposed to—the straightforward organizational factors of streaming or non-streaming. Teachers in streamed schools were found to be largely united in their attitudes and methods, both of which tended to be in accordance with the professed aims of streaming. In non-streamed schools however, about half the teachers held attitudes which were in conflict with the school's organizational policy and which were reflected in the adoption of classroom practices and teaching methods more appropriate in a streamed situation. As the approach of these teachers seemed likely to counteract the effects of organization in non-streamed schools, most analyses were carried out in terms of two teacher 'types'—Type 1, whose attitudes and methods were conducive to the aims of non-streaming, and Type 2, whose approach was more typical of colleagues in streamed schools.

Briefly, the results of the investigation showed that the effects of school organization and type of teacher lay in the pupils' emotional and social development, rather than in the sphere of formal attainment. Little difference was found in the academic progress made during their junior school careers by pupils in the different school environments under study. An analysis of pupils' attitudes, however,

[1] This study, carried out between 1963 and 1967, is fully reported by BARKER LUNN, J. C. (1970). *Streaming in the Primary School*, Slough: NFER.

13

revealed that the children were influenced in their feelings about themselves and about school by both the organizational policy of the school and the approach of their teachers.[1]

Aims of the follow-up study

As the earlier study had drawn attention to the influence of the type of primary school attended on pupils' development in certain non-cognitive areas, the question which then arose was—how far-reaching was this influence? Did it continue to operate after the children had left the primary school or was it more or less swiftly counteracted by factors in the new environment of the secondary school? The follow-up study hoped to throw some light on this question by tracing the progress and development in secondary school of a sample of pupils[2] from the earlier investigation. From this standpoint in the inquiry, attention focused solely on the type of junior school which the pupils had attended, and no attempt was made to allow for the inevitably wide variations in their subsequent secondary school environment.

It was clear however, that factors in the secondary school situation would have acted either to modify or reinforce the effects of the pupils' junior school experience. In order to obtain as clear a picture as possible of the educational development of the pupils in the follow-up sample, it was felt necessary to investigate the effects of different types of secondary school experience also. It was hoped that this part of the inquiry would throw some light upon the effects of streaming and non-streaming in secondary schools, and, where possible, upon the combined effects of primary and secondary school organization.

The sample

As the follow-up investigation was concerned primarily with assessing the long-term effects of streaming and non-streaming in the junior school, it was important to ensure that the pupils from non-streamed schools who were included in the follow-up sample had experienced a 'truly' non-streamed approach, i.e. had been taught for at least the majority of their junior school careers by a pro-non-streaming (Type 1) teacher.

The basis of the follow-up sample was formed by 14 pairs of matched streamed and non-streamed junior schools, which had been

[1] The detailed results in each area of the investigation are presented at the beginning of the relevant chapter in this report.
[2] Limited resources precluded the follow-up of all 5,500 pupils.

14

subjected to more intensive study in the earlier research, and for whose pupils the maximum amount of information was available. However, four of the 14 non-streamed schools were found to have a majority of Type 2 (pro-streaming) teachers on the staff, and these schools were consequently dropped from the follow-up study. Four other non-streamed schools were substituted, in which all or most of the teachers were Type 1. The final follow-up sample consisted of 1,716 pupils, of whom 815 had attended non-streamed schools and 901 came from streamed schools.

The secondary schools

At the end of the earlier study, information had been obtained from each junior school as to which secondary schools its pupils had been allocated to. With the exception of those containing less than five 'follow-up' pupils,[1] all the secondary schools were contacted and invited to take part in the follow-up study. Of the 85 schools approached, 83 indicated that they would be willing to participate in the research programme.

Table 1.1 shows the percentage of pupils from the streamed and non-streamed junior schools in the follow-up sample who where subsequently allocated to grammar, comprehensive and secondary modern schools.

TABLE 1.1: *Percentage of pupils from streamed and non-streamed junior schools who were allocated to grammar, comprehensive and secondary modern schools*

TYPE OF SECONDARY SCHOOL	NON-STREAMED JUNIOR SCHOOLS		STREAMED JUNIOR SCHOOLS	
	Boys	*Girls*	*Boys*	*Girls*
Secondary Modern	63%	61%	62%	60%
Comprehensive	25%	25%	21%	23%
Grammar	12%	14%	17%	17%
Total	100%	100%	100%	100%
Number of pupils	409	406	445	456

[1] This had the effect of excluding the very small number of technical schools which were involved.

Type of organization in the secondary schools

A questionnaire completed by the heads of all the secondary schools in the study provided details of the methods used to allocate pupils to classes upon entering the school. As the pupils in the follow-up sample were now in their second year in the secondary school, information was also obtained about the ways in which these classes had been formed. This revealed a great variety and complexity of organizational methods, which precluded the simple labelling of schools as 'streamed' or 'non-streamed'. For example, should schools which had mixed ability classes but employed 'setting' for most subjects be regarded for the purposes of analysis as 'streamed'? How should a school which divided each year group into several 'bands' of parallel classes be designated? It seemed clear that the extent to which such systems of organization merited the label of 'streamed' or 'non-streamed' would depend upon other factors in the school situation such as the degree of flexibility in grouping methods and the prevalent attitudes towards pupils in different classes, sets and ability groups.

However, some sort of classification was clearly needed in order to obtain a sample of adequate size for the secondary school analysis, and consequently a compromise solution was adopted for the allocation of secondary schools to the category of streamed or non-streamed.[1]

Predictably, streaming was found to be the most prevalent form of organization in the secondary schools. As Table 1.2 shows, the majority of secondary modern and comprehensive schools were streamed and only in grammar schools, with their already restricted ability range, was non-streaming found to be an equally popular method of organization.

TABLE 1.2: *Method of organization within secondary schools*

	STREAMED	NON-STREAMED	TOTAL
Secondary Modern	30	9	39
Comprehensive	11	3	14
Grammar	12	18	30
Total	53	30	83

[1] For details of this and of the number of pupils in schools of different types, see Appendix 2.

Introduction

Of the nine 'non-streamed' secondary modern schools, five employed 'setting' for both maths and English lessons, as did one of the three comprehensive schools included in the non-streamed category. Clearly then, the schools in the sample could hardly be said to constitute a well-defined group for the evaluation of non-streaming in secondary schools. Whilst this was unfortunately unavoidable in a situation where the sample schools were 'inherited' from the earlier study, it must be stressed that the results of comparisons between streamed and non-streamed secondary schools in this study should be interpreted with caution.

Dependent variables

A battery of tests was administered to the pupils in the follow-up study at the end of their second year in the secondary school. In most cases the tests which had been employed in the junior school study were unsuitable for use with this age group (12+), and consequently new instruments were required.

(a) Attainment and Ability Tests[1]

Tests of mathematical understanding and English were constructed especially for the follow-up project by the NFER's Guidance and Assessment Services. The Mathematics test was designed to be as far as possible unrelated to any particular curriculum in that, like the Concept Arithmetic test used in the earlier study, it aimed to measure the pupil's understanding of mathematics rather than his computational skill. The English test concentrated on comprehension and the use of vocabulary rather than the more formal aspects of grammar, punctuation or spelling.

The NFER Secondary Verbal Test 1 was also included in the test battery, being suitable for use with pupils in the age range concerned.

As in the earlier study, a test of divergent or 'creative' thinking was devised, containing items similar to those included in the earlier tests and likewise drawing on material developed in the United States by Torrance (1962) and Guilford (1950).

(b) Non-Cognitive Dependent Variables

As already mentioned, it was in the sphere of personality and social attitudes that differences between pupils in streamed and non-streamed junior schools had been most marked, and an important

---

[1] Full details of instruments used in the follow-up study can be found in Appendix 3.

part of the follow-up study was the further assessment of pupils' development in these areas, as measured by a set of attitude scales.

The attitude scales constructed for use in the junior school study, and containing measures of personality and social adjustment as well as school-related attitudes, were considered suitable for use with the pupils in the follow-up study after being tried out in several schools not involved in the research; only a few very slight modifications were found to be necessary.

As in the earlier study further information on pupils' personality characteristics and behaviour was obtained from teachers, who rated their pupils on such traits as social withdrawal and disobedience.

It was also decided to examine the effects, if any, of different types of learning environment in the junior school on pupils' attitudes and approach to work in the secondary school. Type 1 teachers in non-streamed junior schools had been found to place greater emphasis on learning by discovery and practical experience than their colleagues in streamed schools, who concentrated more on the 'three Rs' and the attainment of set academic standards. It was hoped to discover whether the more 'child-centred', interest-oriented methods characteristic of the Type 1 teachers were associated with more positive attitudes to work amongst pupils than the more formal, 'knowledge-centred' approach typical of streamed schools. Teachers in the follow-up schools were thus asked to rate their pupils on the following traits: ability to work independently, amount of interest shown in school work, and level of contribution to class discussions.

Other areas of inquiry which had produced interesting results in the earlier investigation and which were pursued further in the follow-up study included pupils' degree of participation in extra-curricular activities in the secondary school and their aspirations for their future education and training and subsequent careers.

References

BARKER LUNN, J. C. (1969). 'The development of scales to measure junior school children's attitudes', *Brit. J. Educ. Psychol.*, **39**, 1, 64-71.

BARKER LUNN, J. C. (1970). *Streaming in the Primary School*. Slough: NFER.

GUILFORD, J. P. (1950). 'Creativity', *Amer. Psychol.*, **5**, 444-54.

TORRANCE, E. P. (1962). *Administration and Scoring Manual for Abbreviated Form VII Minnesota Tests of Creative Thinking*. Bureau of Educational Research, University of Minnesota.

CHAPTER TWO

Pupils' Attainments and Performance in Divergent Thinking

A. ATTAINMENTS

The academic progress and level of achievement shown by pupils will clearly be one of the major criteria of success of any system of school organization. The earlier investigation of teachers' attitudes had shown that supporters of streaming and non-streaming both claimed that their preferred system of organization maximized the academic progress of all pupils. Teachers favouring streaming felt that bright children could only be fully 'stretched' when taught in a separate class, while the backward could be best helped by receiving special attention in smaller classes. Supporters of non-streaming, however, claimed that the less able benefited academically from interaction with brighter children in the same class, and that the more able pupils were not held back in any way by the presence of the slower ones.

Academic progress in streamed and non-streamed junior schools

In order to evaluate these differing claims, the earlier research set out to compare the academic progress made by the pupils in the study during their four years in the junior school. A battery of tests was administered to all pupils towards the end of each school year, and included tests of Reading, English, Verbal and Non-Verbal Reasoning, Mechanical and Problem Arithmetic, and Number Concept.

An assessment was carried out of the attainment gains made from year to year, and over the entire junior school course, by pupils in streamed and non-streamed schools. The pupils were divided into three equal-sized ability groups (above average, average and below average) on the basis of their Reading scores at 7+. These groups were further divided according to the pupils' social class background —middle class (social classes 1 and 2), upper working class (social class 3) and lower working class (social classes 4 and 5).[1] The scores of boys and girls were also examined separately.

[1] On the basis of information obtained when the pupils were aged 10+. Father's occupation was categorized according to the Registrar-General's (1960) groupings.

19

The results showed that there was no difference in the average attainment gains made by boys and girls of comparable social class and ability levels in streamed and non-streamed schools. A further analysis revealed that there was also no difference in the progress of pupils taught by Type 1 (pro-non-streaming) and Type 2 (pro-streaming) teachers in non-streamed schools. In other words, academic attainment was found to be largely unaffected by either a school's organizational policy or the attitudes and methods of its teachers.

Academic progress of pupils in the follow-up study

Although no differences had been found in the progress made by pupils in streamed and non-streamed junior schools, the question arose in the follow-up study as to whether the two different approaches had exerted any delayed or long-term effects on pupils' subsequent achievement in the secondary school. It was also hoped to discover whether the type of organization experienced in the secondary school had had any effect on pupils' progress in the two years which they had spent there.

A further assessment of pupils' attainment was carried out towards the end of their second year in the secondary school (i.e. when they were aged 12+). Limited resources made it impossible to cover all the areas of attainment which had been included in the earlier study, and the 12+ battery contained only tests of English, Mathematical Understanding and Verbal Reasoning, which were administered to all the pupils in the follow-up study.

Academic progress between 10+ and 12+ of pupils from streamed and non-streamed junior schools

Firstly, a comparison was made of the attainment gains between 10+ and 12+ of comparable pupils who had earlier attended streamed or 'truly' non-streamed junior schools (i.e. had been taught by Type 1 teachers). As in the earlier study, the pupils were divided into three equal ability groups—above average, average and below average (on the basis of their Reading scores at 10+). These groups were again subdivided according to the pupil's social class background—middle class (social classes 1, 2), upper working class (social class 3) and lower working class (social classes 4, 5). As before, analysis of co-variance (see Statistical Appendix) was employed to compare the attainment gains of pupils from the two different types of junior school. Separate analyses were carried out for each test, and in the case of the Mathematics test, scores at 12+ were analysed

20

firstly in terms of scores on the Number Concept test at 10+, and secondly in terms of scores on the Problem test at 10+.

Results

The results showed that, as before, there was very little difference in the average attainment gains made by pupils who had attended streamed and non-streamed junior schools. Table 2.1 summarizes the results, and the most striking fact to emerge is that of the 72 comparisons made, only seven significant differences were found.

TABLE 2.1: *A comparison of the attainment gains made by pupils from streamed and non-streamed junior schools*

		MATHS/ CONCEPT	MATHS/ PROBLEM	ENGLISH	VERBAL
BOYS					
Above average	social class 1, 2			—	—
Above average	social class 3	—	—	—	—
Above average	social class 4, 5	—	—	—	—
Average	social class 1, 2	*	**	—	*
Average	social class 3	—	—	—	—
Average	social class 4, 5	—	**	—	—
Below average	social class 1, 2	—	—	—	—
Below average	social class 3	—	*	—	—
Below average	social class 4, 5	(*)	*	—	—
GIRLS					
Above average	social class 1, 2	—	—	—	—
Above average	social class 3	—	—	—	—
Above average	social class 4, 5	—	—	—	—
Average	social class 1, 2	—	—	—	—
Average	social class 3	—	—	—	—
Average	social class 4, 5	—	—	—	—
Below average	social class 1, 2	—	—	—	—
Below average	social class 3	—	—	—	—
Below average	social class 4, 5	—	—	—	—

   * = difference favoured non-streamed schools, significant at five per cent level
  ** = difference favoured non-streamed schools, significant at one per cent level
 (*) = significant difference in means was accompanied by a significant difference in regression relationship (see Appendix 4)
  — = non-significant.

In all instances these favoured non-streamed schools, but in most cases the numbers were small (see Table A5, Appendix 5), and the overwhelming majority of comparisons showed no significant differences.

Academic progress between 10+ and 12+ of pupils from streamed and non-streamed secondary schools

A further analysis was carried out to see whether streaming and non-streaming in the secondary school had had any apparent effect on the progress of the pupils in the study.

Limited numbers made it necessary to confine this part of the investigation to pupils in grammar and secondary modern schools. Within the grammar schools, the numbers were too small to control for social class and ability level, although the ability range in these schools was clearly restricted in any case, and the number of lower social class pupils was very small. Pupils in secondary modern schools were divided into two ability groups—(1) above average and average, and (2) below average (on the basis of their Reading score at 10+) and these were then subdivided into two social class groups —middle and upper working class (social classes 1, 2 and 3) and lower working class (social classes 4 and 5). Within both types of school the scores of boys and girls were analysed separately.

Results

As Table 2.2 shows, of the 40 comparisons made, only five revealed significant differences in the attainment gains of pupils in streamed and non-streamed secondary schools. Of these, four favoured non-streamed schools and one favoured streamed schools. These findings thus provided little evidence that pupils' academic performance in the first two years of secondary school is affected by the type of organization adopted by the school.

Summary

The investigation of any long-term effects of junior school organization on pupils' subsequent performance in secondary school reinforced the findings of the earlier study that type of organization bore little relationship to academic progress. The results of this inquiry add further support to the implication that the decision as to whether to stream or non-stream in the junior school must be based on factors other than academic attainments.

The inquiry similarly provided little support for those who advocate streaming or non-streaming in the secondary school in the

TABLE 2.2: *A comparison of the attainment gains of pupils in streamed and non-streamed secondary schools*

		MATHS/ CONCEPT	MATHS/ PROBLEM	ENGLISH	VERBAL
BOYS					
Grammar		—	—	—	—
Secondary Modern					
Average & above average	social class 1, 2, 3	—	—	—	**S
Average & above average	social class 4, 5	—	—	—	—
Below average	social class 1, 2, 3	*N	*N	—	*N
Below average	social class 4, 5	—	—	—	—
GIRLS					
Grammar		—	—	—	*N
Secondary Modern					
Average & above average	social class 1, 2, 3	—	—	—	—
Average & above average	social class 4, 5	—	—	—	—
Below average	social class 1, 2, 3	—	—	—	—
Below average	social class 4, 5	—	—	—	—

*N = difference favoured non-streamed schools, significant at five per cent level
** S = difference favoured streamed schools, significant at one per cent level
— = non-significant.

interests of academic progress. A note of caution should, however, be sounded here. It would be wrong to assume that the approaches and methods found to be characteristic of 'truly' non-streamed junior schools could be attributed to the non-streamed secondary schools involved in this study. For instance, all the 'non-streamed' secondary modern schools in the sample were known to employ 'setting' for Maths, and the majority 'set' for English also (see Appendix 2), an approach which was rarely encountered in junior schools. It would seem likely that the differences in approach in streamed and non-streamed schools were narrower at the secondary than at the junior level, at least as far as the schools in the present sample were concerned.

More information would be needed about the values, approaches and methods associated with streaming and non-streaming at the secondary level, in order to make more than a tentative evaluation of the effects of the two types of organization.

B. DIVERGENT THINKING

Considerable attention has been paid in recent years to the measurement and development of pupils' 'creative' abilities, one aspect of which is the ability to think in a 'divergent' or non-conforming way. Test questions designed to measure this type of ability set out to elicit varied and original responses within an unfamiliar frame of reference, in contrast to the single, correct answer sought by more conventional tests of academic achievement.

The measurement of divergent thinking in the earlier study

On the basis of other research findings (Haddon and Lytton, 1968; Wodtke and Wallen, 1965) it was predicted that greater encouragement would be given to the development of divergent thinking by the more informal, 'child-centred' methods found in non-streamed junior schools than by the more formal academically-oriented approach typical of streamed schools.

Two parallel tests of divergent thinking were constructed especially for the streaming research project; one was administered when the children were aged 9+, the other at the end of the following, final year in the junior school. Three areas of divergent thinking were measured by the tests—fluency, flexibility and originality of ideas.[1]

Results

The results of this inquiry provided some evidence to support the hypothesis that children in non-streamed schools who had been taught by Type 1 teachers would perform better on a test of this type.

Firstly, the *change* of score between 9+ and 10+ was examined. The total distribution of scores in each year was divided into five equal 'bands', each representing 20 per cent of the sample. An examination of the scores at 9+ and 10+ of sub-groups from streamed and non-streamed schools then revealed whether they had moved 'up' or 'down' relative to the other groups in the sample.

It was found that children in streamed schools and those taught by Type 2 (i.e. pro-streaming) teachers in non-streamed schools showed a relative decline on all three aspects of the test between 9+ and 10+, while those taught by Type 1 (pro-non-streaming) teachers in non-

---

[1] For further details, see Appendix 3.

24

streamed schools tended to improve slightly in both fluency and flexibility of ideas.

An examination of the number of pupils obtaining high and low scores on each part of the test (in the top and bottom 20 per cent of the total distribution) showed that the greatest number of 'high' scorers and the fewest 'low' scorers were found amongst pupils who had been taught by Type 1 teachers in non-streamed schools. The poorest performance in terms of scores was shown by pupils who had been taught by Type 2 teachers in non-streamed schools, who tended to have fewer high scorers and more low scorers than pupils from streamed schools.

The test

A further test of divergent thinking was devised for use with the streaming follow-up sample at 12+. The items were of the same type as those contained in the earlier tests; pupils were asked to produce as many varied responses as possible within an unfamiliar frame of reference—e.g. 'Write down all the problems and difficulties that man might meet if he wanted to live at the bottom of the sea'.

Only pupils from whom scores were available at both 10+ and 12+ were included in the analysis; this resulted in a total sample of 685.[1]

Long-term effects of junior school experience on performance on the divergent thinking test

The first step was to discover whether pupils' performance in divergent thinking at 12+ had continued to be influenced by the type of junior school attended, in spite of the intervening effects of varying types of secondary school experience. Did children who had been taught by Type 1 teachers in non-streamed schools continue to perform better than those who had attended streamed schools?

The method of analysis was the same as that employed in the earlier study. Firstly, the *change* of score between 10+ and 12+ was examined; and secondly, a comparison was made of the scores at 12+ of pupils from streamed and non-streamed junior schools.

(*a*) *Change of score between 10+ and 12+* No difference was found in the pattern of score change between 10+ and 12+ of pupils from streamed and non-streamed junior schools. All groups showed a

---

[1] In the earlier study the analysis had been carried out on a sub-sample of approximately 1,800 pupils.

deterioration in score,[1] which reached significance in the case of pupils from non-streamed schools on the flexibility part of the test (see Table A7, Appendix 5).

(*b*) *Scores at 12+* An examination was made of the numbers of pupils from streamed and non-streamed junior schools whose scores lay in each of the five 'bands' of score at 12+. The results showed a tendency for more pupils from non-streamed schools to obtain scores in the top 20 per cent of the total distribution and fewer to obtain scores in the bottom 20 per cent. This tendency was more marked amongst pupils from a higher social class background, and on the originality part of the test the difference was significant ($P<0\cdot01$, see Table A8, Appendix 5).

Effects of secondary school experience on performance on the divergent thinking test

A further analysis was carried out to see whether pupils' performance in divergent thinking was influenced by the type of secondary school attended—grammar, comprehensive or secondary modern—and by the type of organization (streamed or non-streamed) within each school.

(*a*) *Change of score between 10+ and 12+* The most striking finding to emerge when the change of score between 10+ and 12+ was examined was that pupils in both streamed and non-streamed secondary modern schools showed a deterioration in score on all parts of the test. In every case but one the change was significant (see Table A9, Appendix 5).

Little movement was observed in the scores of pupils in either type of comprehensive school, but pupils in streamed grammar schools were found to show a relative decline in score on all three aspects of the test. In the case of originality this drop was significant ($P<0\cdot05$), and approached significance on flexibility also. Pupils in non-streamed grammar schools on the other hand showed little change on any part of the test.

(*b*) *Scores at 12+* No significant differences were found in the pattern of scores of pupils in streamed and non-streamed secondary

---

[1] The finding that scores of *all* groups had moved in a downward direction between 10+ and 12+ was due to a bunching of scores at the lower end of the total distribution on the test at 12+, which resulted in the bottom 'bands' of score containing slightly more than 20 per cent of the total distribution. This finding is of interest in that it lends some support to Torrance's (1963) claim that performance in creative thinking shows a decline at certain ages, one of these being around 13 years.

modern or comprehensive schools. In the grammar school, however, a greater percentage of pupils from non-streamed schools obtained high scores (i.e. in the top 20 per cent) on all three aspects of the test; and in the case of fluency and originality this difference was significant ($P<0.05$ and $P<0.01$ respectively. See Table A10 in Appendix 5).

While these findings would seem to suggest a higher level of performance in non-streamed grammar schools, it should be stressed that the number of pupils attending streamed grammar schools was very small (46), and that the results should consequently be treated with caution. Further research would be needed to see whether streaming in grammar schools is associated with a greater emphasis on the attainment of formal academic goals, to which thinking of a more convergent nature is more conducive.

Summary

This inquiry provided some tentative evidence that pupils from non-streamed junior schools continued to show a slightly superior performance in divergent thinking after two years in the secondary school.

When the effects of different types of secondary school experience were investigated, it was found that only in grammar schools did type of organization appear to be related to performance in divergent thinking. Pupils in streamed grammar schools showed a relative deterioration in score since entering secondary school, and obtained lower scores on all aspects of the test than their counterparts in non-streamed grammar schools.

A marked deterioration in score on all parts of the test was also shown by pupils in both streamed and non-streamed secondary modern schools.

References

HADDON, F. A. and LYTTON, H. (1968). 'Teaching approach and the development of divergent thinking abilities in primary schools', *Brit. J. Educ. Psychol.*, **38**, 2, 171-80.

REGISTRAR-GENERAL'S CLASSIFICATION OF OCCUPATIONS. (1960). London: H.M. Stationery Office.

TORRANCE, E. P. (1963). *Education and the Creative Potential.* Minneapolis: University of Minnesota Press.

WODTKE, K. H. and WALLEN, N. E. (1965). 'The effects of teacher control in the classroom on pupils' creative test gains', *Amer. Educ. Res. J.*, **2**, 2, 75-8.

CHAPTER THREE

Pupils' Attitudes

'THE more important and far-reaching effects of streaming and non-streaming lie much less in formal attainments than in personality and attitudinal factors.' This was one of the major conclusions of the earlier streaming study, which included an investigation of the attitude development of pupils in their final year of junior school. This was measured by a questionnaire to pupils containing a number of scales designed to measure school-related attitudes, and several others concerned with personality and social adjustment.[1]

The results indicated that in both streamed and non-streamed junior schools attitudes varied by ability, with children of above average ability holding the most favourable attitudes, and those of below average ability having the poorest attitudes. School organization and type of teacher had little apparent influence on the attitude development of able children, who seemed to thrive in any situation. Pupils of average and below average ability also tended to develop more positive attitudes when they were taught in a non-streamed school by a Type 1 teacher (i.e. one who supported non-streaming), but those of their counterparts in streamed schools tended to deteriorate—especially on the 'school-related' scales. Membership of a low stream appeared to be associated with the growth of dissatisfaction and negative feelings about one's school class.

Having found that different types of school environment had had some influence on the development of pupils' attitudes towards themselves and towards school, the question which arose in the follow-up study was—how long did this influence last? Did the attitudes of certain pupils from streamed and non-streamed junior schools continue to develop in different directions after they had left junior school? The first part of the follow up inquiry aimed to answer these questions by examining the change in attitudes between 10+ and 12+ of pupils of comparable ability levels[2] from streamed and non-streamed junior schools. A further analysis was then carried

---

[1] For details of the construction of these scales, see Barker Lunn (1969).
[2] Ability was defined, as in the earlier study, in terms of English test score at 9+.

28

out to see whether there were any differences in the attitude development of pupils who had gone to grammar, comprehensive and secondary modern schools.[1]

Sample and analysis

The pupils' attitude questionnaire, which had been constructed especially for the earlier study, was completed by all pupils in the follow-up sample. As before, the questionnaire was administered by research workers who visited each of the secondary schools concerned. The analysis reported here was based on the scores of all pupils (approximately 600) who had completed the questionnaire at both 10+ and 12+.[2]

As in the earlier study the results obtained were examined in terms of change of score between the first and second testing (in this case between 10+ and 12+). The Mann-Witney Sign Test was used to assess the statistical significance of any change in attitude.

The report which follows is in two sections: Part 1 deals with the personality scales and Part 2 with the school-related attitudes. Each scale is treated separately and begins with a summary of the main findings from the earlier study.

Part 1—Personality scales

    (1) Academic self-image
    (2) Relationship with the teacher
    (3) Anxiety in the classroom
    (4) Social adjustment.

(1) *Academic Self-Image*

This scale measured the pupils' self-image in terms of school work and included such statements as: 'I'm useless at school work' and 'I'm very good at Maths'.

10+ Results

(*a*) *General findings* Scores were related to sex and ability, with boys and brighter children having a more favourable academic self-image.

---

[1] Within these types of school a study was also made of the effects of streaming and non-streaming. Although in some cases numbers were very small comparisons showed that trends in streamed and non-streamed schools were the same. The two types of organization were thus combined for further analysis.

[2] I.e. somewhat less than half the total follow-up sample. Only pupils in the '14 schools' (see Chapter 1) had been tested at 9+ and 10+, and of these, only a one in two sample.

(*b*) *Comparisons between schools* Children of above average ability from both streamed and non-streamed schools tended to improve their self-image between 9+ and 10+. Boys and girls of average ability in non-streamed schools also showed an improvement as did boys of below average ability in streamed schools. Other groups showed little change.

12+ Results

(*a*) *General findings* Boys continued to display a more favourable academic self-image than girls ($P < 0.001$) and brighter children again had a better self-image than duller ones ($P < 0.001$).

(*b*) *Change of score between 10+ and 12+ of pupils from streamed and non-streamed junior schools* Girls of above average ability from both types of school had developed a poorer self-image and in the case of those from non-streamed schools the difference was significant ($P < 0.05$. See Table A11 in Appendix 5).

There was little change in the scores of pupils of average ability from either streamed or non-streamed schools, but at the below average level, both boys and girls who had attended non-streamed schools had developed a more favourable self-image (Boys: $P < 0.001$; Girls: $P < 0.05$).

(*c*) *Change of score of pupils in grammar, comprehensive and secondary modern schools* This analysis revealed that both boys and girls who had gone on to grammar schools had developed a poorer self-image ($P < 0.05$ and $P < 0.001$ respectively, see Table A12 in Appendix 5), while boys who went to comprehensive or secondary modern schools had improved their self-image ($P < 0.05$ and $P < 0.01$ respectively). No significant change had taken place in the scores of girls who had gone to non-selective schools.

What do these results mean? Looking first at the scores of the more able pupils—and especially those of girls who had gone on to grammar schools—it would seem probable that the deterioration in their self-image was due to the very different situation brought about by the transition from junior to secondary school. In the junior school these girls would have enjoyed the prestige attached to being a member of the top A-class in a streamed school, or being at or near the top of their non-streamed class. On entering grammar school, however, they would have found themselves competing with their intellectual equals and no doubt all but a few lost the satisfaction of being among the brightest in the class or school.

A similar explanation seems applicable in the case of boys who had gone on to grammar school, although there is an interesting inconsistency in the scores of boys which requires further explanation.

While grammar school boys had developed a poorer self-image between 10+ and 12+, those of above average ability in general had shown a slight improvement (see Tables A11 and A12 in Appendix 5). These findings would suggest that it was the able boys who had gone on to *comprehensive* schools whose self-image had improved, and this might again be explained in terms of the relative ability of these pupils and of the others in the school. Given the full ability range found in comprehensive schools, pupils of above average ability would again find themselves either in a high stream or a high class position, according to the method of organization in the school.

The improvement in self-image shown by boys and girls of below average ability from non-streamed junior schools, and reflected in the scores of boys in secondary modern schools, might also be explained in terms of a change in their *relative* position in the school or class. These pupils would all have been at or near the bottom of the class in their junior school, but in secondary school—particularly in the restricted ability range of the secondary modern—it seems likely that a sizeable proportion of them would no longer find themselves in the very bottom ability group or stream.

(2) *Relationship with the Teacher*

This scale measured the teachers' degree of concern for the pupil, as perceived by the pupil, and contained such items as: 'My teachers are interested in me' and 'My teachers are nice to me'. Clearly the situation in secondary school, where pupils are taught by a number of teachers, is very different from that in the junior school, where most lessons are taken by the class teacher. The statements in the questionnaire at 12+ were altered slightly in order to relate to 'teachers in general', and in view of the difference in meaning at the secondary level, the results on this scale should be treated with caution.

10+ Results

(*a*) *General findings* Girls and brighter children perceived a better teacher-relationship than boys and less able children.

(*b*) *Comparisons between schools* While pupils of all ability levels improved their teacher-relationship in non-streamed schools, only those of above average ability did so in streamed schools, with average and below average pupils tending to deteriorate.

12+ Results

(*a*) *General findings* As at 10+, girls and brighter children were found to have a better teacher-relationship ($P<0.001$ in each case), and again as at 10+, these findings reflected the teachers' feelings

31

about the pupils. Class teachers in secondary schools were asked to rate each pupil on a four-point scale to indicate how great a pleasure it was to have him in the class. These ratings were tabulated against the class teacher's rating of each pupil's ability,[1] and the results confirmed the pupils' beliefs that teachers found girls more pleasurable than boys (P<0·001) and bright children a greater pleasure to teach than dull ones (P<0·001).

(*b*) *Change of score between 10+ and 12+ of pupils from streamed and non-streamed junior schools* Only two groups of pupils showed a significant change in score: above average girls from non-streamed schools perceived a poorer teacher-relationship at 12+ (P<0·05, see Table A13 in Appendix 5), whilst above average boys from streamed schools had moved in the opposite direction (P<0·05).

(*c*) *Change of score of pupils in grammar, comprehensive and secondary modern schools* Here it was found that only one group had made a significant change: girls in grammar schools, who had a poorer teacher-relationship at 12+ than at 10+ (P<0·05. See Table A14, Appendix 5).

The tendency for teachers to look most favourably on bright girls may lie behind the deterioration in attitude shown by girls of above average ability who went on to grammar school. These girls—who were at the top of their non-streamed junior class, would have enjoyed a particularly good teacher-relationship in the junior school. In the grammar school, however, most of them would no longer shine particularly brightly in relation to other pupils and as a result probably felt themselves to be less favoured by their teachers.

A very tentative explanation of the improved teacher-relationship of above average boys from streamed schools may lie in the fact that teachers favoured girls more than boys, and that three-quarters of the boys who subsequently went on to grammar school went to single sex schools, where they would no longer have to compete with girls for their teacher's approval.[2]

(3) *Anxiety in the Classroom*

The items in this scale were concerned with fears or worries in the

---

[1] For details of pleasurability and ability ratings, see Appendix 3.

[2] Also, as the earlier research showed, the system of streaming in junior schools tended to favour girls, so that fewer boys were found in A-streams. (*Streaming in the Primary School*, Chapter Seven, 'Biases in the Streaming System'.) It is probable that some of the above average boys in streamed junior schools had not been in an A class, and this may have adversely affected their perceived teacher-relationship.

classroom, for example—'I'm scared to ask the teacher for help'; 'I would feel afraid if I got my work wrong'.

10+ *Results*

(a) *General findings* Scores on this scale were also related to sex and ability, with boys and more able children showing less anxiety.

(b) *Comparisons between schools* There was an overall tendency in both types of school for pupils to become less anxious, although it was somewhat more pronounced in non-streamed schools.

12+ *Results*

(a) *General findings* At 12+ as at 10+ boys were found to be less anxious than girls (P<0·001), but the difference between ability levels was much less marked, and was not statistically significant.

(b) *Change of score between 10+ and 12+ of pupils from streamed and non-streamed junior schools* No significant differences were found in the change of score between 10+ and 12+ of pupils from streamed schools, although there was a trend for girls of all ability levels to become more anxious. Among pupils from non-streamed schools, however, different ability groups were found to have moved in opposite directions. At the above average level, both boys and girls had become more anxious (P<0·05 in each case. See Table A15 in Appendix 5), while boys of below average ability had become much less anxious since leaving the junior school (P<0·001).

(c) *Change of score of pupils in grammar, comprehensive and secondary modern schools* Boys in grammar schools showed more anxiety at 12+ than at 10+, while those in other schools had become less anxious, and in the case of secondary modern boys the change reached significance (P<0·05. See Table A16 in Appendix 5).

Girls in all types of school became more anxious (P<0·01), and this was especially marked amongst those attending grammar schools (P<0·01).

It would seem, then, that the poorer academic self-image held at 12+ by pupils of above average ability, who had subsequently gone to grammar school, was accompanied by increasing feelings of anxiety on the part of these pupils. Moving from the top of an unstreamed class to the competitive atmosphere of a grammar school class appeared to have seriously undermined their confidence in themselves.

Conversely, less able boys from non-streamed junior schools, who had gone to a secondary modern, may well have had their confidence boosted by finding themselves no longer reminded of their limited abilities by the presence of the most able children among them.

C

(4) *Social Adjustment*

This scale was concerned with pupils' ability to get on well with their peers and included statements such as: 'I have no one to talk to at break' and 'I think other people in my class like me'.

10+ Results

(a) *General findings* The results showed that boys were more socially adjusted than girls, and brighter children had higher scores than duller children.

(b) *Comparisons between schools* No significant differences were found in the social adjustment of pupils in streamed and non-streamed junior schools. Pupils in both types of school were found to have increased their social adjustment score between 9+ and 10+.

12+ Results

(a) *General findings* At 12+ there was very little difference in the social adjustment scores of boys and girls, although the tendency remained for the more able children to be more socially adjusted than the less able (P<0·001).

(b) *Change of score of pupils from streamed and non-streamed junior schools* There was an overall improvement in social adjustment of pupils from both types of junior school. The trend was the same for each ability level, with the exception of average boys from non-streamed schools, but their change in attitude was not statistically significant (see Table A17, Appendix 5).

(c) *Change of score of pupils in grammar, comprehensive and secondary modern schools* Again it was found that both boys and girls in each type of school had increased their social adjustment score between 10+ and 12+ (see Table A18, Appendix 5).

Part 2—School related attitudes

    (1) Attitude to school
    (2) Attitude to class
    (3) 'Other image' of class
    (4) Importance of doing well.

(1) *Attitude to Schools*

This scale was concerned with pupils' attitude to school in general, and included items such as: 'School is fun' and 'I would leave school tomorrow if I could'.

10+ Results

(a) *General findings* Girls had more favourable attitudes to school than boys, and bright children had higher scores than duller children.

34

(*b*) *Comparisons between schools* The direction of change between 9+ and 10+ was similar in both types of school, although the tendency for boys (particularly those of above average ability) to develop more favourable attitudes and girls (particularly those of average and below average ability) to develop poorer attitudes, was more pronounced in streamed schools.

10+ Results

(*a*) *General findings* Again, girls and brighter children were found to have more favourable attitudes to school than boys and less able pupils (P<0·001 in each case).

(*b*) *Change of score between 10+ and 12+ of pupils from streamed and non-streamed junior schools* All groups of pupils from streamed junior schools had developed poorer attitudes to school between 10+ and 12+, and in the case of girls of average and above average ability, this downward move was significant (P<0·001 and P<0·05 respectively. See Table A19 in Appendix 5). Among pupils from non-streamed schools, only girls of above average ability showed a significant change in attitude (P<0·05) which was also in a downward direction.

(*c*) *Change of score of pupils in grammar, comprehensive and secondary modern schools* Girls in both grammar and secondary modern schools showed a deterioration in attitude to school which was highly significant (P<0·001 and P<0·01 respectively. See Table A20 in Appendix 5). There was little change, however, in the scores of girls who went to comprehensive schools.

These results suggest that the tendency for girls to develop less favourable attitudes to school during their final year in the junior school continued after they had proceeded to secondary school, although their actual scores on this scale showed that they still liked school more than boys.

(2) *Attitude to Class*

Items in this scale concerned the favourableness or otherwise of being a member of a particular class—for example: 'I'd rather be in my class than in the others for my age', 'I hate being in the class I'm in now'.

10+ Results

(*a*) *General findings* Scores on this scale were also related to sex and ability, with girls and brighter children having more favourable attitudes to their class.

(*b*) *Comparisons between schools* Pupils of all ability levels in non-streamed schools showed an improved 'attitude to class' between 9+ and 10+, whilst in streamed schools, those in bottom streams of large schools had developed poorer attitudes.

12+ Results

(*a*) *General findings* As at 10+, girls and more able children displayed more favourable attitudes to their class (P<0·001 in each case).

(*b*) *Change of score between 10+ and 12+ of pupils from streamed and non-streamed junior schools* Pupils from both types of junior school had poorer attitudes to their class at 12+ than at 10+; however, when the scores of different ability groups were examined separately, it was found that the poorer attitudes amongst pupils from non-streamed schools were concentrated at the average and below average levels, whilst it was the above average pupils, especially girls, from streamed schools, who had become disenchanted with their class in the secondary school (see Table A21, Appendix 5).

(*c*) *Change of score of pupils in grammar, comprehensive and secondary modern schools* The results of this analysis again showed a deterioration in attitude to class in each type of secondary school (see Table A22, Appendix 5).

The marked deterioration in attitude to class shown by above average pupils—especially girls—from streamed schools no doubt reflects the fact that these children had earlier enjoyed the prestige of being in the top 'A' stream class in their junior school.

In the case of below average pupils from non-streamed schools, it seems likely that those who had gone on to streamed secondary schools would have found themselves in a low stream; there they would no doubt have become aware of the relatively low status of their class—a concept which had been non-existent in their junior schools—and this may well explain the poorer attitudes shown by these pupils.

The general tendency for pupils to show less favourable attitudes to their class in secondary school is not altogether surprising in view of the difference in class organization and teaching methods in junior and secondary schools. In junior school pupils remain in their own class with their own teacher for almost all lessons, while in secondary schools, particularly those employing a complex system of 'setting', pupils are less likely to have lessons in company with all their classmates. This may result in less awareness of their class as an entity and consequently a lower degree of involvement with it.

(*d*) *Change of score of pupils in different secondary school streams* As it had been found at 10+ that pupils' attitude to class in streamed schools was related to the stream they were in, it was decided to examine their 12+ scores in terms of their *secondary* school stream.

36

The change of score between 10+ and 12+ of pupils in top, middle and bottom streams (or 'bands') was examined, and while a downward trend was found in each case, it reached significance only in the case of pupils in middle and bottom streams (see Table A27, Appendix 5).

(3) *'Other Image' of Class*

This scale—clearly more meaningful to pupils in streamed schools —was concerned with the way a pupil felt other classes in the school viewed his own class. For example, 'Other classes make fun of my class', 'Other classes think they are better than us'.

10+ Results

(a) *General findings* As on the 'attitude to class' scale, girls and more able children were found to have a more favourable 'other image' of their class.

(b) *Comparisons between schools* Little change in 'other image' between 9+ and 10+ was found amongst pupils in non-streamed schools. In streamed schools however, above average children had more favourable 'other images' than average and below average pupils, whose 'other image' deteriorated between 9+ and 10+.

12+ Results

(a) *General findings* Girls and brighter children still had a more favourable 'other image' than boys and less able pupils ($P<0.01$ and $P<0.001$ respectively).

(b) *Change of score between 10+ and 12+ of pupils from streamed and non-streamed junior schools* Only one group showed a significant change of score: girls of below average ability from non-streamed schools had a poorer 'other image' at 12+ than at 10+ ($P<0.05$. See Table A23 in Appendix 5).

(c) *Change of score of pupils in grammar, comprehensive and secondary modern schools* Grammar school boys had developed a poorer 'other image' in the secondary school ($P<0.01$. See Table A24 in Appendix 5). There was little change in the scores of other groups.

(d) *Change of score of pupils in different secondary school streams* As the earlier research had shown that pupils' 'other image' scores were related to the stream they were in, it was decided to examine the change of score of pupils in top, middle and bottom secondary school streams.

The results showed that the 'other image' of pupils in top streams had improved ($P<0.05$), while that of pupils in bottom streams had deteriorated ($P<0.01$) (see Table A28, Appendix 5).

37

(4) *Importance of Doing Well*

This scale was concerned with pupils' achievement orientation and included items such as: 'I work and try very hard in school' and 'Doing well at school is most important to me'.

10+ Results

(*a*) *General findings* Girls placed more importance on doing well, as did pupils of higher ability.

(*b*) *Comparisons between schools* All pupils in non-streamed junior schools became more motivated to do well, especially boys of average and below average ability. In streamed schools, however, only boys of above average ability made a significant change, scoring higher at 10+ than 9+.

12+ Results

(*a*) *General findings* There was no longer a tendency for girls to be more highly motivated than boys, and there was no difference between their scores at 12+. More able children, however, still had higher scores than their less able peers ($P<0\cdot001$).

(*b*) *Change of score between 10+ and 12+ of pupils from streamed and non-streamed junior schools* Pupils of all ability levels from both streamed and non-streamed junior schools showed a decrease in motivation to do well. This downward shift in score was most marked amongst girls, particularly those of above average ability from both types of school (non-streamed: $P<0\cdot001$, streamed: $P<0\cdot01$. See Table A25, Appendix 5).

(*c*) *Change of score of pupils in grammar, comprehensive and secondary modern schools* Here again there was an overall decrease in motivation to do well (see Table A26, Appendix 5). Only in comprehensive schools did the change fail to reach significance, although the trend was in the same downward direction.

Why should there be such a general deterioration in motivation amongst children after they had left the junior school? A partial explanation for this may lie in the effects of selection at 11+, as the most marked changes were made by pupils in grammar and secondary modern schools. Those allocated to secondary modern schools may have subsequently rejected the values of an achievement-oriented system, under which they themselves had been conspicuous failures.[1] In the case of those who had 'succeeded', however, and gone on to grammar school, their tendency to attach less importance to school work may be a rationalization of their increasing lack of

---

[1] It may be also the case that the tendency for secondary modern boys to become less anxious merely reflected a growing lack of involvement with their school work.

confidence in their own capabilities as indicated by their scores on the 'self-image' and 'anxiety' scales.

Summary and conclusions

The pupil's sex appeared to be one of the most important single factors associated with attitude development between 10+ and 12+. On the personality scales boys tended on the whole to improve and girls to deteriorate, and on the school related scales, although both sexes showed a decline in score, this was much more marked amongst girls. However, the actual scores on the scales at 12+ showed that, as before, girls still had a better relationship with their teachers, and also had more favourable scores on the 'attitude to school', 'attitude to class' and 'other image' scales. On the other hand, they no longer showed a higher level of motivation to do well in school. Boys, as at 10+, had a better self-image than girls, and were less anxious, although the tendency for boys to be more socially adjusted had disappeared by the time the pupils were 12+.

Attitudes at 12+ were still related to ability, with brighter pupils having more favourable scores on all four school-related scales, as well as on the 'self-image', 'relationship with teacher' and 'social adjustment' scales. In contrast to the 10+ findings, however, there was little difference in the anxiety scores of pupils of different ability levels.

The examination of change of attitudes between 10+ and 12+ revealed that pupils of above average ability, especially girls, had developed a poorer self-image and had become more anxious, while less able pupils, especially boys, had developed more favourable attitudes in both these areas. In both cases the changes were most marked among pupils who had attended non-streamed junior schools.

The deterioration in attitudes shown by girls of above average ability was further reflected in an analysis of change of score according to the type of secondary school attended. Girls in grammar schools had developed a poorer self-image and teacher-relationship and had become increasingly anxious since leaving the junior school. Grammar school boys had also become more anxious and had developed a poorer self-image, but boys in non-selective schools showed more favourable attitudes on both scales.

While the junior school investigation had indicated that pupils of above average ability appeared to thrive in either type of school environment, this favourable development did not seem to have continued after they had left the junior school. Those who had gone on to grammar school—and girls in particular—revealed a growing dissatisfaction and uninvolvement with school and an apparent lack of confidence in themselves and their capabilities.

The nature of the transition from junior to secondary school would seem to offer a tentative explanation of these findings. Pupils of above average ability, especially girls, who, at the end of their junior school careers were enjoying the prestige of being either top of the top class in their non-streamed school, or in the top A-stream of their streamed school—together with the teacher approval known to attach to such pupils—may well have had their confidence and self-image somewhat jolted by finding themselves competing in grammar school with their intellectual peers, in an environment where increasing stress is laid on the achievement of high academic standards (see the case of DAVID in Chapter Six). This change, as the findings suggest, would have been felt most keenly by those from non-streamed schools, who would have experienced even less competition from their classmates than their counterparts in the A-streams of streamed junior schools. Further evidence of the grammar school's role in undermining the confidence of some of its pupils is suggested by the fact that while boys in grammar schools had developed a poorer self-image, the opposite trend was discovered amongst boys of above average ability, some of whom had gone on to comprehensive schools, in which their position *vis-à-vis* other pupils was much different.

A similar argument can be put forward to explain the improved self-image and decrease in anxiety found among pupils of below average ability from non-streamed junior schools. In their non-streamed classes, these pupils would all have been at or near the bottom of their class. On transferring to a non-selective secondary school, however—particularly to the restricted ability range of the secondary modern—many of these pupils would have found that they no longer made up the very bottom ability group. In a streamed secondary modern, some may have found their way into the middle streams, while in a non-streamed school the more limited ability range in the class would mean that at least they were not so far behind the top pupils as they had been in the junior school.

The inquiry produced some tentative evidence to suggest that the attitudes of pupils in comprehensive schools suffered a less adverse development than those in other schools, inasmuch as they showed no significant change in certain areas where pupils in other schools had shown a marked deterioration.[1] It may be the case that a comprehen-

[1] See boys' and girls' scores on 'importance of doing well', girls' scores on 'attitude to school' and also the discussion of comprehensive boys' scores on the 'self-image' scale.

sive system avoids to some extent the deleterious effect on pupils' attitude development to which 11+ selection appears to contribute.

The primary aim of this investigation of pupils' attitude development was to assess the long-term effects of different types of junior school organization. As far as this question is concerned the results were inconclusive. This is perhaps not surprising; for having drawn attention earlier to the differences in attitude development shown by pupils in different environments in the junior school, it would be unreasonable to suppose that their subsequent attitude development would not be strongly influenced by the wide variety of school situations and teachers encountered in the secondary school. Where marked changes in attitude were found to have taken place between 10+ and 12+, this appeared to be due to a combination of factors from both junior and secondary school situations. It is the nature of the transition from junior to secondary school, especially where this has involved a change of stream, class position, or status relative to other children, which appears to have played a major part in the development of pupils' attitudes towards themselves and towards school.

41

CHAPTER FOUR

Participation in School Activities

TAKING part in co-operative group activities outside the formal classroom context can play an important and valuable part in a child's educational development. Apart from the opportunity it offers to pursue personal interests and hobbies, such participation is likely to increase a pupil's sense of involvement with the school and with his fellow pupils and teachers.

The earlier streaming study included an inquiry into pupils' level of participation in school activities—a field in which little or no previous research had been carried out. The results of the inquiry revealed some striking differences in this area between streamed and non-streamed schools. Although in both types of school degree of participation was related to ability level and social class background, pupils in streamed schools were found to take much less part in school activities than their non-streamed counterparts, with the most marked differences appearing amongst children of average and below average ability and from lower social class homes. It seemed that in streamed schools a combination of these characteristics meant that a child was likely to be left out of school activities.

This was clearly an area of investigation which warranted further attention in the follow-up study. The first question to be answered concerned the long-term effects of the pupils' junior school experience—i.e. did the lower level of participation shown by the less able, lower social class pupils in streamed junior schools continue to manifest itself in the different environment of the secondary school—in other words, had non-participation become a habit among these children? Or if, as one might hypothesize, level of participation in the secondary school was influenced more directly by the pupil's experience in that school, were there any variations in the participation shown by pupils in different types of secondary school environment?

A questionnaire designed to obtain information about the activities in which pupils took part during their second year in the secondary school was completed by the pupils themselves towards the end of that year. The questionnaire included all the activities mentioned in the earlier study,[1] with the addition of a number of open-ended questions about other clubs, etc., in which the pupils might be involved.

In order to provide a check on the accuracy of pupils' responses, the head of each school was asked to indicate on a separate checklist the total number of activities available to second-year pupils in the school.

A total of 83 widely different activities were found to be available in the sample schools, ranging from floral art and pottery to bee-keeping and an organization set up to assist elderly local residents. No clear pattern of differences emerged in the type of activities offered by streamed or non-streamed grammar, secondary modern or comprehensive schools, although in most categories the number of schools was too small for any meaningful comparisons to be made. The following table shows the percentage of all schools in the sample offering the most frequently mentioned activities.[2]

TABLE 4.1: *Types of school activity*

1.	School (or house) sports team	100%
2.	School (or house) choir, orchestra, recorder group	100%
3.	School (or class) outing	99%
4.	Individual pupils taking special part in morning assembly	73%
5.	School play, opera or concert	63%
6.	School holiday	60%
7.	School dancing display	32%
8.	School magazine	20%

The most popular school clubs:

9.	Sports club	99%
10.	Chess club	61%
11.	Science club	45%
12.	Art club	38%
13.	Stamp club	37%
14.	Woodwork or metalwork club	35%
15.	Photography club	34%
16.	Geography club	22%
17.	French club	17%
18.	Religious discussion club	12%
19.	Drama club	12%
20.	History club	11%
21.	Transport (railway) club	11%
22.	Debating club	9%
23.	Music club	9%
24.	Cookery club	6%

[1] With the exception of prefects—as the follow-up sample were only in their second year in secondary school, this was inapplicable.

[2] Activities mentioned by less than five per cent of schools are not included.

In order to control for the considerable variation between individual schools in the number of activities available, a *participation ratio score* was calculated for each pupil, relating the number of activities in which he had taken part to the total number available in his school.

Participation in school activities at 12+ of pupils from streamed and non-streamed junior schools

Firstly, a comparison was made of the scores at 12+ of pupils who had earlier attended streamed and non-streamed junior schools. As in the earlier study, the scores of pupils of each social class[1] and ability level[2] were examined separately.

The first point to emerge from the analysis was that the overall rate of participation was considerably lower at 12+ than it had been at 10+, with very few pupils taking part in a large number of activities, and a considerable number being almost completely uninvolved in school affairs. This finding is perhaps not surprising, since children approaching adolescence no doubt have greater freedom and opportunity to become absorbed in interests outside school and home.

Only one significant difference emerged in the participation level of pupils from streamed and non-streamed junior schools. Higher social class boys of above average ability who had attended non-streamed schools took more part in activities at 12+ than did their streamed counterparts (P<0·001). A similar trend was found in the scores of the other groups of boys, with a greater number from streamed junior schools taking little or no part in school activities. In the case of girls, however, there were no differences. As mentioned earlier, the most marked differences at 10+ had been found among less able pupils from lower social class homes; the level of participation of higher social class boys of above average ability had been very similar in the two types of school. While it is possible that the difference between these boys at 12+ reflected the delayed effects of their junior school experience, the pattern of results at 12+ would seem rather to suggest that the influence of type of junior school on level of participation had been largely outweighed by factors associated with the pupils' more recent secondary school experience.

[1] At 10+ pupils were divided into three social class groups: 1, 2 professional and clerical; 3 skilled; 4, 5 semi- and unskilled. Small numbers at 12+ necessitated combining social classes 1, 2 and 3.

[2] Pupils were divided into three ability groups according to their scores on the Reading test at 10+.

Participation in school activities of pupils in different types of secondary school

A further analysis was carried out to discover whether attendance at a streamed or non-streamed secondary school appeared to influence pupils' level of participation in school activities.

Firstly, a comparison was made of the numbers of 'high', 'medium' and 'low'[1] participants in streamed and non-streamed grammar, comprehensive and secondary modern schools. In all three types of school there was a tendency for more boys in non-streamed schools to have a high level of participation and the overall difference was significant ($P<0.05$. See Table A29, Appendix 5). When the scores of girls were examined, significant differences favouring non-streamed schools were found in both comprehensive and grammar schools ($P<0.001$ and $P<0.05$, respectively), although in both cases the numbers involved were small.

It is perhaps of interest to note that the overall level of participation in comprehensive schools was somewhat lower than in the other two types of school. Forty-nine per cent of pupils in comprehensives were 'low' participators, compared with 38 per cent in secondary moderns and 36 per cent in grammar schools. The corresponding figures for 'high' participators were 18 per cent, 30 per cent and 34 per cent respectively. According to the information obtained from the sample schools these differences could not be attributed to fewer activities being available in comprehensive schools, and in any case the use of participation ratio scores would have controlled for any such variation. It would seem possible that size of school and factors associated with this might be relevant in this context, and that in large schools pupils may find it more difficult to become involved in activities within the wider school community.

Participation and class position

In the junior school study, it had been found that both pupils at the top of the class and those at the bottom of the class in non-streamed schools took a greater part in school activities than the corresponding groups of pupils in streamed schools; even although the 'bottom of the class' category in streamed schools included children who were in A-streams. A similar comparison was carried out of the participation level of pupils at the top or bottom of the class[2] in streamed and non-streamed secondary schools. No

[1] High=participation ratio score of 29 and over; medium=15–28; low=0–14.
[2] According to English teachers' ratings.

45

differences emerged in the scores of boys who were at the top of their class, but more girls at the top of non-streamed classes had high scores and fewer had low scores compared with those in streamed schools (P<0·01. See Table A30, Appendix 5). Looking at the scores of those at the bottom of the class, it was found that boys in streamed schools took less part in school activities than their non-streamed counterparts (P<0·05). A similar, though non-significant, trend was found in the case of girls.

Participation and pleasurability

Finally, a comparison was made of the participation level of pupils in streamed and non-streamed secondary schools who had been rated as either pleasurable or unpleasurable to have in the class.[1] In non-streamed schools no differences were found in the participation level of boys and girls who were regarded as pleasurable or unpleasurable. In streamed schools, however, girls who were rated as unpleasurable by their teachers had much lower scores than their more favoured peers (P<0·01. See Table A31, Appendix 5), while there was also a slight trend for boys who were seen as unpleasurable to take less part in school activities than those considered a pleasure to have in the class.

Summary and conclusions

Although children's participation in school activities in the junior school had been profoundly affected by type of school organization, there was little evidence that this influence had continued to operate after the pupils had transferred to secondary school. The results did suggest, however, that organizational factors at the secondary level influenced pupils' participation in the same way as in the junior school situation, with those in non-streamed schools becoming more involved in school affairs. As in the junior school too, it appeared that, in streamed schools especially, pupils whose school careers were less than wholly successful—as indicated for example by a low position in class or a poor relationship with the teacher—were less likely than their peers to find compensatory rewards through involvement in informal activities.

---

[1] English teachers' ratings.

CHAPTER FIVE

Pupils' Aspirations

PUPILS' hopes and ambitions for their future—whether they concern achievement in school or in their subsequent careers—are likely to be influenced to a large extent by what they feel about their capabilities and limitations. Increasing attention has been paid in recent years to the interaction of expectations, motivation and success, the suggestion being that a pupil of whom little is expected will expect little of himself, and will be unlikely to fulfil his potential.

It was hoped to throw some light on the effects of different types of school environment on the educational and occupational aspirations of the pupils in the follow-up study by obtaining information on 1) the age at which they wished or expected to leave school; 2) their choice of further training; and 3) the type of job which they wished or expected to obtain.

The analysis aimed firstly to assess any long-term effects of different types of junior school experience on pupils' aspirations in these areas, and secondly to examine the responses of pupils who had gone on to different types of secondary school.

The pupils in the earlier streaming study had been asked in their final junior school year what they would like to do when they grew up. The responses indicated that occupational aspirations at this age were unaffected by the type of school organization which the pupils had experienced. Girls more than boys appeared to be influenced by ability in their choice of careers; boys tended to be more unrealistic in their ambitions, as evidenced by the large numbers hoping to become professional footballers.

A questionnaire[1] designed to obtain information on the development of pupils' aspirations since leaving junior school was completed by all the pupils in the follow-up study at the end of their second year in secondary school.

1. Pupils' choice of leaving age

Pupils were asked firstly to indicate at what age they expected

[1] For details of the questionnaire, see Appendix 3.

47

to leave school, and secondly the age at which they would ideally choose to leave.

(a) Leaving Age Chosen by Pupils from Streamed and Non-Streamed Junior Schools

There were no differences in the 'desired' or 'expected' leaving ages chosen by boys and girls of comparable social class[1] and ability[2] levels from streamed and non-streamed junior schools.

(b) Leaving Age Chosen by Pupils in Different Types of Secondary School

Streaming or non-streaming within the three different types of secondary school was also found to make little difference to the age at which pupils desired or expected to leave.

The results indicated that in general, pupils expected to stay on at school longer than they would have liked (Boys $P < 0.001$; Girls $P < 0.001$. See Table A32, Appendix 5). Girls tended to wish for an earlier leaving age than boys, although there was less difference between the sexes in the ages at which they *expected* to leave.

Predictably, pupils in grammar schools expected to stay at school longer than those in non-selective schools, with two-thirds expecting to remain until 18. Pupils in comprehensive schools expected to stay longer than those in secondary modern schools, and this difference remained when each social class was examined separately. Lower social class pupils in secondary modern schools seemed particularly lacking in motivation to stay on at school beyond the statutory leaving age. Sixty-four per cent of lower social class girls wished to leave at 15 (or even earlier) and 51 per cent expected that they would do so, while the corresponding figures for boys were 59 per cent and 46 per cent.

Higher social class pupils both wished and expected to stay at school longer than those from lower social class backgrounds $(P < 0.001)$. Only in grammar schools was there no difference in the *expected* leaving age of pupils from different social classes. It would seem possible that selection for grammar school motivates all pupils (and education-conscious parents) to commit themselves to the full course of academic secondary education—at least at this early stage in their secondary school careers.

[1] At 10+ pupils were divided into three social class groups: 1, 2 professional and clerical; 3 skilled; 4, 5 semi- and unskilled. Small numbers at 12+ necessitated combining social classes 1, 2 and 3.

[2] As before, pupils were divided into three ability groups according to their scores on the Reading test at 10+

48

2. Pupils' choice of further training

Pupils were also asked to indicate on the questionnaire whether they wanted to take a job immediately after leaving school; take a job which also involved some sort of training (e.g. an apprenticeship); or enter into a course of full-time training (e.g. university or college of education).

(a) *Choice of Further Training of Pupils from Streamed and Non-Streamed Junior Schools.*

There was little difference in the choice of further training made by boys and girls of comparable social class and ability levels from streamed and non-streamed junior schools.

(b) *Choice of Further Training of Pupils in Different Types of Secondary School*

Type of organization within the secondary school was also found to have little effect on pupils' preferences for further training.

A full-time training course was the most popular choice of both boys and girls in grammar schools (see Table A33, Appendix 5). The fact that a higher percentage of girls than boys indicated this alternative possibly reflects the large number of girls who hoped to become teachers.[1] A combination of a job plus training was the most popular choice of both boys and girls in comprehensive and secondary modern schools. Fifty-seven per cent of boys and 48 per cent of girls in secondary modern schools opted for this alternative and only 25 per cent expected to take a job straight away with no further training. This is perhaps a more encouraging finding than that relating to the expected leaving age of these pupils. It would seem that although more than 50 per cent wished to leave as soon as possible, at least half of these intended to take some sort of training afterwards.

Higher social class pupils were found to attach more importance than lower social class pupils to following some kind of training course after leaving school (P<0·001). Within the grammar schools, although the number of lower social class pupils was small, there was a marked tendency for them to be less likely than their higher social class peers to expect to go on to a full-time training course. Thus, although apparently ready to complete the full grammar school course as indicated by their expected leaving age, it would seem that

[1] See Section 3ii on actual occupations chosen.

many lower social class pupils did not think in terms of continuing their full-time education beyond that point.

3. Pupils' occupational aspirations

Finally, pupils were asked to name the job they would ideally choose for themselves irrespective of talent, qualifications required, or any other limiting factors, and then to state the job they thought themselves most likely to obtain.

(i) Status of Occupational Aspirations

Firstly, the status level of aspirations was studied rather than the actual occupations chosen. All responses were allocated to one of three status groups: 1) professional, 2) skilled; 3) semi- or unskilled.[1]

(a) *Aspirations of pupils from streamed and non-streamed junior schools* As in the earlier study a comparison was made of the choices of pupils of similar social class and ability levels from streamed and non-streamed junior schools, and again it was found that type of organization had no effect on the status level of aspirations.

(b) *Aspirations of pupils in different types of secondary school* An examination of the choices of pupils of similar social class in streamed and non-streamed grammar, comprehensive and secondary modern schools also revealed little difference between the two types of organization.

The results showed an overall tendency for pupils' 'ideal' occupations to be of a higher status level than those which they thought themselves likely to obtain (Boys $P<0.01$; Girls $P<0.001$. See Table A34 Appendix 5), and for the differences between 'ideal' and 'expected' job to be more marked amongst girls and pupils from lower social class backgrounds.

Further interesting results emerged when the choices of pupils in different schools were examined. Not unexpectedly, pupils in grammar schools both desired and expected to obtain jobs of a higher status level than those in non-selective schools. Moreover, there was a higher degree of correspondence between the 'ideal' and 'expected' jobs of grammar school pupils, than in the other schools—especially in the secondary modern. These findings reflect those quoted by Pidgeon (1967) who found that the difference between desired and

---

[1] Responses corresponded closely to those mentioned at 10+ and the same coding frame was used to classify them. Occupations were graded on the basis of the Registrar-General's *Classification of Occupations* and Reiss's (1961) *Scales of Occupational Prestige*.

expected occupation among pupils in selective secondary schools was slight and non-significant.

In secondary modern schools, highly significant differences were found between the 'ideal' and 'expected' occupations of both boys and girls (Boys $P<0·01$; Girls $P<0·001$), which were most marked among those from lower social class backgrounds.

Girls in comprehensive schools also showed a discrepancy between 'ideal' and 'expected' choice of job which was statistically significant, and again the difference was greater in the lower social class group. There were no significant differences, however, in the choices of boys in comprehensive schools.

These results would suggest that sex, social class and type of school attended all play a part in influencing pupils' occupational aspirations. The group who appeared to suffer most from 'depressed' aspirations in terms of the gap between 'ideal' and 'expected' job were lower social class pupils—especially girls—in non-selective secondary schools. No doubt these were the children who had experienced the least success in their school careers, and who, perhaps as a result, had little confidence that they would be capable of fulfilling their ideals in the future.

(ii) Actual Occupations Chosen at 12+

Finally, a study was made of the actual occupations named as 'ideal' and 'expected' job by the pupils in the follow-up study. Table 5.1 shows the percentages choosing each occupation and compares these with the results obtained in the earlier study when pupils were aged 10+.[1]

Not unexpectedly, the most popular ambition of boys at 10+ had been to become a professional footballer or other type of sportsman. Although this was less favoured at 12+ it was still the 'ideal' choice of 11 per cent, and the 'expected' future of a somewhat unrealistic 6 per cent. 'Engineer/mechanic'[2] emerged as the most popular 'ideal' and 'expected' choice of 12+ boys, while the forces maintained their appeal (9 per cent 'ideal' choice, 11 per cent 'expected' choice). Jobs falling in the semi- and unskilled category were seen as less desirable at 12+ than at 10+, but 9 per cent of boys saw this as their likely future.

[1] This comparison must be treated with caution as the 10+ and 12+ samples were not identical. Also, children at 10+ were simply asked: 'What would you like to do when you grow up?'

[2] In a study of the career choices of highly able 13-year-olds in Scottish schools, Butcher and Pont (1968) also found that engineering and teaching were the most popular choices of boys and girls respectively.

As at 10+ girls were found to be somewhat less diffuse than boys in their occupational aspirations; over two-thirds (68 per cent) expected to become a teacher, secretary/typist, nurse, hairdresser or shop assistant.[1] In the case of secretary/typist and shop assistant, however, the number expecting to enter these fields considerablʎ exceeded the number who named them as their 'ideal' choice. Girls

TABLE 5.1: *A comparison of pupils' occupational aspirations at 10+ and 12+*

Boys	Choice at 12+		Choice at 10+ (%)
	Expected (%)	*Ideal* (%)	
Engineer/Mechanic	19	16	8
Forces and Merchant Navy	11	9	10
Sportsman/Footballer	6	11	23
Driver (bus, train, lorry)	6	4	5
Teacher	4	4	2
Carpenter	4	2	3
Electrician	3	3	2
Policeman	3	4	4
Shop assistant	3	1	1
Architect	3	3	3
Pilot	2	8	5
Builder/Decorator	2	1	1
Naturalist/Zoo-keeper/Zoologist	2	1	3
Farmer	1	2	2
Scientist	1	2	3
Veterinary surgeon	1	2	2
Journalist	1	1	0
Doctor	1	1	1
Artist/Art teacher	1	1	2
Actor/Film star	0	1	0
Fireman	0	0	2
Other professions	4	9	4
Other skilled	13	11	7
Other semi- and unskilled	9	3	7
Total	100%	100%	100%
Number of boys giving information	719	719	902

[1] These findings correspond with those of Veness (1962): 'In contrast with the boys there is a much greater concentration of girls' choices. Half intended to work in two major spheres—clerical and distributive. Only in grammar schools do these findings fall below 40 per cent and here teaching beomes important.'

TABLE 5.1—*continued*:

GIRLS	CHOICE AT 12+		CHOICE AT 10+ (%)
	Expected (%)	Ideal (%)	
Secretary/Typist	23	14	13
Teacher	12	16	13
Hairdresser	11	9	16
Nurse	11	13	14
Shop assistant	11	4	6
Work with animals	3	3	4
Dressmaker	3	2	1
Air Hostess	2	9	5
Horse rider/Instructor	2	2	2
Veterinary surgeon	1	4	2
Telephonist	1	1	1
Fashion designer	1	2	2
Model	1	2	1
Artist/Art teacher	1	1	1
Doctor	1	1	1
Librarian	1	1	1
Actress/Film star	0	2	2
Dancer/Instructor	0	1	2
Swimmer/Instructor	0	1	2
Singer	0	2	0
Other professions	2	3	3
Other skilled	5	4	4
Other semi- and unskilled	8	3	4
Total	100%	100%	100%
Number of girls giving information	759	759	899

in particular appeared to adopt a realistic view of their employment prospects; while a considerable number appeared to be attracted by the 'glamour' occupations such as air hostess, film star, actress, singer and model, very few regarded these as attainable ambitions.

A study of the most popular 'expected' jobs amongst pupils from different types of secondary school reflected the findings on the status level of occupational choice. Boys in grammar and comprehensive schools were most likely to opt for skilled white collar jobs, followed by 'teacher' in the grammar schools, and 'engineer/mechanic' in comprehensives. 'Engineer/mechanic' was by far the most popular choice of secondary modern boys.

Teaching was the outstandingly popular choice of girls in grammar schools, with over a third expecting to enter the profession. Secretarial or office work was seen as the most likely field of employment by girls in both comprehensive and secondary modern schools.

Summary and conclusions

The results of this inquiry indicated that the type of school organization experienced by pupils at the primary and the secondary level had little effect on their aspirations at 12+

Pupils in all types of secondary school expressed a desire to leave school at an earlier age than they actually expected to. Pupils in grammar schools expected to stay at school longer than those in non-selective schools, were more likely to continue full-time training after they left, and expected to obtain jobs of a higher status level. Only in grammar schools was there little difference in the status level of desired and expected jobs.

The lowest aspirations were expressed by pupils in secondary modern schools, over half of whom wished they could leave school by the age of 15, and who saw themselves as less likely to obtain the kind of job they would ideally choose.

In each type of school, pupils from a higher social class background were found to have higher hopes and expectations for their future success than their lower social class counterparts. It would seem that pupils' home background and educational experience act together in influencing their aspirations, so that lower social class pupils in secondary modern schools—no doubt the least successful members of a meritocratic society—see themselves as least likely to achieve success in the future. Whether these low aspirations are seen as representing a realistic appraisal of their capabilities on the part of these pupils, or as contributing to a self-fulfilling prophecy is a further question which arouses speculation beyond the scope of this inquiry.

References

BUTCHER, H. J. and PONT, H. B. (1968). 'Opinions about careers among Scottish secondary school children of high ability', *Brit. J. Educ. Psychol.*, *38*, 272–9.

PIDGEON, D. A. (1967). *Achievement in Mathematics*, Slough: NFER.

VENESS, T. (1962). *School Leavers–Their Aspirations and Expectations*. London: Methuen.

REGISTRAR-GENERAL'S CLASSIFICATION OF OCCUPATIONS (1960): London: HM Stationery Office.

REISS, A. J. *et al.* (1961). *Occupations and Social Status*. New York: Free Press.

CHAPTER SIX

Case Studies of Individual Pupils

LARGE-SCALE studies designed to provide information about the overall effects of different types of treatment must of necessity mask wide variations in individual response to different situations. Today more than ever before, however, those concerned with education are becoming increasingly aware of the uniqueness of each child's personality and needs, and it is recognized that the learning situation in which child A appears to thrive may not be the most favourable environment for child B.

In an attempt to assess the effects of different types of junior school experience on the progress and development of individual pupils, the earlier research included a number of pupil case studies. Pupils selected for study included a number whose progress in the junior school had been spectacularly good, and a corresponding group whose performance had shown a notable deterioration. Part of the follow-up study was concerned with a further investigation of the progress and development of four of these pupils after two years in the secondary school.

The case study most closely related to the question of streaming concerned ROBERT, who, according to his annual test scores, had spent all four junior school years in too low a stream. He was subsequently allocated to a secondary modern school, where, in the A-stream, he maintained the high standard of achievement shown earlier, but felt, as before, that he was being insufficiently stimulated in a learning environment which was geared to the pace of pupils less able than himself.

A satisfactory teacher-pupil relationship is likely to be of importance in any learning situation, but especially so in the case of anxious children who are especially in need of sympathy and encouragement. A case in point was SANDRA, a nervous, insecure girl, whose performance deteriorated badly during two junior school years spent in the class of a teacher who had little time for her, and who withheld the encouragement and praise so necessary to such a child. Transfer to secondary school brought new anxieties to Sandra,

55

and her lack of confidence was exacerbated by encounters with other teachers who showed little patience and understanding.

A child's progress and development are likely to be influenced by the interaction of school, home background and personality, with factors in one area serving to reinforce or mitigate those in another. In the case of JULIE it appeared that home circumstances had contributed to her poor progress and lack of motivation in the junior school. Her parents were concerned for her welfare and happiness, but confined their interest in educational progress to that of her young brother. Seeing marriage and motherhood as the most appropriate role for their daughter, they attached little importance to the question of her future career; an attitude which was reflected in Julie's complete lack of motivation to obtain any academic qualifications and her own limited aspirations for her future.

In contrast, DAVID and his parents had had high hopes for his future after the excellent progress he had made in the junior school. His performance in the grammar school, however, did not fulfil these expectations, and it seemed that David's confidence in his ability had been eroded when he was faced with the keener competition from his classmates in the secondary school. His own anxiety and awareness of his parents' disappointment no doubt contributed further to the deterioration in his performance.

Method of investigation

All the pupils whose case histories were reported in the earlier research, and who had gone on to schools in the follow-up study sample, were included in the further investigation,[1] and four are reported here.[2]

Recorded interviews were carried out with the pupils to obtain their views on their work and progress; their attitudes to school and school work; to discover any problems which they may have encountered at school or at home; and to find out about their aspirations for their future training and career.

Each home was visited and a recorded interview was held with the child's mother, to discuss the parents' views of their child's progress and development, their level of interest in the child's education and also their aspirations for his or her future.

[1] This resulted in six of the seven case histories from the earlier research being 'followed up'. The seventh went on to a school not included in the follow-up, and consequently no test data were available to show her subsequent progress.

[2] In the case of two of the children, no parent was available for interview. These case studies have been omitted from this report, although details of them are available.

Discussions were also held with the head of the secondary school concerned, and with a number of teachers who had taught the child, to obtain their views on his or her progress, development and personality.

ROBERT

Robert was one of the pupils identified in the junior school study as having been placed in the 'wrong' stream; his four junior school years had been spent in a B-stream, although his test scores each year suggested that he should in fact have been in an A class. There was a considerable discrepancy between his test performance and his teachers' estimates of his progress; all felt that he was achieving less than he was capable of and that this was due to laziness and a lack of enthusiasm on his part. Robert had not got on well with his teachers, who appeared to have interpreted his quiet, unforthcoming attitude as boredom and idleness. Teachers' assessments played a major part in selection for grammar school in that area, and, in view of his teachers' estimates of his performance, it was not surprising that Robert was not allocated to a grammar school—although his test scores were within the range of those selected.

Robert left his junior school to go to a streamed secondary modern school. The ability range in the school was limited and there were a considerable number of behaviour problems among the pupils. When Robert first went to the school there was no GCE course available, but by the third year this was being developed, in addition to the CSE exam to which the school had previously confined itself.

The majority of Robert's classmates from his junior school had transferred to another secondary modern in the district, which had a 'grammar stream' in each year and was noted for its higher academic standards. That Robert had not also gone to this school was due to an unfortunate error on the part of his mother who had 'misread the date' by which parents' choice of secondary school had to be notified to the education authority. Robert remained 'unallocated' for some while, and by the time this was noticed, the school which both he and his parents preferred had no more vacancies.

According to his mother Robert was 'brokenhearted' over this—'all his friends were going to the other school, and he started off on a bad footing'. Worse still, it was felt that in this school Robert's chances of academic success would be severely limited.

Robert was absent for the English test administered to the follow-up pupils at the end of their second year in secondary school, but his standardized scores on the maths and verbal tests suggested that he was maintaining the good progress which he had shown earlier despite frequent absences due to illness during his second year.

TABLE 6.1: *Robert's test scores*

	MATHS	VERBAL
10+† standardized score	130	110
12+ standardized score	125	117

† In each case study the 10+ Maths test score quoted was the pupil's score on the Concept Arithmetic test, as this was the most comparable with the test used at 12+.

On entering the school Robert had been placed in the A-stream and was considered by his teachers to be an average, and in some cases an above average, member of the class. It was noticeable that these teachers held a much more favourable opinion of Robert than had those in his junior school; perhaps not surprising in view of the fact that he was clearly one of the most able pupils in the year group, while his quiet, sober approach to his work was no doubt appreciated by teachers in a situation where indiscipline seemed the rule rather than the exception.

His maths teachers in particular were full of praise for Robert's work and progress. They found him 'first class—by our standards', and felt that 'he had a real grasp of what numbers are about'. One teacher also commented on his keen, purposeful attitude to work: 'he came and asked for homework . . . didn't mind the others ribbing him'.

Robert seemed to find his work in the A-stream relatively undemanding and expressed the need for the incentive of 'another stream higher up to work my hardest to get into'. He also longed for the opportunity to study subjects not in the curriculum—such as electronics and biology, and clearly found the level of work in some subjects insufficiently stimulating. In science, for example, the work was 'just general—how to mend a washer and that sort of thing, which *I* thought was just common sense!'

In spite of his apparently satisfactory progress, Robert's two years in the school had done little to diminish his regret at having missed allocation to the other school. He was far from satisfied with his progress—'I'm not pleased with it at all. I feel I *can* work better, but don't seem to be able to *make* myself'. He even wished he could be seven years old again—'to realise the possibilities and work harder— to get into a grammar stream'.

Most of his dissatisfaction, however, was directed at the school, and most particularly for the lack of homework. 'I was hoping for a gradual increase from the first year but we don't get much even now.' As a result he found himself devoting more and more time to his many activities outside the school: 'I get taken up in interests outside school, whereas if I had more homework I'd stay in.' His mother had also been disturbed at the small amount of homework Robert had to do in comparison with friends at the other school. 'This is time you can't make up in my opinion—especially if you're going to sit exams.' She had in fact sent a note to the school, saying that her son wished to have more homework, but was shocked at the response. 'One teacher said: "Come to me on a Friday night and you can have whatever books you want for homework." Well! That's no encouragement to any child, is it? After that he just didn't bother . . .' Only one or two teachers had responded positively to Robert's requests for homework, and, where this had happened, Robert was clearly encouraged. 'Mrs. T would always take five minutes whenever you wanted to give individual homework. I really used to enjoy working for Mrs. T.'

Robert also felt that the rowdy atmosphere which seemed to prevail in most classes was having an adverse effect on his work. His criticism, however, was directed at teachers rather than pupils—'I like strictness in the classroom because I can't work in a noisy class'.

Robert had little to do with the 'troublemakers' in his class and simply avoided contact with them—'If I want to work I just go by myself'. One of his teachers found him to be 'rather solitary and distant' and not over-popular. Robert himself felt, as he had in the junior school, that he 'didn't have too many friends' and it seemed that his social relations at this school were even less satisfactory than had been the case earlier. He felt that there had been a 'more homely attitude' at his junior school; in his present school 'there are people you don't like and quite often you feel very uneasy'.

Robert's aspirations regarding his future training and career suggested that he was coming to terms with the limitations imposed on him by his educational experience. He had indicated on the 'aspirations' questionnaire that he would like to stay at school until 18, but expected to leave at 16 (quite the opposite discrepancy to that found among most pupils). His 'ideal' career was a job 'in a research department—in the field of atomic power' but he saw little likelihood of achieving this. His father's suggestion was that Robert should leave school and take up an apprenticeship, and it seemed that Robert was coming to accept this—albeit reluctantly—as the most probable outcome. However he clearly doubted whether this type of work would bring the rewards he sought in a career—'I would like to be happy in a job as well as get on and get good money'.

Robert's educational and occupational aspirations met with little encouragement at home, where his father in particular had never shown much interest in his academic progress. 'He doesn't do much in education—it's my mother that plays the main part.' Robert's mother, however, while clearly more concerned about his academic development, admitted that he received little practical help or advice from either her or her husband—'I didn't have a great deal of schooling and his father just isn't interested anyway.' She appeared to have lost confidence in his academic potential and to have given up hope of him achieving high qualifications, when he was not selected for grammar school. 'I feel if he had had the opportunity at the time he could have got somewhere.' Although not actively opposing Robert's educational aspirations, his parents' attitude was hardly likely to inspire and motivate him: 'He's staying till 16—it's his own preference, so we said we'd let him'.

If Robert does ultimately succeed in his academic and subsequent career, one feels that this success will be due solely to his own perseverance and aspirations; that it will be achieved in spite of, rather than with the help of, his educational and home experiences. Otherwise, his may be a depressing story of waste of ability—and one which may be disturbingly far from unique.

SANDRA

Sandra's four years in the A-stream of a large junior school had not been very satisfactory, either in terms of her progress or her attitude to school. She was a rather nervous, anxious girl, who needed sympathetic encouragement from her teachers if she was to produce her best, and a very poor relationship with one teacher who had taken her class for two consecutive years seemed to have been the chief cause of a marked deterioration in Sandra's performance. She vividly recalled her unhappy two years with this teacher who, she said, had 'really frightened me'. She had in fact been reduced to such a state of nerves at the end of the period that a course of drugs had had to be prescribed.

By the end of her fourth year Sandra had dropped so far back in her work that she stood little chance of obtaining a grammar school place, and, as expected, she left the junior school to go to a large streamed secondary modern school nearby. This school was divided into two geographically, with the first two year groups housed in an annexe some distance from the main building. There were eight classes to a year group and Sandra was assigned to the second from top stream.

Her scores at 12+ suggested that she had made little progress in either Maths or Verbal Reasoning and was slightly below average in each, but that her performance in English showed an improvement over her 10+ score.

TABLE 6.2: *Sandra's test scores*

	MATHS	ENGLISH	VERBAL
10+ standardized score	93	109	101
12+ standardized score	94	116	95

To a nervous, anxious child such as Sandra a change of school could clearly be a somewhat threatening experience, and Sandra admitted that the 'thought of coming to the big school frightened me'. She had not in fact settled down well on entering the school and had soon experienced considerable difficulty with her work, especially maths. According to her mother she was 'terrible at maths' and had been upset by her inability to cope—'the whole two years in the annexe she seemed to spend in tears'. Sandra had been rather overwhelmed by the new fields and processes of mathematics which she encountered in the secondary school—especially algebra. 'There was so much *difference*—I just found I was losing confidence in myself. I thought "I can't do it"—and I couldn't.'

Sandra was very much aware of her lack of confidence as a problem which carried over into other spheres of activity as well as her work. She confessed to feelings of anxiety about P.E. lessons—'I'm self-conscious that I'm not doing what I should be doing correctly'. Similar doubts seemed to have prevented her from taking part in certain extra-curricular activities—'I was asked to join the choir, but I didn't think I was good enough'.

It seemed likely that Sandra's lack of self-confidence and apparent

61

anxiety about her physical appearance (she was in fact only slightly overweight) had been a handicap to her in her social relations with other children. As in the junior school it seemed that she was not over-popular with her classmates. She had one particular friend in her class and had a cousin in another class, to whom she had always been very close, but, as her mother remarked, she 'liked to be alone' and was 'never one for clubs and things'.

Sandra's teachers were almost unanimous in echoing her own opinion of herself as worrying and over-anxious. They all felt that she took her work very seriously, tended to seek assurance that what she was doing was correct, and as one teacher put it, 'seldom looked completely relaxed'. Her form teacher noticed that on occasions when she had reprimanded the class as a whole, Sandra would look 'very tense and worried and would bite her nails'. Another teacher remarked that 'it seemed important to Sandra that she should please', and this would seem to reflect Sandra's continued need for encouragement and praise from her teachers.

Sandra seemed hypersensitive to any form of criticism from her teachers, whether directed at her personally or to the class as a whole. Her anxiety to please the teacher rendered her extremely vulnerable in a situation where she was put to the test—'some teachers expect so much of you—you try to give them the exact answer or you feel you've let them down—that brings you down and you begin to hate the subject'. Understanding, kindness and patience were the qualities which Sandra sought in her teachers, and she clearly related these characteristics to her own personal needs when she added—'so that they can help anyone who is a bit different and can't understand'.

During her second year in the secondary school Sandra had begun to suffer from brief blackouts or, as her mother put it, 'absences'. 'She would go to turn on the TV and just stop dead for a few seconds.' These symptoms had begun to frighten Sandra; at school 'people would keep nudging her and she'd realise she'd missed something'. Numerous tests had been carried out and it was concluded tthat Sandra was suffering from a very mild form of epilepsy.

In spite of these rather disturbing developments, both Sandra and her mother claimed that she had been much happier since transferring to the main building of the secondary school at the start of her third year. Sandra felt that she was 'beginning to gain confidence again' and her mother had been struck by her 'completely different approach to her work—she enjoys going to school'. She felt that the different atmosphere in the main part of the school may have contributed to Sandra's more favourable attitude; in the annexe the teachers 'came and went too quickly' and had had little time to give individual attention to pupils who were in need of help.

In her third year, too, Sandra came into contact with one or two teachers whom she found more approachable, and mentioned her English teacher in particular as being 'very nice and understanding'. This teacher had taken a sympathetic interest in Sandra, whom she saw as a highly sensitive child with considerable tension bottled up inside her. She had been disturbed by the vehement emotions expressed by Sandra in a certain essay in which she had written of her need to 'hit out', which was suppressed by the feeling that this was not 'suitable behaviour'.

Sandra was hoping to remain at school at least long enough to take the GCE 'O' level examinations. She was keen to 'get some qualifications, so that I can get a good job' and hinted that she would like to take 'A' level as well. She felt that her father supported her in this aim, but that her mother was less keen—'I think she thinks for a girl of 18 to be still at school is a bit ridiculous'. It appeared, however, that her mother's reservations about Sandra remaining at school until 18 merely reflected apprehension that Sandra might be aiming for more than she was capable of. She was more concerned about her daughter's well-being, both physical and mental, than about the status level of the career she might obtain. She admitted that her husband was more enthusiastic than she was that Sandra should remain at school as long as possible and obtain high level qualifications. He took a keen interest in Sandra's progress and had made many attempts to help her with her difficulties over maths. Her mother, however, felt that he was 'a bit impatient with her—if she hasn't grasped it after the second sum, he's inclined to have a bit of a shout'. She clearly disapproved of the idea of exerting pressure to succeed, and in the case of a girl like Sandra such an attitude would seem likely to have a salutary effect. Sandra clearly needed sympathy and encouragement from both home and school to overcome her difficulties; if she is fortunate enough to continue to come into contact with sympathetic teachers with whom she can establish satisfactory relationships, there seems every reason to suppose that her work could show the improvement which her early junior school performance suggested would be well within her capabilities.

JULIE

Julie was the elder child of working class parents who showed considerable concern for her welfare and happiness, but little for her educational progress; their aspirations in that area were confined to her younger brother, Paul, whom they considered to be of greater ability and, as a future breadwinner, more in need of educational qualifications.

Julie's progress during her four years in the junior school had been very poor; she was demoted from the A to the B-stream at the end of her first year, and made little progress thereafter. She was subsequently allocated to a four form entry secondary modern school, where she was placed initially in the C-stream. Her test performance at 12+ indicated that she had made little progress in Maths and English, whilst her Verbal Reasoning score showed a marked deterioration.

TABLE 6.3: *Julie's test scores*

	MATHS	ENGLISH	VERBAL
10+ standardized score	83	95	94
12+ standardized score	81	96	79

At the end of her first year in the secondary school Julie was promoted to the B-stream. She claimed that she had found the pace of work in the C class too slow—'I'd be the first to finish and have to wait about 15 minutes for the others'. She was happy in the B class, however, where she found the work 'just about my standard—it's not *hard* work', and was entirely satisfied with her progress—'I've improved a lot—they teach you more in this school'. Her parents, too, felt that Julie's work had improved enormously in the secondary school. Her mother claimed that she 'really enjoyed her schooling now' and she herself had 'seen the progress in her books'. She was convinced that with a little more effort Julie could get into the A-stream. This estimate of Julie's potential, however, seemed merely to reflect the fact that she had exceeded her parents' own limited educational experience, for the view was not echoed by her teachers. They were in unanimous agreement that Julie was a 'B' child who could not go any higher. Only her English teacher saw her as a possible CSE candidate; others, especially her maths teacher, felt she could never attain the required standard.

Maths had always been Julie's greatest problem in school—on her own admission she was 'terrible at maths—it's slow getting through to me'. Her maths teacher's comments on Julie's attitude to the subject were very similar to those made by her junior school teacher. If Julie was in difficulties, she said, she would not dream of coming to ask for help—she would simply ignore the problem. As her junior school teacher had put it—'she thinks things are easy because she only does what she can'.

Julie's ambitions for her future education and career were very limited. She was clearly thinking in terms of leaving school at the earliest possible moment—'I've only got till next Easter to go'—as she saw little point in remaining at school any longer than she was obliged to. 'By the time you're getting to the end of the fourth year, you've learned everything there is to know.'

As one of her teachers put it, Julie was simply not 'school-minded'. She seemed almost totally unaware of any relationship between educational experience and subsequent occupational opportunities. School was merely something which was there to be tolerated, and as long as little pressure was put upon her, Julie would tolerate it with equanimity. However, she resented its intrusion upon life outside, and complained at the amount of homework which had been given during her second year. 'You'd have a hard day's work at school then you'd have to go home and do it there! It's not really fair, 'cos I like to watch the telly.' Julie seemed to look forward to work as a release from the petty irritations and restrictions of school life—'you wouldn't get all those catty girls telling you what do to'.

Julie's father, although more concerned about the education and career of his son, had nevertheless decided that the time had come to settle the question of Julie's future employment, and had suggested that 'tracing' would be an ideal solution as Julie had shown some talent for drawing. Seeing Julie as a 'gentle, home-loving, motherly type' he had decided that she was 'heading for the wedding bells early in life, so that to think of a far-reaching career would be impractical'.

He expressed frustration at having received no indication from the school as to 'which way the child is *leaning*—so that I can push. All the reports do is tell you the *progress* of the child—it's not that I'm interested in.'

Julie's father, a brusque ex-serviceman, had maintained a policy of tight discipline in the upbringing of his children. Although claiming that he would never push his children into a particular job against their will, it seemed from his attitudes and actions in assuming the responsibility for 'placing' them that he was in danger of producing this result. Julie's brother, Paul, was in his first year in secondary school, and his father had already entered him for an apprenticeship at his own factory. Now, he said, he had to be pushed into certain subjects. Determined that his son should have a 'start in life' which he claimed he had never had himself, he appeared to have limited the boy's chances of following any interests and aptitudes which he might already have or might develop in the future.

Julie's mother, on the other hand, was very keen for her daughter to take up some kind of office work—'she could make a decent wage —and have something to fall back on'. She was fully aware however, that such a prospect held no appeal for Julie, whose overriding interest in life was the care of babies and small children. Even in her junior school days Julie had shown a 'strong maternal instinct' and it appeared that this 'instinct' had strenghtened as she had grown older. Baby-minding was still one of her chief pastimes, and her only career aspiration was to obtain a job 'to do with children—like a children's nurse'. If there were no suitable openings in this field, she reluctantly supposed that she would have to take up office work, but—'I don't fancy myself typing'.

Julie was a placid, seemingly contented girl, on whom the education system seemed unlikely ever to make much impact. She was probably achieving less than she was capable of, but was clearly subjected to little pressure or motivation to do better. It seems likely that her greatest satisfaction in life will come from being a 'good housewife and mother', but until that time she would no doubt be happier working in the field for which she has a flair—care of children—than finding herself pushed by a determined parent into a job for which she has clearly little enthusiasm.

DAVID

David was a slightly-built, highly intelligent and articulate boy, the son of very 'education conscious', middle class parents who had high aspirations for his future. He had made spectacular progress during his second and third years in the junior school A-stream, and when, as generally expected, he obtained a grammar school place, his future academic career looked highly promising. He had only one problem—his handwriting. It was suspected that he was a natural left-hander who had been forced to write with his right hand, and throughout his school career he had been under pressure from his parents and teachers alike to improve what was a practically illegible hand.

David's scores at the end of his second year in the grammar school revealed that he had not maintained the progress shown in his junior school results. A comparison of his standardized scores at 10+ and

12+ showed that he had improved slightly in English, but dropped back somewhat in both Maths and Verbal Reasoning.

TABLE 6.4: *David's test scores*

	MATHS	ENGLISH	VERBAL
10+ standardized score	117	115	119
12+ standardized score	112	119	112

.The boys' grammar school which David attended was streamed, and he spent the first two years in a B class. He claimed that he had been quite happy in that class as he 'hadn't expected to go into the A'. At the beginning of his third year, however he was demoted. The head-master felt that the third year C class was too large, particularly as he considered it academically poor by the school's standards, so it was divided into two classes, C and D,—and David was put in the D-stream.

This somewhat drastic demotion clearly came as a shock to David; as his mother put it—'I think it deflated his ego a lot'. The school had apparently given very little explanation of its transfer policy, and when the head was asked how David had reacted to his demotion, he merely replied, 'Theirs not to reason why . . .'

Considerable emphasis seemed to be placed on marks and class positions in the school, and David's demotion was the result of his overall marks at the end of his second year. His low class position was to some extent due to his poor performance in subjects involving manual skills—art, technical drawing and woodwork—for which he had never had any aptitude. His mother felt that this was somewhat unjust: 'He gets no marks at art because he's not good at it—and I think this is wrong—you're either good at art or you're not'.

David himself felt that his handwriting was also 'a big handicap', for even when his work was 'reasonably good' the teachers would 'take two or three marks off for neatness, pushing me down the class'.

It seemed that David had also experienced some difficulty with maths and science subjects in the grammar school, and had complained at home that the maths teacher explained things too quickly for him to grasp. At first he had not approached the teacher to ask for help since he 'did not want people to think me dim'. Later, however, he had swallowed his pride and asked the teacher to explain a step to him again, but the response had been 'Good gracious, I haven't time now—you must ask your father or someone at home'.

In some areas however, David did seem to be living up to his earlier promise. In English his work was considered very satisfactory; he had come second in the B class, and his English teacher in the D-stream felt that he was 'very much ahead' of the others in the class. This teacher had in fact suggested promotion, but was told that since David's maths was not up to standard, there was no possibility of this.

David had also been in the top half of the B class in French, and was distressed to find that in the D-stream, French was no longer on the time-table. After a term, however, the D-stream pupils were given the option of taking French again, and much to David's satisfaction he had 'proved them wrong' by doing well in the examination. He was very keen on languages, and expressed the desire to learn German, which, however, was restricted to the higher streams.

It appeared that David's confidence in his own abilities had been somewhat eroded since entering the grammar school. He admitted that he found the work much harder than in the A-stream of the junior school where he 'used to do things faster than everybody else . . . I wasn't so dim then'. In the grammar school he found that 'they do things a bit too fast for me' and although he was clearly upset at his demotion to the bottom stream he seemed relieved that the work was somewhat easier—'I don't come bottom in everything now'.

David's parents were keenly disappointed by his performance in the grammar school. His father, it seemed, was 'disgusted with the way he's been going on in this school', feeling David had 'just gone steadily downhill since he's been there'. Much of their dissatisfaction was expressed in criticism of the school, and particularly at what they regarded as the utterly inadequate amount of homework given to pupils in the lower streams.

While laying part of the blame for David's poor performance on the school, his parents were also unhappy about their son's attitude to his work. According to his mother he had been 'extremely enthusiastic' in his first year, but then appeared to 'slack off' and subsequently lost ground. She claimed that 'he never bothered with work when he came home' and she was clearly disturbed at David's apparent unconcern about his poor progress. 'I despair sometimes and try to explain how very important it is for him to work—with the great emphasis on 'O' and 'A' levels—you've *got* to have those to get a good job'. Although disappointed at his demotion, she had hoped that it 'might spur him on to work' but felt that this had not been the case.

Both parents seemed to wonder whether the high estimates they had held of David's ability had in fact been erroneous; whether David had shone in the junior school merely because the ability range in that particular school had been restricted. Although both parents firmly believed in the value of education and were keen for David to remain at school as long as possible and take his 'A' level examinations, it seemed that their ambitions for his future career had been somewhat deflated as a result of his performance in the grammar school. They regretfully admitted that David seemed unlikely to obtain a university place and felt that teaching would perhaps be 'more within his ability'.

David's own aspirations seemed also to have suffered considerably, particularly as a result of his demotion. He was depressed by the fact that his chances of obtaining a large number of GCE 'O' level passes were limited by his being in the D-stream—'I won't get entered for as many subjects'. He was still hoping to stay on until the sixth form—'but there again, you need the qualifications—three or four 'O' levels'. Like his parents, he saw little hope of reaching university and had 'sort of resigned' himself to trying for a college of education. The prospect of teaching seemed genuinely to appeal to him, although it was clear that this was very much a second-best choice as far as a career was concerned, and that David would have wished for the chance to follow some of his more far-reaching ambitions.

The views of his teachers on his work and personality suggested that David's rather laconic manner and apparently nonchalant attitude to his work was to some extent a camouflage for a considerable amount of anxiety about his performance. Both his English and maths teachers commented that he seemed to worry about his work; his maths teacher felt that he had 'no confidence', frequently sought assurance that he was correct and was upset when his work was poor—'he doesn't like being wrong'. In spite of his satisfactory performance in English, this teacher too was of the opinion that David was 'sensitive—a worrier, who would be supset if he came low in class'.

These reports suggest that David was much more concerned about his work than his insouciant behaviour at home had led his parents to believe. He could hardly have failed to be aware of his parents' disillusionment over his apparent failure to live up to the high expectations which they and everyone else had held of him, and the 'don't care' attitude which he seemed to adopt at home may well have been a defensive reaction to this.

The case of David would seem to illustrate the possible adverse effects of the change from junior to grammar school suggested in Chapter Three. Leaving the junior school as a highly successful member of the A-stream, David's self-confidence received a blow when he found himself surrounded by the fierce competition in the grammar school, where the work was also considerably more demanding. It is suggested that as his self-confidence decreased, his anxieties increased and his performance deteriorated, thus reinforcing his self-doubts and contributing to an unhappy vicious circle.

Summary

In this study, as in the earlier one, an attempt has been made to highlight the factors in the school and home environment—and in the pupils' personality—which appeared to have contributed to the pupils' progress and development since leaving the junior school. As before, this progress was the outcome of numerous interacting influences—no doubt many more than could be assessed within the scope of this study. However, in the case histories presented here, some indication is given of the factors which appeared to have played a major role in the developing school careers of the young people concerned.

As far as factors in the school situation are concerned, it seems abundantly clear that for the individual pupil the effect of the teacher is far more important than the way the school structures its teaching groups. Also, the need for a system of educational guidance and counselling in the secondary school is well substantiated by these few case studies of boys and girls at educational (and occupational) risk.

CHAPTER SEVEN

Summary and Conclusions

THE primary aim of this study was to examine the long-term effects of streaming and non-streaming in the junior school on the subsequent personality, social and intellectual development of pupils in secondary school. It continued the assessment of a group of pupils whose development during the junior school course had been the subject of an earlier study.

The educational environment of pupils in streamed and non-streamed junior schools had been very different. Those in streamed schools had experienced a more formal approach in the classroom, with greater emphasis being laid on the 'three Rs' and the attainment of set academic standards. In non-streamed schools the approach had been more 'child-centred', concentrating rather on learning by discovery and practical experience in a more informal atmosphere.[1]

Comparisons between the streamed and non-streamed approaches showed that while pupils' academic progress was largely unaffected by the type of school which they attended, their emotional and social development *was* influenced, both by the school's organizational policy and by the approach of their teachers.

The follow-up study focused on the development in secondary school of a sample of pupils from the earlier investigation. Approximately 1,700 pupils were involved, and these were scattered among 83 secondary schools.

The pupils were assessed at the end of their second year in the secondary school, by means of a battery of tests designed to assess their performance in the following areas: (a) Verbal Reasoning, (b) English, (c) Mathematics, (d) Divergent Thinking, (e) Personality and School Related Attitudes, (f) Participation in school activities, (g) Aspirations.

Comparisons were made of the performance in each area of comparable groups of pupils who had earlier attended streamed and non-streamed junior schools. An investigation was also made of the

[1] Only 'truly' non-streamed schools are referred to here, i.e. where teachers supported non-streaming and approaches associated with it.

71

effects of streaming and non-streaming in secondary schools although, as the schools in the sample were not necessarily representative of the two different approaches at the secondary level, the results of these comparisons were interpreted with extreme caution.

1 The investigation of pupil attainment at 12+ showed no differences in the progress made by pupils of comparable ability level and social class who had attended streamed and non-streamed junior schools. This finding reinforces the claim, made on the basis of similar results in the earlier study, that the decision as to whether or not to stream in the junior school must rest on factors other than academic attainment.

No differences were found in the academic progress made by pupils in streamed and non-streamed secondary schools (see Chapter 2A).

2 There was some slight evidence to suggest that pupils from non-streamed junior schools had maintained the higher level of performance in divergent thinking which they had shown earlier.

Pupils in both types of secondary modern school showed a deterioration in divergent thinking performance. Only in grammar schools did type of organization appear to be related to performance, with more pupils in non-streamed schools having high scores on the test (see Chapter 2B).

3 Boys and girls from both types of junior school developed poorer attitudes on the 'school-related' scales, with girls in particular liking school less and becoming less motivated to do well (see Chapter Three).

4 Girls, especially those of above average ability, developed a poorer self-image and became more anxious, while boys, especially those of below average ability, developed more favourable attitudes in each of these areas. These trends were most marked among pupils from non-streamed junior schools (see Chapter Three).

5 Grammar school pupils, especially girls, developed a poorer self-image and became less confident, while boys in secondary modern schools improved their self-image and became less anxious.

It is suggested that many of these changes in attitude are attributable to changes in the pupils' *relative* status in terms of ability resulting from the transition from junior to secondary school (see Chapter Three).

6 A study of pupils' participation in extra-curricular activities showed that factors in the secondary school environment had largely obliterated the marked differences found among pupils in streamed and non-streamed junior schools. The results indicated, however, that organizational factors in the secondary school operated in much the same way as at the junior level, with pupils in non-streamed schools playing a greater part in school activities (see Chapter Four).

7 A study of pupils' choice of leaving age, further training and occupation revealed that type of organization had little effect on pupils' aspirations at either the primary or the secondary level. Pupils' social class background and attendance at a selective or non-selective secondary school were of importance; the lowest aspirations were held by lower social class pupils in secondary modern schools (see Chapter Five).

To sum up, the results of this inquiry suggest that the differences found at 10+ between pupils in streamed and non-streamed junior schools had, on the whole, been eradicated by the end of their second year in the secondary school. The finding is perhaps not surprising since, having drawn attention to the considerable influence of organizational policy and teachers' attitudes in certain areas of pupil development in the junior school, it would be unreasonable to suppose that the children would not be likewise affected by similar factors at the secondary level. The conclusion to be drawn from these findings would appear to be that any decision regarding organizational policy in the junior school should be taken solely in the light of the benefits and disadvantages which have been shown to operate at the junior level.

Ideally, a follow-up study such as this would have focused attention on pupils who had experienced a streamed or non-streamed environment at both the primary and secondary levels. Such an approach was unfortunately beyond the scope of this inquiry, partly because of the relatively small number of non-streamed secondary schools involved, but more especially because it could not be assumed that these schools embodied the same approach and values which characterized non-streaming at the junior level. For example, the widespread use of 'setting' in non-streamed secondary schools might well be regarded as having more in common with a streamed approach. Furthermore, one of the major findings of the earlier study concerned the crucial importance of the teacher's approach—especially in the non-streamed situation. In the secondary schools, however, it was impossible to assess and give weight to the attitudes and methods of the large number of teachers who had taught the pupils in the follow-up study.

Further research will be needed to identify the values, attitudes and methods which characterize streaming and non-streaming in the secondary school, and to establish the extent to which a parallel can be drawn between the two approaches at the junior and secondary level. It might be hypothesized that the more subject-oriented curriculum in the secondary school and the greater pressure from the external examination system would result in a much narrower gap between the streamed and non-streamed approaches than was found in the junior school.

An investigation and evaluation of different types of organization at the secondary level would seem particularly relevant in the light of the continuing move towards comprehensive education. To what extent do methods of organization adopted within these schools reflect the aims associated with a system of comprehensive secondary education? More important, perhaps—how far are these aims supported and put into practice by the teachers working within the system? As the earlier streaming study showed, a mere change of organization, without the support of those whose task it was to put into practice its implications, was insufficient to achieve the aims which it embodied, and represented a change in name only.

APPENDIX ONE

Teacher Ratings of Pupil Behaviour

CLASS, Maths and English teachers in the secondary schools were asked to rate the pupils in the follow-up study in the following areas:[1]

1 Ability to work independently
2 Level of interest in school work
3 Level of contribution to class discussion.

A comparison was made of the ratings given to boys and girls of similar ability level[2] from streamed and non-streamed junior schools. No significant differences were found.

A further comparison of the ratings given to pupils in streamed and non-streamed grammar, comprehensive and secondary modern schools also revealed no significant differences.

Not surprisingly, ratings on each scale were related to ability, with above average pupils receiving more favourable ratings in each case ($P<0.001$).

There were also differences in the ratings given to boys and girls, with girls being seen as showing a greater degree of interest in their work ($P<0.001$), but taking a less active part in class discussions ($P<0.001$). There was no significant overall difference, however, in their perceived ability to work independently.

No differences were found in the ratings given to pupils from either type of junior or secondary school on the other behaviour traits, i.e. disobedience, withdrawn, attitude to school work.

[1] For details of the ratings, see Appendix 3.
[2] Pupils were divided into three ability groups on the basis of their scores on the Reading test at 10+.

75

APPENDIX TWO

Details of the Secondary Schools in the Sample

THE secondary schools in the sample were classified as streamed or non-streamed according to the method used to allocate *second* year pupils (i.e. those involved in the follow-up study) to classes at the beginning of the year. This information was obtained by means of a questionnaire to the heads of all the schools concerned. The results revealed wide variation and complexity in methods of organization, which in many cases prevented a straightforward classification of the school as streamed or non-streamed. For example, many schools employed a system of 'banding', in which each year group contained several groups of two or more parallel classes. Other schools which formed classes of mixed ability made use of 'setting' in basic subjects which many would regard as a form of streaming.

Some sort of compromise solution was clearly required, and it was decided that schools employing a system of 'banding' should be regarded as streamed, since permanent classes were formed on the basis of ability; while those who employed 'setting' in the context of mixed ability classes should be allocated to the non-streamed category. While 'setting' might well serve to modify the effects of a non-streaming policy, it would seem reasonable to suppose that the formation of permanent mixed ability classes was more indicative of the school's approach to the question of organization.[1]

Five of the 30 schools classified as non-streamed contained a remedial class; but as the number of follow-up pupils in these classes was very small, these schools were retained in the 'non-streamed' category in order to maintain a sample of reasonable size.

Table A1 shows the number of schools classified as streamed and non-streamed. Also shown is the number of streamed schools employing a system of 'banding', and the incidence of 'setting' for maths and English within the non-streamed schools.

[1] Or at least, the approach of the head. The importance of the teacher's attitudes for the fulfilment of the aims of non-streaming must not be forgotten, although it was unfortunately beyond the scope of this study to measure the attitudes of the large number of secondary school teachers by whom the pupils in the study had been taught.

TABLE A1: *Methods of organization in secondary schools*

	NON-STREAMED				STREAMED		
	Setting for Maths	*Setting for English*	*No. setting for basic subjects*	*No. of schools*	*Streamed through-out*	*'Banding' with parallel groups of classes*	*No. of schools*
Grammar	4	1	13	18	6	6	12
Comprehensive	2	1	1	3	2	9	11
Secondary Modern	9	5	0	9	20	10	30

TABLE A2: *Number of boys and girls of each social class in streamed and non-streamed grammar, comprehensive and secondary modern schools*

SOCIAL CLASS		NON-STREAMED				STREAMED			
		12	3	45	Total	12	3	45	Total
BOYS	Grammar	(32) 55%	(18) 31%	(8) 14%	(58) 100%	(36) 54%	(21) 32%	(9) 14%	(66) 100%
	Comprehensive	(8) 22%	(14) 39%	(14) 39%	(36) 100%	(29) 18%	(58) 37%	(71) 45%	(158) 100%
	Secondary Modern	(15) 9%	(53) 31%	(101) 60%	(169) 100%	(52) 14%	(178) 48%	(137) 37%	(367) 100%
	No. of pupils	55 21%	85 32%	123 47%	263 100%	117 20%	257 43%	217 37%	591 100%
GIRLS	Grammar	(54) 51%	(38) 36%	(14) 13%	(106) 100%	(12) 38%	(11) 34%	(9) 28%	(32) 100%
	Comprehensive	(4) 15%	(14) 52%	(9) 33%	(27) 100%	(20) 11%	(67) 38%	(89) 51%	(176) 100%
	Secondary Modern	(9) 7%	(54) 39%	(74) 54%	(137) 100%	(57) 15%	(159) 41%	(168) 44%	(384) 100%
	No. of pupils	67 25%	106 39%	97 36%	270 100%	89 15%	237 40%	266 45%	592 100%
BOYS AND GIRLS	Grammar	(86) 53%	(56) 34%	(22) 13%	(164) 100%	(48) 49%	(32) 33%	(18) 18%	(98) 100%
	Comprehensive	(12) 19%	(28) 44%	(23) 37%	(63) 100%	(49) 15%	(125) 37%	(160) 48%	(334) 100%
	Secondary Modern	(24) 8%	(107) 35%	(175) 57%	(306) 100%	(109) 15%	(337) 45%	(305) 40%	(751) 100%
	No. of pupils	122 23%	191 36%	220 41%	533 100%	206 17%	494 42%	483 41%	1,183 100%

APPENDIX THREE

Instruments used in the Follow-up Study

Achievement and ability tests

Maths Test FG

This test, which contained 55 items, was designed to measure the pupil's knowledge and understanding of mathematical concepts, and placed less emphasis than more conventional tests on computational skills. The maximum time allowance was 60 minutes, although strictly speaking it was an untimed test, as most pupils finished within 50 minutes. (See Table A3).

English Test SF3

This test contained 51 items, most of which were designed to test comprehension and vocabulary, but it also included a section on punctuation. As with the Mathematics test, ample time was allowed; a maximum of 60 minutes was permitted, although most pupils finished within 50 minutes. (See Table A3).

Secondary Verbal Test 1

This test was designed to assess the verbal reasoning ability of secondary school pupils aged from 11 to 13½ years. The test contained 90 items and the time allowed was 40 minutes. (See Table A3).

TABLE A3: *Test reliabilities (calculated by the Kuder-Richardson Formula 21)*

TEST	RELIABILITY	RELIABILITY SAMPLE SIZE
Maths FG	·950	1,579
English SF3	·926	1,563
Secondary Verbal 1	·969	1,566

79

Divergent thinking test

Free Writing SF4

This test was very similar in content to those constructed for the earlier streaming study, being likewise based on material devised in the United States by E. P. Torrance and J. P. Guilford.

The items were deliberately designed to present the child with an unfamiliar frame of reference—for example:

'Write down all the problems that man might meet if he wanted to live at the bottom of the sea.'

Another type of question asked the child to think of as many unusual uses as possible for everyday objects, such as a ball of string.

Far from demanding the single, correct answer characteristic of more conventional test questions, children were asked to think of as many, varied responses as possible within the time limits permitted. Each item on the test was strictly timed, the allowance in most cases being two minutes.

The tests were marked for fluency, flexibility and originality of ideas, these being three of the factors scored in Torrance's (1962) Minnesota Tests of Creative Thinking.

Fluency

The fluency score was obtained by adding up the total number of relevant responses to each item (one mark was awarded for each). A response was considered irrelevant if it bore no relation to the situation presented by the question.

Flexibility

The flexibility score was obtained by counting the total number of *categories* into which responses to each item fell, e.g. item 1 asked children to list 'things that are yellow or could be yellow'. The responses 'daffodil, primrose and tulip' would all come under the category 'flowers'. One mark was awarded for each category used, so these three responses would gain one mark.

Originality

Each response obtained an 'originality' score of 0 1, or 2, based on its frequency of occurence in a sample of 400 scripts.

The marks were awarded as follows:

given by five per cent or more of the sample	$=0$
given by two per cent—4·99 per cent of the sample	$=1$
given by less than two per cent of the sample	$=2$

Appendix Three

A marking key was prepared in which all the accepted responses found in the 400 script sample were listed, item by item, and sub-divided into categories. This was done by three independent judges. The originality score for each response was given alongside the response in the marking key. While this key contained a very full list of responses, it could not be expected to be exhaustive. A certain amount of discretion had to be employed in interpreting responses, and where queries arose these were discussed by markers and members of the research team.

The following inter-item correlations were calculated on the results of a trial run of the test:

TABLE A4: *Inter-correlations of items (phi-coefficient)*

(1) *Fluency (number of responses given)*

		1	2	3	4	5
things that are yellow	1	—	0·32	0·34	0·23	0·18
uses of a barrel	2	0·32	—	0·48	0·45	0·36
uses of a ball of string	3	0·34	0·48	—	0·38	0·38
object synthesis	4	0·23	0·23	0·45	—	0·23
living below the sea	5	0·18	0·36	0·38	0·23	—

(2) *Flexibility (number of categories into which responses fall)*

	1	2	3	4	5
Item 1	—	0·31	0·19	0·29	0·21
2	0·31	—	0·39	0·34	0·34
3	0·19	0·39	—	0·29	0·44
4	0·29	0·34	0·29	—	0·27
5	0·21	0·34	0·44	0·27	—

(3) *Fluency and Flexibility correlations*

Item 1	$\emptyset=0\cdot37$
2	$\emptyset=0\cdot67$
3	$\emptyset=0\cdot69$
4	$\emptyset=0\cdot73$
5	$\emptyset=0\cdot77$

81

F

Participation questionnaire

This questionnaire was designed to obtain information on all the extra-curricular activities in which pupils had taken part at any time during their second year in secondary school.

The activities listed on the questionnaire included all those mentioned in the junior school study with the exception of prefects (this was inapplicable), plus a number of clubs etc. known to be popular in secondary schools. Open-ended questions were also included so that pupils could add any activities not listed.

Heads were asked to confirm that all activities mentioned by pupils in their school were in fact available.

Each pupil's level of participation was calculated as a ratio score as follows:

$$\frac{\text{Number of activities in which pupil had taken part}}{\text{Total number of activities available in school}} \times 100\%$$

Aspirations questionnaire

This pre-coded questionnaire was designed to obtain information on pupils' desired and expected leaving age, hopes for further training, and 'ideal' and 'expected' occupation.

Teachers administering the questionnaire were asked to ensure that each pupil understood the distinction between questions asking about 'desired' and 'expected' leaving age and 'ideal' and 'expected' occupation.

Pupil assessment—questionnaire SF5

This document contained all the information which was collected for each pupil during the follow-up study. In addition to test scores it contained ratings by teachers of pupils' ability and achievement and certain behaviour characteristics.

(1) *Teacher Ratings on Ability and Achievement.*

The ratings described below were almost identical to those employed in the earlier study.

(a) *General ability rating.* Second year class teachers were asked to assess each pupil's general ability on a five-point scale:
  (i) superior
  (ii) above average
  (iii) average
  (iv) below average
  (v) dull or backward

(b) *Class position in Mathematics and English.* Second year Maths and English teachers were asked to rate each pupil's performance with respect to his or her class:

    (i) one of the best in Maths (English) (i.e. top 5, 6, or 7 pupils)

    (ii) average in Maths (English)

    (iii) one of the poorest pupils in Maths (English) (i.e. bottom 5, 6 or 7 pupils)

(c) *Attitude to school work.* Class, Maths and English teachers were asked to rate each pupil as:

    (i) a very hard worker

    (ii) a hard worker

    (iii) an average worker

    (iv) a poor or lazy worker.

(2) *Teacher Ratings of Behaviour.*

(a) Several behaviour ratings used in the earlier research were also included in the follow-up study; the design of these was influenced by instruments developed by D. H. Stott (1963) and E. M. Bower (1960).

Class, Maths and English teachers were asked to 'rate each pupil's behaviour as you have observed and experienced it' on the following traits, using a four-point scale:

	4	3	2	1
1. This pupil is disobedient and/or insolent in class	True most of the time (every day or more)	Quite often (at least once a week)	Sometimes (less than once a week)	Seldom or never (less than once a term)
2. This pupil is withdrawn and plays very little with other children		as above		
3. This pupil is a pleasure to have in the class		as above		

(b) Class, Maths and English teachers were also asked to assess pupils' behaviour in other areas, which had not been included in the earlier research. The design of these ratings was influenced by instruments devised by Pauline Sears (1963).

(i) How would you rate this pupil's ability to work independently?

Score: 3—able and willing to organize own work; will get on with a
minimum of direction

2—capable of working independently, but tends to await
directions

1—needs to be told in detail what he/she is expected to do.

(ii) How would you rate this pupil's degree of interest in his/her school work?

Score: 4—seems to genuinely enjoy school work and will do more
than is required

3—shows interest, but less sustained than '4'

2—shows interest only occasionally—rarely does more than
required

1—shows little or no interest—distractable and needs pushing
to achieve a minimum.

(iii) How would you rate this pupil's level of contribution to class discussion?

Score: 4—can be relied upon to contribute

3—quite frequently contributes

2—takes little part in discussion

1—seldom or never participates, or only when specifically
asked.

References

BOWER, E. M. (1960). *Early Identification of Emotionally Handicapped Children in School.* Oxford: Blackwell.

SEARS, P. S. (1963). 'The effect of classroom conditions on the strength of achievement motive and work output of elementary school children', *Co-op. Res. Proj.* No. OE 873. Washington.

STOTT, D. H. (1963). *The Social Adjustment of Children: Manual to the Bristol Social Adjustment Guides* (Rev. ed.). London: University of London Press.

The Statistical Background to the Analysis of Progress of Scores

by Wendy Fader

TWO of the objectives of the Streaming follow-up study are concerned with the pupils' academic progress between the ages of 10+ and 12+. The first of these objectives set out to discover whether academic progress is related to the way in which the primary education of the pupil had been organized—that is by streaming or by non-streaming. A similar set of objectives was concerned with the effects of streaming and non-streaming as a method of organizing secondary schools.

In both cases it was considered important that the standard which had been achieved at the age of 10+ should be taken into account when assessing the 12+ attainment scores. It had been found, when analysing the data from the previous streaming study, that the analysis of co-variance was the most appropriate method of those available. By this means the difference between the average 12+ scores of two groups of pupils can be adjusted for differences between their average 10+ scores. This adjustment can be made only when it is reasonable to assume that the regression of 12+ scores on the 10+ scores is the same in both groups. Tests of this assumption were therefore made prior to all the comparisons which have been reported in Chapter Two. In only one case was the assumption of a common regression relationship found to be untenable, namely in the analysis which compared the progress in mathematics made by boys from social classes 4 and 5 who had been taught in streamed or non-streamed junior schools and who were of below average ability. This particular result must therefore be interpreted with the utmost caution.

The previous streaming research also showed that it would be advisable to group the pupils by social class and ability level and to make a separate analysis of the results recorded for boys and girls.

This procedure was repeated for the follow-up study except when testing for differences between the results which were obtained for pupils from streamed and non-streamed grammar schools. In this case, although the boys and girls were analysed separately, the numbers of pupils were too small to permit separate treatment by social class and ability group.

85

APPENDIX FIVE

Tables

TABLE A5: *Table of initial and final means and final adjusted means*

Boys		N	Initial (10+) Mean	Final (12+) Mean	Final Adjusted Mean	Significance Level
			ABOVE AVERAGE ABILITY			
Social classes 1, 2	Verbal NS	35	112·14	114·29	116·62	—
	S	55	116·55	117·27	117·21	
	English NS	33	108·70	113·91	115·83	—
	S	56	112·82	119·07	118·29	
	Maths/Concept NS	35	115·71	114·43	116·06	—
	S	57	120·32	113·58	113·27	
	Maths/Problem NS	35	110·74	114·43	115·39	—
	S	57	115·42	113·58	113·27	
Social class 3	Verbal NS	38	106·90	106·95	108·22	—
	S	44	107·93	108·59	107·99	
	English NS	42	107·36	108·83	109·34	—
	S	44	108·30	109·48	109·61	
	Maths/Concept NS	37	111·46	112·92	112·73	—
	S	43	114·00	112·70	112·51	
	Maths/Problem NS	37	108·41	112·92	114·29	—
	S	43	108·14	112·70	111·52	
Social classes 4, 5	Verbal NS	27	105·63	105·44	106·34	—
	S	32	108·72	107·09	107·59	
	English NS	25	104·96	107·08	108·18	—
	S	33	107·52	110·24	109·95	
	Maths/Concept NS	26	107·15	108·69	112·04	—
	S	30	110·90	109·27	107·81	
	Maths/Problem NS	25	100·28	109·24	110·36	—
	S	30	107·00	109·27	108·32	

Significance has been indicated by the following convention:
  — = non-significant differences in final adjusted means for streamed and non-streamed schools.

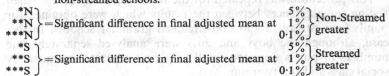

*N
**N   = Significant difference in final adjusted mean at 5% Non-Streamed
***N   1% greater
                                                        0·1%

*S
**S   = Significant difference in final adjusted mean at 5% Streamed
***S   1% greater
                                                        0·1%

TABLE A5—*continued*

Boys			N	Initial (10+) Mean	Final (12+) Mean	Final Adjusted Mean	Signi- ficance Level
				AVERAGE ABILITY			
Social classes 1, 2	Verbal	NS	17	101·47	105·82	103·44	*N
		S	25	100·64	99·16	102·10	
	English	NS	15	100·80	104·40	103·88	—
		S	25	99·48	98·88	99·96	
	Maths/Concept	NS	15	105·13	104·33	108·52	*N
		S	24	108·17	102·00	100·60	
	Maths/Problem	NS	14	100·93	105·36	106·95	**N
		S	24	104·58	102·00	101·15	
Social class 3	Verbal	NS	54	96·93	96·59	97·39	—
		S	53	98·08	97·15	97·79	
	English	NS	47	97·66	98·17	98·03	—
		S	50	98·42	100·08	98·88	
	Maths/Concept	NS	48	102·83	100·29	99·64	—
		S	51	102·57	99·65	98·29	
	Maths/Problem	NS	46	96·61	99·63	99·52	—
		S	51	98·61	99·65	99·19	
Social classes 4, 5	Verbal	NS	54	98·39	97·93	99·04	—
		S	55	98·95	98·80	99·01	
	English	NS	55	97·20	100·35	100·47	—
		S	58	98·10	98·72	98·50	
	Maths/Concept	NS	53	104·11	102·62	103·74	—
		S	57	101·60	100·05	99·27	
	Maths/Problem	NS	52	99·27	103·10	101·56	**N
		S	56	101·05	100·32	101·06	

87

TABLE A5—*continued*

				BELOW AVERAGE ABILITY			
Boys			N	*Initial (10+) Mean*	*Final (12+) Mean*	*Final Adjusted Mean*	*Signi- ficance Level*
	Verbal	NS	6	92·67	95·67	94·72	—
		S	8	86·13	92·13	93·09	
	English	NS	7	84·71	91·29	90·11	—
Social classes		S	10	84·70	88·10	87·47	
1, 2	Maths/Concept	NS	7	95·43	95·71	92·21	—
		S	9	87·22	91·11	94·28	—
	Maths/Problem	NS	7	91·86	95·71	89·87	—
		S	9	86·89	91·11	94·98	
	Verbal	NS	40	90·13	89·73	90·15	—
		S	42	89·86	89·05	89·98	
	English	NS	40	88·68	89·33	89·03	—
Social class		S	48	88·00	87·56	87·83	
3	Maths/Concept	NS	40	96·23	94·78	95·78	—
		S	44	94·02	89·39	90·47	
	Maths/Problem	NS	39	92·13	95·00	94·28	*N
		S	43	91·70	89·88	90·64	
	Verbal	NS	58	86·53	85·48	85·84	—
		S	46	87·07	85·07	85·79	
	English	NS	59	83·63	84·78	84·56	—
Social classes		S	52	83·04	83·15	83·13	
4, 5	Maths/Concept	NS	61	89·97	88·90	87·42	*N
		S	50	86·80	83·18	84·14	
	Maths/Problem	NS	58	89·19	88·78	87·96	*N
		S	50	85·76	83·18	84·16	

Table A5—*continued*

				ABOVE AVERAGE ABILITY		
Girls			*N*	*Initial (10+) Mean*	*Final (12+) Mean*	*Final Adjusted Mean*	*Signi-ficance Level*
Social classes 1, 2	Verbal	NS	37	112·46	113·32	115·90	—
		S	38	120·32	118·66	118·36	
	English	NS	36	114·89	114·67	115·49	—
		S	39	115·82	118·41	118·48	
	Maths/Concept	NS	36	114·11	112·69	113·67	—
		S	36	118·72	115·83	115·49	
	Maths/Problem	NS	34	109·06	112·59	114·83	—
		S	36	111·17	115·83	114·58	
Social class 3	Verbal	NS	48	113·27	112·83	113·41	—
		S	60	112·92	112·38	113·29	
	English	NS	50	111·46	113·76	113·28	—
		S	65	111·28	112·03	111·99	
	Maths/Concept	NS	50	113·46	110·92	111·51	—
		S	64	112·75	109·84	110·47	
	Maths/Problem	NS	48	107·96	111·31	110·70	—
		S	64	107·23	109·84	110·75	
Social classes 4, 5	Verbal	NS	31	111·39	109·10	110·25	—
		S	39	112·18	110·54	110·27	
	English	NS	31	111·10	111·32	111·13	—
		S	38	110·74	112·68	112·57	
	Maths/Concept	NS	31	110·61	109·16	110·66	—
		S	38	113·18	108·82	108·04	
	Maths/Problem	NS	31	104·39	109·16	110·28	—
		S	37	108·27	108·97	107·68	

TABLE A5—*continued*

				AVERAGE ABILITY			
GIRLS			N	Initial (10+) Mean	Final (12+) Mean	Final Adjusted Mean	Signi-ficance Level
	Verbal	NS	23	103·52	106·35	104·92	—
		S	20	103·40	101·45	104·09	
	English	NS	25	105·44	107·32	105·14	—
Social classes		S	23	102·48	104·91	105·49	
1, 2	Maths/Concept	NS	26	107·00	105·15	103·89	—
		S	22	104·46	99·96	99·83	
	Maths/Problem	NS	25	99·56	104·80	103·60	—
		S	22	99·41	99·96	100·65	
	Verbal	NS	42	99·79	100·36	101·36	—
		S	59	105·81	102·05	102·17	
	English	NS	41	102·85	98·44	100·07	—
Social class		S	54	103·32	103·24	103·15	
3	Maths/Concept	NS	44	100·86	99·14	99·97	—
		S	52	102·64	99·71	98·85	
	Maths/Problem	NS	43	96·35	99·35	100·24	—
		S	52	98·27	99·71	98·84	
	Verbal	NS	43	99·67	96·40	98·55	—
		S	44	102·39	100·05	99·33	
	English	NS	39	99·64	98·69	100·09	—
Social classes		S	45	101·69	101·07	99·83	
4, 5	Maths/Concept	NS	41	99·56	96·27	98·43	—
		S	47	103·13	99·79	98·01	
	Maths/Problem	NS	39	95·13	96·36	97·94	—
		S	46	98·74	99·65	98·94	

Appendix Five

TABLE A5—*continued*

GIRLS			N	Initial (10+) Mean	Final (12+) Mean	Final Adjusted Mean	Signi-ficance Level
	Verbal	NS	5	101·80	92·20	92·20	—
		S	8	95·00	91·75	92·25	
	English	NS	3	96·00	94·67	94·72	—
Social classes		S	8	94·50	92·25	91·98	
1, 2	Maths/Concept	NS	4	101·00	96·50	91·48	—
		S	9	95·78	95·33	95·73	
	Maths/Problem	NS	4	95·25	96·50	92·36	—
		S	9	89·00	95·33	95·29	
	Verbal	NS	38	91·08	89·95	90·62	—
		S	45	93·60	90·60	91·26	
	English	NS	37	90·70	91·03	90·73	—
Social class		S	49	90·71	88·71	89·31	
3	Maths/Concept	NS	39	90·21	90·46	91·70	
		S	51	91·88	89·14	88·86	
	Maths/Problem	NS	39	86·72	90·46	91·31	—
		S	49	88·96	89·39	88·68	
	Verbal	NS	68	89·10	87·59	88·22	—
		S	63	89·18	87·40	88·02	
	English	NS	87	87·67	86·93	86·73	—
Social classes		S	63	88·76	86·18	85·39	
4, 5	Maths/Concept	NS	79	90·52	87·70	87·17	
		S	66	88·82	86·23	85·23	
	Maths/Problem	NS	79	85·43	87·70	86·58	—
		S	64	87·28	86·44	86·57	

BELOW AVERAGE ABILITY

91

TABLE A6: *Table of initial means, final means and final adjusted means*

SECONDARY MODERN

Boys			N	ABOVE AVERAGE & AVERAGE ABILITY			
				Initial (10+) Mean	Final (12+) Mean	Final Adjusted Mean	Significance Level
	Verbal	NS	37	98·81	96·00	98·67	**S
		S	125	100·02	100·25	100·17	
	English	NS	36	99·36	100·14	100·58	—
Social classes		S	119	100·63	102·11	101·52	
1, 2, 3	Maths/Concept	NS	37	105·57	103·60	102·57	—
		S	118	104·92	101·72	101·38	
	Maths/Problem	NS	38	100·00	102·97	103·10	—
		S	124	101·00	101·65	101·05	
	Verbal	NS	38	98·37	96·53	98·61	—
		S	71	100·11	99·85	99·81	
	English	NS	38	99·26	99·18	99·39	—
Social classes		S	74	99·58	101·41	101·65	
4, 5	Maths/Concept	NS	37	104·43	100·46	99·19	—
		S	71	101·39	99·37	100·32	
	Maths/Problem	NS	39	100·72	101·08	100·39	—
		S	73	98·73	100·14	100·79	

Boys			N	BELOW AVERAGE ABILITY			
				Initial (10+) Mean	Final (12+) Mean	Final Adjusted Mean	Significance Level
	Verbal	NS	18	91·11	92·39	91·06	*N
		S	54	88·76	87·54	88·76	
	English	NS	18	89·72	90·11	88·54	—
Social classes		S	61	87·49	87·43	87·89	
1, 2, 3	Maths/Concept	NS	18	98·28	97·61	95·12	*N
		S	57	92·53	87·35	88·60	
	Maths/Problem	NS	19	95·74	98·79	95·87	*N
		S	60	90·08	88·12	89·49	
	Verbal	NS	37	85·30	83·19	85·10	—
		S	40	87·83	87·80	86·91	
	English	NS	38	84·71	84·29	84·88	—
Social classes		S	42	86·07	85·74	84·80	
4, 5	Maths/Concept	NS	40	90·25	87·33	87·00	—
		S	42	89·74	87·14	87·16	
	Maths/Problem	NS	39	89·41	87·15	86·96	—
		S	43	89·37	86·79	86·56	

TABLE A6—*continued*

SECONDARY MODERN

				ABOVE AVERAGE & AVERAGE ABILITY			
				Initial (10+)	*Final* (12+)	*Final Adjusted*	*Signi-ficance*
GIRLS			N	*Mean*	*Mean*	*Mean*	*Level*
	Verbal	NS	33	102·33	100·39	103·07	—
		S	135	105·92	104·79	104·96	
	English	NS	31	104·19	102·42	103·63	—
Social classes		S	140	105·43	106·39	105·98	
1, 2, 3	Maths/Concept	NS	35	102·97	100·14	101·29	—
		S	134	104·92	101·82	101·50	
	Maths/Problem	NS	33	97·12	100·39	101·51	—
		S	137	99·18	101·65	101·40	
	Verbal	NS	24	100·38	96·67	99·84	—
		S	74	104·22	101·46	101·20	
	English	NS	24	102·63	100·96	101·60	—
Social classes		S	73	103·56	104·10	103·83	
4, 5	Maths/Concept	NS	24	102·83	100·04	100·24	—
		S	72	102·44	98·76	98·97	
	Maths/Problem	NS	23	99·83	100·65	100·08	—
		S	75	97·57	98·53	98·96	

				BELOW AVERAGE ABILITY			
				Initial (10+)	*Final* (12+)	*Final Adjusted*	*Signi-ficance*
GIRLS			N	*Mean*	*Mean*	*Mean*	*Level*
	Verbal	NS	13	91·69	90·39	90·37	—
		S	53	93·19	90·49	90·99	
	English	NS	11	89·55	90·46	91·14	—
Social classes		S	55	92·06	89·47	89·45	
1, 2, 3	Maths/Concept	NS	15	87·13	89·60	92·84	—
		S	57	93·02	90·44	89·35	
	Maths/Problem	NS	15	86·67	89·60	90·83	—
		S	57	89·35	90·49	89·98	
	Verbal	NS	28	90·04	86·14	87·04	—
		S	71	88·68	86·62	87·01	
	English	NS	39	87·36	84·59	84·26	—
Social classes		S	77	87·60	85·68	85·08	
4, 5	Maths/Concept	NS	35	91·14	85·77	83·23	—
		S	76	87·66	85·08	85·35	
	Maths/Problem	NS	37	86·49	84·70	83·31	—
		S	76	85·04	85·05	84·87	

TABLE A6—*continued*

GRAMMAR

Boys		N	Initial (10+) Mean	Final (12+) Mean	Final Adjusted Mean	Significance Level
Verbal	NS	51	116·47	116·84	118·03	—
	S	58	116·40	117·55	118·05	
English	NS	48	112·79	116·67	117·02	—
	S	59	113·42	116·24	116·12	
Maths/Concept	NS	49	119·37	113·53	113·70	—
	S	58	121·90	119·53	119·61	
Maths/Problem	NS	51	115·94	114·90	115·07	—
	S	60	115·52	119·57	119·69	

Girls		N	Initial (10+) Mean	Final (12+) Mean	Final Adjusted Mean	Significance Level
Verbal	NS	96	119·03	120·08	120·98	*N
	S	28	119·68	117·46	119·14	
English	NS	95	116·85	118·23	118·57	—
	S	30	116·30	116·50	117·09	
Maths/Concept	NS	97	119·93	117·50	117·65	—
	S	29	117·59	115·69	116·85	
Maths/Problem	NS	97	114·06	117·66	118·38	—
	S	30	116·83	115·80	115·23	

TABLE A7: *Change of score between 10+ and 12+ of pupils from streamed and non-streamed junior schools on the divergent thinking test*

	NON-STREAMED				STREAMED			
	No. of pupils			Sign test	No. of pupils			Sign test
	+	=	—		+	=	—	
Fluency	90	104	114	NS	107	137	133	NS
Flexibility	81	108	119	** (2·62)	103	144	130	NS
Originality	101	78	129	NS	122	107	148	NS

+obtained higher score   *=significant at 5% level
—obtained lower score   **=significant at 1% level
=obtained same score   NS=non-significant.

TABLE A8: *Number of pupils from streamed and non-streamed junior schools scoring in each 'band' of score on the divergent thinking test at 12+*

	FLUENCY				FLEXIBILITY				ORIGINALITY			
	Social Class 123		Social Class 45		Social Class 123		Social Class 45		Social Class 123		Social Class 45	
	Non-streamed	Streamed	Non-streamed	Streamed	Non-streamed	Streamed	Non-streamed	Streamed	Non-streamed	Streamed	Non-streamed	Streamed
Low	14%	21%	24%	27%	16%	23%	30%	36%	16%	23%	25%	27%
‖	20%	24%	23%	25%	18%	23%	20%	18%	18%	28%	27%	26%
∨	20%	20%	20%	16%	18%	16%	15%	16%	20%	15%	18%	17%
	22%	15%	18%	21%	25%	22%	19%	13%	24%	21%	17%	20%
High	24%	20%	15%	11%	23%	16%	16%	12%	22%	13%	13%	10%
Total	100%	100%	100%	100%	100%	100%	100%	100%	100%	100%	100%	100%
No. of pupils	183	248	125	129	183	248	125	129	183	248	125	129
Chi-square test	Non-significant		Non-significant		Non-significant		Non-significant		$\chi^2 = 14 \cdot 77$ df$=4$, P$<0 \cdot 01$		Non-significant	

TABLE A9: *Change of score between 10+ and 12+ of pupils in streamed and non-streamed secondary schools on the divergent thinking test*

		NON-STREAMED				STREAMED			
		No. of pupils			Sign test	No. of pupils			Sign test
		+	=	—		+	=	—	
FLUENCY	Secondary Modern	27	37	45	*(2·00)	76	99	108	*(2·29)
	Comprehensive	11	13	10	NS	44	47	36	NS
	Grammar	27	32	27	NS	12	13	21	NS
	All Schools	65	82	82	NS	132	159	165	NS
FLEXIBILITY	Secondary Modern	27	34	48	*(2·31)	75	105	103	*(2·02)
	Comprehensive	9	14	11	NS	39	48	40	NS
	Grammar	24	37	25	NS	10	14	22	†NS
	All Schools	60	85	84	NS	124	167	165	*(2·35)
ORIGINALITY	Secondary Modern	27	26	56	**(3·07)	91	75	117	NS
	Comprehensive	10	14	10	NS	52	31	44	NS
	Grammar	32	29	25	NS	11	10	25	*(2·17)
	All Schools	69	69	91	NS	154	116	186	NS

+obtained higher score
—obtained lower score
=obtained same score

 *=significant at 5% level
**=significant at 1% level
NS=non-significant
 †=approached significance.

TABLE A10: *Number of pupils from streamed and non-streamed secondary schools scoring in each 'band' of score on the divergent thinking test at 12+*

FLUENCY

	Secondary Modern		Comprehensive		Grammar	
	NS*	S**	NS	S	NS	S
Low	28%	25%	26%	19%	6%	9%
	24%	24%	21%	21%	21%	24%
	18%	19%	17%	20%	14%	34%
	16%	19%	21%	21%	18%	9%
High	14%	13%	15%	19%	41%	24%
Total	100%	100%	100%	100%	100%	100%
No. of pupils	109	283	34	127	86	46
Chi-square test	Non-significant		Non-significant		$\chi^2 = 10.98$ $P < 0.05$	

FLEXIBILITY

	Secondary Modern		Comprehensive		Grammar	
	NS	S	NS	S	NS	S
Low	32%	30%	32%	25%	5%	7%
	20%	24%	18%	17%	16%	17%
	18%	12%	15%	18%	20%	28%
	18%	24%	17%	17%	25%	28%
High	12%	10%	18%	23%	34%	20%
Total	100%	100%	100%	100%	100%	100%
No. of pupils	109	283	34	127	86	46
Chi-square test	Non-significant		Non-significant		Non-significant	

ORIGINALITY

	Secondary Modern		Comprehensive		Grammar	
	NS	S	NS	S	NS	S
Low	30%	24%	35%	21%	9%	11%
	28%	29%	20%	22%	9%	24%
	16%	19%	6%	24%	12%	24%
	17%	17%	18%	22%	32%	28%
High	9%	11%	21%	11%	38%	13%
Total	100%	100%	100%	100%	100%	100%
No. of pupils	109	283	34	127	86	46
Chi-square test	Non-significant		Non-significant		$\chi^2 = 13.97$ $P < 0.01$	

*NS = non-streamed

**S = streamed

G

TABLE A11: *Number of pupils from streamed and non-streamed junior schools obtaining higher and lower scores at 12+ on the 'academic self-image' scale*

		NON-STREAMED				STREAMED			
		No. of pupils			Sign	No. of pupils			Sign
		+	=	—	test	+	=	—	test
BOYS	Above average	18	6	15	NS	25	12	23	NS
	Average	22	5	23	NS	19	13	18	NS
	Below average	32	9	6	***	22	13	20	NS
GIRLS	Above average	11	15	24	*	22	22	34	NS
	Average	15	13	13	NS	22	13	15	NS
	Below average	15	4	7	*	12	16	18	NS

TABLE A12: *Number of pupils from grammar, comprehensive and secondary modern schools obtaining higher and lower scores at 12+ on the 'academic self-image' scale*

	GRAMMAR				COMPREHENSIVE				SECONDARY MODERN				ALL SCHOOLS			
	No. of pupils			Sign	No. of pupils			Sign	No. of pupils			Sign	No. of pupils			Sign
	+	=	—	test	+	=	—	test	+	=	—	test	+	=	—	test
Boys	14	16	29	*	46	13	26	*	87	30	52	**	147	59	107	*
Girls	13	24	42	***	33	21	24	NS	57	41	58	NS	103	86	124	NS

+obtained higher score at 12+ than at 10+ (more favourable self-image)
—obtained lower score at 12+ than at 10+
=obtained same score at 12+ as at 10+.

*=significant at 5% level
**=significant at 1% level
***=significant at 0·1% level
NS=non-significant.

Note: The slight discrepancy in the total number of pupils involved in the junior and secondary school analyses is due to the fact that a few pupils had no 9+ English score, which was used to define ability level.

TABLE A13: *Number of pupils from streamed and non-streamed junior schools obtaining higher and lower scores at 12+ on the 'relationship with teacher' scale*

		NON-STREAMED				STREAMED			
		No. of pupils			Sign	No. of pupils			Sign
		+	=	—	test	+	=	—	test
BOYS	Above average	14	11	14	NS	29	18	13	*
	Average	13	16	21	NS	21	11	18	NS
	Below average	18	11	18	NS	20	16	19	NS
GIRLS	Above average	12	11	27	*	27	20	31	NS
	Average	13	17	11	NS	19	15	26	NS
	Below average	12	6	8	NS	12	18	16	NS

TABLE A14: *Number of pupils from grammar, comprehensive and secondary modern schools obtaining higher and lower scores at 12+ on the 'relationship with teacher' scale*

	GRAMMAR				COMPREHENSIVE				SECONDARY MODERN				ALL SCHOOLS			
	No. of pupils			Sign	No. of pupils			Sign	No. of pupils			Sign	No. of pupils			Sign
	+	=	—	test	+	=	—	test	+	=	—	test	+	=	—	test
Boys	24	15	20	NS	36	27	22	NS	59	46	64	NS	119	88	106	NS
Girls	20	21	38	*	26	31	21	NS	52	42	62	NS	98	94	121	NS

+obtained higher score at 12+ than at 10+ (perceived better relationship)
—obtained lower score at 12+ than at 10+
=obtained same score at 12+ as at 10+

*=significant at 5% level
NS=non-significant.

TABLE A15: *Number of pupils from streamed and non-streamed junior schools obtaining higher and lower scores at 12+ on the 'anxiety' scale*

| | | NON-STREAMED | | | | STREAMED | | | |
| | | No. of pupils | | | Sign | No. of pupils | | | Sign |
		+	=	—	test	+	=	—	test
	Above average	11	4	24	*	26	13	21	NS
BOYS	Average	23	14	13	NS	20	14	16	NS
	Below average	28	12	7	***	18	12	25	NS
	Above average	12	10	28	*	23	17	38	NS
GIRLS	Average	13	12	16	NS	22	9	29	NS
	Below average	11	7	8	NS	11	16	19	NS

TABLE A16: *Number of pupils from grammar, comprehensive and secondary modern schools obtaining higher and lower scores at 12+ on the 'anxiety' scale*

| | GRAMMAR | | | | COMPREHENSIVE | | | | SECONDARY MODERN | | | | ALL SCHOOLS | | | |
| | No. of pupils | | | Sign | No. of pupils | | | Sign | No. of pupils | | | Sign | No. of pupils | | | Sign |
	+	=	—	test	+	=	—	test	+	=	—	test	+	=	—	test
Boys	18	12	29	NS	35	20	30	NS	78	39	52	*	131	71	111	NS
Girls	19	16	44	**	25	21	32	NS	52	37	67	NS	96	74	143	**

+obtained higher score at 12+ than at 10+ (less anxious)
—obtained lower score at 12+ than at 10+
=obtained same score at 12+ as at 10+

*=significant at 5% level
**=significant at 1% level
***=significant at 0·1% level
NS=non-significant.

100

Appendix Five

TABLE A17: *Number of pupils from streamed and non-streamed junior schools obtaining higher and lower scores at 12+ on the 'social adjustment' scale*

		NON-STREAMED				STREAMED			
		No. of pupils			Sign	No. of pupils			Sign
		+	=	−	test	+	=	−	test
BOYS	Above average	16	13	10	NS	31	22	7	***
	Average	12	17	21	NS	25	16	9	*
	Below average	23	11	13	NS	21	17	17	NS
GIRLS	Above average	26	17	7	**	30	31	17	NS
	Average	29	7	5	***	24	18	18	NS
	Below average	12	10	4	*	22	11	13	NS

TABLE A18: *Number of pupils from grammar, comprehensive and secondary modern schools obtaining higher and lower scores at 12+ on the 'social adjustment' scale*

	GRAMMAR				COMPREHENSIVE				SECONDARY MODERN				ALL SCHOOLS			
	No. of pupils			Sign	No. of pupils			Sign	No. of pupils			Sign	No. of pupils			Sign
	+	=	−	test	+	=	−	test	+	=	−	test	+	=	−	test
Boys	26	22	11	*	42	24	19	**	68	52	49	NS	136	98	79	***
Girls	32	32	15	*	40	21	17	**	75	45	36	***	147	98	68	***

+obtained higher score at 12+ than at 10+ (more socially adjusted)
—obtained lower score at 12+ than at 10+
=obtained same score at 12+ as at 10+

*=significant at 5% level
**=significant at 1% level
***=significant at 0·1% level
NS=non-significant.

101

TABLE A19: *Number of pupils from streamed and non-streamed junior schools obtaining higher and lower scores at 12+ on the 'attitude to school' scale*

| | | NON-STREAMED | | | | STREAMED | | | |
| | | No. of pupils | | | Sign | No. of pupils | | | Sign |
		+	=	—	test	+	=	—	test
BOYS	Above average	17	12	10	NS	17	17	26	NS
	Average	14	9	27	NS	17	11	22	NS
	Below average	25	8	14	NS	15	18	22	NS
GIRLS	Above average	9	17	24	*	20	22	36	*
	Average	13	15	13	NS	12	8	40	***
	Below average	9	6	11	NS	13	15	18	NS

TABLE A20: *Number of pupils from grammar, comprehensive and secondary modern schools obtaining higher and lower scores at 12+ on the 'attitude to school' scale*

| | GRAMMAR | | | | COMPREHENSIVE | | | | SECONDARY MODERN | | | | ALL SCHOOLS | | | |
| | No. of pupils | | | Sign | No. of pupils | | | Sign | No. of pupils | | | Sign | No. of pupils | | | Sign |
	+	=	—	test	+	=	—	test	+	=	—	test	+	=	—	test
Boys	17	17	25	NS	27	19	39	NS	65	42	62	NS	109	78	126	NS
Girls	13	23	43	***	27	22	29	NS	40	40	76	**	80	85	148	***

+ obtained higher score at 12+ than at 10+ (more favourable attitude)
— obtained lower score at 12+ than at 10+
= obtained same score at 12+ as at 10+

* = significant at 5 % level
** = significant at 1 % level
*** = significant at 0·1 % level
NS = non-significant.

TABLE A21: *Number of pupils from streamed and non-streamed junior schools obtaining higher and lower scores at 12+ on the 'attitude to class' scale*

		NON-STREAMED				STREAMED			
		No. of pupils			*Sign*	*No. of pupils*			*Sign*
		+	=	−	*test*	+	=	−	*test*
BOYS	Above average	14	13	12	NS	16	18	26	NS
	Average	12	10	28	*	19	11	20	NS
	Below average	10	4	33	***	15	16	24	NS
GIRLS	Above average	13	19	18	NS	11	37	30	**
	Average	8	17	16	*	15	20	25	NS
	Below average	9	1	16	*	13	10	23	NS

TABLE A22: *Number of pupils from grammar, comprehensive and secondary modern schools obtaining higher and lower scores at 12+ on the 'attitude to class' scale*

	GRAMMAR				COMPREHENSIVE				SECONDARY MODERN				ALL SCHOOLS			
	No. of pupils			*Sign*	*No. of pupils*			*Sign*	*No. of pupils*			*Sign*	*No. of pupils*			*Sign*
	+	=	−	*test*	+	=	−	*test*	+	=	−	*test*	+	=	−	*test*
Boys	14	20	25	NS	18	21	46	***	55	34	80	*	87	75	151	***
Girls	16	32	31	*	23	23	32	NS	34	54	68	***	72	109	131	***

+obtained higher score at 12+ than at 10+ (More favourable attitude)
—obtained lower score at 12+ than at 10+
=obtained same score at 12+ as at 10+

*=significant at 5% level
**=significant at 1% level
***=significant at 0·1% level
NS=non-significant.

TABLE A23: *Number of pupils from streamed and non-streamed junior schools obtaining higher and lower scores at 12+ on the 'other image of class' scale*

		NON-STREAMED				STREAMED			
		No. of pupils			Sign	No. of pupils			Sign
		+	=	−	test	+	=	−	test
	Above average	11	13	15	NS	18	16	26	NS
BOYS	Average	16	16	18	NS	16	10	24	NS
	Below average	13	12	22	NS	19	13	23	NS
	Above average	21	18	11	NS	24	25	29	NS
GIRLS	Average	13	13	15	NS	29	15	16	NS
	Below average	7	5	14	*	10	16	20	NS

TABLE A24: *Number of pupils from grammar, comprehensive and secondary modern schools obtaining higher and lower scores at 12+ on the 'other image of class' scale*

	GRAMMAR				COMPREHENSIVE				SECONDARY MODERN				ALL SCHOOLS			
	No. of pupils			Sign	No. of pupils			Sign	No. of pupils			Sign	No. of pupils			Sign
	+	=	−	test	+	=	−	test	+	=	−	test	+	=	−	test
Boys	10	20	29	**	27	22	36	NS	61	40	68	NS	98	82	133	*
Girls	21	28	30	NS	27	25	26	NS	61	43	52	NS	109	96	108	NS

+obtained higher score at 12+ than at 10+ (more favourable 'other image')
−obtained lower score at 12+ than at 10+
=obtained same score at 12+ as at 10+

*=significant at 5% level
**=significant at 1% level
***=significant at 0·1% level
NS=non-significant.

TABLE A25: *Number of pupils from streamed and non-streamed junior schools obtaining higher and lower scores at 12+ on the 'importance of doing well' scale*

		NON-STREAMED				STREAMED			
		No. of pupils			*Sign*	*No. of pupils*			*Sign*
		+	=	—	*test*	+	=	—	*test*
	Above average	10	11	18	NS	14	21	25	NS
BOYS	Average	11	8	31	**	14	14	22	NS
	Below average	15	7	25	NS	18	12	25	NS
	Above average	7	13	30	***	16	25	37	**
GIRLS	Average	14	4	23	NS	20	12	28	NS
	Below average	5	2	19	**	16	8	22	NS

TABLE A26: *Number of pupils from grammar, comprehensive and secondary modern schools obtaining higher and lower scores at 12+ on the 'importance of doing well' scale*

	GRAMMAR				COMPREHENSIVE				SECONDARY MODERN				ALL SCHOOLS			
	No. of pupils			*Sign*	*No. of pupils*			*Sign*	*No. of pupils*			*Sign*	*No. of pupils*			*Sign*
	+	=	—	*test*	+	=	—	*test*	+	=	—	*test*	+	=	—	*test*
Boys	10	26	23	*	25	21	39	NS	52	29	88	**	87	76	150	***
Girls	11	24	44	***	30	11	37	NS	42	31	83	***	83	66	164	***

+obtained higher score at 12+ than at 10+ (more important to do well)
—obtained lower score at 12+ than at 10+
=obtained same score at 12+ as at 10+

  *=significant at 5% level
 **=significant at 1% level
***=significant at 0·1% level
 NS=non-significant.

TABLE A27: *Number of pupils in top, middle and bottom streams in secondary schools obtaining higher and lower scores at 12+ on the 'attitude to class' scale*

	No. of pupils			Sign test
	+	=	−	
Top stream	34	40	48	NS
Middle stream	40	34	62	*
Bottom stream	30	29	53	*

TABLE A28: *Number of pupils in top, middle and bottom streams in secondary schools obtaining higher and lower scores at 12+ on the 'other image' scale*

	No. of pupils			Sign test
	+	=	−	
Top stream	55	33	34	*
Middle stream	47	35	54	NS
Bottom stream	26	30	56	**

*=significant at 5% level
**=significant at 1% level
NS=non-significant.

106

TABLE A29: *Comparison of the numbers of 'low', 'medium' and 'high' participants in streamed and non-streamed secondary schools*

Participation Ratio Scores	SECONDARY MODERN				COMPREHENSIVE				GRAMMAR			
	Boys		Girls		Boys		Girls		Boys		Girls	
	Non-streamed	Streamed	Non-streamed	Streamed	Non-streamed	Streamed	Non-streamed	Streamed	Non-streamed	Streamed	Non-streamed	Streamed
Low	36%	42%	41%	33%	53%	51%	28%	50%	39%	42%	27%	55%
Medium	34%	34%	23%	33%	28%	37%	12%	36%	27%	36%	32%	17%
High	30%	24%	36%	34%	19%	12%	60%	14%	34%	22%	41%	28%
Total	100%	100%	100%	100%	100%	100%	100%	100%	100%	100%	100%	100%
No. of pupils	151	334	120	356	32	150	25	155	56	53	102	29
Chi-square test	Not significant		Not significant		Not significant		$\chi^2=29{\cdot}32$, $P<0{\cdot}001$		Not significant		$\chi^2=8{\cdot}52$, $P<0{\cdot}05$	

Participation Ratio Scores	ALL SCHOOLS			
	Boys		Girls	
	Non-streamed	Streamed	Non-streamed	Streamed
Low	39%	44%	34%	39%
Medium	31%	35%	26%	33%
High	30%	21%	40%	28%
Total	100%	100%	100%	100%
No. of pupils	239	537	247	540
Chi-square test	$\chi^2=6{\cdot}89$, $P<0{\cdot}05$		$\chi^2=12{\cdot}80$, $0<0{\cdot}01$	

TABLE A30: *Comparison of the participation ratio scores of pupils at the top or bottom of their class† in streamed and non-streamed secondary schools*

BOYS

CLASS POSITION:	TOP		BOTTOM	
Participation Ratio Score	Non-Streamed	Streamed	Non-Streamed	Streamed
Low	43%	40%	31%	51%
Medium	31%	32%	41%	36%
High	26%	28%	28%	13%
Total	100%	100%	100%	100%
No. of pupils	51	100	54	116
Chi-square test	Non-significant		$\chi^2 = 7 \cdot 89$, $P < 0 \cdot 05$	

GIRLS

CLASS POSITION:	TOP		BOTTOM	
Participation Ratio Score	Non-Streamed	Streamed	Non-Streamed	Streamed
Low	27%	35%	47%	41%
Medium	24%	36%	21%	34%
High	49%	29%	32%	25%
Total	100%	100%	100%	100%
No. of pupils	71	151	53	63
Chi-square test	$\chi^2 = 9 \cdot 31$, $P < 0 \cdot 01$		Non-significant	

† English teachers' ratings were used here

108

TABLE A31: *Participation ratio scores of pupils who were regarded by their teachers† as pleasurable or unpleasurable‡ in streamed and non-streamed secondary schools*

BOYS

Participation Ratio Score	NON-STREAMED		STREAMED	
	Pleasurable	Unpleasurable	Pleasurable	Unpleasurable
Low	39%	39%	42%	46%
Medium	31%	32%	34%	36%
High	30%	29%	24%	18%
Total	100%	100%	100%	100%
No. of pupils	160	79	332	198
Chi-square test	Non-significant		Non-significant	

GIRLS

Participation Ratio Score	NON-STREAMED		STREAMED	
	Pleasurable	Unpleasurable	Pleasurable	Unpleasurable
Low	33%	36%	35%	53%
Medium	25%	27%	36%	24%
High	42%	37%	29%	23%
Total	100%	100%	100%	100%
No. of pupils	166	81	421	119
Chi-square test	Non-significant		$\chi^2 = 12.39$, $P < 0.01$	

† English teachers' ratings were used here.
‡ Those rated 3, 4 were rated pleasurable; those rated 1, 2 were rated unpleasurable, see Appendix 3.

TABLE A32: *Age of leaving 'desired' and 'expected' by pupils of different social classes in grammar, comprehensive and secondary modern schools*

BOYS

Social Class	GRAMMAR						COMPREHENSIVE						SECONDARY MODERN						ALL SCHOOLS					
	123		45		All		123		45		All		123		45		All		123		45		All	
Leaving Age	D†	E‡	D	E	D	E	D	E	D	E	D	E	D	E	D	E	D	E	D	E	D	E	D	E
	%	%	%	%	%	%	%	%	%	%	%	%	%	%	%	%	%	%	%	%	%	%	%	%
15	12	0	13	0	12	0	20	18	40	26	29	21	42	32	59	46	49	38	31	22	51	38	39	29
16	16	13	19	6	17	12	29	33	28	42	29	37	34	43	25	40	30	42	29	35	26	39	28	37
17	31	17	31	25	31	18	25	18	18	17	22	18	12	17	10	10	11	14	19	17	13	13	16	15
18	41	70	37	69	40	70	26	31	14	15	20	24	12	8	6	4	10	6	21	26	10	10	17	19
Total	100	100	100	100	100	100	100	100	100	100	100	100	100	100	100	100	100	100	100	100	100	100	100	100
No. of pupils	93	93	16	16	109	109	102	102	81	81	183	183	268	268	217	217	485	485	463	463	314	314	777	777
Chi-square test	$\chi^2=15\cdot99$ $P<0\cdot001$		NS		$\chi^2=19\cdot53$ $P<0\cdot001$		NS		NS		NS		$\chi^2=11\cdot36$ $P<0\cdot01$		$\chi^2=12\cdot74$ $P<0\cdot01$		$\chi^2=22\cdot23$ $P<0\cdot001$		$\chi^2=10\cdot59$ $P<0\cdot05$		$\chi^2=14\cdot64$ $P<0\cdot01$		$\chi^2=22\cdot92$ $P<0\cdot001$	

GIRLS

Social Class	GRAMMAR						COMPREHENSIVE						SECONDARY MODERN						ALL SCHOOLS					
	123		45		All		123		45		All		123		45		All		123		45		All	
Leaving Age	D	E	D	E	D	E	D	E	D	E	D	E	D	E	D	E	D	E	D	E	D	E	D	E
	%	%	%	%	%	%	%	%	%	%	%	%	%	%	%	%	%	%	%	%	%	%	%	%
15	12	0	18	0	13	0	45	25	50	29	47	27	47	25	64	51	55	37	38	19	58	42	46	29
16	28	17	32	14	28	16	23	32	22	34	22	33	26	45	25	34	26	40	26	35	25	33	25	34
17	28	22	41	27	31	23	20	22	16	17	19	20	14	15	7	10	11	13	19	19	11	13	16	16
18	32	61	9	59	28	61	12	21	12	20	12	20	13	15	4	5	8	10	17	27	6	12	13	21
Total	100	100	100	100	100	100	100	100	100	100	100	100	100	100	100	100	100	100	100	100	100	100	100	100
No. of pupils	109	109	22	22	131	131	98	98	82	82	180	180	255	255	221	221	476	476	462	462	325	325	787	787
Chi-square test	$\chi^2=21\cdot18$ $P<0\cdot001$		$\chi^2=13\cdot24$ $P<0\cdot01$		$\chi^2=31\cdot75$ $P<0\cdot001$		$\chi^2=9\cdot96$ $P<0\cdot05$		$\chi^2=8\cdot04$ $P<0\cdot05$		$\chi^2=17\cdot88$ $P<0\cdot001$		$\chi^2=29\cdot64$ $P<0\cdot001$		$\chi^2=7\cdot85$ $P<0\cdot05$		$\chi^2=32\cdot16$ $P<0\cdot001$		$\chi^2=46\cdot91$ $P<0\cdot001$		$\chi^2=18\cdot50$ $P<0\cdot001$		$\chi^2=59\cdot82$ $P<0\cdot001$	

†D = 'desired' ‡E = 'expected'

TABLE A33: *Further training chosen by pupils of different social classes in grammar, comprehensive and secondary modern schools*

BOYS

Social Class	GRAMMAR			COMPREHENSIVE			SECONDARY MODERN			ALL SCHOOLS		
	123	45	All	123	45	All	123	45	All	123	45	All
Job straight away	9%	6%	8%	14%	23%	18%	19%	31%	24%	16%	28%	21%
Job plus training	30%	56%	34%	50%	52%	51%	61%	53%	57%	52%	53%	52%
Full-time training	61%	38%	58%	36%	25%	31%	20%	16%	19%	32%	19%	27%
Total	100%	100%	100%	100%	100%	100%	100%	100%	100%	100%	100%	100%
No. of pupils	93	16	109	102	81	183	268	217	485	463	314	777

GIRLS

Social Class	GRAMMAR			COMPREHENSIVE			SECONDARY MODERN			ALL SCHOOLS		
	123	45	All	123	45	All	123	45	All	123	45	All
Job straight away	4%	0%	3%	27%	26%	27%	19%	35%	26%	17%	30%	22%
Job plus training	22%	45%	26%	42%	53%	47%	46%	49%	48%	40%	50%	44%
Full-time training	74%	55%	71%	31%	21%	26%	35%	16%	26%	43%	20%	34%
Total	100%	100%	100%	100%	100%	100%	100%	100%	100%	100%	100%	100%
No. of pupils	109	22	131	98	82	180	254	220	474	461	324	785

TABLE A34: *Status level of 'ideal' and 'expected' occupations of pupils of different social classes in grammar, comprehensive and secondary modern schools*

Boys

Social Class	GRAMMAR						COMPREHENSIVE						SECONDARY MODERN						ALL SCHOOLS					
	123		45		All		123		45		All		123		45		All		123		45		All	
Status Level	I†	E‡	I	E	I	E	I	E	I	E	I	E	I	E	I	E	I	E	I	E	I	E	I	E
	%	%	%	%	%	%	%	%	%	%	%	%	%	%	%	%	%	%	%	%	%	%	%	%
1 (high)	29	28	58	17	33	27	31	28	20	17	26	23	23	23	22	9	23	17	26	25	23	12	25	20
2	67	65	42	83	64	67	57	54	70	64	63	59	62	55	54	59	58	56	62	57	58	62	61	59
3 (low)	4	7	0	0	3	6	12	18	10	18	11	18	15	22	24	32	19	27	12	18	19	26	14	21
Total	100	100	100	100	100	100	100	100	100	100	100	100	100	100	100	100	100	100	100	100	100	100	100	100
No. of pupils	85	85	12	12	97	97	87	87	71	71	158	158	211	211	163	163	374	374	383	383	246	246	629	629
Chi-square test	NS		NS		NS		NS		NS		NS		NS		$\chi^2=10.85$ $P<0.01$		$\chi^2=8.08$ $P<0.01$		$\chi^2=6.60$ $P<0.05$		$\chi^2=12.64$ $P<0.01$		$\chi^2=12.44$ $P<0.01$	

Girls

Social Class	GRAMMAR						COMPREHENSIVE						SECONDARY MODERN						ALL SCHOOLS					
	123		45		All		123		45		All		123		45		All		123		45		All	
Status Level	I	E	I	E	I	E	I	E	I	E	I	E	I	E	I	E	I	E	I	E	I	E	I	E
	%	%	%	%	%	%	%	%	%	%	%	%	%	%	%	%	%	%	%	%	%	%	%	%
1 (high)	62	57	36	45	58	55	20	15	28	14	24	15	22	12	16	6	19	9	32	23	21	11	27	18
2	32	37	55	46	36	38	69	62	64	55	67	59	67	71	67	56	67	65	59	61	65	55	61	59
3 (low)	6	6	9	9	6	7	11	23	8	31	9	26	11	17	17	38	14	26	9	16	14	34	12	23
Total	100	100	100	100	100	100	100	100	100	100	100	100	100	100	100	100	100	100	100	100	100	100	100	100
No. of pupils	109	109	22	22	131	131	93	93	77	77	170	170	248	248	207	207	455	455	450	450	306	306	756	756
Chi-square test	NS		NS		NS		NS		$\chi^2=15.01$ $P<0.001$		$\chi^2=18.46$ $P<0.001$		$\chi^2=11.66$ $P<0.01$		$\chi^2=26.07$ $P<0.001$		$\chi^2=34.23$ $P<0.001$		$\chi^2=12.18$ $P<0.001$		$\chi^2=35.61$ $P<0.001$		$\chi^2=4.15$ $P<0.001$	

†I = 'ideal'   ‡E = 'expected'

Index

Ability groups
    definition of 19, 20
Academic self-image, *see* Pupils' attitudes
Allocation to secondary school 15
Anxiety, *see* Pupils' attitudes
Attainment 19-23
Attainment tests
    English 17, 20, 79
    Mathematics 17, 20, 79
    Verbal Reasoning 17, 20, 79
Attitudes, *see* Parents; Pupils; Teachers

'Banding' 16

Creativity, *see* Divergent thinking

Divergent thinking 17, 24-7, 80-1

English, *see* Attainment tests
Extra-curricular activities, *see* Participation

Flexibility 24-7, 80-1
Fluency 24-7, 80-1
Further training 18, 47, 49-50, 82
    and sex 49
    and social class 49-50, 54
    and type of secondary school 49

Leaving age 47-8, 82
    and sex 48
    and social class 48
    and type of secondary school 48, 54

Mathematics, *see* Attainment tests

Non-streaming in secondary schools 16-17, 76-7

Occupational aspirations 18, 47, 50-4, 82
    and sex 50-4
    and social class 50-1, 54
    and type of secondary school 50-4
    status level 50-1
Originality 24-7, 80-1

Parents' attitudes 56, 60, 63, 65, 66, 68-70
Participation in school activities 18, 42-6, 82
    activities available in secondary schools 43
    and ability 42, 44
    and pleasurability 46
    and position in class 45-6
    and social class 42, 44
    and type of secondary school 45
    ratio score 44
Pupils' aspirations, *see* Further training; Leaving age; Occupational aspirations
Pupils' attitudes 13-14, 18, 28-41
    academic self-image 29-31, 68
    and ability 28-39
    and sex 29-39
    and stream 28, 36-7
    anxiety 32-3
    attitude scales 18, 29
    attitude to class 35-7
    attitude to school 34-5
    importance of doing well 38-9
    'other' image of class 37
    relationship with teacher 31-2, 55-6, 57, 60, 62-3
    social adjustment 34

Sample 14-15

113